The Browns
of Providence
Plantations

The Nineteenth Century

The Browns
of Providence
Plantations

The Nineteenth Century

James B. Hedges

Brown University Press
Providence   1968

Designed by Burton J. Jones

Type set in 11/12 Linotype Granjon

Printed by Crimson Printing Company

On Warren's University Text

Bound By Stanhope Bindery, Inc.

PUBLISHER'S NOTE

The posthumous publication of James B. Hedges' last book has been possible only because Mrs. Hedges was willing to oversee its preparation for the printer. In this she was assisted by her son William L. Hedges and Franklin S. Coyle. Mr. Coyle, of the Brown University history department, also supervised the transcription of Professor Hedges' holograph manuscript. Edmund S. Morgan, Sterling Professor of History at Yale University, served as advisor.

Documentation that, had he lived, the author might in some instances have wished to add has not been supplied, but passages written by Professor Morgan conclude the two final chapters, which were left incomplete.

CONTENTS

11 *A New Generation of Businessmen*   248

12 *Investing Capital in the West*   262

Afterword by Franklin Stuart Coyle   275

Notes   281

Index   313

[*A partial genealogy of the Brown family and a list of family companies or partnerships mentioned in the text precedes Chapter 1.*]

ILLUSTRATIONS

[*Following page 140*]

The building occupied by Brown & Ives until 1927. (Courtesy of Rhode Island Historical Society.)

Nicholas Brown (1769–1841). Painted by Thomas Sully, 1847. (Courtesy of Butler Hospital.)

Thomas P. Ives (1769–1835). Painted by James S. Lincoln from the 1835 original by Chester Harding. (Courtesy of Brown University.)

The Brown & Ives ship Asia, *anchored during the War of 1812 at Copenhagen. Water color by the Swedish marine artist Jacob Petersen. (Private collection.)*

Canton factories, or hongs, circa 1810. (Courtesy of Peabody Museum of Salem, Mass.)

Moses Brown Ives (1794–1857). Painted by G. P. A. Healy. (Courtesy of Rhode Island Hospital.)

John Carter Brown (1797–1874). Miniature painted in color on ivory, 1855. (Courtesy of Annmary Brown Memorial.)

Robert Hale Ives (1798–1875). Painted by G. P. A. Healy, 1859. (Private collection.)

View of the Providence water front. Lithograph by J. P. Newell, 1858/59. (Courtesy of Rhode Island Historical Society.)

The Old Slater Mill, the cotton spinning mill built in 1793 by Samuel Slater and Almy & Brown. (Courtesy of Rhode Island Historical Society.)

The Lonsdale mills of the Brown, Ives, and Goddard families. Engraving by Charles Reen on the 1851 H. F. Walling map of Providence County. (Courtesy of Rhode Island Historical Society.)

Broadside of 1823 advertising the Pennsylvania land of Brown & Ives. (Courtesy of John Carter Brown Library.)

INTRODUCTION

In 1952 James B. Hedges published *The Browns of Providence Plantations: Colonial Years,* the fruit of a dozen years of research by an outstanding scholar working with a unique collection of sources. The Brown Papers, deposited in the John Carter Brown Library of Brown University, are perhaps the most complete record in existence of the economic activities of a large-scale American family business over a period of a century and a half. Although the Browns were by no means the largest American house at any time in their history, they were for a long time among the largest. When Professor Hedges' volume appeared, economic historians at once recognized it as the best case history we are ever likely to have of a business firm in early America.

The volume spanned the period from 1723, when Captain James Brown opened his ledger as a shopkeeper, to 1790, when his nephews helped persuade Rhode Island to ratify the federal Constitution. The size of the Browns' business and the range of their activities had expanded steadily through these years. While the War for Independence had counted many established business firms among its casualties, the Browns weathered the war successfully and stood in a strong position to profit from the new opportunities that independence offered to enterprising businessmen. It was clear at the end of Professor Hedges' first volume that the years ahead were to see an accelerating expansion of the firm's activities.

The record of that expansion lies in the chapters now presented. The record is not complete, because Professor Hedges did not live to finish it or to give to it the final polish that distinguished all his writing. It is, nevertheless, not far from complete, and it is an extraordinary achievement, reducing hundreds of thousands of pages of account books and letters to an orderly and lucid narrative. Only those familiar with the breadth of the author's scholarship, his phenomenal memory, and his scrupulous attention to detail will be able to appreciate fully what a work of compression and comprehension has been accomplished in these pages. But every economic historian will be able to observe in them at close range the forces that transformed the United States in less than a century from a struggling and straggling republic into a world power with enormous economic strength at its command.

The transformation had its roots in the past, and it is to be hoped that readers of the present book will not neglect the earlier one. In that volume one of the author's persistent themes was the challenge presented to Rhode Island merchants by the diminutive resources of their colony. Rhode Island produced next to nothing for export, yet it supported first in Newport and later in Providence a commerce out of all proportion to the size of its population. Rhode Island merchants built their wealth by seizing opportunities that businessmen in more favored locations could afford to neglect.

Those opportunities did not lie entirely in commerce. Before the end of the Colonial period the Browns were diverting capital gained in commerce to the establishment of manufactories, most notably their spermaceti candle works and their iron furnace. "Indeed," Professor Hedges remarked, "it may be said that they had come to think primarily in terms of manufacture; their commerce was increasingly conditioned by the needs of the candle and iron business." It had been widely assumed in the eighteenth century that economic forces must make manufacturing unprofitable in America: population was too small, labor too expensive, and land for farming too easily obtained. But the Browns had not been inhibited by the overpowering plausibility of this reasoning. They entered the period of independence with firsthand knowledge of the fact that profits may often lie where the experts least expect them.

The willingness of other Americans to share this view helps to account for the astonishing economic growth of the United States in the nineteenth century. It is true that the abundant natural resources of an all-but-empty continent contributed one ingredient of the American capacity for growth, but a more active ingredient lay in the ideas and attitudes of human beings. It was not simply the fertility of its lands or the richness of its mineral resources or the natural abundance of timber or of any other thing that made Americans a people of plenty. Rather it was the readiness of men to direct their energies and intelligence not merely toward exploiting their obvious natural advantages but also toward overcoming apparent natural disadvantages. As Rhode Island merchants in the Colonial period had learned to prosper in spite of having nothing to export, so Americans in the nineteenth century learned that they need not remain a nation of farmers simply because the environment seemed to demand it of them.

The success of the Browns, then, both in the Colonial period and in the nineteenth century, was more exemplary than eccentric. Although Rhode Island remained in many ways an exceptional state, her merchants and businessmen were exceptional only in that they often led the way for other Americans, as in the Browns' pioneering establishment of the textile industry. What unfolds in Professor Hedges' account is more than the success story of an energetic family: it is the story of American economic growth, and it has seldom been told in such intimate detail by so accomplished a historian.

E. S. M.

The Nineteenth Century

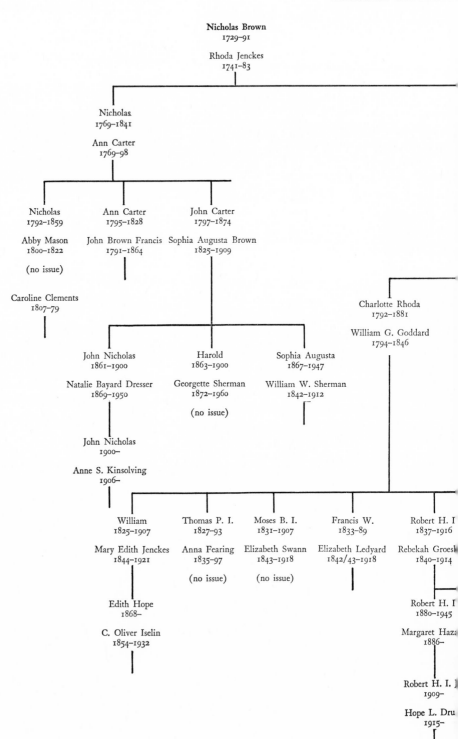

Nicholas Brown
1729–91

Rhoda Jenckes
1741–83

Nicholas
1769–1841

Ann Carter
1769–98

Nicholas
1792–1859

Abby Mason
1800–1822

(no issue)

Caroline Clements
1807–79

Ann Carter
1795–1828

John Brown Francis
1791–1864

John Carter
1797–1874

Sophia Augusta Brown
1825–1909

Charlotte Rhoda
1792–1881

William G. Goddard
1794–1846

John Nicholas
1861–1900

Natalie Bayard Dresser
1869–1950

John Nicholas
1900–

Anne S. Kinsolving
1906–

Harold
1863–1900

Georgette Sherman
1872–1960

(no issue)

Sophia Augusta
1867–1947

William W. Sherman
1842–1912

William
1825–1907

Mary Edith Jenckes
1844–1921

Edith Hope
1868–

C. Oliver Iselin
1854–1932

Thomas P. I.
1827–93

Anna Fearing
1835–97

(no issue)

Moses B. I.
1831–1907

Elizabeth Swann
1843–1918

(no issue)

Francis W.
1833–89

Elizabeth Ledyard
1842/43–1918

Robert H. I
1837–1916

Rebekah Groes
1840–1914

Robert H. I
1880–1945

Margaret Haza
1886–

Robert H. I. J
1909–

Hope L. Dru
1915–

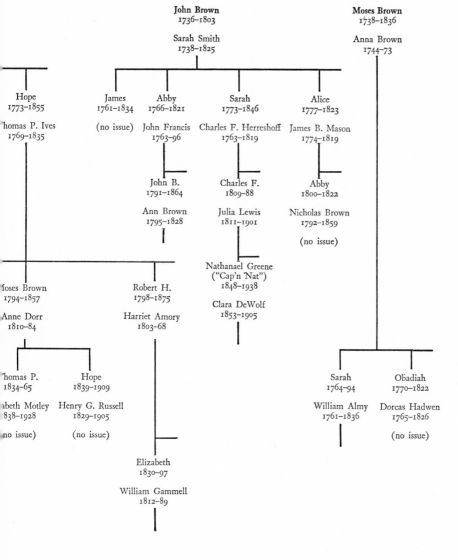

FAMILY PARTNERSHIPS MENTIONED IN TEXT

Brown & Rogers,—*circa* 1786
Brown, Benson, & Brown, *circa* 1791
Brown & Benson, 1783–*circa* 1794
Brown & Francis, 1786–1796
Brown, Benson, & Ives, 1792–1796
Almy & Brown, 1789–*circa* 1856
Brown & Ives, 1796—

CHAPTER 1

A Variety
of Experiments

FOR the Browns the decade that followed the War for Independence was a period of transition. As merchants and shipowners they had long been extensively engaged in maritime commerce. But as candlemakers and ironmasters they had established themselves as a leading manufacturing family, who used the products of their factories as prime articles of their sea-borne trade. With them commerce and manufacturing had been complementary parts of a large and carefully integrated business system.

Eight long years of war had rocked this business structure to its foundations. Gone was whale fishing from Nantucket, and with its passing the close relations that the Browns had long maintained with the leaders of that industry came to an end. Deprived of the chief source of supply for head matter, the candle manufactory was forced into a period of decline and decay. Gone, too, were the days when Hope Furnace played such an important part in the Browns' way of business. Except for one brief period of glory the furnace followed the long, dreary course to oblivion. At the close of the war Nicholas and John Brown, like their mercantile contemporaries, welcomed with enthusiasm the privilege of trading once more with London. But like their fellow merchants they had so greatly overreached themselves in the purchase of British wares that they soon were burdened with debts to London merchants that would require years to liquidate; and so painful was the experience that they never again were tempted to engage in the regular and systematic importation of goods from England.

Although little remained of the many-sided business that the Brown family had so carefully built in pre-Revolutionary days, there had been no comparable impairment of the basic financial resources of the various members of the family. The Browns still possessed the means with which to engage in a variety of experiments, to develop new types of business activity that, while serving the needs of the new nation, would at the same time bring appropriate rewards to their promoters. Some of these experiments involved turning the clock back to an earlier day. Both Nicholas and John Brown for a time engaged once more in the trade to Surinam, which they had known so well in Colonial times. In order to utilize the molasses brought from Surinam, Nicholas and John again became involved in expensive rum distilleries, only to discover within a few years that that kind of business belonged to the past and seemed to have no future. Other experiments, while representing new departures for the Brown family, were doomed to a brief and transitory existence. One such experiment was John Brown's attempt to exploit cod fishing; and another was his gin distillery. But other experiments, although novel to the Browns and to Rhode Island, proved to be successful and worked to the advantage both of the Browns and of their country. One success was the East India trade, first undertaken in Rhode Island in 1787 by John Brown, with some assistance from his brother Nicholas; and another, later, was cotton manufacturing, introduced into America in 1790 through the initiative of Moses Brown and the mechanical skill and knowledge of Samuel Slater.

In 1783 Nicholas Brown entered into partnership with George Benson under the firm name of Brown and Benson. At about the same time John Brown formed with his son-in-law John Francis the house of Brown and Francis. Moses Brown, although less actively engaged in business than Nicholas and John, was occupied with his efforts to perfect cotton manufacturing. Joseph Brown, amateur scientist and architect, although never having been able to commit himself wholeheartedly to business, maintained a connection with trade through the firm of Brown and Rogers (while also serving as a professor at the College of Rhode Island) until his death in 1786.

COD FISHING AND THE SLAVE TRADE

If convincing evidence were needed of the continuing dreary aspect of the Rhode Island economy in the middle 1780's, the spectacle of merchants and mariners of the state turning their attention to cod fishing provided it in abundance. In their happier days they had been content to recognize the pre-eminence of the Bay State in that particular branch of maritime activity and to devote their time, talents, and capital to pursuits in which they enjoyed greater comparative advantage. Their belated interest in cod fishing was therefore born of desperation.

Although certain merchants of Newport became involved in cod fishing at this time, the scale of their operations was dwarfed by the more ambitious effort of John Brown. Never inclined to undertake anything in halfhearted fashion, he now took up cod fishing with enthusiasm; and when, to the surprise of the mercantile community, the cost of labor and materials for the building of ships increased sharply in the Providence area, the reason was found to lie in the fleet of fifteen schooners John Brown was building for cod fishing.[1]

Built at Providence, Taunton, Swansea, Warren, and other places, these vessels were each of twenty-five tons, were named for letters of the alphabet, and were all registered between April 29 and May 31, 1785. They probably went to sea in groups, since on several occasions they returned in that manner. In November, 1785, eight of them arrived at Providence from a fishing voyage, their catch consisting of 1,045 quintals of codfish. Later in the same month three of the schooners docked with a total of 800 quintals. On occasion the schooners caught their fish, returned home to salt them, and then sailed to the West Indian market. The schooner *P* cleared for Cap François with codfish, menhaden, and herring. She returned with molasses, sugar, coffee, claret, and cordials. Occasionally these craft were employed in the coastwise trade. The schooner *H* carried rum, salt, geneva, and chocolate to Baltimore. The schooner *O* returned from that port with flour, bread, and indigo.[2]

The heyday of John Brown's experiment with cod fishing lasted for about two years, although some of the schooners went on fishing voyages as late as 1790. All the evidence, direct and indirect, indicates that the venture was not a spectacular success. John surely was not one to cast aside lightly a profitable branch of trade. Had the business met with the success he had expected he undoubtedly would have persisted in it. And such success might well have drawn into the business Nicholas and his partner, George Benson. The try at cod fishing must therefore be regarded as an unsuccessful effort by a daring and imaginative Providence merchant to find a way out of the economic doldrums into which Rhode Island, along with the rest of the country, was fast slipping in the dark days of 1785/86.

At this time John Brown owed "an Enormus Sum of Money in Europe," an obvious reference to his debt to the firm of Champion and Dickason in London. He was then striving through every trade that appeared lawful and right to pay as much of the debt as possible during his lifetime. Among the trades that he placed in this category was that to Africa. At the moment one of his vessels was on a voyage to Guinea, and for four months he had been assembling the cargo for another venture into the slave trade. News of this brought an anguished protest from Moses, which prompted John to launch forth upon one of his periodic rationalizations of his pursuit of "that Unrighteous traffic." He was convinced that great numbers of the slaves brought from the African coast were better off than those black souls who were left behind. This, he said, was particularly true of those carried among the French, as all accounts agreed that slaves were better treated in the French than in the British West Indies. Both of his slave traders were to sell their human freight in "High spanolia." When, if ever, he became convinced that the slave trade was wrong in the sight of God, he would desist; but as yet he was unconvinced, since the trade had been permitted by the "Supreme Govenour of all things for time Immemoriel." If he should allow experience to be his guide, he would shun the trade, having lost "Very Graitly in allmost Every Voyage to Guiney." Perhaps, John suggested, Moses was correct in his belief that it had been determined by the "power which presides over all Events" that no inhabitant of the town of Providence should ever prosper in the slave business. But John still hoped that one day Fortune would smile upon him as she had upon those gentlemen of Newport whose estates had "beene Got in the Guiney Trade."[3]

Although trade to the coast of Guinea continued to beguile John Brown to the day of his death, that is not to say that it engrossed a major part of his attention. During the years of the Critical Period, John was chiefly engaged in traffic to the Caribbean and to the Cape Verde Islands. He appears to have owned and operated some fifteen different vessels, although not that number at any one time. The import books tell of the arrival of his ships from different ports together with a statement of their cargoes. But because his surviving business papers are so fragmentary, many details of his commercial ventures are lacking.

TRADE TO SURINAM

If John Brown has left a rather sketchy record of his maritime commerce in this era, that is not true of his brother Nicholas, senior partner in the firm of Brown and Benson. During these years trade to Surinam was the major concern of that house. From 1786 to 1793, ships of Brown and Benson made twenty-six voyages to the Dutch colony. In this period, as in pre-Revolutionary days, trade to Surinam served a very special purpose in the firm's scheme of business, although the purpose was very different in the two eras. Before 1775 the great staple exports to the port had been Rhode Island tobacco and horses, spermaceti candles made by the Browns, flour, and meat products. In the postwar era horses disappeared from the invoices of the traffic, their place taken in part by mules from Connecticut sired by jackasses imported by Brown and Benson from the Cape Verde Islands under contract with Dr. Elisha Perkins of Plainfield, Connecticut.[4] Tobacco also was missing, while spermaceti candles were of little importance. In Colonial times the traffic to Surinam had provided the Browns with sugar and molasses (both having a multitude of uses in trade) and good bills of exchange, so necessary in payment at Nantucket for head matter, the raw material of candle manufacturing. After the war bills of exchange were only occasionally the major objective of the business. Much more important were sugar (always highly prized) and molasses with which to feed the rum distillery built by Brown and Benson in conjunction with Welcome Arnold.

Brown and Benson "were induced to be Concerned in a Distillery" because they were often under the necessity of receiving their debts in molasses and at the same time had a "great Occasion for rum" in their business. They were "also Obliged to receive Country produce for Debts" owing them, and this produce they could sometimes sell to best advantage in the West Indies.[5] In exchange for the produce they received molasses in greater volume than they could find sale for. Sound business practice therefore dictated that they distill the molasses into rum, for which the demand was almost constant. The possession of molasses therefore led to the building of the distillery; and once the distillery was in operation, it exerted a powerful pressure for the importation of molasses in ever larger volume.

In spite of the many changes in the objectives and staples of the traffic to Surinam as compared with Colonial days, the ways of transacting business in the postwar era were strongly reminiscent of an earlier time. There were the same laments of the ship captains that the market was dull and glutted, that molasses was scarce and dear, that they had arrived too late, that money was hard to come by, that they were unable to collect their debts, that the ship leaked, and that their goods were damaged by water. There were the same old problems confronting the shipmaster: should he sell at wholesale to a resident merchant, or should he rent a store and retail his cargo. There was the same delay, the same old difficulty in obtaining a full cargo of molasses. There were the same efforts to lower the price of molasses, the same doubts regarding bills on Surinam.[6] And there were the same familiar injunctions of the owners "not to leave any Debts uncollected rather than do it take any article in Pay you can procure" and to "Contract no bad Debts, and leave none behind unsettled."[7]

In the postwar years sugar was almost as much sought after by Brown and Benson as were molasses. They were "Confident the Surinam Trade will not answer to bring only Molasses & Bills [of exchange]—Sugar Must be brought to make a Saving Voyage."[8] The frequent recurrence of this remark suggests that sugar and molasses were almost on a parity. The prime importance of molasses is readily understood. Without it the distillery was useless. The stress placed on sugar is more puzzling, except that it was necessary for a saving voyage. And undoubtedly the importance of sugar increased with the difficulty of its procurement in Surinam.

There was then in force in the Dutch colony a regulation requiring that sugar produced on a Surinam plantation under mortgage in Holland must be shipped to that country.[9] As there were many plantations in this category, the effect of the regulation was to keep in short supply the fund of sugar available for export and to enhance the price of that which was to be had. This in turn placed a premium on contraband trade in sugar by American ship captains. The enforcement of the regulation, of course, varied with the honesty of the "fiscal," or customs officer, on the job at the moment. A lax or dishonest officer could readily lull shipmasters into careless practices that would make them easy victims of a new and more scrupulous official.

In 1786 Captain Simon Smith took on board the brig *Commerce* at Surinam molasses, coffee, cocoa, and fifty-five barrels of sugar. On the eve of his sailing for Providence he had the misfortune to be "arrested by the Fiscal's officer." The sugar on board the brig "brought her in great Danger to be entirely lost in Case she had Come to Strick Examination." But Captain Smith averted complete disaster by "making an agreement with the fiscal to pay him 6500 guilders" and to relinquish thirty-seven of the fifty-five barrels of sugar on board.[10] Although it is a nice question as to whether the 6,500 guilders should be considered a fine imposed for an infraction of a customs regulation or a bribe to the fiscal to secure the ransom of the vessel, this aspect of the case seemed not to disturb Captain Smith. But he did feel aggrieved on another count: he discovered that the sugar taken from him had come from a plantation "not under morgage in Hollan," sugar, therefore, that he had "a Rite to make the most of."[11] A year or so later Brown and Benson wrote in reference to a similar incident involving their brig *Commerce* at Surinam that although "our Prospects were so good we lost a thousand Dollars by his [Captain Benjamin Alger's] Voyage."[12]

Reverses notwithstanding, sugar continued to be a major object of Brown and Benson's trade at the Dutch port. Dispatching their ship *Hope* to Surinam, they directed Captain Seth Wheaton to invest in good molasses and sugar. Their concern was not lest the captain should break the law but that he should not be caught in the act of doing so. He was to exercise the utmost care in taking on board the sugar, "so as to Secure our Property from Seizure."[13]

For a time it seemed that Yankee ingenuity had discovered a way of circumventing the vigilance of the fiscal at Surinam. It was found that a vessel, after legally clearing out, could drop down the bay to a spot called Bram Point, take on contraband goods, and thus elude the officers of the customs. Soon this became standard practice. Brown and Benson, directing Captain Christopher Perry to load fully with molasses and sugar, observed that "those Who now bring sugar . . . take it on board at Bram Point Which appears to us to be the only safe method."[14] But after many months this smuggler's paradise was destroyed when the Governor of Surinam stationed a cutter at Bram Point to inspect outbound vessels. Captain Wheaton remarked that "This circumstance together with the Fiscall's being new, poor, & hungry will make me more circumspect."[15]

The eager quest for sugar by Brown and Benson in no way indicated a lack of interest in other forms of remittance for Surinam. Good bills of exchange and molasses were also in demand. Although these two items without sugar would not make a saving voyage, it was nevertheless true that sugar alone would not answer. Many times they regarded good bills with indifference, but on occasion they considered them a necessity. Such an occasion arose in 1790 when they were preparing to dispatch one of their ships to the Baltic. Finding they could send no cargo to the Baltic that would purchase a return cargo, they appealed to their agent in Surinam to send "all the Good Bills of Exchange you can . . . by[the] first conveyance."[16] Bills of exchange would thus provide the added funds necessary to load a ship with goods from the Baltic.

While good bills were imperative on occasion and while sugar was necessary for a saving voyage, molasses remained the great staple article of import from Surinam. It was the one item that Brown and Benson invariably directed their shipmasters to bring back. And once their new distillery was in operation, the annual procurement of an adequate supply of molasses became a first essential. Their letters reflected the urgency of the problem. They were fearful lest they be forced to "stop our Distillery by the 20th of next Month for Want of Mollasses."[17] As the cost of molasses was an important consideration to distillers, ship captains were enjoined to exert their best "endeavours to reduce the price of mollasses to seven stivers & a half or lower if possible."[18] On at least one occasion Brown and Benson made a conscious choice between sugar and molasses, and their preference was for molasses, even at a high price: "as our Distill House requires large Supply's . . . fill the Brig with Molasses . . . Should it Rise as at 10st per gallon it will Turn more profitable than Sugars."[19]

THE RUM DISTILLERY

As distillers of rum Brown and Benson were to discover that their problem was not confined to the procurement of an adequate stock of molasses. The opening of their new distillery coincided with the launching of the new government under the Constitution; and in that government Alexander Hamilton was formulating his fiscal policies. His funding and assumption plans required for their implementation that the federal government have an adequate revenue system. He planned to obtain the required revenue through the sale of public lands, through impost duties, and through internal revenue duties. Included in the last of these, of course, was the excise tax on distilled spirits. The opposition to the excise, emanating from Pennsylvania and states to the south of it, is well understood by students of history; and the Whisky Rebellion of 1794, occasioned by the excise, is known to every schoolboy in the land. But that the proposed tax elicited warm protests from rum distillers in New England and New York is sometimes overlooked, even in the multivolume general histories of the period.[20]

On January 4, 1791, Welcome Arnold expressed to Benjamin Bourne, Rhode Island member of the lower house of Congress, his belief that unless the proposed excise bill provided for a drawback on spirits exported from the country, it would "destroy [the] spirits Trade in New England."[21] On January 27, 1791, while the proposed excise was under consideration in Congress, four Providence distillers, of whom George Benson was one, addressed to the Rhode Island delegation in Congress a letter pointing to the destructive consequences of the tax not only to the distilling business but to trade and commerce in general. Unless a drawback of the tax were allowed "on all Spirits exported to a foreign market, the importation of Molasses . . . must be reduced to a very small Quantity." As a result "our Vessels will be useless, Ship Building will be discouraged, the Fishery in a great Measure Fail."[22]

The following day twenty "Merchants and Traders of the Town of Providence," representing the most important mercantile houses in the town, affixed their signatures to a petition "to the Senate and House of Representatives of the United States in Congress assembled," in which they pointed out that "a Drawback [of the import duty] is at present allowed upon the Exportation of all foreign imported Spirits." But no similar indulgence was extended to the exportation of spirits distilled within the United States "from Molasses . . . which is itself chargeable with a very considerable [import] Duty." The encouragement of American manufacturing, they said, required that duties on foreign and domestic spirits bear such "a discriminating Ratio" as would "afford the latter a decided Preference." But the proposed excise law contained no such provision. On the contrary, it would "enable Foreigners to prosecute the distilling Business with Superior advantages, and to supply the American, and other Markets to the Exclusion of our own Citizens."[23]

Meanwhile, the Providence distillers were in communication with those of Boston. On January 30, 1791, a committee of the latter forwarded to Providence a copy of the protest against the excise tax that they were placing in the hands of the members of Congress from Massachusetts.[24] The Boston committee had also made their sentiments known to the gentlemen distillers of Salem, Newbury, and other towns to the eastward.

The excise tax as finally enacted by Congress in March, 1791, granted on the export of spirits distilled in the United States a drawback equal to the excise duty thereon, a *quid pro quo* for the remission of the import duty on "all foreign imported" spirits re-exported from the country. But on exports of rum it allowed an additional three cents a gallon in consideration of the import duty on the molasses from which the rum was distilled.[25] Since the bill as originally drawn did not provide for the drawback of three cents on rum, it is a reasonable assumption that the protest of the New England manufacturers of rum was instrumental in securing its inclusion in the law; and the absence of further protest by the distillers in New England would seem to indicate that the drawback had allayed their fears.

But not so with the distillers of New York City. At a meeting held on July 16, 1791, four months after the enactment of the excise, they appointed a committee of three to communicate by means of circular letters with distillers in the different states. The letter they addressed to "The Distillers in the State of Rhode Island" eventually came to rest in the archives of Brown and Benson. The statement of grievances found in the letter offered little that was new or different. But the remedy proposed was distinctly novel. The distillers of New York City were willing, should their brethren in the other states deem it expedient, "to put a total stop to the Business [of distilling] for some time at least for Two or Three Months," in order that some means might be devised to procure the repeal of the excise "or such a modification of it as will relieve us from our present difficulties." They proposed, therefore, the "Twentieth Day of August next for the Period on which we will have our Houses worked off and shut up."[26]

In the years before the War for Independence the American colonies had sought to bring about the repeal of restrictive Parliamentary acts by resort to economic coercion. Nonimportation and nonconsumption had been directed to that end, and sometimes they had achieved a considerable success. What the New York distillers were now proposing was that this same weapon be employed by a segment of American business to bring pressure to bear upon a government of their own choosing. Evidently this medicine was too strong for the New England distillers. There is no evidence of a favorable response by the rum manufacturers of Rhode Island; nor was the distillery operated by Brown and Benson shut down.

Reassured by the drawback, the rum distillers of New England quickly settled down to their accustomed ways of business. Once they had paid the excise tax at the still head, they added the amount of it to the price of their product and passed it along to merchants who distributed the rum. These men in turn included the tax in the price at which they sold to the consumer. Therefore, the one who imbibed the rum, not the one who distilled it, bore the burden of the tax. The distiller's business was unaffected by the tax in any direct or immediate way.

That a sharp rise in the price of rum followed in the wake of the excise, there can be no doubt. In April, 1791, a month after the act was passed, New England rum sold in Philadelphia, considered the best market in the country, at 3s. 3d.; in July it was selling at 3s. 6d.; by March, 1792, the price had advanced to 5s. 3d.[27] The effect of this upon the rum trade is reflected in a letter of George Sears, Baltimore correspondent of Brown and Benson: "Rum at Market, is now selling at 4/10 & 5/ . . . at these prices not so much as formerly will be disposed of, as many of the Country People now substitute Whiskey, which may get at two thirds the Price."[28]

It is clear, however, that the excise was not a major cause of the advance in the price of rum; nor was it responsible for the doldrums in which the New England rum distillers soon found themselves. Basically, the difficulty stemmed from the high cost of molasses in Surinam. This, in turn, meant high costs for distilling rum in the United States. As a result, rum from St. Croix could be "exported from this Country as Cheap or cheaper than our own rum." The high price of American rum "had prompted great Numbers of People to erect Distilleries" all over the country "for the purpose of Making spirits from the various produce of the soil."[29] In these distilleries, corn, rye, wheat, and barley were being converted into whisky and perhaps into gin. These distilleries, whose construction was partially induced by the high price of rum, were turning out spirits that, "together with the great influx of foreign rum," kept the price of domestic rum "far too low for the Cost of Molasses in Surinam," thereby completing a vicious circle.[30] Initially, the high price of rum had encouraged the manufacture of substitutes. These in combination with imported rum were in turn depressing the price of domestic rum to the point where it could no longer bear the high cost in Surinam of the molasses from which it was distilled. Bourbon and rye whisky were making inroads into markets where rum had long held sway. Men who had once imbibed New England rum were now quenching their thirst with whisky from western Pennsylvania or from the back country of Carolina.

Nevertheless, molasses in Surinam remained high in price. Late in 1793 Brown and Benson believed it would answer their purposes only if it was under ten stivers a gallon. Otherwise, it would be better for their ship captain to sell his cargo at Surinam, take a freight for Europe, and invest all his funds in undoubted bills on Amsterdam. When spring came in 1794, they had made no "arrangement for [the] fall & winter supply of Stock for [the] Distillery."[31] They closed it temporarily, planning to reopen it when the times became more auspicious. But the weeks of idleness lengthened into months. A year later it was still in disuse. Soon they sold their interest to Cyprian Sterry. Once Brown and Benson had abandoned the rum business, trade to Surinam lost most of its meaning for them.

THE GIN DISTILLERY

The decision of Brown and Benson to liquidate their interest in the rum distillery roughly coincided with the entrance of John Brown into another kind of distilling business. When in 1793 Brown and Benson complained that the high price of rum had prompted men to erect stills to make spirits from grains, they may well have had in mind, among others, John Brown himself; for by this time John, ever ready to try something new, had directed his attention to the distilling of gin, which became one of the spirits in rivalry with rum. Precisely when John built his gin distillery in Providence cannot be determined; but since it was operating at full blast as early as 1791, it seems altogether likely that it was one of those referred to by Brown and Benson.

If the records of early American business are replete with references to rum distilled within the country, the same cannot be said of gin. Although gin had long been a common article of commerce, it was not the domestic variety but the product so freely imported from Holland at that time. It is not possible to say when American gin first appeared in the market, but evidently domestic gin was being produced by 1784.[32] The number and identity of American gin distillers of 1784 is unknown; but the fact that there are no known records of their operations leads to a strong presumption that they were a rare species. It is unlikely that John Brown was in the business early enough to qualify for inclusion in this select group, but if he cannot claim the distinction of being the first American gin distiller, he surely ranks among the earliest owners of such establishments; and no other gin distillery appears to be so well documented as that built by him.

John's distillery was working at full capacity as early as January 22, 1791. On that day Brown and Francis, through an advertisement in the *Providence Gazette,* announced their desire to purchase for their "Gin Manufactory" a quantity of good rye, barley, buckwheat, and juniper berries, for which they were prepared to pay in cash the highest prices. They also wished to buy forty or fifty young shoats to be fattened on the residue from the fermented grain. John and his partner had ready for sale in large or small quantities American geneva (gin) that had been judged by "the best Connoisseurs" to be the equal in strength and purity of any manufactured in Holland. Reminding the farmers of Rhode Island that gin distilleries would provide a ready market for the grain products grown on their farms, Brown and Francis expressed the hope that patriotism would induce them to foster and encourage American manufacturing by cheerfully discountenancing the importation of foreign gin into the country. In this way they would assure to the United States the advantages of manufacturing gin.

Brown, Benson, and Ives were purchasing gin from John's distillery as early as 1794; and the correspondence between the two houses seems to indicate a flourishing trade in the article. When in 1797 the ship *John Jay,* belonging to Brown and Ives, sailed for Canton, she carried fifty cases of domestic gin, almost certainly procured from John's distillery.

From an advertisement in 1796 by John Brown and his partner John Francis emerges a good picture of the young gin distillery. Brown and Francis wanted 1,500 cords of good oak and pine wood, 6,000 bushels of good barley, 1,200 bushels of good rye, and about 300 head of good oxen, from four to eight years old, to be delivered during the current year at their gin and glass manufactory at India Point. Wanted also were a good foreman and a "Set of HANDS for their GLASS-WORKS," 300 loads of hay, and 20 loads of coal for malting. Brown and Francis had for sale the "best GENEVA, warranted as good as any made in Holland," and a few of the "best fat OXEN in the World."[33]

Fortunately, there have survived numerous letters written by John

Brown from Washington in 1800/1801. He was then a member of the lower house of Congress, and he was keeping in touch with Hezekiah Sabin, who appears to have served as manager of the distillery during John's absence in the national capital. These letters cast a good light upon the operations of the distillery. Power came from both a water mill and a windmill, the latter of which was to be kept "Going Nite & Day when their is wind."[34] Coal was used for malting, while the large number of oxen mentioned in the advertisement suggests their use in a treadmill, should all other sources of power fail. John reminded Sabin that "if aney of the Hoggs at India point is Fit to Kill they ought to be Kild before hot weither." He noted with satisfaction that the returns showed that the distillery was making more gin from the bushel of grain than usual, which he hoped would continue. He thought, however, that use should be made of the information procured in Holland by Colonel Ephraim Bowen, which made it possible to distill 25 per cent more gin from a given quantity of rye.

Although a certain amount of the rye used at the distillery came from the immediate vicinity of Providence, the bulk of it was grown some distance from the area. Hartford and Fairfield, Connecticut, were centers from which the grain was shipped to India Point in quantities up to 1,000 bushels. A New York merchant named Franklin also sent frequent shipments. But the most important source of supply was Baltimore, where the firm of John and Samuel Arnold made extensive purchases on the Eastern Shore of Maryland. In January, 1800, John Brown was expecting a cargo of some 2,400 bushels from that quarter.

The principal outlets for the sale of the spirits produced at the distillery were Providence; New York; Baltimore; and Charleston, South Carolina. None appears to have been shipped to Boston. John sold gin by the gallon, by the pipe of a hundred gallons or more, and by the case of four gallons. Among the extensive purchasers by pipe or case were Brown and Ives, who bought in quantities of fifty or more cases. Sales in gallon lots were made only in the local market. In March, 1800, John set the price at 6s. a gallon "for 60 Days payable at Bank to Good Safe purchessors." Later he instructed Sabin to "Sell all you Can at home, at a Dollar & 90 Days Cr to good Men for their Notes payable at Bank." Gin for the more distant markets was shipped either in pipes or cases. The price per case was $6.00 cash or $6.75 on credit. But should opportunity offer "to Ship a Qty. to a prosperus Market," Sabin was to grant more reasonable terms.[35]

Presumably John Brown continued to operate his gin distillery until his death in 1803, although there is no direct evidence of its existence after 1801. Whether his gin distillery was more profitable than the rum distillery of Brown and Benson, it is not possible to say. John's letters betray no great measure of satisfaction with the profits of the business. This, however, should not be taken too seriously, since his idea of profit was somewhat exaggerated. In one of his letters he refers to the balance for the year 1800 at the distillery as £1,055 lawful money of Rhode Island, or $3,513.[36] As the capital investment in the business is unknown, the rate of return represented by this balance cannot be determined. It was, however, the equivalent of 14 per cent on an investment of $25,000, probably a very generous estimate of the capital fund put into the distillery.[37]

The return of the Browns to the Surinam trade and to the distilling of spirits was a temporary expedient made necessary by the economic dislocations that had come in the wake of the War for Independence. For them, for Providence, for Rhode Island, even for New England, molasses and rum belonged to the past. As for the future, the Browns and New Englanders would seek their fortunes in forms of business that the eighteenth century had not known. The events here considered were but an interlude between a prosperous past and an even more successful future.

CHAPTER 2

To the East Indies

IF independence placed the Americans at a disadvantage in certain areas of commercial activity, it conferred upon them a privileged status in relation to certain other areas. As long as they were British subjects, trade to the Far East had been closed to them in favor of the British East India Company; but now as citizens of an independent country they were under no such disability. Ink of the treaty recognizing their independence was scarcely dry, therefore, when certain Americans began to turn their thoughts to the Pacific, which had been comparatively undisturbed by ships belonging to their Colonial forbears. It was probably inevitable that Robert Morris, conspicuous among businessmen of the day and "financier" of the American Revolution, should be a principal figure in the inauguration of such trade. With his heavy financial support *Empress of China,* launched in January, 1784, became the first ship flying the American flag to sail for the country whose name she bore.[1] Carrying ginseng, brandy, wine, tar, turpentine, and $20,000 in hard money, *Empress* set the pattern that other American merchants trading to China would seek to emulate in the years that followed.

The fortunes of this venture into the unknown were followed closely by the mercantile community along the seaboard. And the interest of thoughtful men in its outcome doubtless quickened as the dislocations in traditional forms of business activity became more marked. By the time *Empress* had returned to her home port, the country was fast settling into the great depression of the Critical Period. Businessmen were ready to grasp at any straw. Trade to the Indies might well prove an acceptable substitute for older trades now lost or impaired.

In no state were the merchants more desperate than in Rhode Island, where the woes normal to a period of hard times seemed to be multiplied by the curse of paper money. The potentialities of trade to China were not lost on them. It would be interesting to know who in the little state first dreamed of sending a ship to Canton. Once it would have been proper that the honor belong to a merchant of Newport. But that town's days of maritime glory were largely in the past; and if any of her sons had the dream, it remained for men elsewhere to transform it into reality. It was a son of Providence who was destined first to implement this idea; and it was appropriate that this son should have been John Brown.

Just when John first directed his attention to the possibility of a China voyage is not known. But it is unlikely that he allowed the idea to remain long in the stage of incubation. By the late summer of 1787 his mind was made up. On August 18 he wrote to Moses that he planned "to Fit the Ship *Gen'l Washington* to the East Indies in which Case Shall not be aney More Concerned in the Ginney Trade." After outlining his plan with some care, he came to the point: "Will you be Concerned."[2] Knowing the strong opposition of Moses to the slave trade, John sought to use his own contingent promise to abjure the evil as an inducement to Moses to invest in the proposed China voyage. There is no evidence that Moses took a share in the venture. But the *Providence Gazette* of September 8 carried the announcement that Brown and Francis wanted for the East India market a quantity of good ginseng (much used in China as a medicine) for which they were prepared to pay well according to quality. In the same month John suggested to Brown and Benson and to Welcome Arnold that they be concerned in the venture. If John expected an eager acceptance of his proposal, he was disappointed. When their delay had worn his patience thin, John set a time beyond which "it may not be Convenient to furnish you with aney part of the Voyage . . . tho you should hereafter wish it."[3] Eventually an agreement was arrived at by which Brown and Benson were to purchase a one-eighth and Welcome Arnold a one-twenty-fourth interest in *General Washington,* which John had selected to make the voyage and which he valued at £3,600 lawful money of Rhode Island. The new investors were to furnish cargo and stores in like proportion. As their combined interest was only a one-sixth, this pioneer East India voyage was primarily the concern of Brown and Francis.

General Washington almost certainly was the vessel that the *Providence Gazette* on November 27, 1779, had announced as the "new Ship GENERAL WASHINGTON, built on purpose for a fast-sailing privateer, to mount 20 six-pounders." Measuring about 340 tons, she was somewhat larger than the average vessel employed in the early trade from the United States to China. She was to sail on a four months' cruise from Boston by "the 15th of December next." Those wishing to take service on board her were advised to apply either to Captain J. Monroe or to the owner, John Brown. In May, 1780, she was about to sail on another privateering voyage carrying 19 guns and 120 men. She then disappeared from the record for a period of three years. On December 27, 1783, the ship *General Washington* sailed for Virginia, John Brown having deposited with the General Treasurer of Rhode Island a bond for £1,000 lawful money guaranteeing that the Old Dominion was her destination.[4] There she loaded tobacco, which Captain Simon Smith sold in London. In October, 1784, she arrived at Providence with a cargo of English goods (which must have augmented John's already swollen debt in London) and with a "large and elegant" clock and a bell of "25 Cwt," both for the First Baptist Meeting House in Providence.[5] She also carried four passengers, one of them Elkanah Watson, once apprenticed to John Brown and agent of the Browns in France during the War for Independence. For the next two years she shuttled back and forth between Providence and the Cape Verde Islands, with occasional visits to the West Indies. In June, 1787, she arrived at Providence with thirty-eight jackasses on board.

THE FIRST VOYAGE TO CHINA

The weeks immediately preceding the sailing of *General Washington* were busy ones for all parties to the concern. Having the largest stake in the undertaking, John Brown shouldered the major responsibility in the preparations for the voyage. "I am Sorry to Trouble you So often," he wrote Brown and Benson, "but without attention the Ship Can Not be Got Reddy, theirfore you'l Excuse Me."[6] He wished to know whether they had any rum to go in the vessel. Discovering that the cargo was short of cordage, he requested them to "Git these Sizes, or otherwise we Shall not have a propotion of Small Cordage."[7] The assembling of the cargo required not only thought and planning but also capital. Always aware of their enormous debt in London, Brown and Benson grudgingly diverted to the venture funds for which Champion and Dickason were pressing them. Even John, whose brainchild the idea was, found it hard to procure funds in the necessary amount. In the course of the autumn the parties to the undertaking sent John Francis, John Brown's partner, to Boston, New York, and Philadelphia to procure various items for the cargo, especially spirits and ginseng. Running short of cash, he was obliged to proffer notes to the amount of £1,300 in payment for brandy, rum, bottled porter, and claret. Six months later, when the notes were yet unpaid, Brown and Francis were still "so much embarrassed for want of Cash" that they found it almost impossible to raise their proportion of the notes.[8]

Procurement of a satisfactory cargo was rendered the more difficult

by the newness of the trade to the Pacific. As yet there was no real con-
sensus as to the items suitable for the East Indian market. Through trial
and error American merchants, ship captains, and supercargoes were
learning, sometimes painfully, the assortment of goods that in the Indies might fetch their first cost. Many of the items, therefore, that
General Washington carried were destined not to find a place on Indiamen dispatched by the Browns at a later time. Among the articles she
carried were anchors, cannon, all weights of shot, gun carriages, some
sixteen different varieties of spirits, sailcloths, copper sheets, blistered
steel, bar iron, cordage, and ginseng. On board also were codfish, beef,
pork, butter, and 9,731 pounds of hams, smoked and unsmoked.[9] En route
to the East *General Washington* was to call at Madeira, where the provisions were to be sold and the proceeds applied in part payment for
Madeira wine to be taken on board there. Including the wine, the cargo
was charged in the invoice at approximately £17,000 lawful money of
Rhode Island, the equivalent of about $57,000.[10]

Eventually all was in readiness. On Thursday, December 27, 1787,
at nine o'clock in the evening, *General Washington,* Captain Jonathan Donnison, weighed anchor at Newport, fired three guns, took leave
of John Brown, and headed for the "heither" Indies.[11] One supercargo
was Colonel Samuel Ward. Also on board in the capacity of a supercargo
was William F. Megee, destined to have a long career in the trade to
the Indies as an employee of both Providence and Boston mercantile
houses. Megee is of special importance because his journal is the chief
source of information regarding this pioneer venture. Megee recorded
in his journal that the first leg of the voyage was completed when the
ship arrived at Madeira after thirty-four days of bad weather. Because
of holy days and continued bad weather, only eighteen of the thirty-six
days spent there were working days. He remarked that English firms
transacted most of the business at Madeira. The currency was sterling,
though the exchange on London ranged from 15 to 25 per cent. A stran-
ger, unless a good judge, was likely to be deceived as to the quality of
the wines.[12]

Samuel Ward's record of the voyage reveals that of the ship's cargo to
be sold at Madeira the codfish occasioned considerable anxiety. When
Captain Donnison began to unload, he found the fish in bad "oder."
It was feared that the stench of them would affect the health of the crew
and occasion complaint to the health officer, with resulting condemnation of the damaged goods.[13] This was the more regrettable because it
was the season of Lent, when good fish would command a handsome
price.[14] But their worst fears were not realized. Although an eyewit-
ness pronounced the fish the most inferior he ever saw, they sold at an

advance of 25 per cent over the invoice figure. This, of course, fell far short of the 100 per cent originally expected, but it was also far short of complete disaster. The proceeds of the provisions sold at Madeira defrayed something less than half the cost of the 200 pipes of wine taken on board there.

On March 7, 1788, *General Washington* again put to sea. For several weeks Megee was able to record in his journal nothing more startling than "a Sheep lambed" or "killed our Milch Goat."[15] Two months out from Madeira, while the crew were cleaning muskets, one of the sows was delivered of twelve pigs. They killed and threw overboard six of them, as "She could not Bring them all up."[16] On May 21 they spoke a Portuguese snow bound for Madras that had sailed from Madeira the night of *General Washington's* arrival.[17] On July 17, having seen no land since Madeira, they anchored among the shipping in Pondicherry Roads. The following day, with a large crowd of people dressed in long white gowns with long sleeves awaiting them on the beach, they went ashore.[18] While hiring rooms in which to live and to display their wares, they were visited by "Black merchants," after which trading began. They bartered ten pipes of Madeira, some brandy, and bar iron for India goods. With another merchant they arranged to sell eighty pipes of wine at fifty-seven pagodas a pipe, "payable in muslins, etc.," on forty days' credit. Within a week Megee had decided the "Merchants . . . was Rogues."[19]

After a sojourn of ten days at Pondicherry, *General Washington* weighed anchor and sailed for Madras, where she arrived the next day. Renting a house and store, the supercargoes made some sales to British officers, but business was dull. During the next fortnight they sold cannon, shot, and gun carriages, and shot sixteen gallons of brandy into the Madeira. In a deal with a Portuguese gentleman, they bartered bottled porter, Madeira, and brandy for goods; and they sold all the cherry rum, much to the delight of Megee, who had feared it would spoil before they reached China. Megee quickly tired of Madras, this "Cursed place" where so many "Rogues" would "Steel a man's Eyes out of his head" if he did not keep a guard. He asserted that the "whole Study of the People . . . is to Cheat you, if Possable which they look on as part of their Religion."[20]

While the details of his experience were yet fresh in his mind, Megee confided to his journal some thoughts on trade to India that he believed would be helpful to his owners in planning future voyages to that part of the world: Ships should arrive on the coast of India in February or March. In stowing cargoes for the trade, the items should be carefully assorted "so that some of each articol may be got at when wanted." On the voyage out, flour and beef could be sold at the Cape of Good Hope and the Île de France (Mauritius). Ships should touch at all the ports on the Indian coast, selling for cash articles in demand at each place. At Madras were to be had book muslins, longcloths, and cambrics; at Calcutta, muslins, calicoes, Bengals, and bandannas; at Pondicherry, bluecloths, coarse handkerchiefs, and niccanees. Freight was to be had at any time on the Coromandel Coast. There were no duties or port charges at Pondicherry, but at Madras there was a charge of 5 per cent, plus the expense of landing goods and "porterage." At Madras one also confronted the "united Power" of Indians and British to "Cheet you as much as they Can." At Calcutta the pilotage fee was a heavy one.

All strangers trading to India must employ an Indian called a "Debauch" to transact business for them, who, Megee went on to warn, must be watched very carefully, for "the whole life and Study of the Indians is to Cheet you, which he Seldom or Ever fails to accomplish, tho not done openly but by Combining with the Buyer." Nor should one be any less on guard against all Europeans in India, for they were there to make a quick fortune. Megee thought it would be of interest to his owners to learn that at Pondicherry the buyers were not aware of the difference between Madeira and Teneriffe wine. At Madras buyers recognized no difference in taste between New England and West Indian rum. He advised that the New England variety be shipped under the West Indian label. Since "they Cannot tell the Difference," it would "fetch as much as the West India [rum]." Ships not calling at Calcutta should procure their chintzes and calicoes at Pondicherry, where "they will sell their Goods for much more" and where the materials would be cheaper than at Madras.[21]

On August 23 *General Washington* sailed from Madras bound for Canton by way of the Strait of Malacca. This leg of the voyage was largely uneventful. Men went ashore on an island in search of eggs and fish. Birds were so plentiful that they could be captured with bare hands. Although the men could have filled the ship with them, they settled for "about 20 doz. of Eggs and as many birds, as Gave all hands a Dinner." They spoke a number of vessels including the ship *Sukey,* Bengal bound. As she was in need of provisions, *General Washington* supplied her with a barrel of pork.[22] October 4 was marred by the first death of the voyage. Frank Malbone, a Negro, was accidentally knocked overboard and drowned in a high sea. The next night they lost a "fine pig over Board" but soon caught two dolphins.[23] Passing Bocca Tigris on October 27, the ship anchored at Whampoa Roads two days later.[24]

Trade at Canton was controlled by the hong merchants, known collectively as the Co-hong. These men were Chinese traders holding a franchise to conduct the foreign commerce of the country. Upon arrival at Canton the captain or supercargo of a foreign ship sought out a hong merchant who agreed to secure or be responsible for the ship and cargo, in return for which he received certain preferential rights to the cargo. Other licensed officials with whom foreign traders dealt were compradors, or stewards, and linguists. Soon the visiting ship received a call from the hoppo, the superintendent of the Chinese customs service, at which time the cumshaw and measurement ceremony took place. In the course of this ritual the port charges and the gift to the hoppo were decided upon. Custom dictated, too, that the captain and supercargo, with all convenient speed, should pay a visit to the foreign factories in the western suburbs of Canton. A series of large buildings connected by arcades and facing the river, the factories, or hongs, were the quarters in which the foreign trader lived, worked, and whiled away his time during his long stay in Canton.

Many kinds of goods were taken to Canton by the American traders. Only by degrees did the merchants who owned and dispatched ships into the Pacific learn that very few of the articles of commerce so familiar to the western world would bring a profit in China. Tea, of course, was the Chinese product most coveted by the American traders. A voyage to Canton that did not procure a valuable cargo of tea was written off as a failure, regardless of other items in the cargo. Nankeens, a coarse type of cotton cloth, also occupied a conspicuous place in return cargoes. Silks, chinaware, and various spices were other articles loaded at Canton in substantial volume. If tea was the most prized of Chinese exports, it was also the most speculative and uncertain. Produced chiefly in Fukien Province, tea was subject to the hazards of drought and flood, of bandits and rebellion, of attempts at engrossment, and of downright fraud.

Always impatient of delay and eager to be the first at market with a cargo of tea, supercargoes were inclined to indulge in competitive bidding for tea, which enhanced its price while correspondingly reducing the proceeds of the goods brought to Canton. Small wonder that resident merchants at Canton viewed such practices with disfavor. The optimum time to purchase tea was immediately prior to the Chinese New Year, when the customary payment of all debts by the Chinese produced such a need for funds that the hong merchants were inclined to sell at bargain prices. Ships plentifully supplied with hard money were able to take maximum advantage of such a favorable opportunity.

Although Americans trading to Canton labored under certain disadvantages, such as their inability to command the large resources of the British East India Company, they were not without countervailing assets. They were unexcelled in seamanship, in Yankee shrewdness, and in the capacity for cutting costs to the bone.

In the early years of the China trade a ship's business at Canton was conducted chiefly by a supercargo. But gradually American merchants resident in Canton came to occupy a controlling position in the trade. So intricate were the processes of the trade that a resident agent ordinarily enjoyed a distinct advantage over a visiting supercargo in the purchase of a valuable cargo on favorable terms. The resident agent was better acquainted with Chinese conditions and regulations, with the hong merchants, and with the fluctuations of the market than was the supercargo. Besides, the resident agent either owned or rented a factory and was thus in a position to spare the trader this very substantial expense. His credit with the hong merchants well established, the agent was in a far better position than a supercargo to procure goods on favorable terms for the ship with limited or insufficient funds.

Probably the first significant resident American merchant in Canton was Samuel Snow of Providence, who went out in 1796 aboard the *Ann & Hope,* owned by the Browns, and who became the second American consul there. In 1799 Sullivan Dorr, later a resident of Providence, established himself in Canton, where he sold goods on commission, bought and shipped Chinese goods to the United States, and re-equipped vessels for trade to the Northwest Coast of North America. In 1803 Edward Carrington, later a prominent Providence merchant, became a resident agent in Canton, where he remained until 1811.

Outstanding among American merchants residing in China was John Perkins Cushing, nephew of Thomas H. Perkins of the Boston house of James and Thomas H. Perkins. Cushing arrived at Canton in the season of 1803/4, at the age of sixteen. With Ephraim Bumstead he set up a commission house under the combined auspices of the Boston firms of James and Thomas H. Perkins and Bryant and Sturgis. He was so successful and showed such great capacity that he soon became the Canton partner of Perkins. Until 1829 he continued to be the foremost American merchant in China.

In 1819 Samuel Russell arrived in Canton, where he established the firm of Russell and Company. In 1824 he formed a partnership with Philip Ammidon, close friend of the Browns and their agent in Canton on several occasions between 1815 and 1820. Before 1830 William H. Low of Salem joined the firm that for many years thereafter remained the leading American house in Canton. It was generally through such resident agents and firms that trade to Canton was carried on by Americans for the next half-century.[25]

To return to *General Washington,* just arrived in Whampoa Roads, the next several weeks were used by her crew in making repairs and painting, while the captain and supercargoes made trips back and forth to Canton. There was also some trading with other vessels at Whampoa, including the delivery on board the ship *Non-Such* of six four-pound cannon. Within a few days the grand hoppo came to measure *General Washington*. Attended by numerous officials, he made a present to the ship of two bullocks, eight jars of samshu, and eight bags of flour. The next month was occupied with the storing of the return cargo.

For the information of his owners and of posterity, Megee compiled a list of ships visiting China in the year 1788, including nationality and dates of arrival and departure. At Canton there had called twenty-one vessels of the British East India Company and twenty-four English country ships (British ships not owned by the East India Company). Compared with this total of forty-five vessels flying the Union Jack, there were four American, four Dutch, two Danish, two Swedish, one French, and three Spanish ships. At Macao, the Portuguese port, there had been a total of thirteen vessels, including five from England, seven from Portugal, and one from the United States. Although American representation compared favorably with that of all countries save England, the fact remained that American trade to China was still in its infancy, both in years and in size.

General Washington set sail for home on January 29, 1789. Two weeks later she sighted Java and Sumatra. At Soenda Strait she stopped for wood and water. There Megee bought a large buffalo for seven dollars, brought him on board alive, and sent a boat ashore for "Broom Stuff" and hay to feed him. After weeks of unrelieved boredom the ship picked up Natal on the southeast coast of Africa, which proved Megee's lunar observations to be correct. At St. Helena her arrival coincided with that of *Albion* of the British East India Company, which had sailed from Canton on the same day as *General Washington* and which Megee referred to as "one of the fastest Sailers that belongs to the English East India Company."[26] On June 7 *General Washington* arrived at St. Eustatius, where nankeens and tea were exchanged for gin and rum. When she cast anchor at Providence on July 6, the first voyage from Rhode Island to the East Indies was at an end.

The return cargo fell far short of John Brown's original calculations, both in variety and in amount. He had expected 850 chests of tea; the ship brought 490 whole chests and 66 half-chests.[27] On board was none of the 25 tons of black pepper or the 2,000 pounds of nutmeg he had anticipated. There was a modest quantity of silks from Canton but no bandannas from any place. From Pondicherry came calicoes, muslins, and cambrics; from Madras came chintz and cambric handkerchiefs but not in the quantity that John had expected. No saltpeter, no red-wood, and no bales of cotton appear in the invoice. Chinaware seems to have been the one article that measured up to expectations.

According to the manifest found in the state records of import cargoes for 1788/89, the goods on board were valued at £29,951 lawful money of Rhode Island, the equivalent of $99,737.[28] John Brown had expected a cargo that would sell for £50,000. No data are extant giving the total proceeds of the wares, but they were clearly less than he had estimated. A calculation by John made in September, 1789, of the profit or loss on the voyage, shows a loss of £500 lawful money.[29] But careful scrutiny of the document casts considerable doubt upon the credibility of John's figures. He charged the outbound cargo of *General Washington* at a figure some £560 in excess of the invoice. He not only charged the venture 6 per cent interest on the capital invested in the ship and her cargo but he reckoned the interest for two full years, despite the fact that the voyage was completed in slightly more than eighteen months. His charge for depreciation on the ship was 44 per cent, although she sailed on her next voyage without any substantial repairs. In these various ways the venture is debited with charges some $12,000 in excess of the amount that today would be regarded as reasonable.

If John's estimate exaggerated the debit side of the ledger, it mini-mized the credit side. One example will suffice. As the cargo had not yet been sold, John assumed that the 139,000 pounds of bohea tea would fetch only the invoice price at Canton. But since Brown and Benson were then selling bohea tea at a figure some 6d. in excess of the invoice price, John's estimate of the return on the tea could well have been on the short side by approximately £3,500 lawful money. Far from showing a loss of £500 on the voyage, *General Washington,* at a conservative estimate, returned a profit of $20,000. In any event, the proceeds were such as to encourage Brown and Francis, Brown and Benson, and Welcome Arnold promptly to dispatch *General Washington* on another errand into the Pacific.

The first visit of the ship to the Indies had provided her owners with information that could have enabled them to avoid a repetition of certain mistakes. The voyage had made clear the importance of arriving at Canton early in the season. Their ship had been not only the last American ship to anchor there but she was the last under any flag. The American ship *Asia,* arriving on July 7, had sold her ginseng at $120 a picul; *Canton,* a month later, disposed of her ginseng at $80 a picul; *Jenny,* at the end of August, had received $70 a picul. *General Washington* appeared on October 28, when the market was glutted; her ginseng sold for $65 a picul.[30] The importance of being early is apparent. This could be achieved in either or both of two ways: by dispatching the ship early or by sending her direct to Canton rather than via India. On their second voyage to China John Brown and his fellow adventurers did neither. Having at the moment no other ship suited to the needs of the East India trade, they were forced to await the return of *General Washington*. Her late return from Canton meant a late departure from Providence on her second voyage, on which she again visited India en route to China.

THE GROWTH OF THE INDIA TRADE

On the second voyage of *General Washington* Brown and Benson increased their share from an eighth to three twenty-seconds, while Welcome Arnold's part was a twenty-second in lieu of a twenty-fourth.[31] John Brown was so optimistic about the trade that he persuaded the other partners in the venture to join with him in fitting out the brigantine *Providence* for a voyage to the Indies.[32] The vessel itself sailed wholly on the account and risk of Brown and Francis, but her cargo belonged jointly to the three houses. If she were sold in India, the proceeds would be taken to Canton on *General Washington;* and goods purchased therewith would be shipped on the account of Brown and Francis. If she were not sold, she would continue to Canton solely on account of the same firm. John Brown was prepared to stake a good deal on trade to the East.

Providence sailed from Field's Point in Narragansett Bay on December 9, 1789, with John Brown on board. At Warwick Neck he went ashore. There is no knowledge of the cargo carried by the brigantine. She touched at Madeira, presumably to take on wine. She also called at Teneriffe, where on January 28, 1790, her crew were busy loading and storing wine. From there the voyage was uneventful, except for a shortage of water that compelled them to use bad rain water. In June she arrived at Bombay much the worse for wear, in need of new sails, spars, rigging, and pumps and also of repairs to her hull.[33]

Of the second voyage of *General Washington* to the Indies a good deal less is known than of the first, although William Megee was again on board and kept his journal. There is no complete invoice of her cargo.[34] Even the instructions to her captain and supercargo must be inferred from the actual course of events. At ten o'clock on the morning of December 30, 1789, the ship weighed anchor in the harbor at Newport. At half-past eleven the crew saluted the town and gave three cheers. At one o'clock they took their leave of "that good man, Mr. John Brown." When he got into the boat and passed "our Quarter we gave him one gun and three Cheers—which he answered."[35] On this voyage, unlike the first one, no call was made at Madeira, perhaps because *Providence* had touched there and at Teneriffe for wine. So empty was the voyage of interesting incident that Megee found little worth recording in his journal. On June 7, 1790, the ship anchored in the harbor at Bombay.

The letters written by Megee from Bombay make it quite clear that the plan of the voyage called for the sale of the cargo there or at other points in India and the procurement of a cargo of cotton for sale in Canton. His first letter could have afforded his owners little hope of the successful consummation of the plan. The cotton crop in India had been a failure, and none was to be had at any price. Bombay merchants had not enough cotton for their own ships, some of which were obliged to remain idle until the next season. Bengal and Madras ships had been under the necessity of returning home in ballast. At Bombay there were seven American ships beside his own, and more were expected daily. Their plans were very similar to that of *General Washington*. But since their cargoes would not sell at Bombay, they would be forced to sail for Bengal or Madras. The ship *Governor Clinton* had been sold because of her inability to purchase or freight a cargo for Canton. The American ships were leaving, and soon *General Washington* would be alone. But Megee planned to stay because of his orders to sell at Bombay, and he was resolved somehow to go on to China even in ballast, as he could not think of breaking orders or of "Loosing the Season." He had samples of his cargo on shore, but had thus far had no offers that were better than half the cost price, except for his iron, duck, cordage, and a few boxes of spermaceti candles. But he planned to keep these "good articols" in order to aid the sale of the others.[36]

A few days after Megee had penned this letter, however, the situation seemed to take a turn for the better. He had closed a bargain with a Parsi merchant to take his entire cargo in exchange for "good last years Cotton Sufficient to load the Ship." He was to receive cotton at the rate of 107.5 rupees a candy of 784 pounds, with the privilege of choosing from 1,800 bales. The merchant was to take everything in his cargo at prices charged in the invoice, plus 12 per cent. Though the cotton was from last year's crop, it had been kept from the weather in a good warehouse. Megee could see little difference between this and the new cotton. Anyway, in the absence of new cotton he was forced to take this offer or lose the season. Except for a few articles his cargo would command no cash, so he would have been compelled to try the other coast of India.[37]

It would seem that Megee had made a good bargain. The cotton remaining in Bombay, after he had purchased (at 107.5 rupees) a sufficient quantity to load his ship, was sold at 127 rupees a candy and would go to Canton on British ships. There would then be not one bale of cotton in Bombay. He thought it fortunate that he had stayed at Bombay instead of following the example of the seven other American ships that, finding no new cotton there, had gone to the other coast and would lose the season. In that his would be the only American ship bound for Canton with cotton, he thought he should make a good profit on the venture.[38]

Meanwhile, Megee had endeavored to arrange a sale of the Madeira wine that *Providence* would bring. But he wrote that he found the market flooded and prices low with no buyers.[39] Three days after the writing of those lines *Providence* arrived. All were well on board except the supercargo, who was vomiting blood, perhaps as a result of drinking bad rain water. Megee was sending the brigantine around to Madras, where the captain was to sell both vessel and cargo. As the wine market at Madras proved better than expected, the Madeira fetched a good price. Receiving only one offer for the brigantine in her bad condition, they sold her for $2,420. Proceeds of the vessel and cargo were to be available for remittance to Canton in two sets of exchange. From Madras, Joseph Rogers, the supercargo of *Providence,* sent to his owners information regarding articles suitable for the Indian market. Bar iron, ducks, cordage, and steel would command cash at some advance. Limited quantities of spermaceti candles would sell, as would tea. There was no market for flour, porter, cheese, planks, or anchors.[40]

As for *General Washington,* Megee wrote on July 16 that he had on board 504 bales of cotton. To make room for it the water, cables, and some of the ship's provisions had been moved to the deck. The lower cabin was stowed with cotton to the sills. With this cargo on board and with bills on China to the amount of 8,300 rupees, *General Washington* sailed from Bombay, bound for Canton by way of Madras, where she called to pick up the officers and crew of *Providence.* She anchored at Canton on October 4, where she found two American ships and fifty other vessels flying various flags.[41] Megee's journal, thus far the most important single source of information regarding both the first and second voyages of *General Washington,* then comes to an end. Nor are there letters from any of the officers describing the weeks spent in Canton. Again the ship had arrived late, but since she carried no ginseng or other products of American origin, it may well be that her lateness was less of a disadvantage than on the first voyage. It would be interesting to know whether the cotton commanded at Canton the handsome price that Megee had expected. Who was the hong merchant with whom Megee arranged for the sale of his cotton and the purchase of the return cargo? What were the details of the day-to-day trading? What were the quantity and prices of tea, nankeens, and other China goods in the market? Unfortunately, details such as these, which would bring the Canton phase of the voyage to life, are wholly lacking. Not even the invoice of the cargo from China is to be found among the papers of any of the owners of *General Washington*.

During the voyage Rhode Island had joined the Union by virtue of her belated ratification of the Constitution. As a result a federal customs office had been established at Providence where *General Washington*'s cargo was entered upon her arrival in June, 1791. She paid duties to the amount of $51,790.53.[42] The customs records list the articles composing the cargo, but there is no record of the cost of the goods at Canton. There are, therefore, only these few facts known about the second voyage of *General Washington*. And this time John Brown did not leave behind an account current of profit or loss for the venture. The probable degree of success achieved can only be inferred from circumstantial evidence. Assuming the duties to average about 25 per cent, the value of the cargo must have been about $200,000. It would seem that the ship's second voyage was rather more profitable than the first.

From John Brown's course of action it appears that he viewed the results of *General Washington*'s second voyage with considerable satisfaction. Within six months he dispatched her entirely on the account and risk of Brown and Francis on a third voyage to the Pacific. As she cleared for Bombay, it seems that the cotton venture at that port the previous voyage was sufficiently profitable to make John willing to repeat it. From Bombay she proceeded to Canton, whence she returned on May 14, 1793, laden principally with bohea tea and sugar. But the fact that the duties paid were only a little more than half those of the previous voyage probably indicates that she was correspondingly less successful.[43] Because Brown and Benson were not concerned in this voyage, no record of it is to be found in their papers; lacking, therefore, are the interesting details that those papers provided for the first voyage.

Meanwhile, in the summer of 1792 John Brown had dispatched his ship *Hope* on a voyage into the Pacific. Nothing is known of the instructions given Captain Benjamin Page, but by design or by chance the ship called at Sydney, New South Wales, thus becoming the first vessel from Rhode Island and the second flying the American flag to touch the continent of Australia. The ship *Philadelphia,* from the city of the same name, had preceded *Hope* by a few days in December, 1792. *Hope* continued on to China, whence she returned to Providence in September, 1793, with a cargo of China goods. Again, there exist no details of the voyage.

Trade from Rhode Island to the East Indies and China was now well begun. The initial impulse, the plan, and most of the capital had come from John Brown, with an assist from Brown and Benson. But the minor share of the latter house in the first two China voyages from Rhode Island in no way committed the partners to a continuation of this kind of maritime activity. It is obvious that Nicholas Brown participated haltingly and with some misgivings. By the time the ship had returned from her first voyage, Nicholas and his partner George Benson were deeply involved in their rum distillery, which not only absorbed a large amount of their capital and energy but committed them heavily to the Surinam trade upon which the distillery depended. There can be little doubt that these old and familiar types of business were more congenial to the cautious Nicholas than the newer kinds of traffic, which still had to prove themselves. Indeed, it may be doubted that he could ever have been won over completely to a branch of commerce so entirely alien to anything he had known when he was younger and more adaptable.

But death spared Nicholas the necessity of making a choice. He died in June, 1791, at about the time of *General Washington*'s return from her second voyage. His place in the firm was taken by his son of the same name. The elder Nicholas had given much thought to the training of his son for his career in business. In 1783 he had taken George Benson into partnership in order that, in the event of his own premature death, young Nicholas might have the benefit of the counsel of an older and experienced man. Serving his apprenticeship with Brown and Benson, the young man became the junior partner of Brown, Benson, and Brown shortly before the death of his father. New blood was thus injected into the business, and before another year had passed, the firm was further strengthened by the entrance of yet another young man. Thomas Poynton Ives, a native of Beverly, Massachusetts, had come as an orphan of fourteen to a clerkship in Brown and Benson. So capable was he and so closely did he apply himself to the business that he soon gained recognition as a young man of great promise. In 1792 he became the junior partner of the house of Brown, Benson, and Ives and in the same year married Hope Brown, daughter of the elder Nicholas Brown.

The death of Nicholas Brown was quickly reflected in a more aggressive and a more venturesome policy on the part of the firm. When John Brown fitted *General Washington* out for her third voyage, Brown, Benson, and Ives gave no thought to obtaining even a small interest in the venture. Instead the partners directed their attention to the fitting out of a vessel entirely on their own account. No longer content to play

second string to John Brown, they declared their independence in relation to the trade to the Indies. For their first venture to the East,
Brown and Benson chose a ship with the appropriate name of *Rising
Sun,* not to be confused with their brigantine of the same name. By
the late months of 1791 their plans were matured to the point of selecting a supercargo for the voyage. Their selection for this part was John
Rogers, a man of long business experience who had served the Browns
in many different capacities. For his services Rogers was to receive a
5 per cent commission on all property arising from the avails of the
outbound cargo, guaranteed to be not less than £10,000 lawful money of
Rhode Island. He was also to have a privilege of one ton by measurement of "Light Goods" on the return voyage. The owners were to furnish
the cabin with small stores on their own account. The master for the
voyage was Captain Pardon Sheldon, whose compensation of thirty
dollars a month was to be supplemented by a privilege of four tons and
by small stores equal to those provided Rogers.[44]

Brown and Benson had thought of employing *Rising Sun* in either
of two ways: to Calcutta and return with a cargo of sugar; or to Canton, via an Indian port, and back to Providence. When young Nicholas
Brown presented these alternatives to John Rogers, the latter made it
evident that a supercargo could be something more than a rubber
stamp for the ideas of the owners. He believed the large number of
vessels from the "Eastward" that "are gone & going" to Calcutta for
sugar would raise the price of that article in India and depress it in
New England. This consideration tended to "Stagger" his faith on a
venture to Calcutta. But he thought a voyage to China via India, with
suitable funds, could be counted on with certainty. *General Washington* and another vessel owned by Brown and Francis would be the only
Rhode Island ships at Canton that season. Rogers had reason to believe
that neither of these had funds sufficient to load with anything more
valuable than bohea tea and chinaware. He would therefore have
Rising Sun bring nankeens and black satins that would sell "quick to
a certain & considerable freight." Rogers seems to have made another
suggestion new to the China traders from Rhode Island. There is no
evidence that *General Washington* carried any specie to Canton on
either of her first two voyages, and Rogers strongly implies that on her
third voyage she was not thus supplied. He thought Brown and Benson should ship Spanish dollars on board *Rising Sun;* he understood
that in Canton the Spanish coin was worth 6s. 7d. sterling, "almost
50% on their worth here." Rogers then submitted calculations showing
that an investment of £20,000 lawful money in nankeens, satins, bohea
tea, chinaware, and fine Japan ware would sell for £33,000 in this

country.[45] After allowing £4,440 to cover all charges, the profit on the voyage would amount to £8,560.

Brown and Benson were sufficiently impressed by Rogers to abandon the idea of dispatching *Rising Sun* to Calcutta for sugar. Instead, they directed Captain Sheldon to proceed to Bombay, the first port of call in the East of *General Washington* on her second and third voyages. And they acted upon Rogers' suggestion that they send Spanish dollars to Canton.[46] *Rising Sun* almost certainly was the first of the Rhode Island East India ships to carry a substantial amount of hard money.

The cargo that her owners assembled for *Rising Sun* bore some resemblance to that of *General Washington* in 1787; but the differences were quite as marked as the similarities.[47] Absent was the great variety of spirits, including Madeira and other kinds of wine. Jamaica rum and geneva had a monopoly of the beverages. Absent, too, were the anchors, guns, and gun carriages; the large quantity of hams and codfish; and the ginseng, so conspicuous on the first Rhode Island venture to the Indies. Present were cordage, bar iron, steel, sailcloths, beef, and flour. Much the costliest items in the invoice were 429 boxes of spermaceti candles, procured from William Rotch, once of Nantucket, now of New Bedford. The goods of various sorts on board were charged in the invoice at £7,594 13s. lawful money of Rhode Island. The entirely new item carried by *Rising Sun* consisted of 17 boxes containing 36,000 silver dollars. For a Providence firm to raise that amount of hard money at that time was no easy task. Not only did it require a vast amount of thought and planning but it also made necessary as not since Colonial times correspondents in the neighboring provinces from whom Brown and Benson could obtain Spanish dollars. Coming at a time when they were deeply involved in their distillery and the ancillary trade to Surinam, the procurement of this amount of specie must have taxed their resourcefulness to the limit.

LEARNING BY EXPERIENCE

Rising Sun weighed anchor at Warwick Neck in Narragansett Bay on Sunday morning, January 15, 1792. Brown and Benson, soon to become Brown, Benson, and Ives, were now in the China trade on their own account. Fair winds made it unneccesssary to tack or wear ship for four weeks. Six weeks out John Rogers wrote that the ship was too deep-laden and very uncomfortable. She moved through the water like a log. The voyage thus far had proved quite uneventful, though not without occasion for concern to Rogers. In the calm latitudes they had opened the main hatch and found some of the candles wet, which he hoped would not hinder their sale. They had "smelt" geneva very perceptibly from the "Ships pumpings," from which they judged there must be some leakage from that article. But his greatest fear was that should existing winds continue, they would arrive at Bombay too late to go to Canton that season.[48] On April 27 they reached the Cape of Good Hope; on May 21, Madagascar; on June 4, Mozambique Channel; and on June 29 they arrived at Bombay.[49] There they found two American ships: one from Boston, the other *General Washington,* which had sailed from Providence only a few days before *Rising Sun* but had been at Bombay for a month and had on board for Canton some 575 bales of cotton. Clearly, *Rising Sun* would establish no records for speed.

As Rogers' instructions were to sell his cargo and invest in cotton, he set about at once to do so. But he had come to a very bad market, which was made worse because of his late arrival. As his alternatives were to sell or lose the season in Canton, he decided to sell, but at ruinous prices. The spermaceti candles in particular proved to be a detriment. They not only sold at a substantial loss but to get rid of them at all he found it necessary to sell other articles at reduced prices. He thought it unfortunate that Brown and Benson had not obtained better information concerning trade at Bombay. Fine wax candles, a product of India, were much preferred to the spermaceti variety. Cocoanut oil, sweet smelling and abundant, was more prized than whale or fish oil. India was a wheat-producing country, and in Bombay, Rogers wrote that he had eaten better bread than could be bought in Providence. To send flour to India was to send coals to Newcastle. He found that there was no demand for beef or pork by the natives, because to eat either meat was contrary to their religion. To add to his problems there had been much leakage of his liquor. But he had 114 bales of cotton on board, and he flattered himself that despite his "unpropitious" beginning, he would make a "tolerable" voyage, since *General Washington* was the only other American ship loading for Canton. However, Rogers unwittingly tempered this mildly hopeful remark with a postscript carrying the ominous news that "60 or 70,000 Bales" of cotton had been shipped "from here to China this Year." It remained to be seen what effect these large shipments in British East India Company and English country ships would have on the price of cotton at Canton.[50]

Much of what Rogers had written was well taken. It comes as something of a surprise to learn that Brown and Benson, through their concern in *General Washington*'s first two voyages, had not discovered the articles suited and unsuited to the Indian market. There were other facts concerning trade to India that they needed to know and were to learn from the pen of John Rogers. Within a week he wrote to express his regret at Brown and Benson's failure to load the ship with fewer goods and more hard dollars. He was convinced that should he make a good voyage, it would be because of the Spanish dollars on board. Sale of the goods would do no more than yield their first cost plus interest. It was his belief that unless his owners could finance the East India trade by the remittance of dollars, they would be well advised to abandon it. American merchants were playing a losing game in their efforts to raise funds for Canton by the exportation of American goods to India. Nothing but the late war between the English and Tipu Sahib had maintained even a tolerable demand for American products. Rogers, however, considered himself fortunate in one respect, that *General Washington* and *Fame* were the only American ships to precede him at Bombay that season. Had there been two more, he believed that he could have sold no part of his cargo.[51]

Even so, from choice or from necessity he carried on to Canton some of his rum, beef, and ducks. The bulk of his cargo from Bombay consisted of 258 whole bales and 20 half-bales of cotton—less than half the amount in *General Washington* on her current voyage.[52] On July 30, 1792, *Rising Sun* sailed for Canton. She had a fine run down the Malabar Coast and across the Bay of Bengal. Within thirteen days she was at the entrance to the Strait of Malacca. Because of tedious calms and light air they were twenty-four days in the Strait. On October 3 Rogers was in Canton. He chose as his security merchant Shykinqua "who is esteemed one of the first in Reputation amongst the Hong." To him he sold the cotton and the rum, taking from him bohea tea, one chest of gunpowder tea, a small amount of white sugar, and one picul of rhubarb.[53] Rogers gave Shykinqua no more of his hard dollars than would pay the balance of this account, plus charges, thinking he could lay his fund of specie out with other merchants to his own advantage. With his Spanish dollars he purchased 150 chests of white sugar (superior to that obtained from Shykinqua), chinaware, silks, cotton stuffs, lacquer ware, and nankeens. Canton had been visited that season by five other American ships, one of which was *General Washington*.[54] In late December, 1792, *Rising Sun* sailed for home, expecting to call at St. Eustatius.

In anticipation of his arrival at that Caribbean port, Brown and Benson, now having become Brown, Benson, and Ives, sent Rogers fresh instructions based on their analysis of the current economic situation within the United States. Trade was suffering, they wrote, because of heavy duties on imports, especially those from Europe. Hitherto the banks had assisted the importer with loans to pay the impost, but lately they had found it advisable to restrict discounting. Since the duties had to be paid punctually, great sacrifices in the sale of property had been and were being made daily. The scarcity of cash was exceedingly distressing and surpassed anything they had yet known. Interest of 2 and 3 per cent a month had been given for money. The 6 per cent funded debt of the country, which had sold for twenty-five shillings on the pound, was now reduced to eighteen shillings. In view of these conditions it was the considered judgment of Brown, Benson, and Ives that Rogers should sell at St. Eustatius all he could of his cargo for cash or good bills of exchange: the scarcity of money had had "a powerful effect in diminishing the price of all our imports." Because of this they hoped he could sell at St. Eustatius his nankeens, china, and silks and also his bohea tea if he could get twenty-five cents a pound for it. They decided that he should bring home money. As they had assembled the "best Materials for building a Ship of 450 Tons," it was their hope that the results of *Rising Sun*'s voyage would encourage them to proceed with the construction of the new vessel.[55]

Within three weeks Brown, Benson, and Ives were to take a more optimistic view of things. They believed that the market in St. Eustatius should be a good one because of "the alarming disturbances in Europe," with the consequent stoppage of "their [European] vessels and increased rate of Insurance."[56] The alarming disturbances, of course, were occasioned by the French Revolutionary Wars. To the best knowledge of the Providence house there was little bohea tea in the United States, most of it bought up in Boston and held speculatively. As the price of tea in Providence was then somewhat above two shillings, Rogers was instructed to bring his tea home unless the price was even higher in St. Eustatius. In the sale of his goods there Rogers was to be guided by the amount of each particular article shipped that season from Canton to America and by the influence of the war in Europe upon commerce in general. But in any event he should get money, "as it is an article very much wanted."[57] A week later their optimism had increased to an even higher point. Because the price of European goods at St. Eustatius must have increased greatly by virtue of the higher cost of "frieghts, insurance, etc.," they were sure Rogers would make a handsome profit. The partners at Providence awaited with some impatience the probable issue of *Rising Sun*'s voyage, eager to go forward with the building of their new ship should Rogers' "success encourage another speculation to Asia & Canton."[58]

In the belief that the British might open their West Indian ports to American vessels, Brown, Benson, and Ives chartered the sloop *Fanny* and dispatched her to St. Eustatius. Aboard her was Ephraim Talbot, a young gentleman of some years' service with the Providence firm, who was to assist Rogers. Should the ports of the British islands be opened, Rogers was to load *Fanny* with silks, chinaware, and nankeens from *Rising Sun*'s cargo to be peddled among the islands. Because of the scarcity of money the silks would not sell in this country, but bohea tea would pay a handsome freight.[59]

The letters addressed by Brown, Benson, and Ives to John Rogers at St. Eustatius provide an interesting analysis of business conditions in the United States in the spring of 1793, and they illustrate the care and thought that a mercantile house of that day gave to a consideration of the various alternatives open to it. But the letters seem to have been void of any practical results. For reasons not apparent, *Rising Sun* either did not call at St. Eustatius, or if she touched there, she did not remain long enough to transact any business. In support of this conclusion is the fact of her arrival at Providence in May, 1793, before some of the letters from the partners could have been received by Rogers at St. Eustatius and also the absence in the papers of the ship of any evidence of a visit to the Dutch island port. What was the reason for the change of plan? Was it because of the "alarming disturbances" in Europe that spring, in the course of which the French quickly overcame Holland, to which St. Eustatius belonged? Such an inference is not unreasonable. The mystery is the more tantalizing because all other aspects of the voyage are so well documented. The circumstances that occasioned the change appear to have been so well understood by John Rogers and his owners that they felt it unnecessary to leave a record for the benefit of posterity.

Instead of selling as much of his cargo as possible in the Caribbean, thereby avoiding the payment of the customs duties, John Rogers arrived in Providence with a cargo on which the duties were in excess of $15,000. It conformed closely to the cargo Rogers had planned before sailing from his home port. Bohea tea, silks, and nankeens were conspicuous. Sugar was the principal deviation from his list of items to be brought home. But the financial returns are of chief interest. Were they such as to encourage "another speculation to Asia & Canton"? Since Brown, Benson, and Ives were concerned in many subsequent speculations to that part of the world, it might be inferred that the venture was a success. According to the calculations of the partners, the voyage was not a failure in the sense of incurring a financial loss; but neither was it the success that Rogers had expected and the owners had hoped for.[60] In spite of the dull market at Bombay the cargo of goods and hard dollars from Providence, amounting to £18,897 lawful money, procured by exchange there and at Canton a cargo that sold in the United States for £23,859 clear of import duties, commissions, etc., an increase of almost £5,000. Deducting from this figure the charges for interest, insurance, depreciation, wages, and all other costs, there remained a balance of £177, which represented the "profit" of the voyage. In other words, the venture yielded that amount in excess of all costs. But the partners reckoned as costs not only all items that would today be regarded as such but also 6 per cent compound interest on the capital invested in the ship and her cargo. Since the capital investment was not less than $70,000, the interest charge for the voyage of sixteen months amounted to some $5,600. If 6 per cent interest on the capital investment be considered profit, as it would be today, instead of a cost, as it was then, the profit of *Rising Sun*'s voyage was about $6,000, not a spectacular figure, but far from a losing one. The capital fund that the partners had put into the voyage was not only intact but substantially augmented and ready to be employed in another venture into the Pacific, should they be so inclined.

Whatever their disappointment at the outcome, the owners of *Rising Sun* should have charged it to experience. The voyage had provided them with a fund of information concerning the trade that should have enabled them to plan more wisely for the future. They should have learned that the trade must be financed less by the export of American products and more by the shipment of Spanish dollars. They should have discovered, too, the folly of sending to India such articles as flour, beef, pork, and spermaceti candles. And they should have come to realize that the East India trade required a larger, faster, stronger ship than *Rising Sun*.

CHAPTER 3

A Rejuvenated Firm

THE more aggressive spirit resulting from the infusion of new blood into the house of Brown, Benson, and Ives was soon to translate itself into action. Replacing caution and conservatism with a measure of daring and imagination, the rejuvenated firm rapidly pushed its business into new areas; and shortly its ships became familiar sights in the Baltic and the Mediterranean as well as in the Pacific. But nothing gave stronger proof of the resolve of Brown, Benson, and Ives to expand the scope of their business than their decision to build a splendid new ship, primarily with an eye to her employment in the East India trade.

On February 28, 1792, they engaged Caleb Barstow to supply them with a quantity of good white-oak timber to be cut "before it will suffer any Injury by the sap" and to be placed in the water at once for purposes of seasoning.[1] A month later they contracted with four men to work under Barstow's supervision "on Taunton River, in & near Bridgewater," Massachusetts, sawing oak timber for shipbuilding.[2] Pursuant to the agreement, Barstow cut timber on many different parcels of land belonging to various persons. By early summer he had assembled at Bridgewater and Taunton thousands of feet of plank, and he had assembled at some seven different places in the same area more than 20,000 treenails. Once cut, the timber was rafted down the Taunton River through Narragansett Bay to Providence.

Although the white-oak plank for the new ship was thus procured within an easy radius of Providence, the white-pine plank and spars came from Maine. On April 4, 1792, Brown, Benson, and Ives arranged for the freighting from "Bath in Kennebeck River" of 4,000 feet of two-and-one-half-inch plank, the same to be delivered in Providence within a specified period of time, "Danger of the Seas excepted."[3] On the following day they commissioned Captain Lemuel Bishop to bring from the Kennebec white-pine timbers suitable for spars.[4] Early in the summer they were able to report that the timber for the new ship "we have in very great forwardness"; and they planned to have it well seasoned "before we sett her up."[5]

When the timber had lingered in the seasoning process for some eighteen months, Brown, Benson, and Ives arranged with one of the most skillful naval architects of the time for the construction of the new ship. In his long career Colonel Benjamin Tallman, a native of Portsmouth, Rhode Island, was to be the builder of about one hundred sail of merchant vessels and at least one man-of-war, the frigate *Warren* built at Providence in 1776 for the Continental navy. Among the merchant craft built by him were the ship *George Washington* (not to be confused with *General Washington*), belonging to Brown and Francis, and the first and second *Ann & Hope,* belonging to Brown and Ives.[6] Some of the vessels designed by him were among the largest in the United States in their day, and two of them were among the fastest sailing of the time. Brown, Benson, and Ives spoke of Tallman as the first shipbuilder of New England.

By the agreement of December 3, 1793, Tallman was to begin at once "to make the moulds & with a small gang of hands prepare the timber," so that the ship could be "set up as soon as the Spring opens." Then he was to employ as many hands as necessary to have her in readiness for launching in September, 1794. The vessel would be "set up" in Tallman's yard, "who is to make no charge for the same nor for his Workshop," which was to be used while the ship was building. To a generation that has witnessed a sharp reduction in the purchasing power of the dollar, it comes as something of a shock to learn that this highly skilled craftsman was to receive compensation at the rate of ten shillings lawful money a day for the first three months, "he finding himself." Thereafter, he was to be paid two dollars a day until the ship was completed, "to be paid every week if demanded." Tallman would build the vessel in the "very best manner" agreeable to the direction of Brown, Benson, and Ives. He promised to keep an exact account of his own work and of every man employed in the yard and to furnish the owners with this account weekly.[7] Thus the partners provided all the materials for the ship and paid all the workers, including Tallman himself. The latter, in turn, gave his skill, his watchful eye in a supervisory capacity, his yard, and his shop in return for a daily wage.

Construction of the craft appears to have progressed according to schedule. In July, 1794, Tallman submitted to the owners a report of the rapid growth of the new ship. The ceiling was all in above deck except one piece that was left out on purpose near the bow "to Run the Beems & knees under the one Side of the waist." The carpenters worked exceedingly well, while the caulkers were faithful and industrious. Tall-man concluded with the remark that since the beams of the upper deck were to go on board that day, "Sum artafisial Spirit" was wanted. Brown, Benson, and Ives would greatly oblige by sending up "Five Quarts of Good W [India] Rum."[8]

The time was fast approaching when this fine ship of 460 tons would slide down the ways into salt water. But prior to that event she must have a name. Party lines had already been drawn within the young country. Federalists and Republicans had made their appearance. And the Browns, like the mercantile element everywhere, had shown their unbounded admiration for the author of the funding plan by rallying instinctively around the Federalist standard of Alexander Hamilton. They would now reaffirm their devotion to Federalist principles by naming the new vessel for one of the leaders of that party. But as they themselves had a ship named *Hamilton* and as John Brown had his *General Washington* and *George Washington,* it was necessary to turn to one of the other prominent Federalists. It would, of course, have been a nice gesture to name the ship *John Adams,* thus honoring a native son of New England who was then Vice-President; but that gentleman had never succeeded in winning the plaudits of the merchant aris-tocracy of his own section. Choice fell, therefore, upon the man who at that very moment was in England negotiating the treaty that bears his name. When launched in September, 1794, the new vessel was chris-tened *John Jay.*

Probably no one in Providence (not even Brown, Benson, and Ives) had followed the building of the new ship with greater interest than John Brown. Alarmed by this convincing evidence of the resolve of his rivals to pursue the China trade on a substantial scale, John sought to dissuade them. The actual construction of the ship had scarcely begun when John, acting for Brown and Francis, expressed the readiness of his house to "Drop all pretentions to the Rum Distillery or Surinam Trade if you will do the Same with Respect to the India Trade..."[9] Not sharing John's belief that "one India House for this Town is Sufficient," Brown, Benson, and Ives proceeded with the building of *John Jay,* which was to be the first step in making them the leading "India House" of Providence and one of the five chief India traders of the country. However, pending the completion of their new ship, Brown, Benson, and Ives were seeking ways to perfect trade to the Baltic.

THE BALTIC TRADE

In the previous decade John Brown, in his restless search for a way of extricating himself from the financial embarrassment of the Critical

Period, had employed a vessel in the Baltic trade. Evidently the adventure did not provide him with great enough returns for his labors, for by the autumn of 1789 he had decided to withdraw from that sea in favor of a possible voyage to Bombay.

During this same period Nicholas Brown and his partner had been assembling data with regard to the Baltic area. From Captain Clarke, who had under the employ of Welcome Arnold been on several voyages to that sea, they requested answers to several questions. From him they wished to know "to what ports or Places Do they sell there Cargoes that go up the Baltick" and the best time of the year to trade in those countries. They understood that New England rum, rice, and tobacco constituted the cargoes, but "What proportions of Each?" Of what proof should the rum be? What kind of tobacco "answers best," since that from the "North part" of Virginia comes cheaper than "James River"?[10] George Benson, writing to his friend William Gray of Salem, asked "where Hemp can be procured cheapest wether at Gottenberg or Copenhagen, what Russia Duck Cost there & what other articles will do to import"? He also asked what month is the most eligible "for a Vessel to sail from here for the Baltic?"[11]

Armed with the answers to these questions, the partners in 1788 loaded a quantity of tobacco, rice, indigo, and New England rum on board their ship *Hope* and dispatched her to the Baltic. They enjoined upon Captain Jacob Westcot the strictest economy. He must not advance money to the crew members on the voyage, nor should he "Suffer them to get at the Rum."[12] *Hope* called at Copenhagen, whence she returned to Providence with a small cargo of Russian goods. She made three more voyages to the Baltic—one to Copenhagen, the other two to St. Petersburg. None of them was a financial success. Although it was the opinion of John Brown that their ownership of the rum distillery placed Brown and Benson in a favorable position with respect to trade to the Baltic (since it supplied them with one of the staples of the trade), the partners found nevertheless that they could not send a cargo aboard *Hope* from Providence that would enable them to bring *Hope* back fully loaded from the Baltic. Trade of the partners to the Baltic, as well as to certain other areas, was still in the experimental stage.[13]

To be loaded on a return voyage a ship to the Baltic had to command greater financial resources than could be obtained from the mere sale of a cargo of American goods. Brown, Benson, and Ives therefore sought to avail themselves of the credit that they enjoyed with their merchant-banker correspondent in London. Loading their ship *Hamilton* with the familiar cargo of tobacco, rice, and rum, they placed in the hands of Captain William Rodman bills of exchange on Thomas Dickason and Company to the amount of £3,000 sterling. Thus equipped, *Hamilton* set sail on March 25, 1792, for Copenhagen to the address of Ryberg and Company. The tobacco and rum sold tolerably well, but not the rice, owing to the prior arrival of two cargoes of that article from Charleston. With a letter of credit from Ryberg and Company for the amount of his sales and with his bills of exchange on London, Captain Rodman proceeded to St. Petersburg, where Smith and Company provided him with a cargo of hemp, iron, Russia ducks, and raven's ducks. The captain was pleased to report to his owners that his funds more than sufficed to load his ship. And the encouragement that the partners derived from this intelligence was appreciably augmented when they found on balancing their books that the voyage had returned a profit of £1,751 lawful money, or about $5,800. They had thus discovered a way of financing business to the Baltic.[14]

Soon the partners thought to try another method of conducting this same traffic, namely, by a voyage to the Baltic via a port in southern Europe. Late in 1792 they dispatched their ship *Hamilton* to Boston, where their friends Head and Amory were preparing for them a cargo of fish for Lisbon. Finding at Boston that he must wait while the fish were brought in from the fishing towns, the captain used his time to put his ship in good order for the reception of his cargo.

But the captain was soon to discover that his weeks of waiting were not to be a period of unrelieved monotony. Boston offered abundant opportunity for "unruly Sailors" to get into trouble. A member of the ship's crew, John Hopkins, alias John Bowen, was committed to jail "for Assaulting a Whore House, Breaking Windows, abusing Both White & Black Prostitutes . . . " Had the fellow behaved properly in the presence of the judge he would have received only a light fine. But so scandalous was his conduct that he was required to pay "Five or Six pounds." When the culprit appealed to Captain Rodman to secure his release from prison by payment of the fine, the latter visited the jail, expressed his sympathy, but refused to bail the man out. He thought "a flaggelation would be of Service to such a fellow." But Captain Rodman wished advice from the owners about this sailor, who had told the judge he was a "Grandson of the late Governor [Stephen] Hopkins" of Rhode Island. The captain had been at particular pains to inform the judge that Hopkins was not a legitimate descendant of Stephen Hopkins, although he might conceivably be a natural one.[15] The owners thought it not prudent to pay the fine. Perhaps the fate of Hopkins would serve as a lesson to the rest of the crew.[16] Being a compassionate man, however, Captain Rodman soon had a change of heart.

When Hopkins had been eighteen days in jail, the captain became convinced of his penitence; and since the intercession of the jailkeeper with the judge had procured a reduction of the fine, Rodman recommended that Brown, Benson, and Ives authorize him to advance the sum necessary to secure the sailor's release.[17] The partners readily acquiesced but with the request that Hopkins be given a "faithful lesson for his own sake."[18]

This affair settled, Captain Rodman could once more concern himself with the loading of fish. Soon he had on board most of the 3,600 quintals he expected to take. But he feared *Hamilton* was "to Lean & Sharp for an Owners Profit."[19] When he cleared from Boston on January 8, 1793, he carried a letter from his owners to John Bulkeley and Son of Lisbon bespeaking their most earnest efforts to procure the highest possible price for the ship's valuable cargo of choice fish. Should this, their "first adventure" to Lisbon, justify their sanguine expectations it would "probably introduce a More frequent intercourse" with that port.[20]

Hamilton arrived at Lisbon after a passage of twenty-seven days, only to find two vessels from New England already there. Captain Rodman "Vallue[d]" on Bulkeley and Son, who sold the fish in "as good a Sale as any made here this Season."[21] Meanwhile the owners were writing to the captain, urging upon him the importance of dispatch. As they expected a "prodigious" importation of Russian goods into the country in the fall, they hoped *Hamilton* would be the first American ship from St. Petersburg.[22] Captain Rodman loaded his ship for the Baltic with oranges, lemons, and cork on freight. As the general war against France had begun, Rodman, as well as Bulkeley and Son, took an optimistic view of its impact upon American trade.[23] American produce would be in great demand; and American ships, covered by a neutral flag, would be in even greater demand. The resulting expansion of the United States merchant fleet would prove a boon to the Baltic trade, since there would be an increased need for iron, canvas, hemp, and shipbuilding materials generally.[24] But not a word did they write of the possibility that American ships might be caught in the cross fire of Anglo-French commercial restrictions.

Provided by Bulkeley and Son with bills of exchange covering the proceeds of his cargo of fish, Captain Rodman embarked for St. Petersburg. But eight days out from Lisbon he was taken by a "French Privateer Called the *Republican*," whose commander forced the second mate and six of the people from *Hamilton,* placed a prize crew on board her, and dispatched her to the nearest port in France. Before reaching this haven, however, *Hamilton* was recaptured by the British frigate *Juno* and sent to Portsmouth, England.[25] After a delay of three or four months, in the course of which the fruit she carried on freight completely rotted, Captain Rodman obtained her release and continued in her to St. Petersburg as originally planned. Brown, Benson, and Ives promptly submitted a bill for some $7,000 covering the losses they allegedly had suffered from *Hamilton*'s capture and detention. Although they pressed their claims upon Paris and London to the point of requesting the official intercession of Thomas Jefferson, then Secretary of State, they obtained from the French only enough to cover the maintenance and passage to the United States of the crew members who had been taken off *Hamilton;* and from the English they received only the freight money for the fruit that had perished on board her.[26] Nevertheless, the voyage was a financial success. *Hamilton* arrived safely at St. Petersburg, where the bills of exchange received at Lisbon in payment for her fish more than sufficed to load her with a large cargo of hemp, old and new sable iron, and ducks. She brought also a small quantity of another article new to invoices of the Russian trade. Her owners had asked Captain Rodman to bring twelve bushels of "Cyberian" wheat, if it was to be had, or Russian wheat—"half winter & half Summer"—for seed.[27] The captain complied with the request. *Hamilton* arrived home on October 23, 1793. Two months later the partners "Settled [the Voyage] in the Book" at a profit of £1,875 lawful money.[28]

The success of this indirect voyage to the Baltic was such that the partners decided to repeat it, but by way of a French port rather than Lisbon. Losing little time, they dispatched *Hamilton* with Captain Rodman again in command to Bordeaux with instructions to obtain all possible information with respect to the business situation there. Thinking the state of war then prevailing in France would overcome the popular aversion there to the products of whale fishing, they loaded the ship principally with whale oil and whalebone, together with a quantity of tobacco. The partners wished the proceeds of the cargo remitted either to Ryberg and Company in Copenhagen or to Dickason and Company in London, upon whom the captain would then be able to draw in payment for goods from the Baltic.[29]

Hamilton arrived at Bordeaux in early February, 1794, where Captain Rodman found a hundred American vessels under an embargo.[30] He observed that the French were much attached to America and were all in high spirits, "Determined to Die or be Free." The guillotine was still in use, and "it is supposed 100,000 Heads is alredy Been taken off." The Algerines had taken nearly thirty American vessels, some of which they had been permitted to carry into Lisbon. To the captain it was clearly the design "of the Infernal Court of Britain" to set those "Hell Hounds of Pirates" on American ships. He declared that the English were fearful that "our Country will Out Rival them in Trade" and that they had been the United States' greatest enemies since "we have become a Free Country." He hoped Congress would "think it time to Build Frigates soon."[31] Captain Rodman without doubt at that moment reflected the resentment of many Americans at the British seizure and detention in West Indian ports of two or three hundred American ships with their cargoes. But he, like the mercantile community generally, would in the long run accept the Hamiltonian idea that British insults were to be borne with patience; and the time would come in a few years when he and they would regard France as a greater offender than England.

Although Captain Rodman liked the French, he was annoyed by their leisurely way of doing business. The people who bought his oil he found especially guilty of procrastination: "I am Daily Put off with fair Promises that the money will come from Paris to pay me very soon. That has been the Say for these 6 or 7 weeks."[32] But he finally received payment in specie, and with "about 10,000 Dollars & Crowns,"[33] 20 ingots of silver, and a quantity of silver plate he set sail for Copenhagen. Finding Russian goods there about 15 per cent higher than in St. Petersburg, he continued to the latter place, where he loaded his ship with a large cargo. *Hamilton* arrived at Providence in the autumn of 1794. When the partners settled her accounts, they found that she had made a profit of £2,055 on the voyage.[34] Brown, Benson, and Ives had perfected a second formula for the financing of trade to the Baltic. On two successive voyages Captain Rodman had successfully combined a call at a port of southern Europe with a visit to St. Petersburg.

Meanwhile the Providence firm had discovered a third method of conducting traffic to the Baltic. This involved a direct voyage to that sea without bills of exchange but with an assorted cargo of both American and Asiatic produce. This plan they first tried when in 1793 they dispatched the brigantine *Three Friends* with a quantity of coffee and the best white China sugar together with tobacco, rice, and rum.[35] With this very valuable cargo Captain John Warner was able to procure a handsome assortment of Russian goods for the return voyage. En route home *Three Friends* was cast away by high winds and heavy seas.[36] The partners calculated their loss at £3,661.[37] But in spite of this seeming disaster the voyage of *Three Friends* is significant. The mixed cargo of American and oriental produce that she carried set a pattern that her owners were frequently to use in their prosecution of this trade.

FREIGHTING

Brown, Benson, and Ives continued to conduct traffic to the Baltic with comparative ease and substantial profit. By the time the partners were well established in the Baltic trade, the French Revolutionary Wars had begun, and the partners soon sought to turn the conflict to their advantage by employing a part of their fleet of vessels in the freighting business. Because of United States' neutrality in the war American shipowners were supposedly reaping a golden harvest by carrying on freight the goods that in time of peace would have been shipped on craft flying the flags of belligerent countries. Their appetites whetted by reports of fabulous earnings, the partners in Providence decided to give freighting a try.[38]

Accordingly, in June, 1793, they dispatched their ship *Rising Sun,* only recently returned from Canton, to Baltimore. In lieu of a typical assortment of New England and West Indian goods she carried chiefly East Indian sugar, chinaware, nankeens, and silks, all imported by her owners from the Pacific. At Baltimore, Captain Daniel Olney was to deliver the cargo to George Sears and to follow his directions in regard to the further employment of the ship. But the "object" of her owners was to utilize the vessel in "freighting to the best advantage." Should Sears direct him to carry a freight to the West Indies (as they hoped he would), Captain Olney was to remit the proceeds to the partners in specie by "some good opportunity," obtain another freight at once either to Europe or to the United States, and continue freighting from port to port. If Sears loaded the ship for Europe on the owners' account, Captain Olney was to arrange with one of their correspondents on the Continent to sell the cargo and remit the proceeds to Dickason and Company in London. It was the partners' hope, though, that *Rising Sun* would be engaged in the freighting business. And, as she was a "good Vessel and well found," the captain was to demand "the highest Price of freight."[39]

En route to Baltimore, in sight of land off Cape Henry, Captain Olney "was fell in with & spoke by the British privateer Schooner *Dolphin,*" whose captain, Archibald Thompson, ordered him to shorten sail, lay by, hoist his boat out, and come on board. Captain Olney's hesitation soon brought from *Dolphin* a "volly of oaths," with the threat of a broadside unless he complied immediately with the order. At this point Captain Olney thought it "most prudent" to observe the command, and he "hoisted out yawl" and sent his mate and two men on board the schooner. Captain Thompson, two officers, and five men, all armed, then came on board *Rising Sun,* "rummaged . . . several Appartments at pleasure untill they were satisfyed," and then permitted her to proceed.[40]

Safely arrived at Baltimore, Captain Olney found that his ship could be freighted "to very great advantage" with flour to the West Indies or Europe or with wheat to Spain or Portugal.[41] Great was his surprise, therefore, when told by George Sears that Brown, Benson, and Ives had changed their minds. They had instructed Sears to load *Rising Sun* with flour on their account and dispatch her to Bordeaux. Sears was accordingly purchasing 1,600 barrels of flour.[42]

But soon the partners had changed their minds again. In the end *Rising Sun*'s voyage from Baltimore represented a cross between their original plan to employ her wholly in freighting and their second one to load her entirely on their own account and risk. Her cargo consisted of coffee, flour, and pig iron on account of the owners. On freight she carried tobacco, deerskins, and rice.[43] The revenue from the voyage was to be further augmented by some human freight. Captain Olney wrote his owners that he had engaged fifteen passengers at twenty guineas a head. They were to support themselves, except that he would "set Ships Beef & Pork before them at times." No one's baggage was to exceed two "Common Size Trunks & beding." The captain was employing his "Joyners" to erect "close births" in the round house and "all that space formerly occupied for a Store room." The accommodations would be erected at minimum cost and of cheap materials. He had resigned the state rooms entirely to the passengers and would endeavor to crowd in thirty persons, "as they are so very earnest for a passage they are no wise nice."[44]

Captain Olney's passengers were Frenchmen, refugees from the recent slave insurrection in Saint Domingue (Haiti), who had arrived in Baltimore "distitute of all property."[45] There a committee of citizens had organized to solicit funds in their behalf; and this committee evidently was instrumental in making arrangements with Captain Olney for their passage in *Rising Sun*. Eventually the captain's passengers increased to thirty-one.

Before sailing from Baltimore, Captain Olney came face to face with another problem born of wartime conditions. He was fearful that some of his crew would put him to a great deal of trouble. As seamen's wages had risen to twenty-four dollars a month, it was difficult to "keep men at their business." He dared not be severe with them, lest they leave him to accept a higher wage, which they could do with impunity in Baltimore, where there were no laws to govern seamen. But he hoped to keep most of his crew together until at sea once more, "when their duty will be executed without so much cerimony."[46] When one compares the nine to eleven dollars' wages of *Rising Sun*'s seamen with the figure quoted by the captain, it would seem that his fears were not entirely groundless. Indeed, the wonder is that he retained any of his crew.

Rising Sun sailed from Baltimore about the first of August, 1793, bound for Bordeaux. Writing to Captain Olney at the latter place, the partners expressed their hope that after delivering his cargo, he might find it advisable to employ the ship wholly in the freighting business. They envisaged the possibility of a "handsome freight" to the Île de France (Mauritius) or elsewhere beyond the Cape of Good Hope. From the Île de France he might procure a freight to Canton and thence to Europe or to the United States.[47] Meanwhile, all had gone well with Captain Olney until September 18, when he was captured by the British privateer *Vulture* and taken to the island of Jersey.[48] Availing himself of the provisions of a British Order in Council of September 3, 1793, he was able to prevent condemnation of *Rising Sun*. Within two months she was restored to him, but without her cargo.[49] Although the Court of Admiralty ultimately allowed Brown, Benson, and Ives some £1,414 sterling on account of the ship's freight and cargo, this was £2,200 short of the claim that they had submitted.[50] Thus flour and rice destined for the French had actually increased the grain supply of their enemies.

Once *Rising Sun* was restored to him, Captain Olney faced the problem of her future employment. The partners, of course, had hoped that she might be used profitably in the freighting business. But the captain found "perfect stagnation of the Freighting trade" in the United Kingdom. Dickason and Company wrote to Amsterdam in a vain effort to procure a freight for him.[51] He thought of calling at the Cape Verde Islands for a cargo of salt but was dissuaded from so doing when he heard that the Algerines were "Cruizing in the Western Ocean," had captured six American vessels, and were demanding $2,000 for the ransom of a seaman and $6,000 for a captain.[52] He therefore had no choice but to return to Providence in ballast. Thus the voyage of *Rising Sun* proved to be neither the disaster it might have been nor the success for which Brown, Benson, and Ives had hoped.

Another venture in freighting was rather more successful. At the outbreak of the European war the partners' ship *Hope* was at Surinam, where she had gone to procure molasses for the distillery. But Seth Wheaton, agent there for the owners, decided to employ her in a different manner. With permission from the governor at Surinam he loaded *Hope* chiefly on freight for Amsterdam but also with a quantity of sugar on the account and risk of Brown, Benson, and Ives, who gave their blessing to Wheaton's decision.[53] Addressing a letter to Captain Charles Sheldon of *Hope* at Amsterdam, they expressed their earnest desire to keep the vessel engaged in the freighting service for the duration of the war in Europe.[54] Unable at Amsterdam to procure a freight either to the United States or to the Caribbean, he obtained one to Lisbon, whence he returned to Providence with a cargo of salt.[55] His visit to Lisbon occurred at the same time that reports of Algerines off the coast of Portugal had discouraged Captain Olney in *Rising Sun* from calling at that port. At Amsterdam the sugar shipped on the owners' account netted $4,000, while the freight money came to $3,800. The freight to Lisbon swelled the total to well over $10,000. Judged by any ordinary test, the experience of *Hope* in the freighting trade must be considered satisfactory to her owners. Yet either from choice or from lack of opportunity they did not continue her in this kind of employment.

In this first year of the war Brown, Benson, and Ives had yet another try at freighting. Their correspondent at Philadelphia procured for their ship *Harmony* a freight of flour from the Quaker City to Puerto Cabello, near Curaçao, at the rate of eight shillings a barrel Pennsylvania currency, the money to be paid in "good heavy Spanish milled Dollars." The captain was to remit the proceeds from the freight by some American vessel to the partners' correspondent in Boston, New York, or Philadelphia. From Puerto Cabello he was to proceed to Curaçao, where he would take a freight for Amsterdam; there Hodshon and Son would remit the freight earnings to Dickason and Company in London to the account of the Providence house.[56]

Harmony arrived at Puerto Cabello in twenty-eight days from Philadelphia. Captain John Crumby delivered his freight, received 1,813 Spanish dollars, and proceeded to Curaçao.[57] There he lay for ten days while seeking a freight to any place. Failing to find one, he procured letters from French gentlemen to merchants in Jérémie, Saint Domingue. Upon his arrival off that port a cruiser came out, boarded him, and informed him that the town had been captured by the British. He then headed for St. Marc on the same island, where he planned to take on a cargo of salt. On the very day of his arrival there an "Extrordinery" storm attended by a "Verry Large Sea" destroyed all the salt. Thereupon, he agreed to take a freight to Charleston, South Carolina, for $1,800, payable on safe arrival there.[58] Upon reaching that port he received the freight money, which he placed in the hands of Hazard and Robinson, correspondents of his owners. These men procured for him a freight to Bilbao, Spain, at four to five dollars a ton, payable in good bills on London at thirty days' sight. From this he expected to make £680 sterling, which he would remit from Bilbao to Dickason and Company in London.[59] In the end, however, he decided to forego the voyage to Bilbao because of the danger from the Algerines off the coast of the Iberian Peninsula.[60] Instead he procured one to Hamburg for £532 sterling. The partners in Providence directed him to continue from Hamburg to St. Petersburg for a cargo of Russian goods. This Captain Crumby chose not to do, probably because of the extensive repairs that his ship required, including a new keel and new sheathing. Even after the repairs were made, the captain considered *Harmony* a hazardous vessel. In lieu of a Baltic voyage, therefore, he agreed to take wheat on freight to San Sebastián, Spain, for which he would receive £510 sterling. He expected to make "two of those voyages and Return home Early in the fall."[61]

Early in the fall he was not in Providence but in Hamburg, although in the six months' interval he had employed his ship in freighting to and from Le Havre rather than to San Sebastián. At this point Captain Crumby vanishes for a year, but only after he had sold *Harmony* without authorization from the men who owned her. After many months the partners wrote to Caspar Voight, their correspondent in Hamburg, conveying to him their power of attorney to recover from Captain Crumby the sum of "10,396 Dollars besides what interest may be due thereon."[62] While the captain had remitted more than $4,600 of the freight money to various of their correspondents, he had withheld the remainder of his earnings as well as the proceeds of the ship's sale. Eventually, Captain Crumby turned up in Boston, where he paid to Head and Amory (for the account of the owners) a sum equivalent to £1,273 lawful money of Rhode Island, the amount he had received from the sale of *Harmony,* valued by the partners at £1,350.[63] The record is not clear as to the balance of the freight money, but since no further charges were preferred against the captain, it seems likely that Brown, Benson, and Ives recovered. It is apparent that in the course of her brief freighting career *Harmony* earned for her owners some $10,500 over and above the cost of her extensive repairs.

These examples may be regarded as fairly typical of the freighting business in which several ships of Brown, Benson, and Ives were engaged in the years 1793 and 1794. These vessels made some money, but their earnings undoubtedly fell short of the hopes of their owners. One wonders, therefore, whether the partners were guilty of faulty planning, whether they were merely unlucky, or whether the supposedly fabulous earnings of the freighting trade were more the exception than the rule.

SPECULATION IN RICE AND FLOUR

By 1795 the partners were no longer involved in freighting, in part, perhaps, because they had become interested in the shipment on their own account of American produce, especially rice and flour, to war-torn Continental Europe. Like all wars of major proportions, the one then prevailing had created a marked demand for the great agricultural staples; and the hazards of transporting these articles across the seas in the face of existing obstructions to maritime commerce had greatly increased the speculative character of such traffic. Many ships engaged in this business failed to reach their destination; but such failures seemed merely to make more glittering the prospect of profit to be realized on a cargo that was fortunate enough to make port in safety. To this highly precarious, yet alluring, type of trade Brown, Benson, and Ives now for a season committed their attention and their resources without reservation.

In February, 1795, they dispatched the chartered ship *Ann,* George Page supercargo, to Bilbao with a cargo consisting chiefly of rice, flour, and whale oil.[64] As they expected to have an urgent need for a substantial sum of money within a few months, they directed Page to sell the cargo for Spanish dollars and return at once to Providence.[65] Two months later George Page wrote them, not from Bilbao, but from Bordeaux. As his ship was "standing" along the coast near Bilbao, he saw a number of vessels to windward. Soon two French frigates came up to him, sent officers on board, and informed him that Bilbao was under blockade. Thereupon he had proceeded to Bordeaux, where he sold the rice and flour for specie. The whale oil commanded only a moderate price in assignats, payable in brandy. A decree of the National Convention interdicting the export of specie in vessels "which did not import it" posed something of a problem for Page. Although large sums in specie were illegally carried from the country every day, the hazard involved was a considerable one. After careful consideration, Page decided to take his specie with him, at the risk of confiscation if apprehended in the act. As he prepared to sail from Bordeaux, he had on board 5,000 hard dollars, 9,555 gallons of brandy, and 1,099 yards of silesia cloth.[66] Although *Ann*'s return was somewhat later than her owners had hoped for, her voyage was a successful one, yielding a profit of £2,231 lawful money, or $7,439.[67]

In June of the same year the partners chartered the brig *Rambler;* loaded her with rice, flour, and bread; and dispatched her to Dunkirk under command of Captain Jacob Westcot.[68] The captain was to sell his goods for cash (no assignats) and return directly to Providence.[69] But *Rambler* never saw Dunkirk. En route she was stopped by the British frigate *Diamond,* Captain Sir William Sidney Smith, who examined her papers, and "alltho they ware all Clear for Hamburgh," put a prize crew on board and sent her into Portsmouth.[70] It is apparent that Captain Smith was undeceived by this attempt to establish a neutral port of destination for *Rambler*. Captain Westcot went up to London to enlist the aid of Dickason and Company, who told him his ship was only one of 150 American vessels then detained in British ports and that the government would in due time discharge the brig and pay for the cargo and all costs incurred by her capture. Eventually the owners received £3,667 sterling for the cargo and costs of *Rambler's* detention but nothing for the two seamen she lost to a British man-of-war.[71] Thus the partners were spared an actual loss on the voyage, but they were denied the possible profit—and perhaps a handsome one—of the sale of the cargo at a French port.

Before the summer of 1795 had run its course, Brown, Benson, and Ives sent yet another craft on her way to a port of France. This time it was *Charlotte,* George Tyler supercargo. Heavily loaded with rice and flour, *Charlotte* set sail for Bordeaux, where Tyler was to sell his wares for specie.[72] En route to Bordeaux he was intercepted by three British men-of-war, taken into Portsmouth, and then ordered to London for the discharge of the cargo.[73] Again Dickason and Company came to the rescue, providing Tyler with advice and with the funds he needed pending disposition of the case. In the end the owners of *Charlotte* received from the British government, by way of Dickason and Company, the sum of £6,712 sterling for the cargo and costs.[74] And the ship had lost one more seaman to the Royal Navy, for whom there was neither restitution nor reimbursement. Brown, Benson, and Ives, far from supplying the French with provisions at the expected profit to themselves, were providing sustenance to the British at cost.

Another voyage of that same year began in a most auspicious manner, only to end in near disaster. The partners sent their ship *Hope,* Captain John Warner, Ebenezer Thompson supercargo, to Brest with a valuable cargo consisting of rice, flour, whale oil, and small amounts of hemp and Swedish iron imported into the United States from the Baltic. Thompson was free to sell his cargo either to "Agents of the Republick" or to private parties; and since very valuable prizes had supposedly been carried into Brest, he might be able to make an investment in articles promising a good advance either in the United States or in the Baltic ports. Or he might proceed to the Baltic in ballast, invest his funds in Russian goods, and return to France for the sale thereof.[75] It seemed reasonable to suppose that France in wartime would have need for the naval stores of the Baltic.

Upon arrival at Brest, Thompson decided to sell his goods to the "national agents." Being in great demand, the rice and flour sold the entire cargo to advantage.[76] But in general Russian goods were selling cheaply in France, owing to the plentiful supply received by way of Denmark and Sweden. Investing his proceeds, therefore, in wine, raisins, figs, and coffee, Thompson headed for the Baltic, where he would purchase Russian goods, not for sale in France, as his owners had suggested, but for a return cargo to Providence. Selling his cargo at Copenhagen, he remitted £3,000 sterling to Dickason and Company in London, invested the balance of his funds in iron and ducks (hemp being too high), and set sail for home via the northern route instead of the English Channel.[77] North of Scotland a severe gale drove *Hope* onto a reef in the Orkney Islands. Unloading her in order to remove her from the rocks, they placed her upon a sandy beach while they conducted an investigation into the extent of the damage. Much of her keel was gone, "the after part intirely," and her bottom was much chafed and damaged, but none of her timbers was broken. For six months the weather was so severe and stormy that it was impossible to make even temporary repairs. But in the next two months she was patched up enough to allow her to sail for Leith, Scotland, where she underwent an extensive renovation. In early autumn of 1796 she arrived at Providence after an absence of eighteen months.[78] To the time of the wreck *Hope* had made a highly successful voyage. But the cost of repairing and rebuilding her was so great that a potentially fine profit was transformed into a loss of £854 lawful money.[79] The elements had conspired with British seizures to make the year a bleak one for Brown, Benson, and Ives.

Nor was their misfortune at an end. Late in 1795 they dispatched the brigantine *Friendship* to Le Havre with George Page as supercargo. Her cargo consisted of rice, flour, and whale oil that Page was to sell for specie or good bills, the proceeds to be remitted to Dickason and Company in London. After sending *Friendship* back to Providence or on a freighting voyage, Page himself was to remain at Le Havre, where he would serve as agent for the partners. In this capacity it would be his duty to gather the "earliest & best" intelligence as to the state of the different European markets for American rice, flour, and other products.[80] Having given Page these instructions covering his conduct at Le Havre, the owners, with an obvious eye to British naval officers, handed him another order directing him to proceed to Hamburg, a neutral port.[81] *Friendship,* of course, set her sails for Le Havre, and probably because of a relaxation in British policy toward neutral vessels, arrived there in safety. But Page found Europe glutted with American produce and commerce in France completely prostrated because the National Convention had ordered a new emission of paper money. Remaining behind, Page sent *Friendship* on to Rotterdam, where she could do no worse than in Le Havre.[82] Already in bad repair, the brigantine appears to have disintegrated while at sea. Only a few casks of rice were salvaged. The loss was a heavy one.

Thus in the single year 1795 Brown, Benson, and Ives had dispatched five vessels to the Continent with cargoes of rice and flour. One had returned a good profit, two had been seized by the British, one had been wrecked and repaired at great cost, and one had vanished from the seas. The trade in American staples had been a disappointment, not because of any lack of demand for the products, but because of the hazard involved in getting ships through to their ports of destination. Nevertheless, the partners were undismayed. Believing that rice would be in extraordinary demand at very high prices, their plan for 1796 called for a highly speculative venture in the purchase and shipment of that article to France.

With George Page stationed at Le Havre to keep a watchful eye on the state of the market, the partners dispatched the ship *Charlotte* and the brig *Harriot* to Charleston, South Carolina, where their several correspondents were making large purchases of rice for them. And they sent Ephraim Talbot to the same city with instructions to take up on charter or freight a third vessel, to load her with 1,000 casks of rice, and proceed in her to Europe.[83] The three vessels were expected to carry a total of 2,500 casks of rice to markets abroad.

Unfortunately for Brown, Benson, and Ives so many other American merchants were also making purchases of rice in Charleston that the price quickly advanced from twenty shillings a hundredweight to thirty shillings—an unhappy augury for their speculation. They expected *Harriot* to carry 600 casks of rice to Le Havre, where George Page would receive and sell the cargo, remit the proceeds to Dickason and Company in London, and send the brig to St. Petersburg for a return cargo of Russian goods.[84] Actually *Harriot's* cargo consisted of only 398 whole casks and 68 half-casks of rice. Upon her arrival at Le Havre the business situation was so adverse that George Page ordered her to Copenhagen. There Ryberg and Company agreed to advance £4 sterling a cask on the rice for remittance to Dickason and Company, but as this was less than half the cost of the rice in Charleston, the remittance fell far short of the £9,000 sterling that Brown, Benson, and Ives had expected.[85] Discouraged by the unfortunate turn of events, George Page ordered the sale of *Harriot* in Europe, as his instructions gave him the discretion to do. The owners calculated their loss on the voyage at £2,926 lawful money, or $9,744.[86]

While *Harriot* was en route to Le Havre *Charlotte* was on her way to Dunkirk with 423 whole casks and 121 half-casks of rice. Finding business there in a state of extreme stagnation, George Tyler continued to Copenhagen.[87] Leaving his cargo in the hands of Ryberg and Company, who agreed to advance £4 sterling a cask of rice for remittance to

Dickason and Company in London, he proceeded to St. Petersburg for a return cargo of Russian goods.[88] Sale of the rice by Ryberg and Company was bitterly disappointing. The partners' loss on the venture amounted to $14,000.[89]

Meanwhile, Brown, Benson, and Ives had given Ephraim Talbot at Charleston new instructions. To avoid the payment of exorbitant freight rates he was not to take up a vessel on charter or freight. Instead, he might spend up to $10,000 for the purchase of a suitable ship of 250 tons.[90] He thereupon purchased the ship *Elizabeth* at $8,500, which he would load with rice on his owners' account.[91] He was to invoice the rice at 12.5 per cent above the cost at Charleston, "as in case of any restraint it may be usefull," and to conceal all evidence of the real cost.[92] The higher the invoice price, the greater would be the payment for the cargo in the event of the detention and subsequent discharge of the ship by the British. The owners were mindful of the fact that this had been the fate of two of their vessels in the previous year.

Talbot soon developed misgivings in regard to this speculation, believing that prices in Europe would not make it profitable.[93] But for some time the partners were not disposed to share his doubts. They did not "wish to be Defeated in the Shipments" of rice, so confident were they "of its going to a great market in Europe."[94] So the purchase of rice at Charleston continued. Within a few weeks Talbot wrote that the quantities of rice "are all *secured*" but at high prices. He soon suggested that the partners should not anticipate "too great proffits" from shipping rice at thirty shillings exclusive of other charges. Among the other charges was the high wage of seamen. As Talbot thought, "The wages that I am obliged to give for a Crew is Enormious." Only with great difficulty were they to be had at less than thirty dollars a month.[95]

After *Elizabeth* had sailed from Charleston, her owners began to receive the unpleasant news that the price of rice in Europe was declining sharply. Soon it became apparent that their speculation must end in disaster. Like all mortal men, they were reluctant to admit that they were the victims of their own folly. Accordingly, they looked about for a scapegoat and found one in the person of Ephraim Talbot. They were "mortified & shagrined" at his purchase of rice at the "Enormous price" of thirty shillings. As for the ship *Elizabeth,* they wished never to see her again; and they regretted that when Talbot could have "freighted [rice] on such easy terms," he purchased the ship.[96] All this, of course, was grossly unfair to Talbot, who had complied with their instructions in the rice purchase against his better judgment. As for the "easy" terms on which he could have freighted the rice, it was precisely to avoid paying what they termed a "high freight" that they had directed him to buy the ship rather than to freight the goods. When they again wrote to Talbot, they were even more "mortified." His invoice amounted to an enormous sum, his disbursements at Charleston were very great, and he should have "persuaded" himself to have "no more Rice purchased at the monstrous price" of thirty shillings.[97] This was wisdom after the event.

Pursuant to instructions, *Elizabeth* called at Cowes for directions from Dickason and Company, who advised Talbot to take the ship to Amsterdam to the address of Hodshon and Son. Knowing how eager the partners were to place funds in the hands of Dickason and Company, Talbot requested and received from Hodshon an advance of 40,000 guilders ($16,000) on the cargo for remittance to London.[98] Hoping the rice market might recover from its state of demoralization, Talbot for a time held his cargo in storage. But, accepting Hodshon's opinion that the price would not soon rise, he ultimately sold it, incurring thereby a loss of more than $10,000 on the cost at Charleston.[99] Talbot hoped to purchase at Amsterdam a cargo that he would take to Cadiz, where the markets were said to be good, but the refusal of Hodshon and Son to advance the necessary funds forced him to relinquish that plan. He then decided to go to Cadiz in ballast in quest of a freight, but a "general disturbance," amounting almost to a mutiny on board his ship, caused a delay in the execution of this design. After discharging the entire crew and hiring a new one at lower wages, he was finally on his way.[100] At Cadiz he engaged a freight of wine to the island of Guernsey at £850 sterling.[101] On October 20, 1796, *Elizabeth* sailed from Cadiz on what, with good weather, should have been an easy voyage to Guernsey. For a few days all went well. Then the ship became caught in adverse winds that buffeted her back and forth between the coast of Ireland and the English Channel. After struggling with the gales for seventy days, facing a shortage of water caused by the rats gnawing the water casks, and with the crew members either sick or exhausted, Talbot made one last desperate effort to reach a haven on the Irish coast. But amid the anguished cries of his crew to the Almighty for mercy, he was caught in a fresh gale that between three and four o'clock in the morning of December 29 threw the ship on a rocky ledge near a place called "Blind Harbour" in Ireland. At the cost of five lives *Elizabeth* was so completely wrecked that she would not "fetch much." Among the survivors was Ephraim Talbot himself, who lost everything except his "sea dress" and who found himself "at the Mercy of a parcel of Irishmen" who behaved "mor like brutes than Sivilized people." Upon Talbot devolved the solemn duty of relating to the partners in Providence the sad tale of disaster.[102]

While he was in Europe, Talbot was amazed to learn that the owners had been speculating in flour as well as rice, "both of which articles is *Very low* [and] of dull sale."[103] While the three rice ships were crossing the Atlantic, the brigantine *Hiram* was carrying on freight for Brown, Benson, and Ives 975 barrels of flour from Baltimore to Le Havre, where George Page was to take charge of the cargo.[104] Because of the low price of flour at that port Page sent the brig to London but at the cost of an additional freight charge. Dickason and Company sold the flour at a loss of $2,727 from the cost at Baltimore. Adding the freight charges of $3,037, the partners were out of pocket to the amount of $5,764 on this particular venture.[105]

Brown, Benson, and Ives had lost $35,000 on the three rice cargoes of 1796. Assuming that *Elizabeth* was insured for as much as half her purchase price (a generous estimate), they incurred an additional loss of at least $4,250 by her wreck. Adding the loss suffered on *Hiram*'s cargo of flour, their total loss in the rice and flour speculations of 1796 was no less than $45,000.

As they surveyed the ruins of their much-cherished plans, the partners may well have taken solace in the thought that they were not alone in their folly. One company in New York had speculated in rice to the amount of £100,000 with correspondingly large losses. The firm of Thayer and Sturgis in Charleston was supposed to have lost £50,000 to £60,000, which would break it.[106]

One naturally wonders what the reasons were for the sudden collapse of the market for rice in Europe in the spring of 1796. Ephraim Talbot, in a letter written at Amsterdam on June 23, 1796, said it was owing to the "effectual methods" the government in England had taken to prevent a scarcity of grain in that country and to the arrival in Europe that spring of "many ships laden solely with Rice from the East Indias." The decline had begun in England, whence it had spread to the neighboring countries, which were "governed by the price in England."[107]

IMPROVEMENTS IN THE INDIES TRADE

While thus deeply engaged in commerce with Europe, Brown, Benson, and Ives were gradually developing the methods required for conducting the East India trade to maximum advantage. Late in 1794 their new ship *John Jay* was made ready for her maiden voyage. For command of the vessel the owners selected Daniel Olney, who had served in a similar capacity in another of their ships.[108] Olney was also to serve jointly with Samuel Snow as supercargo for the voyage. A graduate of Rhode Island College (subsequently Brown University), Snow was later to occupy the post of American consul at Canton. His business connection with the partners had begun as early as 1791, when he served as their agent in New York for the sale of commodities and the purchase of state securities.[109]

When they turned their attention to the cargo of *John Jay,* the Providence firm faced a still-unsolved problem of the East India trade: What were the items suitable for the markets in question? Although they failed to solve the problem to their satisfaction, they did introduce certain deviations from cargoes hitherto regarded as standard in the trade. The most distinctive feature of the cargo, as compared with previous ones, was the prominence of Russian goods. Bar iron, cordage, and Russia ducks and raven's ducks accounted for about two-fifths of the total amount of the invoice. Now quite well established in trade to the Baltic, the partners thought to use imports from that area in their traffic to the Pacific, thereby combining two different facets of their business. The category of goods ranking next in value may best be described as "spirits": rum, Holland gin, London brown stout porter, London porter, and bottled porter, which were valued at only a slightly lower figure. Pig iron, beef, pork, boards, anchors, anchor stocks, manufactured tobacco, and spermaceti and tallow candles constituted the balance of the cargo, which was rather more diversified than those of earlier voyages. The presence of spermaceti candles occasions some surprise in view of the sad experience of John Rogers with them on *Rising Sun's* voyage of three years before. The entire cargo was charged in the invoice at £10,365 lawful money.[110] Even if these wares were to sell in India at prices surpassing the wildest dreams of the owners, the proceeds would be insignificant when compared with the cost of purchasing a return cargo that would fill a ship the size of *John Jay.* To augment the funds at the disposal of the supercargoes, therefore, the owners placed on board 46,000 Spanish dollars assembled with much effort by them and their correspondents in the various coastal cities.[111] Thus the total resources of the ship as she sailed from Providence on Sunday, December 28, 1794, amounted to $80,550.

However much the partners were disposed to include new items in the cargo, they once more decided upon a voyage to Canton by way of India. Captain Olney's instructions directed him to make all possible dispatch to Bombay, where he was to call upon Dady Nassereang, who had assisted John Rogers on the occasion of *Rising Sun's* call at that port. After disposing of his cargo, the captain was to load the ship with cotton, preferably on freight, and proceed to Canton for a return cargo. He was reminded that conservation of space on board ship must be his watchword. To this end the pig iron that served as ballast on the voyage out was to be sold at Canton to make room for chinaware with which to "floor" the vessel. In a further effort to save space the partners placed on board the frame for a coach house that the ship's carpenter would begin putting up after they rounded the Cape of Good Hope. The officers were to live in the coach house from Bombay to Canton to Providence, "as the Cabin as well as every other part of the Ship must be compleatly full on both those Passages."[112]

A few days out from Providence *John Jay* ran into a rough gale that blew for thirty hours, but she took the punishment well. The supercargoes found her a "good Sea boat," very swift and free from any fault whatever. Because some of their water casks were damaged in the gale, they put in at São Tiago in the Cape Verde Islands for water. There they bought a milch goat and kid together with some other provisions. From there to the Cape of Good Hope *John Jay* and *Belvidere* of New York took turns outsailing each other. At the Cape they spoke *Columbia* of New Bedford, hoping to find a sea-going physician who could treat an ailing member of the crew. Finding none, they borrowed some medicines not to be found in their own deficient medicine chest.[113]

In the Indian Ocean when the monsoons changed they were caught in a severe gale in which they "just escaped from Death" and in which they lost their "foremast, Bowsprit & every yard sail and spar," except their main and mizzenmasts. In this perilous situation they remained for twenty-four hours, when the storm abated sufficiently to enable them to rig a "small Jury Foremast." With this and with the help of "some spare light sails" they reached Bombay seven days after the disaster, their arrival looked upon by the natives as "next to a Miracle." But to their great satisfaction they found the ship entirely tight, although the cargo had suffered a good deal from breakage.[114]

At Bombay they found three other American ships. Markets were very bad, and no freights were to be had. Sale of their cargo was disappointing. The gin and bar iron sold readily, but the porter would not fetch half its first cost. There was no sale for cordage or anchors nor for beef or pork, because of the religious scruples of the natives. Early in their stay Snow and Olney were at pains to warn their owners not to expect much profit at Bombay in view of the dull market and the high cost of repairs to the ship's rigging. Not the least of their difficulties was the necessity of using their best men for repairs, leaving only raw hands and "Slow Moulded Lascars" to handle the cargo.[115]

Unable to procure cotton on freight to Canton, the supercargoes decided to purchase cotton on the owners' account. But there was in the market only half the usual supply for the reason that early in the year Bombay merchants had agreed among themselves upon a ceiling price for the cotton purchased by them. This so displeased the merchants of Surat, the chief source of supply, that they withheld cotton from the market. The result was a short supply of cotton at Bombay. Snow and Olney were able to procure a full cargo, however, "by the particular exertions of Dady Nassereang." Although Nassereang was the most influential, respectable, and wealthy merchant in Bombay, they nevertheless kept an eye on him, for "like most of the Eastern Gentlemen he looks out a little for himself as well as for us."[116]

Sales of the cargo at Bombay amounted to $23,000, a loss of $11,500 from the invoice. As the cotton cost $36,000, it was necessary to use in payment some 13,000 of the Spanish dollars on board, while additional dollars had to be used to pay for repairs to *John Jay*.[117] These facts spoke eloquently in support of John Rogers' view (at the time of the *Rising Sun* voyage) of the folly of attempting to finance the East India trade with goods instead of dollars. Brown, Benson, and Ives would one day grasp that idea, but they had not yet done so.

John Jay sailed from Bombay on July 22, 1795, with 1,000 bales of cotton. A few days after passing the Strait of Malacca she fell in with the ships *America* and *Sampson,* which had sailed from Bombay a week before her own departure. With these two vessels "nearly within Hale of us," *John Jay* again narrowly escaped disaster. In a tremendous thundersquall she was struck by lightning that "Shivered the Main Top Gallant mast quite to pieces, & rent a large piece out of Main Top mast." It then "quit" the mast, passed over the ship's side, and "expired in the water." Snow and Olney thought this a most happy ending, for had it followed the mast into the hold, both ship and cargo would probably have burned. One seaman was killed, one lay lifeless for half an hour, the carpenter received a considerable shock, and most of the crew were knocked down. But generous assistance came from the masters of *America* and *Sampson,* who came on board *John Jay* with physicians, carpenters, and ordinary seamen. After repairs were made and the nerves of everyone calmed, *John Jay* continued her course toward Canton. In the China Sea she ran into two "Tuffoons," which were severe but from which no damage was suffered. The supercargoes found the passage long and tedious, with calms and headwinds, but they remarked with pride that they arrived at Whampoa ahead of five ships that had sailed from Bombay before them. They had made it in eighty-five days, while *America* required ninety-five.[118]

Writing from Canton a fortnight after their arrival, Snow and Olney reported the presence of seven other American vessels, one of which was supposed to have 250,000 hard dollars. They arranged with Mouqua, "one of the first Characters in Canton," for the sale of the cotton and the procurement of the return cargo. Mouqua agreed to absorb the grand hoppo's charge for measurement of the ship. Although the cotton sold for somewhat more than $54,000 (representing a profit of $18,000) and although Snow and Olney had part of the Spanish dollars brought from Providence, they were nevertheless short of funds. They found that nankeens and silks, in which the owners expected them to invest a considerable sum, could not be had on credit. As for bills on London, they first reported the Chinese to be as ignorant of them as "an American is of their language," but they later discovered that such bills could be negotiated at a discount of 20 per cent.[119]

With wholly inadequate funds and being unable to draw on London to advantage, the supercargoes had no choice but to procure credit from the hong merchants, reserving enough of their cash for the purchase of nankeens and silks. Thus they took tea from Mouqua to the amount of $8,000 and from Geoqua for about $20,000 on a credit of twenty months, Geoqua "risquing" 580 chests of bohea tea to Providence without insurance. But even with this amount of credit, they were unable to purchase a cargo sufficient to load a ship the size of John Jay. They procured 1,611 whole chests, 360 half-chests, and 312 quarter-chests of tea, the cheaper bohea variety accounting for more than 90 per cent of the total. Only small amounts of the more expensive Souchong, hyson, and gunpowder teas were included. But the different varieties of tea represented more than 85 per cent of the invoice value of the cargo. Of nankeens, of which the owners had expected 40,000 to 60,000 pieces, the supercargoes purchased only 12,000 pieces. Two boxes of silks, an assortment of chinaware, and small amounts of various other items completed the cargo. The ship was far from being loaded to capacity, and the supercargoes found it unnecessary to tax their ingenuity in stowing her. They had no occasion to take to the coach house in order that goods might be stored in the cabin. A large vessel whose cost of operation was very great, John Jay made the long voyage from Canton with a short cargo.

Nevertheless, this cargo, charged in the invoice at only $83,886, had in Providence a value that must have been a pleasant surprise to Brown, Benson, and Ives.[120] According to the customs duties levied, the goods on board John Jay had an estimated value of $256,000.[121] Evidently under the stress of wartime conditions a ship that returned safely from Canton could hardly make a losing voyage.

If the voyage paid to the partners a good dividend in dollars, it could have provided them with an even larger return in experience. It should have convinced them that beef, pork, cordage, spermaceti candles, and porter were not to be sent to India. Indeed, it should have cast doubt upon the wisdom of shipping to India goods of any sort. It should have made it obvious that ships to India should go in ballast, load with Indian cotton, and proceed to Canton, all in full recognition of the fact that the India trade had to be financed in hard dollars and not in goods. Above all, the voyage should have made it clear that at Canton a large ship must have funds to purchase a full cargo. Only in this way could the owners be sure that their vessel could safely bear the heavy cost of navigation.

Meanwhile, the ship *Hamilton,* Captain William Rodman, property of Brown, Benson, and Ives, had also been on a voyage to the Pacific. Sailing from Newport on January 26, 1795, less than a month after *John Jay,* she carried a small cargo valued at only £2,443 lawful money. Included were spermaceti and tallow candles and cordage, none of them easy to sell in India. Present, too, were American gin (probably the product of John Brown's gin distillery), Holland gin, Russian bar iron, and Russia ducks, all more readily saleable. She also carried rice, flour, codfish, and pipe staves on freight to Madeira. For the financing of the voyage the partners counted heavily on wine, which had occupied such a prominent place in the cargo of *General Washington* on her first voyage to the Pacific. They had, therefore, placed the necessary funds in the hands of two different houses in Madeira, who were to have the wine in readiness when Captain Rodman called en route to India.[122] Conspicuously absent from her cargo were Spanish dollars.

From the very beginning *Hamilton*'s voyage was a disappointment. Delay in getting out of the Providence River prevented a fine run before the easterly winds set in. Because of the "Deficiency of the Crew to take in Sail in Case of emergency," Captain Rodman was unable to take full advantage of the good winds when they came. The result was that, "Dutchman like," he was obliged to carry short sail during the night, much against his own inclination and much to the detriment of his owners' interest. But with the aid of "Divine Providence" he arrived at Madeira after a shorter passage than several other American ships. Nevertheless, Captain Rodman thought he must augment his crew with one or two good men or "Give up the Voyage." Some of his men were so inexperienced in the ways of a sailor that they did not know the difference between the bowsprit and the "Mizen" mast and were "no better than Dead men in a Gale of Wind." One was homesick, one was physically sick, one was suffering from "Sore Afflictions," and one "Got both his feet Frost Bit." Rodman had discharged one "very Indolent Person and no Part of a Carpenter," and he had advised another to go home. In their stead he had hired two new sailors, one American, the other French.[123]

Captain Rodman was fearful lest the Indian market be flooded with wine from Madeira. Two American ships had sailed prior to his arrival, and two more were then loading with wine.[124] His fears were not shared by his owners, however, who counted upon the war in Europe to prevent the usual shipments from Continental countries, thus creating an unusual demand in India for the wine of Madeira.

At Madeira nothing worked out according to plan. The captain had expected to be there sixteen to eighteen days, but his visit consumed more than seven weeks. He was compelled to employ laborers from ashore at considerable cost to stow the wine. He was obliged to buy boards to secure the wine. A scow loaded with boards sank alongside the ship, forcing him to pay dearly for replacements. The presence of a large number of English ships en route to the West Indies prevented the prompt dispatching of American craft. The captain thought that dealing with two houses, far from expediting matters, had caused further delay. Bad weather and numerous holidays had occasioned further loss of valuable time.

At last the captain was able to report that his cargo of Madeira— 250 pipes—was safely on board, with one pipe to carry "the Voyage Round" for the partners to drink at *Hamilton*'s return. But he was worried lest the ship was loaded too deep, "as She is Naturly an Indifferent Sailor." He thought her a very unfit vessel for such a voyage, and he believed he should have left two months earlier "to have Prosecuted the Voyage you wish for."[125]

Captain Rodman's orders allowed him a large measure of discretion once he had sailed from Madeira, although it was the hope of Brown, Benson, and Ives that he would sell his cargo at Madras and procure a freight from there to Canton. But events were to prove that the captain was not entirely the master of his own fate. A short time out from Madeira he encountered light winds and calms for seventy-five days. He mistook the southeast trade wind for the southerly, sighted the coast of Brazil, and worked to the southward until he came into the path of the variable winds. Six months out from Madeira he was still far from India, and his crew was suffering from scurvy, three of them unfit for duty and three more "at times on the Point of Giving up doing anything." In a hurried conference with his mates he decided to make the nearest port. He headed for Calcutta, hoping later to continue to Madras. But a severe squall played havoc with the rigging, causing a delay of two or three weeks. Once at Calcutta, Captain Rodman was compelled to hire ten or twelve lascars, as only three of his crew were able to work. Reflecting upon his experiences, he thought "Poor *Hamilton*" ill suited to such a voyage. In light wind, he wrote, "she goes but Little." She was improperly built for the China trade, her masts and yards being too short. The captain thought that beyond the Cape of Good Hope vessels needed a quarter more canvas than those engaged in trade to Europe, an observation the owners later took to heart.[126]

As time passed nothing occurred to lift the captain's spirit. Within a few days he reported the death of one of his men. Two others were in a critical condition, while three more were very ill with scurvy. Two weeks later his crew was mostly under a doctor's care, forcing him to employ natives at enormous expense. His cook had run away, but he hoped for his return in order that he might "have the Pleasure of Flogging him to my Satisfaction." His ship was in no better condition than his crew, her upper works leaking and in need of caulking, her spars and masts rotten, her sheathing cut "all to Pieces."[127]

Captain Rodman doubted the wisdom of going on to Madras, where according to all reports there was no market for wine. He had hoped to sell his wine to advantage at Calcutta, but the arrival of the new ship *Ganges,* owned by Willing and Francis of Philadelphia, with 600 pipes had depressed the price. Nevertheless, he decided to dispose of his entire cargo at Calcutta, partly at auction, partly at private sale. The results were, of course, disappointing. He realized only about a rupee (forty-six cents) for each dollar of his merchandise. His only solace was that he had fared no worse than most of his countrymen. The ones who had done better were those who "Brought Out the Dollars and therefore did not depend on the Goods they Had as Cargo."[128]

As it was too late to continue to Canton, Captain Rodman loaded *Hamilton* with sugar, pepper, and piece goods on the owners' account and with a freight of forty-eight tons for Boston at £125 sterling a ton. His disbursements at Calcutta were enormous, the charge for pilotage amounting to 6,000 rupees. The captain again emphasized the importance of bringing dollars to India.[129]

In July, 1796, *Hamilton* arrived in Boston with her freight after a voyage of eighteen months. As her owners had scant reason for wishing to see her in Providence again, they directed Captain Rodman to sell her at Boston. As it was a "Dull time for Navigation," there was no deluge of offers for her. Israel Thorndike of Beverly finally bought her for $3,000, even though he thought her "Very Ugly."[130]

The voyage of *Hamilton* was as unprofitable for Brown, Benson, and Ives as it was unpleasant for Captain Rodman. According to their calculation they had incurred a loss of £4,977 lawful money, the equivalent of $16,590.[131] But what they had lost in dollars they should have gained in knowledge of the business: To achieve a consistent success in this distant traffic they must be equipped with the tools of the trade. And what were the tools? Fewer goods and more dollars, as they had been told repeatedly; a large, sturdy, fast-sailing ship, with funds sufficient to load her completely; more canvas once the ship had turned the Cape of Good Hope; and adequate provision for the health of the crew, which meant a well-stocked medicine chest, vegetables and fruits to guard against scurvy, and perhaps a physician on board. The disastrous outcome of the voyage of *Hamilton* appears to have raised doubt in the minds of the partners as to the wisdom of trying to combine a visit to India with a call at Canton. Such a voyage was too time consuming. Henceforth, their trade to Canton was a direct one.

The year 1796 was an eventful one in the annals of Brown, Benson, and Ives. It was the year of the rice speculation in which they lost so heavily. It saw the return of *John Jay* with a valuable cargo of China goods, but it also witnessed the return of *Hamilton* from a losing venture. In December of that year Colonel Benjamin Tallman began building for them a fine, large, fast-sailing ship of 536 tons at an estimated cost of $44,834. To be named *Ann & Hope,* for Ann Carter Brown and Hope Brown Ives, wives of two of the partners, this vessel would prove a worthy companion of *John Jay,* thus giving them two ships well suited to the requirements of the East India trade. Finally, this same year brought the reorganization of the partnership. George Benson, senior partner, withdrew, leaving the two brothers-in-law—Nicholas Brown and Thomas P. Ives—in complete control, under the name of Brown and Ives. This firm was to be for the next seventy-five years one of the leading business houses of Rhode Island, indeed of all New England.

A CHANGE IN POLICIES

The reorganized house of Brown and Ives began business under conditions that were most auspicious. The elder Nicholas Brown had at his death in 1791 left to his son and daughter, wife of Thomas P. Ives, $200,000 in public securities alone. By 1796 their holdings of various kinds of corporate and government stock had grown to $270,000. Included in the total was $147,000 in 6 per cent, 3 per cent, and deferred stock of the United States, issued in accordance with the funding plan of Alexander Hamilton; $58,000 of the state debt of Rhode Island, assumed by the federal government under Hamilton's assumption plan; $9,000 of the debt of Rhode Island that was unassumable; $15,000 in stock of the first Bank of the United States; and $37,600 in the stock of the Providence Bank, an altogether handsome portfolio for that day when a dollar would purchase so much.[132] With proper attention to business and with ordinary prudence the possessors of this fortune could not fail to do well.

While their new ship was building, Brown and Ives dispatched

John Jay on her second voyage to the Pacific. Her destination again was Canton, but she was not to call en route at an Indian port as she had on her previous voyage. Once more Daniel Olney was her captain and joint supercargo with John Bowers, who appears to have been a last-minute substitute for Samuel Snow. Not having been to China before, Bowers seems to have been at pains to acquaint himself with the ways of the trade. By Benjamin Dexter he was told he should engage a good linguist, who would procure the factory and put him in touch with the security merchant. He should use his cash to buy goods cheap. Care must be taken to see that all tea packed was equal in quality with the sample. Particular vigilance was necessary in shipping chinaware lest the boxes be opened and the china stolen. Some linguists were faithful, but for the most part they were rogues who "act for themselves."[133] Another person warned Bowers that "there is the Greatest Duplicity practiced there of any where Els."[134] A third gentleman advised him to be on guard "against the best Chinaman you meet."[135]

Mindful of the short (yet valuable) cargo *John Jay* had brought home on her previous voyage, Brown and Ives planned in great detail a return cargo that would fill the ship. Estimating the cost of such a cargo at $155,000, they aimed to provide Olney and Bowers with funds sufficient both to purchase the cargo and to take up notes given to Mouqua and Geoqua on the previous voyage, making a total of $183,000. Hard dollars would have been the ideal way of providing the funds. But the partners found hard dollars difficult to come by in 1797. Because of their heavy losses of the previous year and the high cost of their new ship, *Ann & Hope,* they felt they could afford no more than 50,000 silver dollars for the voyage of *John Jay.* But after paying $28,000 on the two notes at Canton, little of the specie would remain; and since they were shipping goods of only trifling value, credit instruments of one sort or another must make up the deficiency. Accordingly, they provided Olney and Bowers with bills of exchange on Hodshon and Son in Amsterdam for $241,000 (60,000 guilders), with bills on Dickason and Company in London for $22,222 (£5,000 sterling), and with a letter of credit authorizing drafts on Brown and Ives up to $40,000. But this would still leave them far short of the necessary amount. The deficiency could be met in only one way—by giving their notes at Canton, payable in twenty months.[136]

Thus Brown and Ives were avoiding the mistake of trying to finance the voyage with goods. They would send a quantity of hard dollars, but their chief reliance was to be on credit in various forms. They realized the disadvantage at which this placed them, but it appeared to be the only alternative to letting *John Jay* lie idle.

John Jay sailed from Providence on April 9, 1797. She found the weather comparatively favorable to that of her first voyage. She was chased for some six hours by a ship of unknown nationality, but when night came on, *John Jay* lost the ship, and when morning came, she was nowhere to be seen. From her size and "appearances," however, the supercargoes were sure she was a "Ship of Force."[137] Otherwise no untoward incident broke the day-to-day routine. Arriving at Canton in 164 days, Olney and Bowers soon realized that they were headed for trouble. Although they paid promptly the money owed Mouqua and Geoqua from the previous voyage, they found it impossible to procure a cargo from either of them. The best terms to be had from Geoqua required 80,000 hard dollars, for which he would grant a credit of $40,000 for twenty months. But the goods supplied on credit would be at an advance of 20 per cent, a grim reminder of the importance of having cash. As Olney and Bowers had a balance of only 22,000 hard dollars after paying the debt of the last voyage, they could not avail themselves of Geoqua's offer. With their bills on London and Amsterdam and with their letter of credit they could do nothing, even at a heavy discount. A scarcity of specie at Canton placed a high premium on it. Specie was necessary in dealing with the hong merchants because they "are all so much involved that they cannot procure the Goods you want unless you have it in your power to advance them Specie, at least for two thirds of the Amount" of the goods purchased.[138]

Thus the supercargoes of *John Jay* were in the embarrassing situation of having the largest of eleven American ships at Canton but of lacking funds so completely that they were unable to procure a cargo for the account of Brown and Ives. What were they to do? They tried in vain to procure a freight to the United States. At their wits' end, they chanced to meet a Danish gentleman, Michael Fabritius of the house of Conrad Fabritius and Company in Copenhagen, who was desirous of chartering a neutral vessel to take a freight to Hamburg. Accordingly, they entered into an agreement with Fabritius to carry chinaware, tea, etc., to the extent of 750 tons at 100 Spanish dollars a ton, payment of the money to be contingent upon safe arrival at Hamburg.[139] Thus they might earn $75,000 for their owners; but there was a possibility that the voyage might end in complete disaster. That, however, was a chance they thought they must take. Actually, Fabritius was acting for the Dutch East India Company, which sought to reduce the risk of capture by giving to the transaction the appearance of one between private citizens of two neutral countries and one involving a neutral port of destination.

Arriving at Hamburg after a voyage of 162 days from Canton, Olney and Bowers delivered their cargo and received payment for the freight.

Now they faced again the problem of what to do with *John Jay*. They thought of a freight to some part of the world, but the strained relations between France and the United States made European shippers unwilling to risk their goods in American vessels. They weighed the wisdom of going on to St. Petersburg, but that involved a "great hazard" so late in the season. In spite of the hazard, however, they decided to go, rather than to purchase Russian goods in Hamburg.[140] Taking a letter of credit from Caspar Voight, the partners' correspondent in Hamburg, they went on to the Russian port. On September 1, 1798, they wrote that the ship was "Compleatly filled and very deep" with Russian goods. Since they had been unable to invest all their funds, they were remitting the balance to Dickason and Company in London. Returning, they had a fast run through the Kattegat on the North Sea, but in the English Channel *John Jay* sprang her rudder. Putting in at Lisbon for repairs, she was delayed for some seven weeks.[141] She arrived at Providence on March 18, 1799, after an absence of almost two years.

John Jay had made a saving, but a very indifferent, voyage, which again demonstrated the necessity of an adequate fund of hard dollars for the proper conduct of the trade at Canton. A successful freighting venture was no satisfactory substitute for a full cargo of China goods shipped on the account and risk of the owners of the vessel.

While *John Jay* was absent on her long voyage, the new ship *Ann & Hope* was completed and dispatched to Canton on her maiden voyage. For command of this fine vessel, Brown and Ives selected Benjamin Page, who had been master of John Brown's ship *Hope* when in December, 1792, she became the second vessel flying the American flag to enter the port of Sydney, New South Wales. He had also commanded *Halcyon* of Providence when she called at Sydney in 1794. He therefore brought to his new assignment a considerable fund of experience in traffic to the Pacific, including China. For his services Page was to have a privilege of eight tons and was to receive the sum of $2,000 upon the ship's safe return to Providence.[142] For the post of supercargo the partners chose Samuel Snow, who had served in a similar capacity on the first voyage of *John Jay* to Canton. Snow's privilege was ten tons, and upon arrival of *Ann & Hope* at home port he would receive $8,000.[143] That Brown and Ives regarded this voyage as an important one is shown not only by the caliber of the men they placed in charge of it but also by the scale of compensation allowed them.

This voyage is significant, too, because for the first time Brown and Ives accepted the fact that the trade to Canton could not be financed either with goods or mainly by credit. Accordingly they placed on board 80,000 hard dollars, not a dollar of which was mortgaged to hong merchants on account of previous voyages.[144] Thus the resources of *Ann & Hope* would substantially exceed those of any ship the owners had previously sent to China.

Brown and Ives were sure that the specie at Snow's disposal would readily enable him to procure whatever credit he would need to complete the loading of the ship. And they expected that the "respectable situation" in which he would appear at Canton (an obvious reference to his prospective consular position) would be of assistance to him, since it would be evident to the hong merchants that he possessed the "distinguished regard" of the government of his own country. They were "Build[ing] Considerably on this Circumstance."[145]

Going out as an understudy to Snow was Thomas Thompson, a young man in whom Brown and Ives placed the greatest confidence. He was to reside with Snow in the factory and to assist him in the business. Snow would keep the young man informed and would explain to him his plan of procedure in procuring his cargo. It was understood that should Snow remain in Canton, he would send by Thompson any information that he deemed useful to Brown and Ives.[146] Another young man making the voyage, for whom Brown and Ives bespoke the special attention of both Snow and Page, was Dr. Benjamin B. Carter, brother-in-law of Nicholas Brown, and the ship's surgeon. The voyage of *Hamilton* to Calcutta had shown the partners that illness, even among a small and modestly paid crew, could prove costly. It would have been false economy, therefore, to gamble with the health of a crew of fifty-seven men receiving high wages. Hence the decision to have on board a physician. Although Dr. Carter's monthly pay of seventeen dollars was no greater than that of several of the crew members, he was entitled to a privilege of one ton. He was to live in the factory with Samuel Snow in Canton and was to dine at the officers' table.[147] Being a young man of "good understanding" and possessing a mind well informed, he kept a journal of the voyage that is exceptional for its wealth of information as well as for its perceptiveness.[148]

In the interest of safety Brown and Ives instructed Captain Page to pass "round or Easte of New Holland" (Australia) on the voyage out, as the insurance was made "on this representation." Returning, he might exercise his discretion, but they strongly recommended that he avoid Soenda Strait. Since this was "a Voyage of Serious Consequence" to them, the ship must be "Completely filled, in every part." Captain Page was to have some light accommodations made up on deck for the carpenter, gunner, and all those men "which are provided *now* with Births Between decks in the after part of the Ship," as those berths and the "bulk head forward of them *must* come away." The owners expected the captain to improve to advantage the storeroom under the cabin and to stow provisions in the space forward between decks occupied by the crew, all without inconvenience to the occupants. He was, of course, to have packages of all sizes for efficient stowing.[149]

Relations between the United States and France at the time were so strained that the government was commissioning privateers, among them *Ann & Hope*.[150] Captain Page was instructed to avoid speaking any vessel and, "without exhibiting any signs of fear," he was to keep out of the way of any craft he might "discover" on the passage. But they would depend on him, they wrote, to defend the ship, were he attacked by any "Corsair or Cruizers." He was by all means to avoid the Cape Verde Islands and give the Cape of Good Hope and the Île de France "good births." In short the captain was to be at great pains to avoid involvement with any ships flying the flag of France.[151]

Ann & Hope sailed from Providence in July, 1798. Because of the progressive depletion of the water supply on board, it became necessary on September 6 to ration water, each man receiving one quart in the morning for tea and three pints for the remainder of the day. From October 12, because of the exhaustion of their rum, each man was allowed one gill of gin a day (probably gin from John Brown's distillery).[152] But in spite of these measures of conservation, a shortage of water combined with the need to replenish his livestock forced Captain Page to put in at Botany Bay, Australia, thus further contributing to the prominence of Providence vessels in Australian waters in the last decade of the century. En route from Botany Bay to Tinian, Captain Page fell in with the ship *Jenny,* formerly of New York, then of Boston, and "reported to be [the] fastest ship in America." It was with great pride, therefore, that Captain Page reported, "with her I proved the *Ann & Hope* superior by at least one fifth."[153] After a passage of five months and one day the ship arrived at Macao and a day later anchored at Whampoa. In celebration of the event the steward made in his book the entry: "No bread allowed from this day but plenty of Rice" and "Also Fresh Meat & Vegitables."[154]

At Canton, Snow secured the ship with Mouqua. His return cargo included somewhat less tea than Brown and Ives had expected, which enabled him to make a larger investment in nankeens and silks than planned. The total cost of the cargo was $121,014, two-thirds of which was paid in hard dollars.[155] For the balance Snow gave the partners' note to Mouqua, with notes for small amounts to Poonqua and Pinqua, the silk merchants.

Although his 80,000 hard dollars had enabled him to purchase a good cargo, Snow urged upon his owners the importance of "sending out large funds" in specie, since he, like Olney and Bowers before him, had been unable to dispose of bills on London. He hoped Brown and Ives would send the ship back to Canton promptly; and should they not be in cash to the necessary amount, it would be "an object" worth their attention to borrow even at an extra interest rather than lose the advantage the hard dollars would confer upon them.[156]

At Canton not all went well between Snow and Captain Page. According to Snow, Page's inattention to the stowing of goods on board created confusion, occasioned delay, and prevented *Ann & Hope* from loading as large a cargo as she was capable of taking. But over and beyond that, Snow doubted that Page was in "his Senses," as he had at times been "considerably *cracked*." Snow further thought it would be a "deed of Charity, to believe he was really delirious when he left Canton."[157] For his part Captain Page shed no tears when Snow decided to remain in Canton to serve as United States consul there.

In his consular capacity Snow was surprised at the "confidence & respect" he received from the people of China. He reported that the Chinese government "is very well pleased that some person is appointed to superintend . . . American affairs." With the permission and approbation of Chinese authorities Snow "for the first time erected the American Flag in Canton." The occasion was the birthday of President John Adams, October 30, 1799, when Snow had the "English Company, Spanish, Danes, Hong Merchants, & all the Americans in port" to dine with him.[158]

Ann & Hope arrived at her home port on June 15, 1799, after an absence of eleven months. Her cargo, which had cost $121,014, was valued at $314,987. Her teas were of fine quality and found a ready sale in a good market.[159] Her maiden voyage had been a highly profitable one. Small wonder that Brown and Ives promptly dispatched her on another voyage to Canton.

Just a month before the return of *Ann & Hope* the partners had sent *John Jay* on a voyage to Batavia on the island of Java, a part of the world not previously visited by one of their ships.[160] Java had emerged as the chief producer of coffee, since the slave insurrection in Saint Domingue in 1791 had brought to an end that island's primacy in coffee. Captain Olney of *John Jay* was to speak no vessel while en route to Batavia, and he was to avoid the Western Islands (the Azores), the Cape Verde Islands, the Cape of Good Hope, and the Île de France. He was to give the greatest attention to his crew while in port, taking care not to expose them to disease and keeping them "temperate, that their Health may be Preserved." Carrying a commission making his ship a private man-of-war, he would, if attacked, defend the vessel to the utmost.[161]

John Jay had on board 52,000 hard dollars with which the owners hoped the supercargoes would be able to purchase 800,000 pounds of Java coffee and sugar in sufficient amount to ballast the vessel. If the price of coffee was prohibitive, however, the captain was to seek a freight from Batavia to Canton, where all available funds were to be used to purchase a cargo on the partners' account.[162]

At Batavia the price of coffee was only slightly in excess of $0.08 a pound, which was so satisfactory that the captain was relieved of the necessity of going on to Canton. Within the brief period of three weeks *John Jay* was loaded with a cargo of 735,221 pounds of coffee and 63 tons of sugar. The total cost was 64,272 Spanish dollars.[163] As their fund of Spanish dollars was somewhat less than this figure, the supercargoes made successful use of their letter of credit to procure the additional funds. *John Jay* arrived in Providence on March 19, 1800, after an absence of ten months.

Within three weeks the ship *Charlotte* sailed from Providence with 242,117 pounds of the coffee, slightly less than a third of the amount *John Jay* had brought from Batavia.[164] Invoicing the coffee at $0.20 a pound (it had cost a little more than $0.08), the partners dispatched *Charlotte,* Ephraim Talbot supercargo, to Amsterdam to the care of Van Staphorst and Company, although Talbot was free to seek another market, if that should seem desirable. At Amsterdam, Talbot found awaiting him a letter from Dickason and Company, saying there was no better market than the great Dutch port. The coffee sold at 15 to 17.25 stivers, or $0.30 to $0.35 a pound.[165] The coffee, costing about $18,000, sold for $55,386, a profit of more than $37,000, all in spite of Van Staphorst and Company's charges, which were so enormous that Talbot questioned the honesty of the firm. Assuming that Brown and Ives did equally well with *John Jay*'s entire cargo of coffee, they made a net profit of $111,000 on an investment of $60,000, an altogether auspicious beginning in the coffee trade.

Although Brown and Ives at the turn of the century had not yet completely mastered all the problems of the East India trade, they had made substantial progress in that direction. Voyages to both Canton and Batavia were returning a good profit.

Meanwhile John Brown, who had planned and largely executed the first voyage from Rhode Island to Canton, had not neglected the East India trade. While the destruction of his papers makes it impossible to speak in detail of his business in these years, certain features of it are revealed from other sources. *Hope,* a ship belonging to Brown and Francis, in 1792 became the second American ship to call at Sydney, New South Wales. The *Providence Gazette* of January 8, 1791, reported that "On Thursday Morning a most elegant coppered Ship, called THE

PRESIDENT [*President Washington*], belonging to Messieurs BROWN and FRANCIS, was launched at the Ship-Yard near Fox-Point. She is intended for the India Trade, is 950 Tons Burthen, and allowed to be the best Ship ever built in New-England."

The *Providence Gazette* for September 14, 1793, stated that "A few Days past a Waggon, with between 50 and 60,000 Dollars in Specie, was unloaded at the Bank in this Town, and the Money deposited in the Vaults—the Property of Messrs. BROWN and FRANCIS, Merchants, and Part of the Proceeds of the Ship *President Washington,* and her Cargo, sold at Calcutta in 1792."

Not content with having owned the ships *General Washington* and *President Washington,* John Brown built for the Indian trade the *George Washington,* described as a vessel of 624 tons. She sailed from Providence on her first voyage in January, 1794. She made a visit to China and Batavia in 1796. By the time she had returned to her home port, the United States was engaged in the undeclared naval war with France. The resulting demand for cannon with which to arm the ships of the enlarged navy brought to Hope Furnace one final brief moment of prosperity. And the program of governmental purchase of merchant ships for conversion to men-of-war offered to John Brown an opportunity that he was quick to improve.

In the summer of 1798 John Brown offered, through the Secretary of the Treasury, to sell to the government his ship *George Washington,* "built of Cedar and live Oak," coppered, with two suits of sails, completely rigged, and "fitted in all respects for a Ship of War." She could be sent on a cruise with little expense and without delay. "One of the best Sailers in America," she was capable of carrying twenty-four twelve-pound cannon.[166] When this letter finally came into the hands of the Secretary of the Navy, he wrote to John expressing his very genuine disappointment at his inability to accept the offer of sale. Funds appropriated by Congress would not pay for more than half the number of ships needed. "The public Spirit of the Country must be relied on for the rest." The "Towns distinguished for Federalism and public Spirit" were striving to furnish the vessels still wanted. The Secretary chided John on the fact that the town of Providence, "not less able, and not less patriotic," had not yet "taken up the Subject." It would be gratifying if Providence would furnish one of these vessels; and if John Brown would use his influence to bring this about, he "would lay an additional obligation" on his country.[167]

These words from the Secretary of the Navy could have given John Brown but the slenderest reason to hope for a sale of his ship to the government, least of all on his own terms. But within three weeks the

Secretary, for whatever reason, had changed his mind and apparently had solved his financial problem. For the sake of "adding one more to the number of the ships capable of immediate service," he had now decided to buy John's ship, if on examination she proved to be sound, strong, and fast sailing. Accordingly, the Secretary asked Captain Silas Talbot of the Navy to visit Providence and there "examine strictly, and critically" the ship belonging to John Brown and to report every particular that he deemed necessary to a decision regarding purchase of the vessel. In particular the Secretary desired to have the dimensions of the ship (which John Brown had not given), the alterations that ought to be made in her, and the probable time and expense involved in making the changes. He thought Talbot might require the advice and opinion of a carpenter in making his examination of the ship; and since John Brown was a gentleman of "very great Influence in Providence," Talbot must determine the chances of finding one in that town who would not be "under the influence of Mr. Brown." At his discretion, Talbot might take a carpenter with him from New York.[168]

Within another three weeks Talbot had made his examination of *George Washington*. That his report was a reasonably favorable one is to be inferred from the fact that on the very day of its receipt the Secretary wrote to John Brown telling him he had decided to take the vessel on John's original terms. Those terms had been $40,000, a fourth in cash and the balance in 6 per cent stock of the United States. But since the Secretary's acceptance of these terms had been a tardy one, John Brown exacted a penalty for the delay. With respect to this the Secretary remarked that it was not "worth disputing about Trifles, and if you insist on it, I must add the 400 Dollars for the expense since your offer; tho' I really think you ought not to ask it."[169]

The purchase completed, the Secretary of the Navy again sent Talbot to Providence, this time to supervise the fitting out of *George Washington* as a man-of-war. For this purpose the Secretary made available the sum of $2,500, with the promise of any further amount when needed. John Brown was to furnish the cannon that Talbot would receive at an early opportunity and for which he would have a sufficient quantity of "Ball, Grape & round headed shot cast in time." The Secretary warned Talbot that John Brown, "a complete Master of the Art of bargain making," would probably ask more than a fair price for these articles. Talbot would do the best he could with John "and let the public be Screwed as little as possible."[170]

Events were to show John's mastery of the art of bargain-making. Within nine months the Navy was completely disillusioned. Far from being a fast sailer, *George Washington* was "a dull Vessel—not fit to chase

French Privateers."[171] Late in 1799 she was extensively overhauled at Newport and found to be in extremely poor repair, her timbers badly decayed, her copper of poor quality, "the thinnest kind used for any Vessel."[172] The cost of these repairs, combined with the high purchase price and the expense of fitting her for sea at Providence in 1798, must have made *George Washington* a costly luxury.

The most notable incident in the naval career of the ship occurred after the difficulties with France had come to an end. In 1800 she was dispatched to Algiers with tribute from the government, whence she was forced by the Dey to carry an Algerian embassy to Constantinople, her cargo consisting of the ambassador and his suite, 100 Negro women and children, 4 horses, 150 sheep, 25 horned cattle, 4 lions, 4 tigers, and specie to the value of $500,000. She was the first vessel to fly the American flag at the capital of the Ottoman Empire.

The 1790's had been a period of great activity for the Browns. They had perfected ways of conducting trade to the Baltic. In the early stages of the war in Europe they had tried their hand at freighting. They had indulged in a rice speculation in which they had lost heavily. They had built two fine ships especially designed for the East India business, and with these they were beginning to discover the secrets of profitable trade to Canton and Batavia. These years had also revealed the new role that Dickason and Company in London were henceforth to play in the Providence firm's scheme of business. No longer were Dickason and Company the purchasers of English goods for Brown and Ives. Instead, they now rendered a number of services for the partners. They received remittances from Brown and Ives correspondents all over Europe. They honored drafts on them by Brown and Ives and their supercargoes in various parts of the world. They gave the partners advice as to market conditions. They provided aid and counsel to ship captains of Brown and Ives who were the victims either of wind and weather or of British seizure and detention. It was the aim of Brown and Ives to maintain in the hands of Dickason and Company funds sufficient to meet all contingencies. But on occasion they drew upon Dickason and Company in anticipation of remittances yet to be made to the London house. In this way Dickason and Company played the part of merchant-banker to the partners. This illustrates in miniature the function of British mercantile firms in financing American business expansion. In the early days of the Republic when the United States was a debtor nation, the prime need of American business was credit. And as Alexander Hamilton had observed, credit could be had only in Britain.

CHAPTER 4

A South American Interlude

AT the beginning of the nineteenth century Brown and
Ives turned their attention to the Spanish empire in South
America. For decades ships owned by the Browns had traded regularly
at the Dutch port of Surinam on the northern coast of that continent,
but never had one of their vessels attempted to break through the commercial monopoly that Spain maintained in her vast dominions on
the mainland. And it was precisely because this monopoly was weakening that the attention of American merchants, including the Browns,
was now drawn to the Spanish colonies in South America.

In the French Revolutionary Wars Spain was cast in the role of an
enemy of England. In consequence, she found her colonial empire increasingly at the mercy of British sea power. Unable to maintain trade
with her colonies in her own ships, she thought to avert their economic
strangulation by relaxing her restrictive regulations. By a royal decree
of November, 1797, Spanish colonial ports were opened to neutral ships
sailing from a neutral or a Spanish port with "goods and effects not
prohibited" by the laws of Spain. Although designed to spare the colonials "very serious if not . . . irreparable injuries," the decree succeeded in arousing the bitter opposition of many Spanish merchants
intent upon preserving their monopolistic privileges. This fact, combined
with the flagrant abuse of the new regulations by neutral traders, soon
prompted His Catholic Majesty Charles IV to reconsider. Accordingly,
a new decree of April, 1799, directed that "Spanish ports in South
America be shut against all neutrals as well as the subjects of belligerent
nations."[1]

If governmental fiat required that the door be closed to neutrals, the
wartime needs of the people of South America dictated otherwise. In
practice, therefore, neutral ships were allowed to call at the forbidden
ports, subject always, of course, to the caprice of the local viceroy. Thus
American ships actually visited the Río de la Plata in greater numbers

immediately after the ban was reimposed than during the period when the ports had been officially open. An observer at Buenos Aires thought it "one of the most extraordinary things in nature that this so lucrative trade ... should have been open for two years, & scarce a ship from the United States been to this part until they were prohibited."[2] To Spanish colonials neutral trade had become a wartime necessity. To neutrals the hazards of the trade were enormous. But the rewards of success were so lucrative that they were deemed worth the risk. The result was a thriving illicit trade to the Río de la Plata.

Although this trade has received considerable attention from historians, their accounts of it have been based principally upon government documents and contemporary newspapers. Those writing upon the subject appear not to have had access to the records and papers of merchants who were actually engaged in the business. Their narratives, therefore, sometimes miss the meaning and significance of the events described. The archives of Brown and Ives, however, reveal in detail the nature of the traffic to the Río de la Plata in 1800.

THE FIRST VOYAGE TO A NEW CONTINENT

In the spring of 1800 Brown and Ives dispatched their ship *Charlotte* to Amsterdam with a cargo of coffee. Within a fortnight they wrote to Ephraim Talbot, supercargo, that they had recently received some information regarding trade "at the River La Plata."[3] One source of this information was Captain Trotter, then in the service of John Innes Clark, prominent Providence merchant.[4] As this intelligence describes the devious means by which a neutral ship could deliver a cargo of goods at Buenos Aires without running the risk of seizure and confiscation, it is clear that the edict of April, 1799, again closing Spanish colonial ports to foreigners, was then known in Providence. Captain Trotter had cleared from London for Madeira but actually touched at São Tiago, one of the Cape Verde Islands. He had then proceeded to Rio de Janeiro, where he met the agent of a Spanish house, who arranged for the delivery of his cargo at Buenos Aires at an advance of 133 per cent, free of all risk to either ship or cargo. But it was imperative to take a Spaniard on board at Rio de Janeiro to conduct the vessel to Buenos Aires.[5]

That American ships frequently called at Rio de Janeiro in those years has been known for some time. But the purpose of their visits has not been so well understood. Supposedly they called there in distress or to refit and to replenish their supplies. Actually, they visited Rio de Janeiro either to sell goods there or to make contact with Spaniards possessed of influence at Buenos Aires.[6]

Brown and Ives, impressed by the word received from Captain Trotter, suggested to *Charlotte*'s supercargo an investment in European goods suitable for a voyage to the Río de la Plata.[7] Talbot thought so well of the idea that his combined purchase at Amsterdam and London amounted to over £7,000 sterling. While in London, Talbot met Captain Trotter and from him obtained further information as to the procedures to be adopted in South America.[8] Clearing for Madeira, he there again crossed the path of Captain Trotter, who had charge of the ships *Patterson* and *Palmyra,* both the property of John Innes Clark. Evidently by appointment, Talbot again met Captain Trotter at Rio de Janeiro, where he arranged to place *Charlotte*'s cargo on board *Patterson,* bound for the Río de la Plata. Talbot himself proceeded in *Charlotte* in ballast for Buenos Aires with a letter from Captain Trotter to a merchant of "large Property" at that place.[9]

Talbot soon reported from Buenos Aires that all the goods had been discharged from *Patterson* and deposited in places of safety. But he added that the great quantity of merchandise recently received at Buenos Aires had so excited the envy of the customs officials at Montevideo that a large detachment of them had descended upon Buenos Aires. In consequence, the valuable cargoes of *Juno* of Boston and of *Palmyra* of Providence had been seized. With some show of satisfaction Talbot remarked that "we have Experienced no loss" because "our cargo was . . . deposited in different places."[10] Surely, these letters from Talbot could have left no doubt in the mind of Brown and Ives that any trade conducted by Americans in the Río de la Plata was strictly of an illicit character.

In spite of enormous port and other charges at Buenos Aires, the goods brought out by *Charlotte,* costing slightly in excess of $23,000, netted $63,000, a sum that Talbot brought home in the form of Spanish milled dollars, gold dust, and gold ingots. In addition, *Charlotte* carried from Buenos Aires on freight oxhides and copper that yielded another $13,000 to her owners. The voyage of *Charlotte* had been a thoroughly successful one. Her coffee had sold at Amsterdam at a fine profit. At Buenos Aires the amount invested at Amsterdam and London had almost doubled. Talbot had returned to Providence with $75,000 for the account of Brown and Ives.[11]

A SECOND TRIP TO FORBIDDEN PORTS

Before they had received the glad tidings of *Charlotte*'s profitable venture in the illicit trade to the Río de la Plata, Brown and Ives had become involved in another try at this same forbidden traffic. Their young friend Thomas Lloyd Halsey, Jr., while pursuing his study of the French and Spanish languages in Boston, had made the acquaintance of Joseph Antonio de Sanzetenea, agent for Thomas Antonio Romero, a Spanish merchant at Buenos Aires. Sanzetenea repeatedly urged Halsey to undertake an enterprise to the Río de la Plata to the consignment of Romero. The Spaniard painted for Halsey a bright picture of the opportunities awaiting American traders at Buenos Aires, where the acute scarcity of dry goods and wearing apparel meant that huge profits would undoubtedly ensue; and Romero, by virtue of the privileges he enjoyed from the Spanish monarch, would be able to procure special favors for his American friends.

Halsey obviously relayed this intelligence to Brown and Ives and to John Corlis, another Providence merchant. Things began to move. Corlis sold to Brown and Ives a half-interest in his handsome new ship, *Mary Ann,* for a consideration of $17,000. On April 23, 1800, Brown and Ives, John Corlis, and Halsey jointly entered into a contract with Sanzetenea, acting in behalf of Romero of Buenos Aires. By this agreement the Providence merchants pledged their sincere intentions to have *Mary Ann* arrive at Rio de Janeiro in October with goods to the value of not less than $80,000. Sanzetenea, on his part, engaged to furnish the ship with a certificate and "every other Necessary Paper or Documents" that would "Infallibly" procure her a "Free, secure, & lawful" entrance at Buenos Aires. At Rio de Janeiro, *Mary Ann* would be met by a "Confidential, & Capable" agent of Romero, who would proceed in her to the Río de la Plata.

Sanzetenea's guarantee against seizure applied only to *Mary Ann,* not to her cargo. Having "exposed & made known" to the owners the hazards of landing goods "which are prohibited in the Spanish Settlements of Monte Video & Buenos Ayres," he merely undertook to the "Utmost of his Power, Abilities, & Influence" to land the cargo "in Safety from Confiscation."[12]

On April 23, 1800 (the date of the contract discussed above), the owners of *Mary Ann,* "for and in consideration" of the sum of $20,000, "granted, bargained, & sold" to Sanzetenea (in behalf of Romero) "all the Hull, or Body of the good Ship *Mary Ann*" together with "all & singular her Appurtenances." On the same day Sanzetenea "granted, bargained, & sold the good Ship" to Brown and Ives, Corlis, and Halsey for a consideration of $20,000.[13]

For the command of *Mary Ann* the owners selected Daniel Olney, a man of wide experience in the service of Brown and Ives.[14] As they planned to send a cargo of manufactured goods, largely dry goods, to South America, it was necessary first to dispatch the ship to Europe to procure these wares. Brown and Ives seized the opportunity to ship on board her to Amsterdam a large quantity of the coffee *John Jay* had brought from Batavia that same spring. This visit of *Mary Ann* to Amsterdam is notable for the reason that her cargo was sold by Daniel Crommelin and Sons, who thereafter remained the leading correspondent of Brown and Ives in Continental Europe. The coffee came to a good market, thus making possible large remittances to Thomas Dickason and Company in London. These funds in turn would pay for the dry goods that the ship was to carry from London as the principal part of her cargo. At London the captain was to have the vessel sheathed with copper designed to last for seven years.

From London, Captain Olney was to clear *Mary Ann* for São Tiago in the Cape Verde Islands, unless obstacles should prevent him, in which case he was to head for Madeira. But he was instructed to make "the best of your way" to Rio de Janeiro, where upon entering the harbor he was to display a blue flag on his fore-topmast head and "appear to be in distress."[15] The captain also carried a letter from Sanzetenea to Romero, a certificate and a passport from the Spanish consul (in Boston), and the bills of sale of *Mary Ann* to and from Sanzetenea. Sanzetenea had been at great pains to impress upon the owners that without these documents entrance to the Río de la Plata could not be expected.

In the meantime the owners, with a view to a safe and advantageous disposition of *Mary Ann*'s cargo in South America, had decided to dispatch Thomas Lloyd Halsey, Jr., to the Río de la Plata to meet that ship. For this purpose they purchased from Halsey's father the schooner *Eliza,* for which they paid the sum of $3,400. Sanzetenea then obligingly offered to purchase the vessel for $6,400. The partners had scarcely accepted this generous offer when Sanzetenea proffered them the privilege of putting a cargo on board *Eliza* on their own account, free of freight and consigned to Halsey as supercargo. Availing themselves of this opportunity, they placed on board *Eliza* an assortment of wares, largely dry goods, which they charged in the invoice at $6,717. To the command of the schooner they appointed Henry Olney, brother of the captain of *Mary Ann*. *Eliza* sailed from Providence late in June, 1800, about a fortnight after *Mary Ann*'s departure for Amsterdam. Although she cleared for Madeira, her invoice was for the Cape of Good Hope and her bill of lading, for Buenos Aires.

As supercargo Halsey carried two sets of instructions from Brown and Ives and Corlis, both bearing the date of June 23, 1800. One set directed him to proceed to the Cape of Good Hope, dispose of the cargo, and let Captain Olney rig the schooner into a brig. Halsey was then to dispatch her to St. Paul Island, where he was to endeavor to procure a cargo of sealskins. Once he had his skins on board, Captain Olney was to proceed to Canton. But Halsey was to wait at the Cape of Good Hope for the arrival of the ship *Ariel,* which they were dispatching from Providence. Halsey was then to proceed in *Ariel* to Canton, where he would meet Captain Olney in *Eliza.*

The ship *Ariel* had an astonishingly brief career in the annals of Brown and Ives. The one time she appears is in the document just mentioned. The Providence merchants, of course, had never owned a vessel of that name, nor is it likely that they ever chartered one. She was invented solely for the purpose of misleading inquisitive officials who might have occasion to examine the papers of *Eliza.* And *Eliza* was not transformed into a brig; nor did she go sealing.

Halsey's second set of instructions, of course, directed him to proceed directly to Buenos Aires, where he was to inform himself of the "Character and abilities" of Romero. Like Halsey the captain of *Eliza* carried two sets of instructions. The one ordered him to call at the Cape of Good Hope, preparatory to his sealing venture and his voyage to Canton. His bona fide orders required that he observe carefully the directions of Sanzetenea in entering the port of Buenos Aires. He was to have his "Spanish papers Seperated from the others, to hand to the officer that will board" him, keeping out of sight all the American papers except the portage bill. Brown and Ives emphasized that the captain must ever be mindful that "great Care and Circumspection is Necessary."[16]

Eliza arrived safely in the Río de la Plata after a passage of 101 days. Within three hours Sanzetenea "came on board, with two officers— (in favor) who staid on board." The second night the dry goods were removed from the vessel but were taken only to Ensenada, "a small village . . . where all the Ships lay."[17] Pending removal to Buenos Aires, the goods were in constant danger of seizure, notwithstanding the freedom with which money was used to purchase their safety. But ultimately they were sold, and despite high charges, netted $15,000. This amount in Spanish dollars Halsey placed on board *Gladiator* of Boston for the account of Brown and Ives, Corlis, and himself. He selected this particular vessel in preference to others because she was fast sailing and was armed with twelve guns. En route to Boston, however, *Gladiator* had the misfortune to be captured by a British man-of-war and taken to Halifax. The Providence men, of course, claimed the 15,000 Spanish dollars, and the judge of the Court of Vice-Admiralty, strange as it seems, was sufficiently impressed to order the restoration of the money to them.[18]

Pending the arrival of *Mary Ann* from London, Halsey negotiated with Romero in regard to the terms governing the sale of her cargo. For a time he was inclined to believe he was outsmarting the Spaniard; but the latter's *froideur* soon convinced him that his wiles were ineffective. For weeks Halsey had an opportunity to observe firsthand the art of procrastination of which Romero was a complete master. Eventually on November 24, 1800, Halsey, in behalf of the owners of *Mary Ann,* entered into a "treaty" with Romero. By the first article Romero agreed to purchase *Mary Ann*'s cargo on board the vessel in whatever port of the Río de le Plata "shall be agreed on." The purchaser undertook to assume all risk and expense from the hour the ship anchored in the "place signalised"; and he was to be responsible for "any Confiscation which may orriginate from the Spanish Government to either the Ship or Cargo." Romero covenanted to pay a modest advance of 68 per cent over the first cost of the goods, which was assumed to be $80,000. As soon as the ship was unloaded (at some spot in the river sheltered from the eyes of Spanish officials), she was to be brought to the port of Ensenada, where she would enter as a Spanish vessel (by means of the passport she brought from the Spanish consul in Boston), "benifitting of the same exemptions & priviledges which the Spaniards enjoy."[19]

Although the terms of the "treaty" were less favorable than Halsey had expected, he solaced himself with the thought that, with one exception, it was an "infinitely better negotiation" than that of any other American. He considered a 68 per cent advance on board ship the equivalent of 135 per cent on shore, since it would cost, he alleged, $59,000 to land the cargo. Furthermore, by selling on board, he was spared all risk.[20]

SEIZURE AND CONFISCATION

Meanwhile, developments boded ill for *Mary Ann.* Romero refused to abide by his agreement to send *Eliza* to Rio de Janeiro to meet the ship, saying her return to the Río de la Plata in so short a time would excite the suspicion of Spanish officials. When *Mary Ann,* detained by adverse winds, arrived at Rio de Janeiro some three months late, she found no confidential agent of Romero there to meet her. As the weeks passed, Captain Olney's initial surprise changed to anxiety for the safety of the valuable property in his care. He seriously thought of selling his cargo at Rio de Janeiro, which would have spared both his owners and himself no end of trouble.[21] Before he could do this, however, Sanzetenea appeared on the scene to say that instructions from Romero were at last under way. After several weeks instructions arrived in a felucca, which was to accompany *Mary Ann* to Buenos Aires. Spanish procrastination does not suffice to explain this delay. Romero had delayed the dispatch of the felucca in order to "collect & amass" money to send in her for the purchase of goods at Rio de Janeiro. On his part, Sanzetenea then delayed the departure of *Mary Ann* in order to carry on trade with ships at Rio de Janeiro, "few or none of which he left unattempted & until the crew of the falucho, from the Patron to the Cook could make their purchases."[22]

His patience worn thin, Captain Olney set sail for the Río de la Plata without the felucca but with the understanding that his ship would, at a stipulated place in the river, await the arrival of the felucca. But again the captain waited in vain while Sanzetenea dispatched the felucca on a leisurely trading voyage along the Brazilian coast. Olney then sought to communicate with Halsey, only to have the message intercepted by the Spaniards. As the message included an invoice of *Mary Ann*'s cargo, it was most welcome intelligence to Joaquín del Pino, the viceroy, who now had every reason to be on the alert for such a valuable prize.

Soon Romero received news of the presence of *Mary Ann* in the river; but his message to Captain Olney was intercepted by a British man-of-war, which thus became aware of the presence of *Mary Ann* in the river. Pursued by both British and Spanish cruisers, Captain Olney was in a most precarious position, his difficulty being compounded by his own illness. Meanwhile, Romero watched and waited for the opportune moment to land the cargo illicitly, as his "treaty" had plainly anticipated. When the right moment failed to appear, he twice petitioned the government for the lawful entry of the cargo with payment of the regular duties. Both requests were refused.

Finally Romero arranged that the cargo be put ashore at a desolate spot up the river until it could be taken to some other country or entered at Buenos Aires, should the government there become more tolerant of neutral traders. Accordingly, he sent feluccas, which received the goods from *Mary Ann,* his agent giving receipts for the merchandise. But since officials at Buenos Aires knew, both from Romero's petitions to enter the goods and from Captain Olney's intercepted messages, that the ship had brought a cargo, they easily found the place of deposit, seized the goods, and brought them to Buenos Aires. Final decision with respect to the cargo was deferred pending trial of those involved.

Since the treaty made Romero answerable for the confiscation either of the ship or her cargo, Halsey requested that gentleman to make payment. He was told that payment would be made the next day. But on that day, to Halsey's amazement, Romero bluntly refused to pay, denied the existence of a treaty, and warned Halsey that he would pay with his life should he attempt to invoke the aid of the government at Buenos Aires. In an effort to save the ship from confiscation, however, Romero pretended to the Spanish officials that he was her owner.

At this point Halsey thought he had found a friend at court. Don Pedro Dewal, a merchant at Buenos Aires, came forward with professions of deep solicitude for Halsey, the nephew of his particular friend, John Innes Clark. About the cargo Dewal said he could do nothing. But he would be responsible for the ship. He assured Halsey that *Mary Ann* would be allowed to sail unmolested within four months and with the very valuable freight she had engaged. Unfortunately there was one condition attached to this offer, namely, that Halsey should leave the country, a condition imposed at the request of Romero. Seeing no prospect of redress, fearing for his life should he attempt any action against Romero, and wishing to salvage so valuable a property (the ship and her freight were valued at $170,000), Halsey agreed to accept Dewal's terms. Taking Dewal's signed contract, together with his bond for $170,000, Halsey in July, 1801, departed for home, hoping to enlist later the aid of his government in his efforts to obtain redress at Madrid for the confiscation of *Mary Ann*'s cargo.[23]

Soon after Halsey sailed from the Río de la Plata, the government at Buenos Aires seized *Mary Ann*, placed Spanish soldiers on board her, and threw Captain Olney into prison. While confined, the captain was compelled to undergo numerous and prolonged interrogations without being allowed to sit down and without the benefit of counsel. Finally two physicians (who attended him when permitted) and numerous friends, all outraged by the severity of his treatment, made such strong representations to the Viceroy that the captain was released from prison and confined in the house of a friend. Romero was also placed under house arrest.

Meanwhile, Romero claimed *Mary Ann,* in accordance with the Spanish papers she carried, but disavowed the confiscated cargo. At length, in March, 1802, His Catholic Majesty issued a decree directing that the cargo be sold and the proceeds (amounting to more than $300,000) be deposited in the royal treasury pending final determination of the case. When Halsey sailed for the United States, he naïvely hoped the case would be settled quickly. Actually it was more than two years before a decision was rendered, an interval that Romero availed himself of to send agents to Madrid to present his case against the Viceroy and to endeavor to recover *Mary Ann*. Halsey, too, had visited the Spanish capital to present the case of the Providence owners of *Mary Ann*.

At long last Romero's agents at Madrid, either through moral suasion or through bribery, obtained a decision in the case. In October, 1803, it was announced at Buenos Aires that Romero, Captain Olney, and all others who had been proceeded against as criminals in the "cause" were "absolved from the accusations alledged agt. them," declared free, and "their persons put at liberty." *Mary Ann* was decreed free from confiscation and "the rightful property of Romero"; and the proceeds of the sale of the cargo, still on deposit in the royal treasury, were "declared to be confiscated to the benifit of the King & others" and were to be divided among them.[24] Before the division of the funds could be carried out, however, the Viceroy, Del Pino, foiled in his designs upon *Mary Ann,* sought to satisfy his vengeful spirit by appropriating the $300,-000 for the benefit of himself and his friends. The protests and representations of Romero, Halsey, and others elicited a royal decree condemning Del Pino's actions and ordering the restoration of the sequestered funds to the royal treasury. But in the absence of a final decision of *Mary Ann*'s case at Madrid, no decree was ever issued directing the return of the money to the ship's owners in Providence.

But what of Dewal, who had agreed to be responsible for the safety of the vessel and who had given Halsey his bond as a guarantee that she would be allowed to sail undisturbed with her valuable freight? When Captain Olney, upon Romero's refusal to hand over the ship, requested Dewal to pay the bond, that gentleman not only refused to do so but declared in the presence of witnesses that the bond was worthless because he had bribed the notary at whose office it was registered to write clauses into it that had the effect of making it invalid. This was the final proof that Dewal had been in league with Romero to defraud the rightful owners of *Mary Ann* and her valuable cargo.

A DISAPPOINTING OUTCOME

An epilogue rounds out the story of *Mary Ann.* Although a Spanish decree of 1803 had declared her to belong to Romero, that gentleman, out of deference to a widespread suspicion at Buenos Aires that the ship was not his property, soon relinquished his claim to her.[25] In consequence, of course, title reverted to her rightful Providence owners, with Captain Olney once more in command. But under regulations then prevailing she could not sail with a cargo from Buenos Aires while flying the American flag. Frustrated in his every effort, Captain Olney decided to accept Romero's offer of a bona fide purchase of *Mary Ann,* which would enable her to take her departure from the Río de la Plata under Spanish colors. The sale price was $40,000, but as usual Romero was unable to make payment in cash. He proposed, therefore, that he pay in two equal installments of $20,000, to be derived from the sale of the cargo she would carry to Europe. In view of Romero's known record of default on his engagements, this was hardly a safe arrangement for the American owners of *Mary Ann*. Nevertheless, Captain Olney accepted in the belief that no better disposition of the vessel could be effected.[26]

Mary Ann sailed for London late in 1804 with a cargo of hides and tallow, just at the time of the renewal of war between England and Spain. Early in 1805 she was captured by a British cruiser, condemned (with her cargo) as Spanish property, and later sold at public auction at Halifax. Captain Olney subsequently went to London, where he sought in vain to collect the purchase money from Romero. As a last resort, he tried to convince the British Court of Admiralty that the sale of the ship to Romero had been a fictitious one. When this too ended in failure, there vanished the last lingering hope of the owners that they would recoup the losses they had suffered.

Brown and Ives and their associates in the adventure of *Mary Ann* were not alone in having trouble with the Spaniards in the Río de la Plata. In spite of the official ban on neutral ships in Spanish colonial ports, officials there pursued for two years an indulgent policy toward United States vessels in the river. But this tolerance was always dependent upon the caprice of the Viceroy; and in 1802 Del Pino decided to detain a large number of United States ships then in the river. On March 31, 1802, "sundry Citizens of the United States" restrained at Buenos Aires protested to the Viceroy the unlawful detention of themselves and their ships in the Río de la Plata. They had come there at a time when Spain was at war with a "powerful Nation," and they had come to carry to market for the subjects of His Catholic Majesty "the perishing Produce" of the area, which could not be shipped with safety under the Spanish flag.[27] When this document, signed by twenty-three of the Americans, was received by the Viceroy in contemptuous silence, the same citizens appealed to Charles Pinckney, American minister at Madrid, enclosing a copy of the protest to which the Viceroy had turned a deaf ear.[28] The protesters charged that a distinction had been made between them and the citizens and subjects of other nations; and in support of their charge they could point to the forty-one American vessels with a combined tonnage of 10,299 tons then confined in the three ports of the Río de la Plata.[29] But Jonathan Russell (then in the Río de la Plata on business but later one of the American commissioners to negotiate the Treaty of Ghent) testified that no other American ship captain was "treated with the same severity" as Captain Olney. Nor had any vessel other than *Mary Ann* been deprived of her rudder and sails.[30]

In these protests blame for the plight of the Americans and their ships was placed on the Viceroy; and no mere subjects of the Spanish Crown were held culpable. But Brown and Ives, Corlis, and Halsey were originally more outraged by the conduct of Romero and Dewal than by that of the Viceroy. It was these men who were alleged to have broken their contract, repudiated their bond, and conspired to defraud the owners of *Mary Ann*. It was these men who had inflicted upon the owners such grievous loss. It was against Dewal that they brought legal action in a vain effort to compel compliance with the bond. And it was to invoke the aid of the Spanish Court against these men that Halsey went to Spain in 1802.

Only when they failed to obtain satisfaction from Romero and Dewal did the owners turn their fire upon the Viceroy. From 1804 on they consistently chose to regard the Viceroy as the villain in the piece. Briefly stated, theirs was a plea of innocence. As the argument ran, they had been induced to undertake the voyage of *Mary Ann* by the royal decree of 1797, opening Spanish colonial ports to the ships of neutral nations. That decree they understood to be still in effect when *Mary Ann* sailed from Providence in June, 1800. The revocation of the decree was not made known to Captain Olney until after his ship had been seized and he had been thrown into prison. The captain and the ship were the victims of the Viceroy's avarice. From the day the ship arrived in the river, the Viceroy had been determined that the vessel and cargo should be sacrificed. In a tyrannical and mercenary spirit he had resorted to persecution as an instrument of plunder. His cruel treatment of Captain Olney had had but one purpose: to shake his faith in his employers and to torture him into abandoning the ship.

In this fashion the owners of *Mary Ann* pressed their case through the years. When they had almost despaired of recovering anything from the disaster, the treaty of 1819 with Spain gave their hopes a new lease on life. That treaty provided for the appointment of a joint commission to adjudge the claims of citizens or subjects of each country against the government of the other. In 1822 Brown and Ives were busy assembling data, procuring affidavits, and perfecting their arguments in support of their claim to indemnification for the injury they had suffered. They estimated at $390,000 the loss incurred by the detention of the ship and the confiscation of her cargo, and charged compound interest on this sum for a period of twenty years. Their total claim, therefore, amounted to $843,264.14. But the commissioners were not impressed. On December 12, 1823, Brown and Ives reported to their counsel the melancholy intelligence of "the rejection by the Commissioners, of the claim for the *Mary Ann*" on the ground that "they suspected the Voyage to have been an illicit one."[31]

The preponderance of available evidence supports the correctness of this decision. When Brown and Ives dispatched their ship *Charlotte* to the Río de la Plata in 1800, they were clearly aware that the ban upon neutral vessels in Spanish colonial ports had been reimposed. In the absence of countervailing evidence it must be assumed that they knew the ports in the Río de la Plata were still closed to them when *Mary Ann* sailed from Providence a short time later. Why, if the owners of *Mary Ann* believed trade by neutrals to the river was lawful, did they surround her voyage with all the trappings of an illicit enterprise? Why the false clearance, the false papers, the fictitious bill of sale designed to give the ship the character of a Spanish vessel? The contract signed by Sanzetenea in behalf of Romero specifically referred to the goods to be shipped on *Mary Ann* as "prohibited in the Spanish Settlements of Monte Video and Buenos Ayres." Furthermore, Brown and Ives stated under oath that the schooner *Eliza* cleared for Madeira in June, 1800, because "the Spanish Government did not allow of any commerce in American vessels . . . to Buenos Ayres or to any of their colonies in South America."[32] Since *Mary Ann* sailed in the same month, her owners knew that her projected voyage was in contravention of those same Spanish commercial regulations.[33]

CHAPTER 5

Distant Enterprises of Magnitude and Hard Money

IN 1800 the maritime commerce of the United States entered upon an era of marked expansion as Europe's preoccupation with the French Revolutionary and Napoleonic Wars provided American merchants with the chance to trade in various quarters of the globe against reduced competition. In response to the opportunity the volume of American foreign trade increased sharply, and the shipbuilding industry boomed. Unprecedented prosperity prevailed until 1805, when England became concerned about the size of the trade being carried on indirectly by American shippers between England's European enemies and their colonial possessions. This trade was allowed under a decision of the British Court of Admiralty rendered in 1800 in the case of the ship *Polly.* In 1805 the *Essex* decision modified the ruling of the *Polly* case, making the trade between belligerent ports more difficult and less profitable. Furthermore, American shipping was soon afterwards caught in the cross fire of Napoleonic decrees and British Orders in Council; and when the Jeffersonian embargo of December, 1807, sought to save United States ships from this cross fire by keeping them in port, it rang down the curtain on an important commercial epoch.

The business of Brown and Ives during the years from 1800 to 1807 reflected the maritime expansion of the period. In 1800 they possessed but two ships—*John Jay* and *Ann & Hope*—suited to the requirements of the East India trade. But in 1801 they contracted with Colonel Benjamin Tallman for the building of a new ship of 236 tons, to be named *Isis.* In the same year they purchased a one-third interest in the new ship *Arthur,* of which they soon became the sole owners. And in 1804 they purchased the newly built ship *Asia* of 350 tons. Apart from these five vessels, which were to be employed in the trade to the Pacific, they had the ships *Charlotte* and *General Hamilton,* which they used in their traffic with Europe. Rounding out their fleet were nine smaller craft, which carried to Europe much of the tea, coffee, sugar, and other products brought from Canton and Batavia in their ships.

TRADE TO CANTON WITH SKINS AND GOODS

At the dawn of this era of commercial prosperity *Ann & Hope* sailed on her second voyage to China. With a view to spreading the risk, Brown and Ives let a seven-twelfths part of the ship to Gibbs and Channing of Newport; John Innes Clark of Providence; and the firm of Munro, Snow, and Munro, also of Providence.[1] In command was Captain Christopher Bentley, while Thomas Thompson, a veteran of the first voyage of the ship, went along as an assistant. The owners directed Captain Bentley to "have the Ship, between Decks & in the lower hold, aired as much as possible on the passage." He was to keep the vessel clean and the men's berths "as well as other parts of her, frequently washed with Vinegar," as this would tend to keep the "Crew in Health & to preserve the Timber & plank." In Canton he must have her well smoked, which would dry the wood and "destroy all Vermin that may be in her."[2]

Ann & Hope carried 100,000 hard dollars and a quantity of sealskins, charged in the invoice at $22,596. Sealskins, a new item in the invoices of ships sent to Canton by Brown and Ives, were another of the many articles employed in the trade in an effort to more nearly equalize the value of the east- and westbound cargoes, thereby reducing the amount of specie required. Brown and Ives were thus recognizing, though somewhat tardily, an important fact of the China trade, namely, that furs and skins were in greater demand than other goods that Americans could send to Canton. The high esteem in which these articles were held had been discovered quite by accident on Captain James Cook's third voyage, when fur of the sea otter taken on board off the northwestern coast of North America was ultimately carried to China. This intelligence, brought to the eastern seaboard of the United States, prompted enterprising Boston merchants to load trinkets on board their vessels, send them to the northwestern coast, and exchange these cheap but gaudy wares for the very valuable fur of the sea otter. While on such a trading venture Captain Robert Gray, a native of Tiverton, Rhode Island, sailing *Columbia* out of Boston, discovered the great river to which he gave the name of his ship.

In the beginning only a limited number of Boston merchants of relatively large means appear to have participated in the sea otter trade. But merchants of lesser means gradually entered the business. By 1801 each of the numerous vessels arriving at Canton from the northwestern coast brought anywhere from a few hundred to several thousand sea otter skins, which sold within a price range of $17 to $25 a skin.[3] Thus a really good cargo of sea otter skins could provide as much as $80,000 toward a return shipment of China goods. But such cargoes were the exception rather than the rule. A competent observer thoroughly familiar with the situation at Canton wrote that "The Northwest trade is compleatly overdone." He thought it must be neglected for a few years "unless the old and first adventurers unite and make a monopoly of the business." Individuals who had entered "into a competition of late" had not met with the "greatest success."[4]

With the supply of sea otter furs rather limited, American merchants turned to other kinds of skins in their efforts to find a satisfactory substitute for hard dollars at Canton. Of these the most successful were sealskins. More plentiful but much less valuable a skin than sea otter, sealskins arriving on a single ship at Canton numbered from 20,000 to 65,000 and sold at prices ranging from $0.85 to $1.25 a skin.[5] Sealskins were procured at numerous places, one of the most important being South Georgia, located east of the Falkland Islands in the South Atlantic. At the beginning of the new century a large proportion of the American vessels arriving at Canton brought either sea otter skins or sealskins.

Although skins were the most acceptable type of goods at Canton, they were in no sense an adequate substitute for hard dollars. As one observer wrote, "Goods of any kind at this market are not to be esteemed ... if you send a money Ship you may expect the best of goods at less prices than for skins. I can never promise you great quality Teas ... unless I procure them with Cash."[6] Two years later the same observer wrote that "Barter business in this Country is attended with great uncertainty as it respects the quality of goods had in return, and I assure you that I can transact business with specie 10 or 20 per Cent better, and with certainty in point of the quality of the Merchandize received in return."[7] Such statements leave no doubt that specie conferred a great advantage at Canton; and it was only because goods, even otter skins and sealskins, cost less than specie to procure, that anyone sent other than hard dollars to that market.

Brown and Ives had not participated in the sea otter trade on the American northwestern coast, probably because the Boston merchants were so well established there. Nor is there any evidence that they had ever tried sealing. It is probable, therefore, that the sealskins shipped on board *Ann & Hope* were brought to Rhode Island by one of the other parties interested in this particular voyage. But with these skins and 100,000 hard dollars *Ann & Hope* had resources in greater amount than any previous ship sent to Canton by Brown and Ives.

Although his ship was armed, Captain Bentley was warned to take no undue chances. He was to proceed to Canton by the "Eastern Passage, round new Holland, & Norfolk Island"; he was to stop nowhere, except from absolute necessity, and to give the Cape of Good Hope, the Île de France (Mauritius), and Bourbon (Réunion) "good births." Returning, he was to avoid the Soenda Strait unless he sailed in convoy or had adequate assurance from that quarter and to be out of the China Sea before the southwest monsoon set in.[8]

From Providence to the South Cape of New Holland (Australia) *Ann & Hope* had a fine run; from there to Canton the passage was disagreeable and dangerous. They soon encountered head winds that for a fortnight prevented them from making any progress. Where they had every reason to expect a regular trade wind from the southeast, they experienced nothing but a constant succession of northerly winds and disagreeable calms. They passed around the New Hebrides and through the Caroline Islands, falling in with several islands "not noticed" in their charts. Thirty miles from Macao they lost their stream cable and anchor, which for a time kept them in a precarious situation.[9]

At Canton, Samuel Snow (serving as American consul) received *Ann & Hope,* disposed of the sealskins, and procured the return cargo. He reported that he was holding the skins at $2.00 a skin but that he had been offered no more than $1.25. Nankeens were high in price because of the large quantities taken by American, Danish, and Swedish vessels. At the moment they were in short supply, but more were expected at market within a fortnight. Pending their arrival, he refused to disclose the amount he wanted, as that "would rise them immediately up." The late arrival of the English ships operated against him. Since the English captains had brought their money ashore only a few days before the New Year, the timely supply of specie had enabled the hong merchants to discharge their obligations without sacrificing their property. They were therefore "under no necessity of reducing the price [of their goods] to obtain a preference in the Sale." But by practicing his wiles on Mouqua, Snow was able to obtain his teas at a reasonable price—half-cash, half-credit.[10]

Even with the substantial credit allowed by Mouqua on the teas, *Ann & Hope*'s fund of hard dollars was not sufficient to load the ship. Snow found it necessary, therefore, to draw fifteen bills of exchange payable on London at twelve months' sight, totaling £16,113 sterling, or $71,541. Samuel Snow sent back by *Ann & Hope* a document that presents an admirable view of the American trade at Canton at that time.

Specifically, it is a record of American ships that called at that port between August, 1799, and March, 1800. Of the seventeen vessels, six were from Boston, five from Philadelphia, three from New York, two from Providence, and one from Salem. Total tonnage from the respective ports was 1,093 tons from Boston, 2,302 tons from Philadelphia, 940 tons from New York, 1,025 tons from Providence, and 331 tons from Salem. Boston's ships were the smallest, and Philadelphia's were the largest, one being of 700 tons. Four of the Boston vessels came from the American northwestern coast, where they had obviously called for sea otter skins.

The cargoes taken home from Canton are equally interesting. Those of the Philadelphia ships had an aggregate value of $1,117,000; those of New York, $363,000; of Providence, $357,000; and of Boston, $305,000. The six Boston vessels with their low average tonnage had taken from Canton cargoes that were correspondingly modest. Providence, which ranked fourth in number of ships, was third in total tonnage and in value of the cargoes shipped from Canton. *Ann & Hope,* Brown and Ives's representative among the seventeen American vessels, was third in tonnage and in value of the cargo taken from Canton.[11]

From the data assembled by Samuel Snow certain conclusions may be drawn with respect to the American trade to Canton as of the year 1800. Philadelphia merchants were engaged in the traffic on a larger scale, employed larger ships, and used hard dollars in greater quantity than their rivals in the other cities. Boston shipowners were trading to China chiefly by way of the northwestern coast, but on a relatively small scale, and they were obviously trying to finance the business mainly with sea otter skins. Only the Dorrs of Boston had sent more than one vessel to Canton, but the combined tonnage of their two craft was only 320 tons, compared to 550 tons for *Ann & Hope* or 700 tons for *Canton,* owned by Willing and Francis of Philadelphia, who undoubtedly ranked first among American houses then trading to China. *Ann & Hope* sailed from Canton on March 12, 1800. No invoice of her cargo has been found, but Snow had estimated its cost at $243,900.[12] Upon her arrival in Providence, these goods were valued at $324,388, an advance of 33 per cent.[13]

Before the return of *Ann & Hope,* Brown and Ives had dispatched *John Jay,* Captain Benjamin Dexter, to Canton to the care of Samuel Snow. Although the partners were placing at the disposal of Snow 140,000 hard dollars and perhaps $10,000 in goods, approximately a third of this amount was owed to Mouqua on account of the credit given to complete the cargo of *Ann & Hope.* As the fund of specie remaining would not suffice to load the ship, the partners authorized Snow either to draw bills on London or Hamburg or to procure a credit for the largest possible time, interest free.[14]

Before *John Jay*'s arrival at Canton the report had circulated that drought in certain parts of China and frost in other areas had seriously damaged the tea crop. Realizing that this rumor probably was nothing more than a pretext for the hong merchants to raise prices, Snow remarked that could those gentlemen "place a perfect confidence in each other so as to form a combination to raise the price . . . they certainley would have it in their power to command it from us." Fortunately, so great was their mutual suspicion that price agreements, although frequently attempted, had never been observed "two months at a time."[15] Carried on as it was through one port in terms of a limited number of great staples eagerly sought after, the China trade could have been susceptible to monopolistic control.

Snow's fund of hard dollars was sufficient to pay for the silks and nankeens of *John Jay*'s cargo, but he was obliged to draw bills on London for two-thirds of the cost of his teas. As the bills were accepted only at a discount of 15 per cent, he was once more reminded that nothing succeeded so well in Canton as hard dollars.[16]

Snow himself took passage on *John Jay* as she sailed from Canton at the end of January, 1801. Through the China Sea and the Soenda Strait she was in the company of four other American vessels. Except for an outbreak of smallpox, which necessitated the inoculation of twenty members of the crew, the passage was quite uneventful. Captain Dexter put in at St. Helena to obtain water and to "Endever to find" a leak in the ship. Seventeen days out from that station he wrote that the ship was "Very Fowl and Sails Monsteras Heavy." He reported that Snow was very impatient, but he had not "Discovered as the Ship sails any the faster for it."[17] At Providence the cargo, which had cost $178,832, was valued at $318,315, an advance of 78 per cent.[18]

From Canton, Samuel Snow had advised Brown and Ives that some of the American vessels visiting that port had come by way of England, where they had taken on board large quantities of camlets for sale in Chinese markets. Since the partners wished to have *Ann & Hope* well coppered, which at that time could not be done in the United States, they decided to dispatch her to London for the twofold purpose of sheathing her and loading her with English goods for Canton.

Snow had also informed Brown and Ives that several American ships had brought to Canton ginseng in various amounts, although he had not indicated the prices at which it had been sold. They therefore placed on board *Ann & Hope* some 5,000 pounds of the herb, cured and uncured. The cured variety, supposedly "Clarified, in the same manner

. . . as the Tartars manufacture theirs," had repeatedly sold in Canton at $70 to $100 a pound.[19] To avoid depressing the price in Canton the partners advised that knowledge of the amount of the clarified sort on board the ship should be withheld from the Chinese. It would be well, they thought, to repack it in small catty boxes to be fed gradually to the market.[20]

The great expectations of profit entertained by Americans exporting ginseng to China were based in part upon a misconception. It was true that ginseng was a Chinese "nostrum applied to all diseases," possessing "every virtue in their estimation." It was believed to be a good diuretic and sudorific, to promote digestion, stimulate the appetite, calm the mind, induce sleep, conquer any debility, procure easy births, give vigor to old and young, and excite people "to Coition when nature would not."[21] Surely for an herb so highly prized by millions of Chinese the demand must be unlimited, reasoned the American skipper. A picul of "first Quality Tartar Ginseng" sold at retail in China for the enormous sum of $700,000. But ginseng from Tatary was procured only for the Emperor's account and produced for him a very handsome revenue. The American merchants failed to realize that ginseng from the United States could not command in China either the esteem or the price of the Tatar variety and that a small quantity of the herb went a long way. In 1802 a competent witness estimated that the 160 piculs of ginseng then on the Canton market were sufficient for "ten years consumption."[22] The Americans were about to overwork a good thing.

Besides the ginseng destined for Canton, *Ann & Hope* carried to London a cargo of tobacco, flour, sugar, and coffee invoiced at $83,670, together with 30,000 hard dollars.[23] Captain Christopher Bentley was again in command, with Thomas Thompson as supercargo. Provided by the partners with a letter of credit for £10,000 sterling, Thompson had the means of augmenting in London the resources at his command.

At London the flour, coffee, and sugar netted $86,540. Assuming that the tobacco brought in no more than the amount of its invoice, the total return was in excess of $95,000 on the invoice of $83,670. Thomas Dickason and Company introduced Thompson to a packer for the British East India Company who gave him a memorandum of the goods that the company found suited to the Chinese market: camlets, broadcloths, and long ells, a cloth similar to serge, put up in pieces of twenty-four yards. Thompson engaged the goods from the firm of John and William Jacobs, who in turn arranged to "billet & pack the Camblets & long Ells . . . in every respect equal to those Shipped by the India Company." He also purchased watches, glassware, cutlery, and porter for which he paid cash because he could thus procure them on much

better terms. In London, Thompson invested in goods to the amount of
£19,566 sterling, or $86,873, a sum more than covered by the sale of the
wares he brought to London. But as Brown and Ives desired that a substantial balance be left in the hands of Dickason and Company, he
drew on his owners in favor of the Jacobs house at twelve months for
£9,652 sterling.[24]

Ann & Hope thus sailed from London with British goods costing
$86,873, ginseng of unknown value, and 30,000 hard dollars. The voyage
to Canton was comparatively uneventful, broken only by a stop at the
Bali Strait for wood and water, "with some other refreshments." At
Canton, Thompson found awaiting him 20,000 hard dollars that
Brown and Ives had sent on freight to his care. With his total fund of
specie increased to 50,000 hard dollars and with a valuable cargo of
goods on board ship he expected to transact business to his positive
advantage. But he soon discovered that his prospects, "both as respects
our Sales & purchases," were most unpromising. He had learned that
his funds' being in goods placed him in a situation "very different
from what it would [have been] had [they] Consisted of Specie only."
The large quantity of British goods remaining on hand from the
previous year, coupled with the belief that the British East India Company ships would soon arrive, made the security merchants wary of
contracting for large purchases of his goods. Thompson had flattered
himself that Mouqua would secure his ship and purchase the entire
cargo; but when that gentleman discovered the meager fund of specie
on board ship, he flatly refused to secure her. In the end Ponqua secured
the ship, took part of the goods, and provided part of the return cargo,
leaving Thompson free to make supplementary arrangements with other
merchants.

The ginseng on board *Ann & Hope* proved a disappointing investment. The quality was not good, and it was a bit moldy from its
long stay in the ship. Thompson sold all of the common variety and
part of the clarified, but it did not command the high prices the owners had expected. The remainder of the root he left behind to be sold
on commission. Upon a final accounting it appeared that the ginseng
invoiced at $10,084 had sold for $9,463, clear of all charges.[25]

The cargo taken on at Canton consisted chiefly of tea, sugar, nankeens, and cassia and cost $194,986.[26] As the goods purchased in London
at $86,873 netted in Canton only $84,106, Thompson's funds, including
the hard dollars, were far from sufficient to cover the cost. Only a very
large credit at twenty months enabled him to purchase so costly a cargo;
and being short of specie, he paid high prices for goods that were less
than the best.

While *Ann & Hope* was at Canton, a total of twenty-two American ships called there, of which *Ann & Hope,* of 550 tons, was the largest, the next being of 430 tons.[27] Philadelphia was represented by six vessels, two of more than 400 tons. All of the craft from the Quaker City had come to Canton direct. Six vessels of the smaller variety had touched at the American northwestern coast; two had been to South Georgia and one to the Falkland Islands for sealskins. Only *Ann & Hope* had come from a port in Europe. In 1801 it was again the shipowners of Philadelphia who were prosecuting the China trade on the largest scale; and it was also they who were conducting it in the most efficient way, namely, by means of hard dollars. Boston merchants, operating small ships, were still financing the business chiefly with skins; and the scale of their business was dwarfed by that of Philadelphia. As for Brown and Ives, although represented by the largest ship, they were unwilling or unable to send specie in large volume; nor had they found goods suited to the Canton market. Ginseng was a disappointment, as were camlets and cloths from England. It is significant that in 1801 no other American ship had been to London before visiting Canton. Perhaps other shipowners had discovered earlier what Brown and Ives were just now learning: that it was difficult for American merchants to compete with English traders (British East India Company and private) in English cloths at Canton. Obviously skins, next to hard dollars, provided the most efficient means by which Americans could finance the trade. And Brown and Ives, shunning the traffic in furs, should have recognized that specie was an imperative of the business.

But in spite of the disadvantages under which Thompson had labored, *Ann & Hope* made a successful and profitable voyage. Judging by the duties paid at Providence, the cargo that in Canton had cost $194,986 had a value in the United States of perhaps $390,000.[28]

TRADE TO CANTON WITH HARD DOLLARS

In the years 1803–4 Brown and Ives finally accepted without reservation the idea that they must continue to finance their trade to China mainly with hard dollars. Accordingly, when they fitted their ships *Arthur* and *Isis* for voyages to Canton with Samuel Aborn and Thomas Thompson as the respective supercargoes, the ships together carried 230,000 hard dollars.[29] The partners realized, of course, that even with this quantity of specie it would be necessary to procure some goods on credit in order to completely fill the two vessels. But their instructions to the supercargoes show their thorough conviction that a plentiful supply of hard money made it possible to obtain credit on terms of advantage. Aborn was to negotiate a credit payable in Canton within twenty months, interest free, without an addition to the customary price and with the hong creditor risking the goods to Providence. Aborn was to have it "fully expressed" in the notes given by him in behalf of his owners that they were to be "absolutely null, & void, & of no avail" in the event the property should not "reach America" in safety. In short, no goods, no pay. When specie could work such miracles, it is hard to understand why they ever had resorted to anything else.[30]

On her outward passage *Arthur* arrived at the Soenda Strait in 117 days, after having experienced a "very uncommon Proportion of Calms, & light adverse Winds." Samuel Aborn reported her to be very strong, entirely tight, and "an excellent Sea Boat." If she was "no high flyer," neither could she be called a "dull Sailor." They had crowded her up to ten knots, and in very heavy squalls for a few moments she would "run off Eleven"; but beyond that it was "out of the power of Wind & Canvas to carry her." After leaving the Strait, the ship had a "moderate run" through the China Sea until near Macao, where she encountered violent gales that continued for three days, dismasting three English ships and leaving one a complete wreck. *Arthur,* however, proved rugged and durable. Aborn again termed her "an Excellent Sea Boat."[31]

At Canton, Aborn found nine American vessels, four from New York, four from Philadelphia, and one from New Haven.[32] But within a fortnight there arrived four more from the American northwestern coast, all of them small, each carrying about 2,000 sea otter skins, and all destined, in Aborn's opinion, to make very unprofitable voyages. After spending four or five days in learning "how the Different Security Merchants stood," Aborn applied to Mouqua, who showed no inclination to secure the ship. He had secured a large number of English craft and had become somewhat embarrassed through "an immense purchase" of Bombay cotton. Besides, Mouqua's goods were much higher priced than those of other hong merchants. Aborn accordingly decided to secure with Conseequa, reputed to be as punctual and honorable as any.

Arthur had brought to Canton two bales of American cotton, the first of that article ever carried to China by a ship of Brown and Ives. Aborn sold it without difficulty and reported that the Chinese were not only much pleased with it but thought it preferable to that from Surat. He believed that if cotton could be obtained in the United States at twelve or thirteen cents a pound, it might well become an article of considerable export to China.[33]

Aborn believed some Americans trading to Canton were too much inclined to abuse the confidence placed in them by allowing their notes to hong merchants to go unpaid for long periods of time, with the result that other Americans, more punctual in their payments, paid the penalty for the delinquency of the few. "The Strictest Punctuality," he wrote, "ought to be Observed towards People who are so liberal & generous in their Credits as the Chinese."[34]

When *Isis* sailed for Canton, Brown and Ives enjoined Captain Benjamin Dexter to be attentive to the health of his crew. This could best be done by keeping the ship well ventilated and by providing the men with fresh vegetables and "such things as you have, that are considered antiscorbutic."[35] One day out from Block Island, *Isis* encountered a gale in the Gulf Stream in which she lost her main-topmast and topgallant mast. Six days elapsed before they could be replaced. She was also brought to by a French ship of twenty-two guns, which took Captain Dexter on board. But the master of the French craft dismissed him with "civility" after an examination of his papers. The chief difficulty of the passage out came from a succession of head winds and calms that caused much delay.[36]

Arriving at Canton, Thomas Thompson, the supercargo, found the market largely drained of teas. After negotiating with the various hong merchants, especially Mouqua, Houqua, Junqua, and Conseequa, he contracted with the last named to secure the ship. Conseequa had more teas than the others and could afford to give a larger credit.[37]

In the year 1804 two ships of Brown and Ives, *Arthur* and *Isis,* had returned with cargoes costing $363,000, payment for which was made chiefly from the fund of hard dollars the vessels had carried to Canton. The partners had plumbed the secrets of the trade to China. The heyday of their traffic to that quarter of the world was at hand. In the course of the next two years ships owned by them made four additional visits to Canton. First was their new ship *Asia* on her maiden voyage. Her master was Nathaniel Pearce, but the business of the voyage was to be transacted by Thomas Thompson, who had remained at Canton after his passage out on *Isis* the previous year. Consigned to him was a quantity of gin and brandy and 102,213 hard dollars on board *Asia*.[38] This, together with 30,000 hard dollars sent to Canton by Brown and Ives aboard ships from Philadelphia and Boston, provided Thompson with some $130,000 in specie toward the purchase of a cargo of China goods.

These dollars had been collected by dint of great effort; and the instructions of the partners to Thompson cast a significant light upon the difficulties under which the trade to China was carried on. To procure hard dollars a merchant must have "funds" or assets to offer in exchange. But even with the necessary funds in hand the quantity of dollars required for a China voyage could not be procured and assembled in less than three or four months and then only after careful planning. Of the specie carried by *Asia* much the largest proportion came from J. R. Wheaton in New York, but Isaac Moses and Sons of the same city provided 10,000 dollars. From Philadelphia the partners received 15,000 dollars, while they procured 10,000 dollars in Newport. From the bank in Warren, Rhode Island, they received 5,000 dollars; from the Providence Bank, 6,000 dollars. And one box containing 2,000 dollars had been "packed in the Compting House."[39] In Europe dollars were even higher than in the United States, "owing in some measure" to the use of them in England as a "currency at the rate of 5/ St. each." The time and trouble they had "in collecting the Money now remitted" to Thompson almost discouraged them from a further prosecution of trade to China. In an unduly pessimistic vein they wrote that "under its present embarrassments—the prospect of profit is by no means equal to the labour and perplexity attending the collection of a large number of Spanish Dollars, & without them the trade cannot be pursued."[40] The profits of *Asia*'s voyage would show such gloom to be entirely without warrant.

As Brown and Ives planned to send no other vessel to Canton that season, they requested Thompson to ship them by some good American vessel or vessels "the bulk of one hundred Tons of Teas—provided those of a suitable quality can be obtained on reasonable terms" and shipped at a moderate freight. Any deficiency of funds was to be obtained by Thompson on credit payable in Canton in twenty months, unless he was able to negotiate bills on the firm payable in Amsterdam or London at twelve months' sight.[41]

Upon Captain Pearce the partners urged every attention to the health of his crew by providing them occasionally with "such vegetables as you have, and small beer." And they remarked that the "Woart, or new Beer, made of the Essence of Spruce, and drank when first made is considered useful in preventing and checking the Scurvy."[42]

Sailing from Providence in mid-July of 1804, *Asia* was in the Bali Strait on November 1. She passed through the Makasser Strait, which Captain Pearce found "a very Safe and Easy Navigation," then sailed by way of the Sir Edward Pellew Group and the Formosa Strait. He reported *Asia* a "very fine Stanch and fast Sailing Ship." He fell in with the ship *General Washington* and "out Sailed her very Much." In the China Sea he spoke the ship *Rousseau* (owned by Stephen Girard of Philadelphia), whose captain said that *Asia* was the "first Ship that he Ever fell in with that Could Sail with him."[43]

Asia arrived at Canton on December 10, 1804, after a fine passage of

145 days. Thomas Thompson, who was there to receive her, chose to secure the ship with Houqua rather than Conseequa because the latter, though liberal in credit, sometimes sold tea of inferior quality. He did, however, contract with Conseequa for 650 chests of teas of the varieties in which deception was more difficult. The cargo, consisting principally of teas and 156,000 nankeens, cost $202,816. As this was some $70,000 in excess of his fund of hard dollars, Thompson gave his "obligations" in behalf of Brown and Ives for the balance, payable in twenty months.[44]

Taking her departure from Canton in January, 1805, *Asia* arrived at Providence at the end of May. The partners removed from the ship a minor portion of the teas and the major part of the nankeens. They then invoiced the teas remaining on board at a figure almost exactly twice the cost at Canton. Short nankeens costing $0.45 they charged at $0.84, while the "Yellow Company" nankeens purchased at $1.00 were marked up to $1.55. Teas and nankeens whose total cost had been $109,000 were thus charged in the new invoice at $201,000. Other assorted items brought the total invoice to $210,000.[45]

Brown and Ives consigned *Asia* with this cargo to the care of Daniel Crommelin and Sons in Amsterdam. Since 1801 Crommelin and Sons had become, next to Dickason and Company, the most important of the European correspondents of the partners, selling on commission a large part of the tea, coffee, and sugar imported by them. Captain Pearce's orders directed him to call at Texel, where he would report his arrival and await instructions from the Amsterdam house. His owners hoped the cargo could be sold at Amsterdam, but they recognized that it might be necessary to discharge it at Emden.[46]

On July 9 the captain wrote from Texel Roads that Crommelin and Sons had not yet determined the disposition of the cargo. But while he waited, he was not suffering from boredom. Some of his men had celebrated the Fourth of July by becoming so unruly that he was compelled to put three of them in irons. Two of these succeeded the first night in freeing themselves and throwing their irons overboard, but Pearce again put them in irons and confined them to the cabin. With good order restored aboard ship, he received directions from Crommelin and Sons to proceed to Emden to discharge his cargo.[47]

Asia was the first ship owned by Brown and Ives that carried to Europe a major part of the cargo that she had brought from Canton.[48] The Crommelin and Sons account of the sales shows that the net proceeds were 645,935 guilders, or $258,374, an amount $48,000 in excess of the invoice and some $149,000 above the first cost of the goods.[49] The teas sold at a figure at least 125 per cent above the price paid for them. *Asia* had made a handsome voyage.

Her cargo discharged, *Asia* returned to Amsterdam, where Captain Pearce put her in order, procured the necessary stores and provisions, advanced to each man a month's wages, and received on board a quantity of Dutch camlets and gin from Crommelin and Sons. Crommelin and Sons then directed *Asia* to Lisbon, where they had asked John Bulkeley and Son to purchase 100,000 hard dollars for her. Although dollars were in great demand, Bulkeley and Son procured the necessary amount without delaying the ship, drawing upon Crommelin and Sons for the funds with which to complete the purchase. If it be remembered that Crommelin and Sons then remitted to Dickason and Company in London the balance of the proceeds of *Asia*'s cargo, a good view of the commercial system of Brown and Ives emerges.

Sailing from Lisbon with gin, camlets, 100,000 Spanish dollars for her owners, and 50,000 dollars on freight for other American houses, *Asia* arrived 127 days later at Macao, where Thomas Thompson was awaiting her.[50] Since Crommelin and Sons had let it be known that for the next year the Dutch East India Company would admit for sale at Amsterdam entire cargoes of China goods in American ships, Thompson was careful to place on *Asia* no goods to be disposed of in America. She could thus call at Providence, procure new papers, and continue to Amsterdam with her cargo intact.

Thompson disposed of the Dutch camlets at $50 a piece in barter for Souchong tea, which he considered a handsome sale. Together with the gin they netted $17,860, a profit of some 35 per cent on the cost at Amsterdam. In Thompson's opinion the prospects of the China trade were not especially flattering, but since Brown and Ives could carry it on "to more advantage than many others," he thought they should continue in one or two ships having a capacity of 5,000 to 6,000 chests of tea. He was sure that with the continuation of the war tea would be in demand in Europe. Nankeens were too high to justify large purchases, while silks were not an "object worth Speculating in."[51]

Asia sailed from Canton on February 19, 1806, with a large amount of tea, 50,400 pieces of nankeens, and a small amount of cassia, all charged in the invoice at $152,464.[52] Touching at Providence for orders, she carried to Europe the identical cargo invoiced at $225,088, a markup of $72,624, or 47 per cent. Brown and Ives directed Captain Pearce to proceed to Texel, whence he would advise Crommelin and Sons of his arrival. En route to Holland, Captain Pearce was taken by the ships *Janvrin* of London and *Alarm Lugger* of Guernsey and sent to the latter place, where the owners of the privateers "Cawled to Day a Coart of Enquirey" before which Captain Pearce was closely questioned. From what he could "Discovour" he had reason to believe he had "fell into very bad hands."[53] But his worst fears were not realized.

In the lower court the judge restored the ship and cargo to the captain, only to have the captors appeal. In the High Court of Admiralty, however, on September 25, 1806, Sir William Scott directed that *Asia* be handed over to Captain Pearce.[54] The remainder of the voyage was without incident. The cargo arrived at Texel in good condition, and Crommelin and Sons arranged for its disposal at the sales of the Dutch East India Company. Thanks to Crommelin and Sons' careful records of payments received from the India Company, detailed data exist respecting the outcome of the venture. The goods that in Canton had cost $152,464 netted in Amsterdam 789,211 guilders, or $315,684, an advance of 107 per cent. *Asia* had made a second handsome voyage.[55]

Meanwhile, Brown and Ives had dispatched their ship *Isis,* Samuel Aborn supercargo, on another voyage to Canton. Sailing from Providence with a cargo of flour and bread, she called at Lisbon, where Bulkeley and Son were under instructions to purchase for her 80,000 Spanish dollars.[56] There Aborn, by sale of the cargo and by drafts on Amsterdam and London, procured the funds needed to finance further purchases of hard dollars by Bulkeley and Son. As a result *Isis* sailed from Lisbon with 156,000 Spanish dollars on board, a sum that was to be augmented by 47,000 hard dollars that Brown and Ives were shipping to Canton on board John Jacob Astor's ship *Beaver.* Thus Aborn would have at his disposal some 203,000 Spanish dollars.[57]

Isis arrived at Canton on September 20, 1805, after a passage of 124 days from Lisbon. Aborn found that a large part of the return cargo had already been purchased by Thomas Thompson. The two men secured the ship with Conseequa, from whom they obtained an abatement of $5,000 on a note given him on account of *Isis'* cargo of the previous voyage. This concession came from no generous impulse on Conseequa's part but rather was the result of spirited protests by Brown and Ives of the inferior quality of the teas he had sold them. Both Thompson and Aborn were sure that Conseequa would provide goods of the highest quality for the current cargo. They were equally certain that Brown and Ives had received from him credit in "such amounts" as not given to any other house in the United States.[58] The partners had learned how to turn their large supplies of hard dollars to their own immediate advantage.

When in 1806 *Isis* arrived at Providence with her China cargo, which had cost $204,292, Brown and Ives were pondering the question of the further employment of *Arthur;* and they considered the prospects of another China voyage were good enough to warrant dispatching her again to Canton, even though it would be late August before she could be made ready for the sea. The fact that *Arthur* was a fast-sailing vessel and newly coppered weighed heavily, no doubt, in their decision to disregard the lateness of the season.

The monotony of the voyage out was broken on October 14 when *Arthur* was chased by another vessel, which after an hour gave up and stood on a different course. On December 31 in the Banda Sea she was boarded from the British frigate *Sir Francis Drake*. The boarding officer carried Captain Solomon Townsend on board the frigate but, finding his papers in order, soon released him. More serious than pursuit by men-of-war were the hazards of nature herself. Along the northwest coast of New Holland at eleven o'clock at night, the darkness was so extreme that the man stationed on the foreyard was unable to see land. But for the fortunate discovery of their position from the deck, the ship "had perhaps in 10 or 15 minutes been drove on the rocks or ashore." *Arthur*'s charts of the coast of New Holland, as of other areas, were found to be erroneous, the whole area being "laid down" too far to the westward. But in spite of everything, when he arrived at Canton on January 31, 1807, William Carter, supercargo, could report that *Arthur*'s was the "best run" of any ship arriving since the previous September.[59]

At Canton there was some delay in loading the return cargo, occasioned by the celebration of the Chinese New Year, the necessity of smoking the ship to destroy the rats, and an outbreak of smallpox among the crew members. Houqua, the hong merchant who secured the vessel, was more than ordinarily willing to grant liberal credit, owing, no doubt, to the 140,000 hard dollars at Captain Townsend's disposal.[60]

The return of *Arthur* from Canton in 1807 completed the fourth successful China voyage by ships of Brown and Ives within a period of about thirty months, two by *Asia* and one each by *Isis* and *Arthur*. On each voyage the ship was amply supplied with hard dollars, which made possible the purchase of maximum cargoes on terms advantageous to the partners. Between midsummer, 1804, and March, 1807, their trade to Canton attained its high water mark, whether judged by the number of ships employed, profits obtained, or efficiency in the conduct of the business. Properly to appraise the China trade of Brown and Ives, however, it is necessary to compare it with the traffic carried on at Canton by other American mercantile houses.

Thanks to the industry and the thoughtfulness of supercargoes aboard the ships of Brown and Ives at Canton, the names, tonnage, and owners of the American ships that called at and cleared from the port of Canton between July 1, 1804, and March 20, 1807, are recorded. The number of hard dollars and the quantity of goods brought to Canton by each vessel are also recorded, along with much information regarding the cargoes loaded at Canton. These data show that Philadelphia still dominated the trade in terms of number and size of ships and the fund of hard money brought to Canton, although her pre-eminence was less marked than a few years before. New York ranked second, followed closely by Boston, whose merchants generally employed ships of the smaller variety, financed largely with otter skins and sealskins.[61]

When these data are examined in terms of the merchants who owned the ships instead of the cities from which they came, it is apparent that five American houses stood out above all the rest. Of these Philadelphia claimed two, one being Willing and Francis, the other Stephen Girard. John Jacob Astor resided in New York, while James and Thomas H. Perkins directed their commercial empire from Boston. Brown and Ives rounded out this select circle of commercial giants.

The very fullness of available data invites comparison among these five firms. Within this period ships of Willing and Francis, totaling 1,675 tons, in five visits to Canton brought 438,000 hard dollars. Those of Stephen Girard, of 959 tons, paid three visits, bringing 405,000 Spanish dollars. Vessels owned by John Jacob Astor, of 1,210 tons, made three calls with 346,000 hard dollars. Craft belonging to James and Thomas H. Perkins, of 720 tons, made two calls with a total of 510,000 dollars in specie. Brown and Ives were represented by ships of 1,260 tons, which made four visits and brought 575,000 Spanish dollars. Thus the Providence house was second in total tonnage and in number of visits but first in the fund of hard dollars brought to Canton. Since hard dollars were a pretty accurate index of the scale on which trade to Canton was then conducted, it is clear that Brown and Ives were the equal of any American house then engaged in the tea traffic. Their prominence seems remarkable in view of the general insignificance of Providence's role in the trade.

TRADE TO BATAVIA

If Brown and Ives mastered the China trade slowly and with great effort, that was not true of the business they carried on at Batavia, the great Dutch colonial port situated on the island of Java. Early in the year 1800 *John Jay* had returned from that quarter with a fine cargo of coffee and some sugar; and the re-export of the coffee to Amsterdam netted a handsome profit. Once embarked on this trade, the Providence firm conducted it on a large scale with comparative ease and with uniform profit to themselves. In the period of great commercial prosperity beginning in 1800 and terminating with the Embargo Act of 1807, the partners maintained a nice balance between the tea of China and the coffee and sugar of Java, their five large ships making ten voyages to Canton and eleven to Batavia.

Late in 1801, when Brown and Ives were confronted with the problem of providing sufficient funds to send *John Jay* to Canton, Willing and Francis of Philadelphia asked for the hire of the ship for the freighting of a quantity of sugar and coffee from Newport to Amsterdam. Although the Providence firm thought that the proposed rate of £6 sterling a ton was too little, they accepted it because of the opportunity it gave to load Dutch goods at Amsterdam for a voyage to Canton.[62] Besides the freight *John Jay* carried sugar, tobacco, rice, and yellow nankeens on account of her owners to the amount of $23,283. As the partners had recently shipped from Providence to Amsterdam a quantity of tea, they reasoned that the proceeds of the tea, of the goods by *John Jay,* and of the freight would procure hard dollars and Dutch goods sufficient for a venture to China. The ship's arrival at Amsterdam was coincident with the signing of the Treaty of Amiens, which "deranged the plans of all those that calculated on a continuance of the War." Tea in Europe was low in price, and a further decline was likely owing to the large supplies on the market. The Dutch East India Company had just received three large cargoes previously thought lost. A voyage to Canton would be the very essence of folly.[63]

John Bowers, the supercargo, weighed the relative merits of going to Bombay to procure cotton for the European market on the owners' account (the war having occasioned a shortage) and chartering *John Jay* to the Dutch East India Company for a voyage to Batavia and back to Amsterdam and decided the latter course promised the greater return to Brown and Ives. Estimating that the ship would stow 462 tons of freight, he calculated that he could earn a tidy sum over and above all costs.[64] Besides, he was free to take to Batavia a quantity of Dutch goods on the account and risk of the partners. Accordingly, *John Jay* sailed from Holland on March 28, 1802, arriving at Batavia on August 18. The crew was in good health, and the ship "remarkably tight."[65]

Bowers and Captain John F. Fry quickly discharged the cargo and put the vessel in readiness to receive her freight according to the charter. But after weeks of delay a committee from the Dutch East India Company examined her and decided that the decayed condition of some of her timbers rendered her unfit to carry a cargo to Europe for the company.[66] When Bowers offered to make the necessary repairs, he was told the facilities for making them no longer existed at Batavia. Thus the company repudiated its contract with Bowers, with most of the freight money yet unpaid.

Bowers was in a dilemma. Expecting to carry freight to Europe for the Dutch East India Company, he had left most of his funds in Amsterdam; and the goods taken to Batavia just about brought their original cost. He could, of course, advise his owners of his situation and wait for them to make the necessary financial arrangements. But such a delay would be very costly. To make matters worse, government officials were forbidden to sell East India goods for bills of exchange. A bad situation was saved from becoming completely hopeless by a business connection of Brown and Ives at Batavia, William Vincent Helvetius Van Riemsdyck, who in return for bills of exchange on Amsterdam at nine months' sight agreed to provide Bowers with 6,000 to 7,000 piculs of sugar. In March, 1803, *John Jay* arrived at Providence with 910,709 pounds of sugar (slightly less than 7,000 piculs at 136.16 pounds to the picul) for the account of her owners.

Before the return of *John Jay,* Brown and Ives had dispatched *Ann & Hope* to Batavia.[67] Knowing of Bowers' agreement with the Dutch East India Company to freight goods for them from Batavia via *John Jay,* the partners hoped that *Ann & Hope,* once at Batavia, might find similar employment. But realizing that the ship might not procure a freight, they were at pains to provide the supercargo with funds necessary to purchase a cargo on their own account. With merchandise (consisting chiefly of various kinds of cloth previously imported from Holland) charged in the invoice at $41,000 and with 20,000 hard dollars, they ordered *Ann & Hope* to Batavia, where Thomas Thompson, the supercargo, was to pretend to be calling for provisions while en route to Manila. After gaining admittance in this fashion, he was to inquire discreetly as to the possibility of obtaining a freight. Or he might indicate a willingness to purchase a cargo of coffee, sugar, and pepper. Failing to obtain either a freight or a cargo (on the owners' account) at Batavia, Thompson was at liberty to proceed to Manila in quest of a cargo or to Canton for a freight or a cargo.[68]

Brown and Ives directed Captain Thomas Laing to take particular care of the crew while at Batavia, which they considered an unhealthy place. No one should be allowed to go ashore there; and Java boats were to be employed to carry Thompson and himself to and from the ship. Nor did they fail to remind the captain that Dr. Benjamin Carter, the ship's doctor, had a good medicine chest.[69]

Ann & Hope arrived at Batavia on August 22, 1802, after a passage of ninety-four days from Providence. Contrary to all expectations of Thompson and his owners, he found the Dutch East India Company disinclined to take up his ship on freight to any place on any terms whatever. But he was told he could dispose of his cargo to individuals for paper rix-dollars with which he could purchase company sugar. And with his Spanish dollars he could procure coffee at $13 a picul. Convinced by all the information he could gather that he could do no better, if indeed so well, at either Manila or Canton, he decided to "make up his voyage" at Batavia. Selling his merchandise for paper rix-dollars, he invested 50,241 of these dollars in sugar.[70] For the 1,531 piculs of Djakarta coffee loaded on the ship he paid 19,908 Spanish dollars (virtually his entire supply). Thus his cargo cost the equivalent of 53,158 Spanish dollars.[71]

On October 3, 1802, *Ann & Hope* was ready for sea, bound for some port in Europe. On January 24, 1803, she anchored in Portland Roads in England, whence Thompson went to London, expecting to find that Brown and Ives had lodged instructions for him with Dickason and Company.[72] In this he was disappointed; and his uncertainty was increased by the news that the ports of Holland were closed by ice. Dickason and Company twice sought permission to unload the cargo in London under the direction of the British East India Company but were twice refused. Waiting in England until the Dutch ports were ice-free, Thompson proceeded in the ship to Amsterdam where he placed the cargo at the command of Crommelin and Sons. He arrived at an opportune moment, since British preparations for a renewal of the war with France promised a rise in the price of sugar and coffee. At Amsterdam there was no chance of a freight to Batavia, as no one at the moment was allowed to take up other than Dutch vessels for voyages to the colonies. Without awaiting the sale of the cargo, Thompson took a letter of credit from Crommelin and Sons for 160,000 guilders and set sail for St. Petersburg, leaving instructions for them to remit the balance of the proceeds to Dickason and Company in London. At the Russian port he purchased new sable iron, hemp, and ducks costing 104,870 rubles and headed for his home port. When Crommelin and Sons had completed the sales of the coffee and sugar, they reported net proceeds of 366,234 guilders, or $146,493, a profit of $93,335 on the $53,158 invested at Batavia.[73]

Thus both *John Jay* and *Ann & Hope* had visited Batavia, supposedly on freighting ventures, only to load with highly profitable cargoes on the account and risk of the owners. But so obsessed were Brown and Ives in the year 1802 with freighting that they also dispatched their new ship *Isis* to Batavia on such a mission. With a small invoice of goods and with 30,000 Spanish dollars, *Isis,* Ephraim Talbot supercargo, sailed in January for the Javan port.[74] The partners strongly urged (but did not command) Captain Benjamin Dexter to call at one of the Cape Verde Islands for salt with which to season the ship. A few hundred bushels of that article "judiciously thrown between the timbers" would "very much help the frame." As the vessel was going into a warm climate to load with coffee, pepper, and sugar, they "apprehended" the steam would injure the wood. This they devoutly hoped to prevent, as

Isis was a valuable ship that they had taken "great pains with in the building." They had imported from New York two ventilators, which they had installed on the ship. These Captain Dexter was to keep constantly in good order, "that fresh air may be conveyed into the hold."[75]

Isis anchored at Batavia in July, 1802, after a voyage of 140 days from Providence, apparently without calling en route for the salt. Talbot reported *Isis* to be a fast-sailing vessel, the long passage being caused by adverse winds and calms. For a fortnight he tried in vain to procure a freight. Since the price of coffee was so high as to preclude all thought of loading with that article, he purchased sugar and sailed for Masqat on the Persian Gulf, where he hoped to sell the sugar and buy coffee at a reasonable price. If that were impossible, he would go elsewhere to load cotton for Europe. And should that fail he might visit the Bay of Bengal, procure piece goods, and return to Providence.[76]

Leaving Batavia on July 19, 1802, *Isis* arrived at Masqat in forty-five days, the first ship of Brown and Ives ever to visit that part of the world. There Talbot found the market less favorable than he had expected because disturbances among the "petty princes up the Gulph of Persia" had seriously impeded the sale of imported wares. He termed Masqat the "ware House" for the whole gulf area as well as for part of the Sind country. Receiving cotton from Surat and Bengal; indigo from Surat and the Sind; sugar and spices from Batavia and Bengal; coffee, gums, and drugs from Mocha; saltpeter from the Sind; and brimstone from the Gulf, it exported all these articles. Sugar, coffee, and cotton went up the gulf; the other articles went largely to Europe. Masqat also exported fine Arabian horses to Bombay and Bengal and "Vast quantitys" of dates, the staple article of the country. Business at Masqat was conducted through a person who "stiles himself Broker," appointed by the sultan, receiving a commission together with 5 per cent of the duties on imports.[77]

At Masqat, Talbot sold for $31,149 the sugar for which he had paid $26,061 at Batavia and purchased Mocha coffee that cost him $38,422. He believed the prospect "extremely dull" for making a "prosperous Voyage." He was "too well convinced" that he had this time paid " 'Very-Very dear for the Whistle.' " Believing his cargo would sell better in the Mediterranean than elsewhere in Europe, he was strongly tempted to return to Providence direct, whence the coffee could be sent to that sea in smaller vessels at slight expense. But suspecting that Brown and Ives had some plan for his ship in northern Europe, he set sail for England.[78] In London, Dickason and Company advised him to seek a market at Rotterdam. There the cargo was discharged and *Isis* dispatched to St. Petersburg with a letter of credit from Roquette, Beldamaker, and Company for £9,000 sterling, Talbot remaining behind to attend to the sale of the cargo. Upon the advice of several mercantile houses, including Dickason and Company, Talbot decided to advertise the coffee for sale at auction. But because the bids were too low he withdrew it from public sale and offered it in small lots. The delay thus caused was undoubtedly a godsend to Talbot and his owners; for during those weeks the market experienced that fillip that had so greatly increased the profits of *Ann & Hope*'s cargo in Amsterdam that same spring. When the sales of coffee from *Isis* were completed, the proceeds, clear of all charges, were 273,281 guilders, or $109,312, a profit of $70,890 on the investment at Masqat.[79] At St. Petersburg the iron, hemp, ducks, and sailcloths for *Isis* cost 68,152 rubles.

Encouraged by three successive profitable voyages to Batavia, Brown and Ives decided to dispatch their two largest ships on new ventures to the same port. In November, 1803, *Ann & Hope* sailed from Providence with John Bowers as supercargo.[80] She carried ten pipes of geneva and 80,000 hard dollars. The partners expected to derive considerable advantage from Bowers' knowledge of the business situation at Batavia, gained through his recent visit to that port on board *John Jay*. Especially important, they thought, was his acquaintance with William Vincent Helvetius Van Riemsdyck, whose friendship had previously been so helpful to Bowers.

The supercargo was to procure sugar in sufficient amount to ballast the ship and then to fill her with coffee. The owners expected the price of coffee at Batavia to decline from ten to eight cents a pound because the resumption of the war in Europe would prevent the export of that article in Dutch ships. It was their hope, too, that he would obtain a relaxation of the rule that American ships must take a certain proportion of pepper in order to procure coffee. Bowers was to explain that he possessed the specie necessary to purchase coffee and that he would go elsewhere rather than take pepper. Bowers was also to inform officials that *John Jay* would soon arrive, prepared to load solely with coffee to the extent of her supply of specie.[81]

Brown and Ives urged Captain Laing to pay strict attention to the health of his crew while at Batavia. The men must not be unnecessarily exposed to that "sickly climate." The ship was well supplied with stores of all sorts, especially "roots," which would conduce to the wellbeing of the men. They advised the captain to have coffee "started loose" in the ship, "that every vacancy" might be filled.[82]

Ann & Hope arrived at Batavia on March 15, 1804, after a passage of 128 days. The Governor General and Council received Bowers with much politeness and expressed a desire to serve him as far as circumstances would permit. The Council had recently increased the price of coffee and sugar, but Bowers believed this was more than balanced by the lifting of the requirement that American ships take a certain amount of pepper.

The cargo purchased by Bowers consisted of 2,310 piculs of sugar and 5,406 piculs of coffee for which he paid 82,774 Spanish dollars, plus 22,684 paper rix-dollars. As 100 paper rix-dollars were then the equivalent of 50 Spanish dollars, the cost of the cargo was 94,116 Spanish dollars.[83]

Meanwhile, *John Jay,* Captain Fry, with Daniel Tillinghast as supercargo, had arrived at Batavia with 60,000 hard dollars. The ship was not only strong and tight but she steered and sailed better than ever before. The passage to St. Paul Island was the fastest of any American ship that season. At Batavia there were six other American ships, including *Ann & Hope,* the only one with greater tonnage than *John Jay.* Although prices of sugar and coffee were somewhat higher than the supercargo had expected, he nevertheless decided to purchase a cargo at that port. From the Dutch East India Company he bought sugar and coffee, "both of an excellent quality," and from Van Riemsdyck he procured more sugar and some long pepper.[84] His cargo consisted of 3,593 piculs of sugar, 147 piculs of pepper, and 4,251 piculs of coffee for which he paid 68,745 Spanish dollars, plus 31,552 paper rix-dollars. At the current rate of exchange the rix-dollars were the equivalent of 15,776 Spanish dollars. The cost of the cargo was therefore 84,521 Spanish dollars.[85] As this was in excess of his fund of hard money, Tillinghast drew on Brown and Ives payable in New York or Philadelphia; and he drew directly on Crommelin and Sons in Amsterdam at nine months for 14,000 guilders.

When *John Jay* appeared in the Providence River in August, 1804, she was met by a messenger bearing a letter from Brown and Ives with the notation "to be delivered below the light House." The purpose of the communication was to instruct Tillinghast to add the words "or Europe" to the ship's manifest. The owners explained that "the addition must be made before" the manifest was seen by "any Custom-House Officer." Omission of the words would subject the partners to the "great expense and delay" of unloading and reloading the cargo at Providence. In this way they indicated their intention of dispatching *John Jay* to Europe for the sale of her cargo.[86]

Before dispatching *John Jay* to her European destination, however, Brown and Ives were at pains to give her cargo a new invoice in which the goods that had cost $84,521 in Batavia were charged at

$172,618, an advance of $88,097, or 104 per cent. According to Crommelin and Sons, who sold the cargo at Amsterdam, the net proceeds of the sugar and coffee amounted to 566,859 guilders, or $226,743, an advance of $54,125 over the invoice price and of $142,222 over the $84,521 paid for the goods at Batavia.[87] Thus on *John Jay*'s cargo Brown and Ives realized a profit of 168 per cent on the original investment.

Since *Ann & Hope*'s cargo from Batavia was unloaded at Providence for reshipment to Europe in smaller craft, data with respect to profits are necessarily somewhat incomplete. In the summer of 1804 Brown and Ives placed on board their ship *Charlotte* and the brig *Polly* part of the coffee from *Ann & Hope* and dispatched the two craft to Amsterdam to the care of Crommelin and Sons. There the coffee invoiced at $106,921 netted $143,294, an advance of $36,373, or 34 per cent.[88] But if it is assumed that the coffee was invoiced at a figure 100 per cent above its cost at Batavia (a reasonable assumption in view of the 104 per cent markup in *John Jay*'s invoice), the shipments by *Charlotte* and *Polly* returned a profit of about $90,000, or 169 per cent, on the initial cost of the goods. It can hardly be doubted that the voyage of *Ann & Hope* was quite as profitable as that of *John Jay*.

So satisfied were Brown and Ives with the success they had achieved in the trade to Batavia that they laid their plans for a continuation of their two large ships in the traffic to that port. With a small invoice of goods and with 83,000 hard dollars that the partners had instructed Crommelin and Sons to purchase in Holland, London, or Lisbon, depending on the price, *John Jay* sailed from Amsterdam on March 11, 1805, in command of Captain Fry with John Bowers as supercargo.[89] The owners had urged the closest cooperation between the two men because "when difficulty or jealousy takes place between the Captain . . . & a Supercargo—the interest of the owners is very much neglected." The two had very quickly complied by agreeing to hire a Dutch physician to serve as ship's surgeon at twenty dollars a month. The presence of a doctor on board was thought to be a wise precaution on a visit to "a sickly Port" such as Batavia.[90]

John Jay made Batavia in 130 days from Amsterdam. There Bowers purchased sugar, tin, coffee, and tea, the coffee accounting for $85,000 of the total outlay of $114,361. Whether because of the skill of the Dutch doctor or not, all enjoyed good health; and on September 28, 1805, *John Jay* sailed from Batavia bound for Providence. Writing at sea on November 26, Bowers reported a comfortable and safe passage that far, with only one death since leaving Amsterdam. The ship leaked somewhat in her upper works but a five-to-ten-minute spell at the pumps every two hours was sufficient to free her, "so that she only makes water enough to keep her sweet." Some three weeks later he wrote that they had stopped at Ascension Island for turtles for which they waited in vain for two days. Discovering a piece of sheathing off the bends, they replaced it and thus stopped the leak. Bowers hoped to see the owners at Providence early in January.[91]

A SHIP CAPTURED AND TWO SHIPS LOST

But on January 6, 1806, at about four o'clock in the afternoon, *John Jay* fell in with His Majesty's sloop-of-war *Driver*, Captain Simpson. On boarding *John Jay*, Captain Simpson took possession of the logbook and all papers relating to the voyage. Believing that *John Jay* had violated the "Law of Nations" by trading between Holland and Batavia, he thought that the ship should be sent in for adjudication by a British Court of Admiralty. Captain Simpson removed most of the men from *John Jay*, placed a British crew on board, and ordered her to follow *Driver*. The two vessels arrived at St. George's Island, Bermuda, on January 12, whence Bowers informed Brown and Ives of his misfortune.[92]

A closer look at the Court of Admiralty decisions in the cases of *Polly* (1800) and *Essex* (1805) will make clearer the plight of *John Jay*. Neutral vessels, according to the earlier decision, were allowed to trade indirectly between France or one of her allies and their colonies. Goods shipped on board an American vessel, for instance, in the French West Indies might be carried to an American port and reshipped to Bordeaux without interference. This "broken-voyage" trade had become a lucrative business. En route between two belligerent ports ships frequently touched at an American port without taking the trouble either to break bulk or to pay duties. In the *Essex* decision, however, British sanction of neutral trade between belligerent ports was made contingent upon the actual discharge and reshipment of the cargo at the American port of call. The British Navy was now understandably suspicious of the sort of trade in which *John Jay* was engaged.

Brown and Ives, having heard the bad news from Bowers, engaged the services of Samuel Ward, a capable attorney, and sent him aboard the chartered sloop *Sally* to Bermuda with all pertinent documents. Ward's first concern was to be the release of *John Jay* and her cargo from detention. Realizing that large funds might be needed for this purpose, Brown and Ives were quick to capitalize upon their undoubted credit and high financial standing. To the directors of the Providence Bank, in which they were large stockholders, they wrote:

We now have to propose that your President & Cashier furnish us a letter to Col. Ward. for the sum of Sixty Thousand Dollars, to be used by him in Case

of need. You will make Security to the Bank for that Amt. in a Deposit of
Funded Stocks [of the United States], to the full Value of sd. Credit, which
stocks you [are] to hold, Until it maybe ascertained whether the letter is used
& until it maybe returned to you. We presume the security now offered will
be to the Entire satisfaction of each Director.[93]

The same day the bank provided Samuel Ward with a letter expressing the belief that *John Jay* belonged entirely to Brown and Ives, "highly
esteemed by this Institution as well as by the Inhabitants of this
Town," and affirming their desire to be of service "in recovering this
property." The letter said, "It is well known here that this House com-
menced business with a large Capital which has unquestionably been
increased by their Mercantile operations & that they had the ability
to undertake distant enterprizes of Magnitude with their own means."
The particular object of this letter was to furnish Col. Ward "with an
undoubted Guarantee for the sum of Sixty Thousand Dollars to be
given to such person or persons in Bermuda or elsewhere as may
become sureties or Bondsmen."[94]

Ward also carried a circular letter from Moses Brown, uncle of
Nicholas Brown, senior partner of Brown and Ives, addressed "To all
whom it may Concern," declaring that he would be "responsible for the
said Brown & Ives for any Contract their said Agent may make in their
Behalf . . . for the amount of Ten Thousand Dollars."[95]

From these two sources and from various insurance companies
Brown and Ives were able to deliver to Samuel Ward "undoubted
Guarantee" to the amount of $175,000 together with a statement from
Judge David Leonard Barnes attesting to the solid financial standing
of the various guarantors.

Samuel Ward also carried a letter from Moses Brown addressed to an
unknown "Esteemed Friend," the one person in Bermuda, he wrote, of
whom he had "particular knoledge." Designed as a further testimonial
to the strong financial situation of Brown and Ives, the letter traced the
development of the house from his "Eldest Brother Nicholas Brown,"
who "Died in 1791 Leaving Much the Largest Propperty" that had been
left "by any of Our Citizens, who had Died before him . . . " Moses described the partners as "young, Enterprizing & active"; he explained
that they had "Extended their Trade as their Capital Increased," until
the firm had become "one of the Most Oppulent and Respectable Mercantile Houses in the State Trading on their Own Capital in Such
Manner as to have Manifested as Much Integrity & Punctuality in
Business as any in the State, or of my acquaintance in New England . . . "

Brown and Ives, according to Moses, had "Steadily Owned Upward of
one hundred shares" in the Providence Bank, "the Current Price of

which has been 470 to 500 Dollars a Share." Nicholas Brown had long been a director of the bank and his partner, Thomas P. Ives, was a director of the Providence Insurance Company, "who do their Business at the said Bank." In the insurance company

as well as divers Other State Institutions they are Large Stockholders, as also in the Public Fund of the United States, and tho' they have now several sail of Ships at Canton and on the India Sea, yet it is well understood here that no Merchants of their Extensive Trade among us do their Business upon their Own propperty so generaly as they do, that We who are Intimate with them, and know their Business so well . . . are fully Sattisfyed that no foreigner is concerned with them . . . in Ship *J[oh]n Jay* now at Bermuda.[96]

If unable to secure the ship's release on bond, Ward was to remain at Bermuda for the trial; and should the decision be in favor of the captors he was to enter an appeal and try to purchase the vessel and cargo, if this could be done on terms of advantage.

Brown and Ives had assumed they could procure the release of *John Jay* and her cargo merely by proving that no foreigner was concerned with them in the ownership of the property. But in April, 1806, the Court of Vice-Admiralty at Bermuda condemned the ship and cargo on the grounds that: (a) she had made a voyage direct from Amsterdam to Batavia, contrary to His Britannic Majesty's instructions of 1803; (b) she had made false declaration in clearing for Sumatra and China, though actually bound for Batavia; (c) she had contraband on board in the form of flat bars of iron destined for Batavia, a Dutch naval base; and (d) there was want of proof of the neutral character of the property.[97]

However, Bowers and Ward secured the release of *John Jay* and her cargo (pending the decision of the appeal court in London) on condition that Brown and Ives deposit in London by June 1, 1807, the sum of £35,096 sterling to be invested by trustees for the account of the owners. The ship arrived at Providence on June 29, 1806.

To deposit £35,096 sterling ($155,826.24) in London taxed both the resources and the resourcefulness of Brown and Ives, for the times were not propitious. The seizure and detention of *John Jay* not only occasioned costs unanticipated by them but it also prevented them from realizing quickly on her cargo. To make matters worse, the partners at this same time had the misfortune to suffer another exceedingly heavy loss, the wreck of the *Ann & Hope*. To meet the deposit deadline, therefore, they directed their correspondents in Continental Europe to remit to Dickason and Company in London the proceeds of the various cargoes discharged by their ships. On May 27, 1807, the process was completed when a notary certified that Dickason and Company had deposited with two London banking houses exchequer bills in the prescribed amount.[98] The conditions of the bond fulfilled, Brown and Ives could only await the decision on the appeal. On December 4, 1807, the court in London reversed the decree of the Bermuda court, declared *John Jay* and her cargo to be the lawful property of Brown and Ives, and ordered her restored to them on payment of the captor's expenses in both courts. So ended the case of *John Jay*. Although her owners were at no little trouble and expense in prosecuting her case, they had saved both the ship and the cargo, thereby averting what had threatened to be a total disaster.

The voyage of *John Jay* had almost exactly coincided with the last visit of *Ann & Hope* to Batavia. In November, 1804, the latter ship sailed from Providence for Lisbon, where Bulkeley and Son were under orders to purchase 80,000 Spanish dollars for her. Continuing to Batavia, she was at first refused permission to load with sugar and coffee because of the scarcity of produce. But Samuel Greene and George Page, her supercargoes, chanced to discover through a friend that the Dutch East India Company was desirous of placing a sum of money at the Cape of Good Hope. Arrangements were therefore made for the ship to load at Batavia with sugar, pepper, and coffee, on condition that she touch at the Cape to deliver $60,000. *Ann & Hope* thus took on board a cargo costing 102,960 Spanish dollars.

Having directed *John Jay* to return to Providence from Batavia, Brown and Ives were strongly tempted to seek greater variety by ordering *Ann & Hope* to Cowes, England, where she would receive instructions from Dickason and Company as to the most suitable market on the Continent. When advised of this plan, Dickason and Company, ever attentive to the interests of Brown and Ives, sought the opinion of Sir John Nicholl, the King's counsel, as to the legality of such procedure. In the opinion of that gentleman it would not be prudent to direct the vessel to proceed from Cowes to "any Foreign Port in Europe." She should therefore deliver her cargo either in England or in Providence.[99]

When *Ann & Hope* weighed anchor at Batavia in June, 1805, her owners could have had little reason for concern. She could make the best of her way to Cowes, where Dickason and Company would direct her to unload her cargo in England. But if the supercargoes should elect to head for Providence, they could expect to make home port without interference from any source. En route from Batavia the ship was obliged to put in at the Île de France for repairs. To locate a serious leak the cargo was unloaded. Removing the sheathing, recaulking the bottom, and putting on an entirely new covering consumed both time and money.[100]

Because of the long delay at the Île de France, it was late October before the ship arrived at the Cape of Good Hope. There the supercargoes decided in view of the lateness of the season to head for Providence instead of Cowes. From the cape all went well until the ship was in the very shadow of her home port. On January 10, 1806, there was a heavy fall of snow along the coast of southern New England; but in the evening clearing skies brought very pleasant weather. After making Montauk Light at the eastern end of Long Island, *Ann & Hope*'s course "was shaped" for Block Island, which was sighted about eleven o'clock at night. Supposing he was far enough from shore to avoid all danger, Captain Laing intended to steer to the eastward of the island, as was usual with large vessels. But the presence of snow on the ground completely deceived the captain as to his distance from the island. Before the hour of midnight the ship struck a reef of rocks projecting from the south shore. By "Noon of the following day she was beaten almost to pieces & the Cargo washed into the sea." The disaster was the more inexplicable to Brown and Ives because Captain Laing had "the Character of being remarkably timid when approaching Land." They found it hard to reconcile "this instance of apparent want of attention to his otherwise uniform caution."[101]

The wreck of *Ann & Hope* had followed the capture of *John Jay* by only four days. Nicholas Brown wrote that had the two ships arrived at Providence without detention or delay they would have been worth nearly $500,000 to their owners.[102] *Ann & Hope* and her cargo were insured in London for only £12,000 sterling.[103] Ruminating upon the fate of this ship, the owners remarked that it was "beyond all comparison worse, than the great risk of capture that was contemplated [in touching at Cowes] could have been."[104] And being thoughtful men, they must have reflected upon the contrasting fortunes of *John Jay* and *Ann & Hope*. The former had been captured, but her owners had recovered her and her cargo, both of which were very heavily insured. *Ann & Hope,* but lightly insured, had averted capture only to be wrecked by the fallibility of man. The ship that the owners, in all the circumstances, could better afford to lose was the one that was saved.

Their reverses notwithstanding, Brown and Ives in October, 1806, again dispatched *John Jay* to Batavia with 50,000 hard dollars and goods valued at $17,000. When he anchored at the Dutch port on February 25, 1807, Captain Fry found produce so scarce and dear that he needed almost six months to accumulate a cargo; even then he procured no sugar and only a small quantity of pepper. Composed principally of coffee, his invoice of $131,000 was the highest of any ship of Brown and Ives that had sailed from Batavia.

During the long weeks of waiting for his cargo, Captain Fry's letters to his owners were punctuated with somber references to his crew.

Dr. Westcott died on April 15, and the men generally were "very sickly." A month later the men were still very ill; nine were down with the fever, and three more had died. By the end of July he had lost two more, making a total of six.[105]

John Jay sailed from Batavia Roads on August 16, 1807. At about eight o'clock in the evening of that day she struck "on a point of a Reeff . . . in Consequence of which the Ship got on the Rocks" and entirely disintegrated.[106] One who visited the scene of the wreck attributed it to "a strong current & a high tide that almost compleatly covered the land and left scarcely any thing . . . above the water," a situation in which the "most experienced seaman may be deceaved in his distance from the land."[107] The recent loss at the same spot of a Dutch ship of seventy-four guns seemed to confirm the opinion that no particular blame attached to Captain Fry. Nevertheless, the captain was a profoundly shaken man. One witness described him as "the most depressed and altered man I ever knew."[108]

Sales of goods salvaged from the wreck netted $16,000 on an invoice of $131,000. Beyond that Brown and Ives retrieved nothing from the disaster. Because of uncertainty as to whether Captain Fry would procure a cargo at Batavia, they had taken out no insurance, pending word from the captain as to his success. When the word arrived in Providence, *John Jay* was already a total loss.[109]

Within a period of nineteen months Brown and Ives had suffered the loss of their two largest ships while en route home from Batavia. Three times in those same months, however, other ships owned by them set their sails for that same port. *Isis* made two voyages, both direct from Providence. *Asia* touched at Lisbon, where the supercargo drew on Crommelin and Sons and Dickason and Company for the funds with which to purchase 95,000 Spanish dollars. On the three voyages the ships carried a total of 218,000 hard dollars with which to purchase cargoes having a combined cost at Batavia of $255,476. One cargo arrived at Providence in the spring of 1807; the other two in the spring of 1808, after the Embargo Act of 1807 had become effective. The partners thus had on hand a vast quantity of coffee, which they were to ship to Europe in the years that followed.

Trade to Batavia in the era of commercial expansion before the Embargo Act had a dual attraction for Brown and Ives. It was extremely profitable, the loss of *Ann & Hope* and *John Jay* notwithstanding, and it could be financed on a large scale with a smaller fund of Spanish dollars than was required in the trade to Canton.

In this era of maritime prosperity trade both to Canton and to Batavia had assumed new forms. Brown and Ives had finally come to recognize the paramount importance of Spanish dollars in financing the trade. The primary source of the dollars, like the principal market for the tea and coffee, was now in Europe. Ships on occasion sailed direct from the East Indies to Amsterdam. Discharging their cargoes, they procured Spanish dollars at a European mart, whence they returned to the Pacific for fresh cargoes of tea and coffee. On other occasions ships en route from the Indies merely touched at Providence for fresh orders, continuing to Europe without breaking bulk. In some instances the cargoes were discharged at Providence and reshipped on smaller craft to Europe. But whatever the precise procedure they employed, Brown and Ives were no longer engaged in the importation of tea and coffee for American consumption. Their chief concern now was the carriage of these products from the countries of origin to markets in northern Europe.

THE SHUTTLE TRADE TO EUROPE

While keeping their five larger vessels so constantly employed in the trade to Canton and Batavia, Brown and Ives maintained a whole fleet of smaller craft in their traffic to Europe. The ships *Charlotte* and *General Hamilton;* the brigs *Polly, Argus, Juno, Abeona,* and *Pilgrim;* the brigantine *Eliza;* and the schooners *Venalia* and *Minerva* all shuttled back and forth across the Atlantic, carrying to Europe the tea, nankeens, sugar, and coffee their larger ships had brought from the Pacific. But they were also freighted with the flour, tobacco, and rice produced in the United States. Returning to home port they brought gin and linseed oil from Amsterdam; wine, brandy, fruit, and specie from the Mediterranean; and hemp, new sable iron, and ducks from St. Petersburg.

Between 1801 and 1807 *Charlotte* made one visit each to Bilbao, Bordeaux, and Málaga and six to Amsterdam. Cargoes of tea, sugar, coffee, and nankeens, charged in the invoice at a figure far in excess of the cost in the Pacific, sold at a substantial (frequently a handsome) advance over the invoice. Thus 38,000 short nankeens, which had cost $0.48 a piece in Canton, were invoiced at $0.7067. At Malta they sold for $1.0667 each. Expressed in other terms, an investment of $18,240 in nankeens yielded a net profit of $22,295. A cargo of coffee invoiced at $63,000 "Neated per their Sales" $85,000 at Amsterdam. Another consignment of the same article invoiced at $43,000 netted $58,000, and a cargo of pepper, sugar, and coffee, which had cost $88,000 at Batavia and was invoiced at Providence for $173,000, sold at Amsterdam for $226,000.[110]

Profits from the shipment of American staples to Europe were usually more modest but not inconsiderable. In 1806 *General Hamilton* carried rice, tobacco, and cotton, which cost $22,000 at Charleston, South Carolina, and netted $32,000 at Amsterdam. The next year her cargo from Charleston, invoiced at $24,000, produced a net return of $32,000 in Holland.

But the trade of Brown and Ives with Europe in these years cannot be told completely in terms of their own ships. So great were their importations of tea and nankeens from Canton and of sugar and coffee from Batavia that their own vessels did not suffice to carry to Europe the quantity of goods they wished to export. In consequence, they frequently freighted oriental goods across the Atlantic on vessels belonging to others. In their account with Crommelin and Sons are recorded the proceeds of the sale of tea and sugar received in Amsterdam from *Yarico, Ida,* and *Hope,* all owned by others.[111] In July, 1806, the partners wrote Dickason and Company that they were loading the "new Ship *Mary & Eliza,* owned & commanded by Capt. [Thomas] Simmons of this Town," with sugar and coffee from *John Jay*'s cargo.[112] This cargo netted at Amsterdam the sum of $102,000.[113] Later in the same month they shipped by *Abby & Sally* more "Coffee & Sugar out of the *John Jay.*"[114]

On one occasion Brown and Ives shipped on freight oriental goods not of their own importation. In 1807 they purchased on speculation at Newport a quantity of sugar and coffee for which they paid $109,000. Freighted on board the ship *Pacific* to Bordeaux, this produce netted $160,000.[115] After paying the freight charges, their profit on the transaction was not less than $35,000.

Of the goods imported from Europe, special interest attaches to the new sable iron from St. Petersburg and Swedish iron from Göteborg. Ships of Brown and Ives visiting the Baltic in this period usually returned with cargoes of the metal ranging up to 375 tons. In pre-Revolutionary days one of the centers of the iron industry in New England was at Taunton, Massachusetts. And the Browns, as proprietors of Hope Furnace, had enjoyed rather close business relations with ironmasters in that area. It is not surprising, therefore, that when Brown and Ives became extensive importers of iron from the Baltic, they should have found their principal market for it in Taunton. Over a period of many years Samuel Crocker, Charles Richmond, and Horatio Leonard, individually or collectively, purchased entire cargoes of iron brought in by a long succession of ships owned by Brown and Ives. From this iron they then fashioned nails, hoops, shovels, and a variety of other metal products. When these men joined with Bostonians such as Harrison Gray Otis, Samuel A. Eliot, and Israel Thorndike to form the Taunton Manufacturing Company, that firm in turn became an important customer for iron from the Baltic. With the growing dependence of these ironmongers upon Brown and Ives for their raw material, the Taunton area became part of the economic hinterland of Providence.[116]

The close ties that Brown and Ives thus forged with the iron interests of Taunton were later strengthened when the Providence house began to invest funds in Taunton industrial enterprises. In time the Old Colony Iron Works came to occupy a dominant position in the economic life of that area. And with the coming of the railway it was relatively easy to apply this skill and knowledge of the iron business to the building of the iron horse. Accordingly, the Taunton Locomotive Manufacturing Company emerged as the other important industrial establishment of the town. Brown and Ives were among the chief stockholders in both of these concerns—an interesting example of the manner in which a commercial connection paved the way for the later investment in industry of capital accumulated in maritime trade.

As their trade to Europe expanded, the importance to Brown and Ives of their correspondents in various countries of Europe also increased. During the years 1800–1807 the important role of Crommelin and Sons in the commercial system of Brown and Ives first became apparent. Crommelin and Sons obtained for the partners permission to enter cargoes in Holland and, on occasion, to dispose of them at sales of the Dutch East India Company. Crommelin and Sons sold most of the sugar, tea, and coffee shipped to Europe by Brown and Ives. It was Crommelin and Sons, too, upon whom the Providence house frequently drew for the purchase of Spanish dollars at Lisbon and later at Gibraltar. And the large balances that Crommelin and Sons remitted to Dickason and Company were of vital importance to Brown and Ives.

But first place among the correspondents of the partners must go to Dickason and Company. The London house performed a multitude of services for them. It constantly gave advice on the market situation in Europe. It directed ship captains and supercargoes to particular ports in Europe. It procured insurance on ships of Brown and Ives. It made arrangements for the coppering of ships in London. It was always at the service of shipmasters whose vessels were in distress either because of wind and weather or because of capture by a belligerent. The prime role of Dickason and Company, though, was in the field of finance. As merchant-bankers they served as a clearing house for the world-wide business operations of the Providence firm; and they provided the credit then so essential to Brown and Ives, as it was to other business firms in the young Republic. It is not strange that the letters passing between London and Providence give a fine over-all picture of the various facets of the commercial edifice of Brown and Ives.

CHAPTER 6

A Growing Fleet
in Trade to Europe

WITH the imposition of the embargo in December, 1807, the flush times that had prevailed in the maritime business since 1800 came to an abrupt end. For the next several years seaborne trade was to be carried on within the framework of commercial coercion and war. Business did not cease, but its tempo slowed, and its scale underwent a drastic reduction.

SHIPBUILDING AND THE TEA TRADE

Notwithstanding the adverse effects of the restrictive measures of Jefferson and Madison, Brown and Ives added four ships to their merchant fleet in the years 1808–9. But since two of these were necessary replacements for *Ann & Hope* and *John Jay,* there was a net increase of only two ships. Shortly after the loss of *Ann & Hope* they had decided to build a fine new ship to bear her name. By June, 1806, work on her had begun under the expert supervision of Colonel Benjamin Tallman. As the carpenters worked through the long summer days the vessel began to take form. In late autumn with the shortest days of the year at hand Brown and Ives asked the workmen to take a reduction in their daily wages from eight to seven shillings. Although the men called the new wages "insufficient for our daily Support," they cheerfully acquiesced, considering that "the days were Short & Cold." They assumed, of course, that on the return of warm weather wages would again be raised. The winter passed, spring arrived, and the days grew steadily longer, but wages remained at seven shillings. In mid-April, 1807, eighteen of the carpenters respectfully submitted their case to Brown and Ives. "Now Gentlemen," they wrote, "the weather is Sufficiently mild & days nearly thirteen hours Long a full sufficiency of time for a Good days work to be performed." They addressed "these few Lines with full assurance that you will raise our wages to something competent to the service which we are determined to render you." In conclusion the craftsmen asked their employers to "do us the Justice to believe that should Necessity compell us to leave your employment it would be with the Greatest reluctance to each of your hbl Servts."[1]

The thinly veiled threat of a strike contained in the last sentence produced the desired result. Although Brown and Ives made no direct reply to the carpenters, they asked Colonel Tallman to propose to them that wages remain unchanged "for the remainder of the present Month," to be increased to eight shillings beginning the first Monday in May.[2] With the acceptance by the men of this compromise proposal all further danger of labor strife over the building of the ship seems to have vanished. Work progressed so steadily during the months that followed that she was ready for the sea early in the next year. Of 558 tons, the new *Ann & Hope* was undoubtedly a finer and a faster ship than her namesake.

The second new ship was *Robert Hale,* of 291 tons, built at Marietta, Ohio. That ocean-going vessels were then being constructed in the heartland of North America meant that enterprising local citizens were making an effort to provide the means of shipping the produce of the upper Ohio Valley to the markets of the world.[3] Without doubt this was an important incentive. Another, perhaps equally important, factor was the desire of merchants in the cities of the eastern seaboard to avail themselves of the substantially lower cost, compared with that on the coast, of building ships at Marietta.[4] Marietta had been established by the Ohio Company, whose shareholders were almost exclusively New Englanders. The settlers in the town had come from the same states. There is impressive evidence of the close ties prevailing between the pioneers at Marietta and their friends and relatives who remained behind in New England. It is not surprising, therefore, that New England shipowners should have discovered that ships could be built on the banks of the Ohio to their own advantage as well as that of their relatives residing in the Middle West.

There was a very special reason why Brown and Ives should have contracted for the building of their ship *Robert Hale* at Marietta. One of the original settlers in the town was a young man named Benjamin Ives Gilman. The favorite cousin of Thomas P. Ives, junior partner of Brown and Ives, young Gilman, a graduate of Phillips Academy at Exeter, New Hampshire, quickly became a person of importance in Ohio.[5] He provided much of the initiative and enterprise that resulted in the development of the shipbuilding industry at Marietta. By correspondence and by frequent visits to Providence Gilman had kept the

Providence house well informed about Ohio and about his interests in shipbuilding. Thus when Brown and Ives needed a new ship, they arranged for Gilman to build it.[6]

Work on *Robert Hale* began in the spring of 1807.[7] In anticipation of her completion Brown and Ives engaged a captain and crew in Providence and sent them by ship to Alexandria, Virginia. From there Captain Charles Holden, Jr., set out on horseback for Marietta in the January snows of 1808, the crew crossing the mountains later by wagon.[8] In May *Robert Hale* passed the falls of the Ohio at Louisville and continued on her course to New Orleans, where Captain Holden found the sails, anchor, and water casks awaiting him, all having been sent from New York. Loaded with cotton and tobacco, *Robert Hale* sailed from New Orleans in June, 1808, arriving in Providence a month later. She was to enter the trans-Atlantic service whenever her owners thought the time propitious.[9]

The third ship new to the fleet of Brown and Ives was *Patterson,* of 447 tons, built at Providence in 1800. This vessel was originally owned and operated by John Innes Clark, prominent merchant of Providence, from whose estate Brown and Ives purchased her in 1809 at the price of $20,000.[10] The final addition to their list of ships was *Hope,* purchased in 1809 for the sum of $7,000.[11] Built at New Haven in 1781, she was of 239 tons, and she took her place as one of nine ships flying the flag of Brown and Ives, the others being *Arthur, Asia, Isis, Charlotte, General Hamilton, Ann & Hope, Robert Hale,* and *Patterson.* With an aggregate of 2,852 tons these ships were complemented by numerous smaller craft owned by the partners. Thus it was in a period of obstruction to American navigation that the fleet of Brown and Ives attained its maximum proportions.

Because of the embargo the maritime business of Brown and Ives in the year 1808 all but came to a standstill. Although six of their vessels (all in foreign ports when the Embargo Act became effective) returned to Providence in the course of the year, not one ship sailed for a foreign destination. American trade with Europe and with other parts of the world came to a halt.

When the Embargo Act was supplanted by the Nonintercourse Act in 1809, which permitted American ships to trade with all countries except England and France, maritime commerce began to revive. *Ann & Hope,* the handsome new ship of Brown and Ives, sailed from Providence to the Orient on her maiden voyage. For command of the vessel the owners selected Daniel Olney, who had been master of *Mary Ann* on her ill-fated voyage to the Río de la Plata several years before. The supercargo was Samuel Aborn, now a veteran of many voyages in that capacity. Funds for the venture consisted of goods invoiced at $11,000; Spanish dollars on board to the number of 90,000; and 60,000 hard dollars that the partners were freighting to Canton by three different vessels belonging to other ports.[12]

For several weeks after leaving Block Island strong gales and a rough sea, new rigging "Continually on the Stretch," and a crew "composed mostly of raw, unexperienced lads" gave the officers some anxious moments. And their situation was the worse because "those few who professed themselves Seamen, came to Sea in a State of Intoxication." But writing from the Soenda Strait, Aborn described *Ann & Hope* as "a most Charming Ship, . . . an excellent sea boat . . . and a remarkable fast Sailer."[13] Arriving at Macao in ninety-seven days from Providence, Captain Olney remarked that it had remained for his ship "to distance all other Ships & vessels, of whatever *description* or *direction,* in the accomplishment of her outward passage." And he thought she perhaps "challenges a parallel where equal distance has been run in equal time." The captain was happy to report that "the utmost harmony & good understanding" had prevailed on board ship throughout the passage, a statement he somewhat contradicted when he added that, "notwithstanding our every vigilence to guard against the vice," some of the men had been very "troublesome when getting in liquor" and were "mutinously disposed." But "timely corrections" had proved "efficacious," and "quiet & obedience" had been restored. The young lads had all "behaved themselves with propriety."[14]

Five American ships were at Canton when *Ann & Hope* arrived. Aborn soon discovered that the arrival of each additional vessel was made the occasion by the security merchants "to raise (by degrees) the price of their goods," which made him hasten to secure with Houqua. The return cargo for *Ann & Hope* cost him $210,784, and the teas and nankeens that he was freighting for his owners brought his total outlay to $227,661. As his supply of hard dollars was not equal to this large sum, Aborn obtained from Houqua a substantial credit, interest free for twenty months.[15] Rarely had a ship of Brown and Ives sailed from Canton with such a handsome cargo.

TO PORTS IN NORTHERN EUROPE

The safe return of *Ann & Hope* from Canton in the year 1810 clearly demonstrated that American ships could once more trade to the Pacific at no hazard except those of wind and weather; and this continued to be the case until the declaration of war on England in 1812. Nevertheless, in the course of these two years not a single ship of Brown and Ives paid a visit to either Canton or Batavia. At that time tea and coffee were imported into the United States largely with a view to their re-export to Amsterdam, which was the great market for these staples. But British Orders in Council had declared the coast of Europe from Copenhagen to Trieste in a state of blockade; and British sea power was able to make the blockade effective. Thus inability to re-export freely to Europe deprived Brown and Ives of all incentive to continue the importation of either coffee from Batavia or tea from China. As they wrote to a correspondent, "there being no export from this Country of China goods to Europe, no demand . . . exists . . . for [the import of] Teas the quantity now in the Country is supposed sufficient for two or three years consumption. Every chest that was imported by us last year in the *Ann & Hope* remains in Store & what to do with the teas we know not."[16]

In this situation it would have been folly for Brown and Ives to import any more tea and coffee from the Pacific. On the contrary, it was necessary to cut down the large supplies they already had on hand. This could be done only by shipping them to European markets, the hazards of war notwithstanding. They decided to take the risk and dispatched their ship *Asia* to Europe with the identical cargo of coffee she had brought from Batavia in 1808. It was their original hope and expectation that she might be permitted to go directly to Holland in conformity with the Erskine agreement; but before she could set sail, news came of the repudiation of that covenant by the government in London.[17] Accordingly, the partners directed Captain John H. Ormsbee to proceed to Cowes, England, where he would seek the advice of Thomas Dickason and Company.[18] Upon his arrival at Cowes he found two letters from the London house with advice that, after a delay of several weeks, he followed, proceeding first in a convoy to Heligoland and then sailing to Tönning, where he arrived late in October.[19] There he was permitted to unload his cargo, which was sold by Schwartz Brothers of Hamburg for the account of Brown and Ives.

The coffee that *Asia* carried to Tönning had cost $102,354 and was charged in the invoice from Providence at $172,000. Unfortunately, Schwartz Brothers' account of the sales covers only 3,395 of the 8,157 bags of coffee composing the cargo. These netted 436,611 marks banco, which at the current rate of exchange was the equivalent of $173,000, an advance of $71,000 over the first cost of the whole cargo at Batavia.[20] Assuming that the balance sold at the same rate, the net proceeds of the entire cargo amounted to $418,000, a profit of more than 300 per cent. *Asia*'s voyage seems to have been fantastically successful.

Believing it was too late in the season for a voyage to St. Petersburg for Russian goods, Captain Ormsbee set his sail for Portugal. After a passage of twenty-three days "coming North about" [around Scotland and Ireland], *Asia* arrived at Setúbal. ". . . the first 19 days . . . it blew gales and some of them Tremdous," which required that six of the crew "lay by thro fatigue."[21] Captain Ormsbee left the ship at Setúbal for a visit to Lisbon, where he arranged with John Bulkeley and Son for a load of salt to be taken on at Setúbal, Bulkeley and Son drawing on Dickason and Company for the amount of the cargo. On February 15, 1810, *Asia* anchored at Newport.

Meanwhile, Brown and Ives had loaded the ship *Hope* entirely with tea and cleared her for Bremen but with some hope that the Erskine agreement might permit the landing of her cargo in Holland, a hope in which they were again disappointed.[22] Finding that the British blockade would not allow them to enter any port between Ostende and Texel, Captain Uriel Rea put into the Jade River, which runs into Jade Bay on the North Sea coast of Germany. There he obtained permission to land his cargo and transport it in wagons to Emden and from there to Amsterdam by water. Freight by wagons came high, as they were in demand for the harvest season and for the "Smuggling trade."[23] At Amsterdam, Daniel Crommelin and Sons sold the cargo for the account of Brown and Ives. As the tea had been imported from Canton on board the ship *Arthur,* it is possible to determine its cost in China. A comparison of the invoice from Canton with that from Providence shows that tea costing $65,000 was charged in the invoice of *Hope* at $156,000.[24] At the great Dutch mart the cargo netted 335,470 guilders, the equivalent of $134,000.[25] Although this fell short of the invoice, it nevertheless represented an advance of more than 100 per cent over the cost at Canton.

His cargo discharged, Captain Rea set sail for St. Petersburg, but at the Sound he was brought to by an English man-of-war and told that the whole area was in a state of blockade. He then went to Göteborg to find a pilot to take him up the Great Belt but found them all engaged for a convoy up the Baltic. He applied to the commodore of the fleet for permission to sail with him but was refused because *Hope* had no English license. When the convoy got under sail, however, Captain Rea decided to go along, copying the signals from another vessel, "which answered every purpose." Arriving at Kronshtadt, he wrote that he considered his "situation very criticall." As the British would forbid him to return by the Sound, he must try the Great Belt, where the "Danes takes all vessels." However, he trusted "to Providence" that he might be fortunate enough "to arrive safe in the United States."[26] At Kronshtadt, *Hope* took on a cargo of bar iron and other Russian goods costing 136,000 rubles, which her owners later estimated to be the equivalent of not less than $36,000 and not more than $40,000.

Returning from Kronstadt, Captain Rea was captured by the Danes and condemned by the Danish Court of Admiralty.[27] The ship herself, old and leaking, was no great loss to the partners, but the condemnation of the cargo was a substantial blow, partially offset, however, by two insurance policies for a total of $20,000.

In May, 1811, the partners again dispatched *Asia,* this time with tea, to "a permitted port in the North of Europe." Captain Ormsbee was to proceed in the direction of Vrangö Roads near Göteborg, where he would ascertain the state of European markets, being careful to conduct himself in accordance with the intelligence thus obtained. As Samuel W. Greene had for some time been in Europe as an agent of Brown and Ives, Captain Ormsbee would get in touch with him, if possible, upon arrival at Vrangö and obtain his suggestions regarding markets. The partners thought that Kiel or some other port in Denmark "on this side of the Baltic" might be open to American vessels. Captain Ormsbee would also address Schwartz Brothers in Hamburg and Crommelin and Sons in Amsterdam. Perhaps he would be permitted to land his cargo in Swedish Pomerania or Prussia or even Russia.[28]

Arriving at Göteborg in the early summer of 1811, the captain communicated at once with Samuel Greene, with Crommelin and Sons, and with Ryberg and Company in Copenhagen. In their report Crommelin and Sons expressed regret that their friends Brown and Ives had "not Kept the Property at home," as they were at a loss to know how it could be realized.[29] Ryberg and Company held out some hope that the cargo might be admitted at Copenhagen, but in the end permission was denied them.[30] As Greene was then in Berlin, Ormsbee received no assistance from him. Weeks passed while he tried in vain to find a port at which he might be permitted to land the cargo. As late as September 20, 1811, he had not succeeded. The record of the captain's procedure for the next year is virtually nonexistent. All that is known is that he was allowed ultimately to discharge *Asia*'s cargo at Copenhagen. Perhaps Ryberg and Company, despite their initial failure, obtained the necessary permission. But, in any event, the teas were not to be sold in the Danish city. Instead, they were shipped first to Hamburg, whence they were moved to Amsterdam for sale, according to Crommelin and Sons' account of the sale of the teas, dated October 22, 1812. The teas, which had cost $68,623 at Canton, were charged in the invoice at $104,493. The net proceeds were 669,440 guilders, or $267,776, an advance of $199,000 over the original cost.[31] The success of this tea venture was almost unbelievable.

After discharging his cargo of teas at Copenhagen, Captain Ormsbee, thinking a visit to St. Petersburg too hazardous, proceeded to Stockholm, where he purchased a cargo of iron, steel, and deals. Sailing from Stockholm on June 18, 1812, bound for Lisbon, *Asia* put in at Karlshafen, took a pilot for Malmö Roads, and almost immediately ran aground. In spite of assistance from the Swedish brig *Maria,* they were unable to float her until several tons of her iron were thrown overboard. Fortunately, *Asia* had suffered no damage. Captain Ormsbee then set out for Elsinore to pay the sound dues, where he learned from a schooner just arrived from America that England and the United States were at war. Hearing that the Kattegat was infested with British cruisers, he decided for the safety of the ship and cargo to return to Copenhagen. There *Asia* remained for the duration of the war.

Ships of Brown and Ives in those troubled times had made three visits to ports of northern Europe laden solely with coffee or tea. In none of the three cases was it possible to land the cargo at a port of Holland, although in two instances the goods were ultimately sold at Amsterdam. Two of the ventures were almost fabulously profitable, the other highly successful. Aside from these large shipments of East India produce, various small vessels of Brown and Ives frequently carried lesser consignments of coffee and tea to the Baltic. Typical of these was the brig *Hector,* which in 1811 arrived at Kronshtadt with 870 bags of coffee that sold at a net advance of 127 per cent over the invoice for Providence.[32]

AMERICAN PRODUCE TO DUTCH PORTS

During the three years immediately preceding the outbreak of the War of 1812, Brown and Ives were largely concerned with trade to Europe in American produce. But this, like all traffic to Europe in those years, was subject to all the hazards involved in the unsettled state of international affairs then prevailing.

The ship *Robert Hale,* built at Marietta and floated down the western rivers to New Orleans, arrived at Providence in July, 1808, bearing a cargo of cotton and tobacco from the South. Having decided to send her to Europe with the goods on board, her owners instructed Captain Martin Page to proceed toward Göteborg via the English Channel, calling for information at Cowes or some other convenient port in England.[33]

When he arrived at Cowes, the captain was not encouraged by what he learned. He could not safely proceed to the Continent, since "the danes Take all American Ships bound to Sweedland the Sweeds Take all bound to Russia the Russians Stops all in Their Ports."[34] With the passing of the weeks the prospect became ever less promising. As a correspondent at Cowes wrote Brown and Ives, *"Rob' Hale* being *cleared for Sweden* could not go to Holland" because she would be subject to the British blockade. And if she were lucky enough to run the blockade and enter a Dutch port, "She would be seized for having been in England."[35] Eventually Captain Page was rescued from his dilemma by word from Dickason and Company advising him to proceed to London.[36] Although the Nonintercourse Act of the Madison administration made London a forbidden port of call for American ships and although his owners had instructed Captain Page to avoid all places interdicted by the laws of his country, he appears not to have hesitated to act upon the word from Dickason and Company. On August 22, 1809, he reported to the partners the safe arrival of *Robert Hale* at the London docks. While he recognized that sales at London might be bad, he thought this preferable to a destination in Holland, "Where all goods in american Ships are Stored in the Kings Ware houses there to Remain Until a peace."[37] In view of his gloomy forebodings Captain Page, as well as Brown and Ives, must have enjoyed a pleasant surprise at Dickason and Company's report of the sales of the cargo. The tobacco and cotton that at New Orleans had cost $20,330 netted $41,254, a profit of 100 per cent.[38]

Never again would *Robert Hale* know such happy days. When she returned to Providence in the autumn of 1809, the partners loaded her with cotton and coffee and cleared her for the port of Rustersiel on the Dutch side of the Jade River or "any other permitted port in the north of Europe."[39] She arrived at the Jade without untoward incident. There Captain Charles Randall thought he had permission of the Dutch authorities to sell his cargo, but he soon discovered that he was a French prize, his property confiscated.[40] But before a final adjudication could be had, the ship (minus the cargo) was seized by a British man-of-war and sent to England in expectation of salvage. But to Captain Randall's surprise *Robert Hale* was restored to him upon payment of the captor's expenses. For his owners his voyage had been a costly one. Years later they estimated that the confiscated cotton and coffee would have sold for $148,000 at prices prevailing in Holland in 1810.

When *Robert Hale* returned to Providence in the fall of 1810, the Nonintercourse Act (interdicting commerce with England and France) had been superseded by Macon's Bill No. 2, permitting American ships to visit those two countries.[41] Accordingly, Brown and Ives dispatched her to Liverpool with a cargo of cotton charged in the invoice at $39,782. In this decision they were doubtless influenced by their recollection of the handsome sale of *Robert Hale*'s cotton and tobacco in London in 1809. They hoped for the safe return of the ship by the first of March, 1811, at which time they had "a particular object for the vessel."[42] Unhappily, there was to be no return of *Robert Hale*. En route to Liverpool she was wrecked on the rocky coast of Wales with the loss of one member of her crew and most of her cargo.[43]

There is reason to believe that during the voyage all had not been well on board the ship. According to testimony of four of the seamen, for some days before the disaster Captain Randall "appeared to be very much in liquor," abusing "all hands onboard," including his officers. He was still "very much in liquor" at the time of the accident and was with difficulty "prevailed on to Save himself from the wreck." It was the considered opinion of the four men that had Captain Randall "Conducted in a proper manner . . . the Ship would not have been lost."[44] But the full force of this testimony is largely offset by the official protest of Captain Randall and his first and second officers, in which the wreck is made to appear as an act of God.[45] More curious is the fact that the two officers were the witnesses to the statement of the four seamen. Whatever the actual cause of the wreck may have been, the owners appear to have accepted Captain Randall's version.

The loss of *Robert Hale* was a heavy blow to Brown and Ives. Yet they were not without certain crumbs of comfort. The ship was insured for $9,000, while three different policies on the cargo came to a total of $21,000, about half the figure at which the cotton was charged in the invoice.

Nor was this the only reverse suffered by the partners in the year 1810. Loading their ship *Arthur* with cotton and clearing her for the Jade River, they gave to Captain Joshua Rathbun instructions that appear to have been designed to be so ambiguous as to afford him maximum freedom of action. He was free to go to Texel should he hear that the British Orders in Council were rescinded and that Dutch ports were open to American trade. Or he might proceed to the Ems, a passage into which was supposed to be left open by British Orders. But should the Ems be completely blockaded, he would sail to the Jade. The proceeds of the cotton, wherever realized, he would place in the hands of Crommelin and Sons in Amsterdam.[46]

It must have been a great surprise to the owners when the first intelligence from Captain Rathbun came under a London date line; and their disappointment must have been even greater as they read the story of his misfortune. After entering the North Sea, he had thought it imprudent to "run to the mouth of the Jade . . . without a pilot on board." Accordingly, he had "made" Texel, where he was boarded by the British frigate *Desire*, whose commander informed him he would be unable to procure a pilot at that port and that he should not be found "long hovering about the place." Leaving Texel but still finding no pilot, he "ran into the Ems," where he was taken by "his B M Gun Brig *Blazer*" and sent first to Yarmouth and then to London. He expected to be tried for "breach of blockade," but it was his hope that "the situation of the Ship with my ignorance of the coast" would be a sufficient plea for his release.[47] This hope was not realized. On February 25, 1810, Captain Rathbun wrote Brown and Ives the melancholy news of his trial before Sir William Scott, who had condemned both ship and cargo. He remarked that the "disposition of the courts seem very unfavorable towards the Americans at this time of the many which are sent in and tryed but few are Cleared ... "[48]

Notwithstanding the hazards involved, trade to the ports of northern Europe, especially of the Baltic, continued to engage the attention of Brown and Ives until the outbreak of war in 1812. Besides the voyages already mentioned, their ships made nine different visits to the Baltic between 1810 and 1812. In every instance the voyage was completed. One vessel was seized by the Danes, forced to unload and reload the cargo, and compelled to submit to other indignities, but in the end both the vessel and the cargo were restored to the captain. In the main these craft carried American cotton, rice, and tobacco, returning sometimes with iron, hemp, and sheeting and sometimes in ballast. In 1810 *General Hamilton* called at St. Petersburg with a cargo of the three great staples loaded at Wilmington, North Carolina, and charged in the invoice at $21,567.[49] Although there are no figures respecting the net proceeds, they were sufficient to purchase a return cargo costing 212,400 rubles, the equivalent of at least $60,000.[50] This must be reckoned a successful venture.

The voyage of *General Hamilton* to Russia in 1812 was on a level somewhat above mere maritime enterprise. True, she carried cotton and Brazilian sugar to the value of $43,000.[51] But more interesting was the human freight on board. Taking passage was Glade Gabriel, a Negro domestic at the court of the Emperor of Russia, who had returned to the United States the previous autumn for the purpose of taking his family back to Russia. Embarking with him were his wife, two children, and a colored woman named Patience Mott. To all of them Brown and Ives wished a safe arrival, bespeaking for them the "humane attention" of Captain Charles Holden. Gabriel and his party were to find their own stores, excepting water, but should their stock of provisions become depleted en route the captain was to see that they did not want for sustenance.[52] Gabriel carried a passport from the Russian minister resident in the United States. With the papers of Captain Holden was a letter from the minister to a Russian nobleman concerning Gabriel, together with a bill of exchange covering the passage of the party, half of which was to go to the captain. Glade Gabriel had been steward on the ship *President Adams,* owned by Jonathan Russell of Providence, when that vessel paid a visit to St. Petersburg. For reasons not known he had been detained in Russia when the ship sailed for her home port. Left stranded in the land of the czars, he had found employment in the royal household.[53]

Little did Captain Holden realize as he sailed out of the Providence River into the waters of Narragansett Bay in early April, 1812, how prolonged would be the absence of *General Hamilton* from her home port. Before her arrival in Russia the United States and England were at war, which, as the partners remarked, placed their commerce in imminent danger. Once safely within the Gulf of Finland, Captain Holden gave no thought to an immediate return. Just as *Asia* spent the war years in Copenhagen, so *General Hamilton* lingered at St. Petersburg. Not until 1815 did she return to Providence.

FOODSTUFFS TO SPAIN AND PORTUGAL

While thus engaged in a lively trade to the Baltic countries, Brown and Ives were well aware of opportunities awaiting them elsewhere. Britain was then involved in the Peninsular War with Bonaparte, which assured the maintenance by her of large military forces in Spain. For the sustenance of this army England was dependent upon American provisions of various kinds. Although President Madison had banned the shipment of American grain to England when he invoked Macon's Bill No. 2 in February, 1811, this in no way interdicted the movement of foodstuffs to ports of Spain and Portugal, whence the goods easily came into the hands of the British troops in Spain. American merchants required no urging to take advantage of this bonanza. Lisbon, Gibraltar, and Cadiz soon began to teem with ships engaged in this lucrative traffic.

Ships flying the flag of Brown and Ives were frequent visitors to these ports. At first they carried some cotton, tobacco, cassia, and nankeens, together with provisions of various sorts, but soon the partners discovered it was foodstuffs that were really in demand. Flour, rice, bread, crackers, wheat, rye, and coffee became the great staples of this trade.

Typical of this traffic was a venture to Cadiz in 1809 with rice, tobacco, cotton, and Indian corn. For the cotton there was no sale in Cadiz, but when reshipped to Liverpool, it sold well. Goods charged in the invoice at $21,000 netted $35,556, a good profit. The same year *Patterson*'s cargo of wheat and flour, which had cost $23,700 at Baltimore, brought a net return of $45,590 at Lisbon.[54] Two years later *Charlotte* sailed from Providence with flour and rice invoiced at $14,000, which yielded a net return of $20,550 at Cadiz.[55] She next carried to Lisbon flour and rice charged at $13,000, which netted $23,000.

Within a period of some thirty months ships flying the flag of Brown and Ives made as many as twenty-five visits to ports of the Iberian Peninsula. Nor did the trade stop with the outbreak of war. On the contrary, the exigencies of war for a time provided a further stimulus to it. Dependent as she was upon the grain products of the United States to feed her troops in Spain, England in that first summer of the war freely resorted to the licensing of American ships for the transport of produce to Spain and Portugal. In short, England was officially condoning trade with the enemy.

Between July 29 and the end of October, 1812, nine different vessels owned in whole or in part by Brown and Ives sailed from Providence for either Lisbon or Cadiz, carrying flour, rice, and rye.[56] Of *Hector, Argus, Pilgrim, Charlotte,* and *Patterson* they were the sole owners. In *Munn, George, Warren,* and *Little Ann* they held a part interest. The voyage of *Hector* is fairly typical. On September 1, 1812, she sailed from Providence with flour costing $13,000. At Cadiz the cargo brought a net return of $27,000.[57]

In at least one instance, however, possession of a license did not prevent a vessel from running afoul of the English fleet. On September 10 the brig *Argus* sailed for Cadiz with flour and rice. En route she was seized and sent to Gibraltar. There the Court of Vice-Admiralty ordered that *Argus* be restored to Captain John M. Noyes under an Order in Council directing the release of all American vessels laden with grain and flour for Spain and Portugal that carried passports and certificates of protection granted by Vice-Admiral Sawyer of Halifax Station.[58] From this it is clear that one source of the licenses protecting American ships was Vice-Admiral Sawyer himself.

But there were other sources. On August 28, 1812, Dickason and Company of London wrote Brown and Ives that British officials there were granting licenses: "we have procured and inclose two authorizing you to Import into Lisbon and Cadiz: grain, etc."[59] The next day the London house forwarded additional certificates that the Providence partners considered "very acceptable."[60] On November 23, 1812, Dickason and Company wrote that "Mr. Larned [agent of Brown & Ives at Gibraltar] wishes us to forward him Licences for Flour but this cannot be done, as Government ceased to grant them . . . "[61] Trade under the protection of licenses had not lasted for long, but for a season it was a robust and lucrative business.

Since licenses conferred a privilege on those who possessed them, they came to be highly prized and much sought after, and they therefore became an object of speculation. In January, 1813, Brown and Ives received from Amasa and William H. Mason a letter saying: "agreeably to your request we have consulted together respecting the license for Lisbon which is dated 12 September [1812] running for nine mo., and have concluded to offer it to you for $1350. Your answer before the closing of the Western mail will oblige."[62] This letter indicates not only the continuing interest of Brown and Ives in this trade but also a lively traffic in the buying and selling of licenses. That the partners purchased the document seems doubtful. They have left no record of a voyage, actual or projected, to Lisbon in 1813.

The trade to Spain and Portugal, before and after the United States went to war with England, with and without licenses, was very profitable and comparatively safe. In the course of it Brown and Ives lost but one ship. On April 1, 1812, their ship *Isis* sailed with rice and flour for Gibraltar; en route she was intercepted and sunk by a French squadron. She thus joined *Hope, Robert Hale,* and *Arthur,* all of which were lost while on voyages to England or the Baltic.

These reverses were substantial but not catastrophic, considering the scale and diversity of the trade of Brown and Ives. In 1813 and 1814 their maritime trade was virtually nonexistent. But they were well prepared to weather the storm, for as David Parish of Philadelphia, the American agent of the Barings of London and of the Hopes of Amsterdam, had written to the firm headed by his father, John Parish, the great Hamburg banker, "the credit & solidity" of Brown and Ives were "equal to that of any other commercial establishment on this Continent."[63]

CHAPTER 7

An End to the
Maritime Business

THE return of peace in 1815 marked the beginning of a new
chapter in the commercial and economic history of the
United States. Within a few years New York was to emerge as the
greatest American port, drawing within its orbit traffic once controlled by the smaller towns on the coast of southern New England and
making inroads upon the trade of Boston itself. Coincident with
maritime decline in New England was an increase in the importance, both actual and relative, of manufacturing; and nowhere was
the growth of industry more marked than in Rhode Island, where a
member of the Brown family had already been instrumental in the
introduction of cotton manufacturing. In 1808 Brown and Ives had
diverted some of their capital from sea-borne trade to cotton manufacturing when they with others organized the Blackstone Manufacturing Company with a capital of $150,000. In the years after Waterloo
they turned increasingly to newer forms of economic activity. In 1838
they were to sell their last ship, bringing to an end a maritime history
that for the Brown family had begun in 1721.

The story of the shipping interests of Brown and Ives from 1815 to
1838 is anticlimactic, the doleful story of gradual decline and decay.
But the decadence did not show itself immediately. Until 1821 their
commercial system seemed to possess much of the health and vigor that
had characterized it before 1808. The scale of their operations was only
somewhat diminished. In 1820 they employed eight ships and three
brigs, compared with nine ships and six lesser craft in 1807. In the six
years immediately following the overthrow of Bonaparte their vessels
paid twenty-one visits to Canton or Batavia, an average of more than
three a year. The ships *Ann & Hope, Asia,* and *Patterson* and the brig
Rambler were almost constantly employed in this fashion; and the new

ship *Washington* entered the service beyond the Cape of Good Hope in 1819.

During the War of 1812 it was the confident belief and expectation of many American merchants that with the end of hostilities their trade would once more flow smoothly and uninterruptedly in the old and familiar channels. They forgot that the unparalleled maritime prosperity of the United States in the years 1800–1807 was largely the result of opportunities created by the Napoleonic Wars in Europe and that with the return of peace to the Continent, American shipping would once more meet with stiff competition in the carrying trade. They failed to realize, too, the degree to which tea and coffee would move to Europe in European bottoms. Nor did it seem to occur to them that American ships might encounter discriminatory treatment in European ports.

CARRYING BETWEEN CANTON AND EUROPE

So eager were some men to resume the old ways of trade that their planning began before the formal return of peace. In June, 1813, Brown and Ives received a letter from their friend Philip Ammidon of Boston expressing his desire to visit Canton, provided he could "procure the agency of funds to make it any object." He believed the war would "drive down" the price of China goods, especially those not much prized by the British, such as green teas and nankeens. Men therefore might well invest funds in China goods that could be stored at Canton pending safe shipment through the agency of a neutral. The goods could be paid for with English bills, particularly those on Bengal.[1]

Brown and Ives were interested but wanted more details.[2] Later in the year their interest may have been whetted by news of the arrival at New Bedford of the brig *New Hazard* with a full cargo of teas brought around the Horn from Canton.[3] For some weeks both Ammidon and the partners were undecided whether to attempt the voyage in a neutral or an American ship. Should the latter course be decided upon, Ammidon thought that *Rambler,* a brig of 327 tons owned by his friend Captain Benjamin Rich, would be a likely craft, as she had made Bordeaux from Boston in seventeen days and had easily outsailed British cruisers.[4] Brown and Ives were prepared to purchase a share in her on condition that she sail directly to Canton rather than first have a try at privateering, as Ammidon had suggested. When the latter yielded the point, the partners purchased a quarter share in *Rambler,* the other investors being Samuel G. Perkins and Company, Israel Thorndike, and Bryant and Sturgis, all of Boston.

By common consent of the owners, Philip Ammidon was to go out as their agent. Brown and Ives placed in his hands £25,000 sterling in bills on Calcutta and Bombay. With these funds Ammidon was to purchase their share of *Rambler*'s return cargo, together with tea for a ship they would dispatch to Canton once peace returned.[5] Sailing from Boston on May 18, 1814, *Rambler* anchored at Canton on September 13 after a passage of 118 days. En route she captured two prizes, one off the Cape Verde Islands, which yielded a small quantity of Madeira wine. (Since the remainder of her cargo consisted of salt, she was quickly released.) The other prize was a Bengal ship taken in the China Sea. From her *Rambler* took five boxes of opium, sixteen bales of Calcutta goods, and some medicines. Captain Rich succeeded in getting this prize into Macao, his object for doing so being that she might serve as a decoy to any frigates he might meet, thereby giving *Rambler* a better chance of escape.[6]

Going up the Pearl River to Whampoa, *Rambler* had a close call. The pilot, who had been taken "off the Great Ladroon," assured the captain that there were three British frigates in Macao Roads. Accordingly, he took them up a back passage about three leagues to the eastward of the Ladrone Islands. But meanwhile two of the frigates had moved up the river. *Rambler* ran between them at night, not suspecting they were there until they were close alongside. The frigates hoisted lights and "sent two boats after us full of men." But *Rambler* sailed away from them and anchored three hours later at Whampoa.[7]

From Canton, Philip Ammidon reported to Brown and Ives that Houqua still was the most powerful of the hong merchants, his business being "immense." Silks were the principal article that had fallen in price, being 25 per cent lower than before the war. *Rambler*'s disbursements at Canton were higher than Ammidon had expected because Captain Rich, inexperienced in the Canton trade, had neglected to purchase at Boston many things needed for the voyage. As a result articles had to be bought at Canton at higher prices.

Rambler sailed from Canton on a very dark and stormy night in January, 1815. She was at Boston in early May. All the stockholders in the venture seem to have agreed that the cargo should be sold at auction. Accordingly, advertisements were inserted in four Boston newspapers announcing the sale to be held on May 23, 1815. For the occasion there was prepared and circulated a printed catalogue describing the goods to be sold at auction. The results were highly gratifying. The gross proceeds came to $277,222.41. Total costs, including the price paid for *Rambler,* outfitting, disbursements at Canton, return cargo, wages, insurance, etc., were $130,596.45. Thus the total profit of the voyage was $146,625.96, of which Brown and Ives's one-quarter share was $36,656.49, a 112 per cent return on their investment of $32,649.36. So well impressed were they that they bought out the other owners of *Rambler*.[8]

Meanwhile Brown and Ives had instructed Philip Ammidon, who

had remained in Canton when *Rambler* sailed, to purchase and store a cargo for *Ann & Hope,* which they planned to send out once hostilities were at an end. The ship sailed from Providence in June, 1815, carrying a small cargo of goods together with 40,000 hard dollars, all consigned to Ammidon. The latter, the partners believed, would have at his command funds sufficient to provide a valuable cargo. They estimated that the Bombay bills sent to Canton by Thomas Dickason and Company would amount to $115,000. Calcutta bills to be forwarded by the same house would add another $25,000, and they were shipping 20,000 hard dollars by other vessels. These sums, with the specie on board *Ann & Hope,* would amount to $200,000. The deficiency would have to be covered by a credit "at as distant a period as possible free of Interest."[9]

These instructions were written the day before Waterloo, and Brown and Ives were well aware that the unsettled state of affairs in Continental Europe might make it unwise to dispatch *Ann & Hope* direct from Canton to Amsterdam. But the return of peace in Europe that summer and the seating of Louis XVIII on the throne of France brought a change in their thinking. Writing to Captain Wilbur Kelly on August 29, they requested him (should he receive the letter before sailing from Canton) to make all possible speed direct to Texel. The chances were good, they thought, that should he arrive in Holland by April, 1816, the cargo might be included in the public sale to be held at Amsterdam in May. The teas would do better in Holland than in the United States in view of heavy duties and the large importations expected direct from Canton.[10]

Captain Kelly anchored at Macao Roads in 108 days from Rhode Island Light, having made "the best Passage of anny Ship heer by 20 Days," except for a privateer that had made it in 90 days. The ship *Pacific,* which had sailed from Philadelphia a month before *Ann & Hope,* had not yet arrived. The captain reported that since his arrival his men had given him some trouble. Discovering that every ship arriving before him had been robbed, he had ordered quarter watches with an officer in each watch until the hard dollars were all out of the ship. The first night all of his men refused to stand watch, saying it was not "customary in the Port." But the captain's threat of stopping their wages persuaded all hands to obey except the "two greatest vileins" on board, who obliged the captain by running away. Otherwise all had gone well.[11]

At Canton, Philip Ammidon provided the return cargo with such dispatch that Captain Kelly was ready to sail by November 20. Contrary to his instructions to proceed directly to Amsterdam, he called at Providence, where Brown and Ives issued new orders directing him to Texel. As Daniel Crommelin and Sons had made a contract for the admission of the cargo into Holland for sale on condition that it "should be entire," the partners touched not a single article, "not even small matters put onboard at Canton for our families."[12]

Ann & Hope arrived at Texel after a very tedious passage of thirty days from Providence, during which a heavy snow and ice storm had frozen the fingers of several of the crew members, rendering them temporarily useless. Captain Kelly had some very miserable men aboard. He complained that four of them had "Shipped for Seamen [and] don't know anny thing about a Ship." The captain's wish that they would run away was soon granted, for within a month three deserted, while nine were in prison. But in Holland seamen willing to work for low wages were so plentiful that Captain Kelly had his full complement of men in short order.[13]

But no amount of difficulty with his men could obscure the fact that Captain Kelly had made for his owners a very profitable voyage. His ship had brought from Canton goods costing $207,395, of which teas accounted for $176,000.[14] Although the cargo failed to arrive in time for the government sales of May, 1816, most of the teas were sold "under Controul of Government at Auction" in November, 1816, and May, 1817. The teas netted 973,314 guilders, or $389,325, an advance of $213,-325 upon the cost at Canton.[15] Assuming a very modest price for the other items in the invoice, the entire cargo netted not less than $430,000.

Supplied with 200,000 Spanish milled dollars that Crommelin and Sons had procured partly in Amsterdam and partly in Paris, *Ann & Hope* sailed from Nieuwediep, Holland, in early June, 1816, arriving at Canton on October 17 in "rather a bad Staite." Before her arrival in Canton a "very hard tempest of thunder & Lightning" seriously damaged the ship's masts, took a piece out of the main yard, and "tore up Several pieces out of the deck."

But again Captain Kelly's main problem was men and not the weather. He could place no dependence on his first officer, whose conviviality forced him to keep the "Liquor Locked up," in spite of which it was not unusual to find gin bottles in the officer's bed. If "anny missfortune had befallen" the captain on the voyage, "God Only Knows what would become of the Ship." In the opinion of Captain Kelly, "Justis" to his owners demanded that he should not go to sea again with "Such a man for Chieft officer."[16] So he sailed with a new first officer and with a cargo that cost $238,658.[17]

Ann & Hope arrived off Beachy Head in 104 days from Canton, having had a pleasant passage except for a hurricane off the Île de France

(Mauritius). But as she approached the coast of Holland she was caught in a very hard gale in which only "the blessings of God & great good Luck" prevented a shipwreck. Had not *Ann & Hope* been "one of the finest Ships in the world," she must have gone on shore, where many a ship had gone that winter. The captain wrote from Amsterdam that Dutchmen would not believe that *Ann & Hope* had been to Canton; they thought it impossible that the voyage could have been made in so short a time—eight months and twenty-seven days from anchor to anchor, Amsterdam to Canton and back to Amsterdam.[18]

If Captain Kelly was pleased with his ship, he was pessimistic about the sale of the cargo she had brought, largely because of the attitude of Dutch officials. "... one of the Dutch Creeds," he wrote, "[is] to make Every thing out of the Americans they can." Captain Kelly reported that the King had decreed that none of *Ann & Hope*'s teas were to be sold at the spring sale. He said that the King was ruled entirely by his minister, who as an ardent promoter of the East India Company was willing to take advantage of an occasional bit of intrigue. But the captain readily conceded that Crommelin and Sons had done all they could in his behalf.[19]

Because the Americans were forced to wait, this cargo of *Ann & Hope* was much less profitable than the previous one. When Crommelin and Sons finally rendered their account of the sales, the net returns were only some 771,160 guilders, or $308,469.[20] This represented an advance of only $69,811, or 29 per cent, over the cost at Canton, a modest profit compared with the 121 per cent of the previous voyage.

Brown and Ives had intended to dispatch *Ann & Hope* from Amsterdam to Batavia on a coffee voyage, but word from Captain Kelly regarding his substandard officers and the damage the ship had suffered en route to Canton the previous year caused them to change their plans. Accordingly, they directed the captain to return to Providence for repairs, bringing 100,000 hard dollars. Arriving at her home port in the early summer of 1817, *Ann & Hope* sailed in good order for Canton on October 1 with 120,000 Spanish dollars on board. To provide funds adequate for a large return cargo the partners were sending 130,000 hard dollars to Canton on other vessels, thus increasing the funds for the voyage to 250,000 dollars, all consigned to John Bowers, who for the moment was to supersede Philip Ammidon as their agent in China.

Captain Kelly arrived at Macao Roads in 133 days from Providence, the last 40 the worst he had ever experienced at sea. But compared with other ships *Ann & Hope* had had a short passage. He was told by John D. Cushing (of Perkins and Company) that "it was the best Passage ... ever ... maid this Sesen of the year" since he had been at Canton.

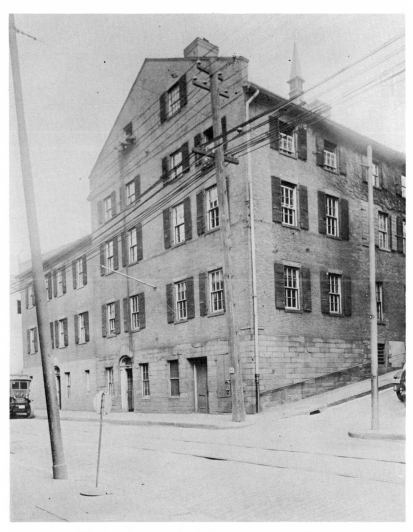

The building occupied by Brown & Ives until 1927.

Thomas P. Ives (1769–1835). Painted by James S. Lincoln from the 1835 original by Chester Harding.

Nicholas Brown (1769–1841). Painted by Thomas Sully, 1847.

The Brown & Ives ship Asia, anchored during the War of 1812 at Copenhagen. Water color by the Swedish marine artist Jacob Petersen.

Canton factories, or hongs, circa 1810.

Robert Hale Ives (1798–1875). Painted by G. P. A. Healy, 1859.

John Carter Brown (1797–1874). Miniature painted in color on ivory, 1855.

Moses Brown Ives (1794–1857). Painted by G. P. A. Healy.

View of the Providence water front. Lithograph by J. P. Newell, 1858/59.

The Old Slater Mill, the cotton spinning mill built in 1793 by Samuel Slater and Almy & Brown.

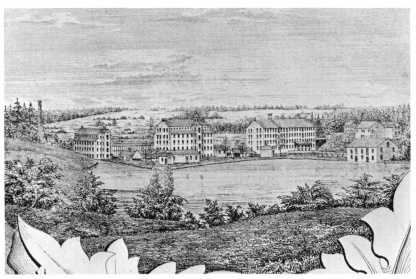

The Lonsdale mills of the Brown, Ives, and Goddard families. Engraving by Charles Reen on the 1851 H. F. Walling map of Providence County.

Land in Pennsylvania,
FOR SALE.

A VALUABLE tract of Ten Thousand acres of Land, in the counties of Bradford and Susquehannah, State of Pennsylvania, and belonging to Brown & Ives, of Providence, Rhode-Island, is offered for sale to actual settlers. The climate is healthy—the land of excellent quality, well watered, and in a good neighbourhood. The timber, principally beach and maple, mixed with hemlock, pine, birch, basswood, oak and some chesnut. There are now about thirty families settled on the land, and well made roads through it in various directions. The Milford and Owego Turnpike passes within two miles of this tract. It is about ten miles (by this Turnpike) to Owego, a flourishing village on the Susquehannah, in the State of New-York, from which, lumber and any other articles may be sent to Baltimore and other markets, by water.— It is twenty-five miles from Chenango Point, and about ten miles from the Court-House of Mont-Rose, in Susquehannah county—there are a grist and saw-mill on the land, and other water privileges.

The present price is three dollars per acre, two years without interest, payable in eight annual instalments, secured by a mortgage on the premises. An indisputable title will be given.

For further particulars, persons, disposed to settle in that part of the country, are referred to the subscriber, who resides in the vicinity of the land, and is duly authorized to make contracts and transact any business relative to the concern.

PARLEY COBURN.

Warren, county of Bradford, State of Pennsylvania, June 1823.

Farmers, disposed to remove with their families on to the above tract, may, perhaps, have an opportunity of exchanging their farms for new land, on advantageous terms.

Broadside of 1823 advertising the Pennsylvania land of Brown & Ives.

Within a month the captain was ready to sail for Texel with a cargo for which he had paid $183,707.[21] On August 4, 1818, he wrote his owners from Amsterdam, telling them the goods were discharged in good order.[22] The account of the sales forwarded by Crommelin and Sons must have been gratifying to the partners in Providence. The proceeds, clear of all charges, amounted to $289,648, an advance of $105,941, or 57 per cent, above the cost at Canton.[23] As Brown and Ives expressed it, "Nothing has saved us from experiencing an indifferent Voyage . . . but the rise of Teas"[24] in Holland.

The rise in the price of teas led the partners to a change of plan with respect to the immediate employment of *Ann & Hope*. The previous spring Moses Brown Ives, son of Thomas P. Ives, had embarked in *Rambler* for Texel, his first stop on a mission designed to give him experience in the maritime business. With him he carried instructions that he was to deliver to Captain Kelly upon the latter's arrival at Texel. The purport of the orders was that the captain should head for Batavia on a coffee voyage. This would obviate a trip to Canton, where it was difficult to go with a ship as large as *Ann & Hope*. But upon learning of the increase in the price of teas in Europe, the partners directed Moses Brown Ives to send Captain Kelly to Canton to the address of Philip Ammidon, who had in the meantime returned to China. At Canton, Captain Kelly would not divulge the rise of tea prices in Amsterdam in order to avoid tempting the hong merchants to raise the price unreasonably.

As *Rambler* had only recently procured Spanish dollars at Gibraltar at a very high price, Crommelin and Sons arranged with Dickason and Company in London that *Ann & Hope* should load her complement of hard money at Portsmouth, England, where Brown and Ives feared the cost would be but slightly less. After pondering the problem of financing trade to Canton, they came to the conclusion that the "Scarcity and high price of Spanish Dollars, makes it very important, that some substitute may be found to raise a Capital in Canton." Captain Kelly and Philip Ammidon were assigned to make inquiry in this regard. They pointed out that should quicksilver answer as a remittance, it could be had in large quantities from the Mediterranean on very reasonable terms. Pig lead also came "very low." The day would come, they believed, when these two items would largely replace Spanish dollars in trade to China.[25]

Sailing from England in the autumn of 1818, Captain Kelly arrived at Macao on January 12, 1819, after the lapse of 122 days, and reported that it was "one of the best Passages that ever was Maid from England to this Country this Season of the year and Very Much to the Astonnishment" of British residents in China.[26] By mid-February he was en route to Amsterdam, which he reached after a long voyage to a heavy market. The fears that the word heavy may have aroused in Captain Kelly's owners must have been largely dispelled by the receipt of Crommelin and Sons' account of the sales of the goods on board. The wares that had cost $177,008 netted in Holland 625,749 guilders, the equivalent of $250,299, an advance of $73,000, or 41 per cent.[27] As Brown and Ives believed Spanish dollars were to be had in the United States as cheaply as in Europe, they directed Captain Kelly to return to Providence in ballast.

CARRYING BETWEEN BATAVIA AND EUROPE

In the years when *Ann & Hope* was plying between Canton and Amsterdam, freighted chiefly with teas, Brown and Ives were employing their ship *Patterson* in a rather different manner. In March, 1815, they ordered her to Savannah, where she loaded with rice on freight and with 400 bales of cotton on their own account.[28] On arrival at Amsterdam in July the general business stagnation was such that Nathaniel Pearce and John Rogers, the joint supercargoes, were unable to obtain a freight around the Cape of Good Hope as the owners had expected. So, with goods costing $8,500 at Amsterdam and with 31,000 dollars in specie, *Patterson* set sail for the Île de France, where she arrived in January, 1816.[29] After selling the goods on board for $13,000, the supercargoes loaded the ship with sugar and coffee at a cost of $64,000, covering the deficiency of their funds with bills on London, which were in demand. When *Patterson* arrived at Providence, the partners marked the cargo up to $98,496 and ordered her to Amsterdam.[30] There the goods produced a net return of $101,000, an advance of some 58 per cent over the first cost. *Patterson* had made an auspicious postwar beginning. From Amsterdam she went to Göteborg, where she loaded with iron for the American market.

In January, 1817, she sailed from Providence with goods valued at $10,000 and with 50,000 hard dollars. Brown and Ives instructed the supercargoes to proceed to Java for coffee and sugar, if coffee were to be had there; if not, they might head for Calcutta for sugar and cotton. On arrival at Batavia they found no coffee for sale and none on the island of Java except for 15,000 piculs in the hands of the government.[31] They considered a visit to Calcutta but were deterred by reports of a sharp advance in prices following the arrival of twenty American vessels seeking cargoes. They therefore decided to remain at Java to await the new crop of coffee. Meanwhile they chartered *Patterson* to the government for the transport of troops and military supplies from Semarang to the island of Amboina for a consideration of $7,000.[32] This mission accomplished, they began taking on cargo for Holland. On November 10 they sailed with 2,000 piculs of sugar and 2,767 piculs of coffee.

While *Patterson* was en route to Amsterdam, Crommelin and Sons notified Brown and Ives that coffee prices were advancing slowly, given a lift by the speculative activity of a house in Antwerp. They wrote that "as this consumption is . . . great, and the Stocks . . . proportionlly small," they expected good prices throughout the year.[33] The sale of *Patterson*'s cargo strongly attested to the accuracy of Crommelin and Sons' diagnosis. The goods that had cost $65,000 produced a net return of 401,000 guilders, or $160,000, an advance of $95,000.[34] Although Brown and Ives conceded that this would make the voyage quite profitable, they were disappointed that the cargo included so much sugar. Had the proportion of sugar to coffee been more wisely chosen, the profit would have been $20,000 more.

The question of the future employment of *Patterson* brought a sharp difference of opinion between the owners and Pearce and Rogers, the supercargoes. Both supercargoes were fearful lest the large number of vessels leaving the United States and Europe in search of coffee should make it difficult to procure a cargo of that article at satisfactory prices.[35] Brown and Ives, however, were convinced that coffee prices would advance because of the poor condition of the West Indian crop.[36] As the weeks passed Crommelin and Sons retreated somewhat from their earlier optimism with regard to coffee. They confirmed the report of the supercargoes that many ships were sailing in search of coffee. But they conceded that with a plentiful supply of hard dollars and with the letters that they would furnish the supercargoes a coffee venture in *Patterson* might do well.[37]

Whatever course the evidence may have dictated, the weight of authority was on the side of coffee. Accordingly, when *Patterson* went to sea from Nieuwediep on April 29, 1818, with 100,000 hard dollars supplied by Crommelin and Sons, she headed for Batavia. There the market was miserable. Nothing could be bought except at the so-called monthly sales, which were held at irregular intervals of four to eight weeks. At the sales the potential purchasers were so numerous that their competitive bidding forced prices sky-high. The only alternative was to scour the coast of Java, where prices were usually lower than at Batavia. This Pearce and Rogers did but without much success; and the coffee they purchased at $19.50 a picul they resold in Batavia at $25.00. "You may form some idea from this Sale," they pointed out, "of the extent of the Coffee mania." Every port in Java was crowded with adventurers and speculators of every name and nature.[38]

Having decided against a cargo of coffee and fearful of a voyage to either Bombay or Calcutta, Pearce and Rogers set sail for Soerabaja, where they purchased 5,000 piculs of rice for the Canton market. It was their hope that the rice would return a profit sufficient to defray the ship's expenses in China. At Soerabaja they were detained by sickness among the crew, several of whom died and were replaced by Chinese and Europeans at a wage of ten dollars a month.[39]

The decision of Pearce and Rogers to forego the coffee venture in favor of a tea voyage must have produced mixed emotions, for the news of this change of plan was followed quickly by a letter from Crommelin and Sons telling of the rising price of coffee in Europe. Nor could the partners have been comforted by further word from the Amsterdam house, written after hearing that *Patterson* was bound for Canton, expressing the belief that a cargo of coffee even at the enormous high prices at Batavia would have done well.[40]

Once at Canton, Pearce and Rogers felt compelled to rationalize to their owners the procedure they had employed. They had reasoned that the high price of coffee would bring a rise in the consumption of tea in Europe and America, thus making an investment in that article a highly profitable one. Their first concern was to sell the rice, which they accomplished at prices yielding a profit nearly sufficient to defray the ship's expenses. Securing the ship with Houqua, they purchased teas, sugar, and cassia costing $107,000.[41] When *Patterson* arrived at Providence in the early summer of 1819, Brown and Ives promptly dispatched her to Amsterdam. As she had proved to be an expensive ship to run for the amount of goods she carried, they instructed Pearce, now the captain, to sell her in Holland if she would command a price in excess of $20,000. Otherwise, he was to ballast her and return to Providence with 50,000 hard dollars.[42]

Crommelin and Sons awaited with concern the arrival of *Patterson*. They feared the taste of the teas would be adversely affected by the presence of the sugar on board. They were also worried over the generally low price of teas, the scarcity and dearness of hard dollars, and the improbability that the ship could be sold at the price her owners demanded. But their worst fears with respect to the teas were not realized. Although damaged by the presence of the sugar, they nevertheless sold at a substantial profit. The entire cargo, which had cost $107,000 at Canton, netted at Amsterdam the sum of $136,000.[43] This was not a spectacular success, yet it was far from a losing venture.

Because Spanish dollars were not to be had in quantity at Amsterdam, even at a heavy premium, *Patterson* returned to Providence with nothing more valuable than 2,000 empty gin cases. Loaded with super-

fine flour, she sailed for Gibraltar, where the proceeds of the flour were
to be invested in Spanish dollars. Although three sailors deserted in
the longboat while at Gibraltar, the boat was recovered and new men
hired in time to allow *Patterson* to sail only sixteen days after arrival,
carrying 78,000 silver dollars and gold doubloons to the value of $20,000.
Upon reaching Batavia, Captain Pearce found there many vessels in
search of coffee, which was not to be had on the open market. The government had on hand some 18,000 piculs that it would sell at a very
high price.[44] No more was expected until the new crop entered the
market the next year. Sugar was scarce and dear. Calcutta, Canton, and
Manila were reported to be overrun with ships, so that produce was
to be had there only at exorbitant prices. The captain therefore had no
choice but to procure a cargo on the island of Java. The prices at the
government sales of coffee were so fantastic that he abandoned all hope
of procuring a cargo of the old crop. Accordingly, he proceeded to
Semarang (where coffee was less expensive), there to "wait for Coffee
to grow."[45] During his six months' delay the plague carried off
thousands of the inhabitants of Java and turned *Patterson* into a hospital. Eventually, Captain Pearce procured a cargo of coffee at prices much
reduced from the previous year, the total outlay amounting to $78,584.[46]
En route to Amsterdam he reported that *Patterson* "Sails very heavy being
a bed of Barnacles."[47] After a long, slow voyage of five months he arrived
at Nieuwediep with his ship in a very "foul" condition.[48] The coffee
sold well, netting 322,561 guilders, the equivalent of $129,024, an
advance of $50,440 over the cost in Java.

Such were the distinctive features of nine of the twenty-one voyages
made by ships of Brown and Ives into the Pacific in the six years after
Waterloo. One of these nine voyages was by *Rambler,* four by *Ann &
Hope,* and four by *Patterson.* Six of them were to Canton, three to
the island of Java. Only *Rambler*'s cargo was sold in the United States.
The other cargoes were not only disposed of in Amsterdam but in five
of the voyages the ship had proceeded direct from the Pacific to Holland. In the other voyages the ships merely touched at Providence for
fresh instructions. In the absence of the hazards of war the trade was
fast becoming a direct one from Canton or Batavia to Amsterdam.
Shuttling back and forth in this fashion, ships anchored at home port
less frequently than ever before. The trade was now being conducted
more nearly on a cash basis than was the case even in the golden years
from 1800 to 1807. A ship carried to the Indies Spanish dollars equal
in amount to 80 or 90 per cent of the cost of the return cargo. Shipment
of the goods to Amsterdam directly obviated the heavy expense of breaking bulk at Providence. In these respects Brown and Ives were conduct-

ing the trade with greater economy and efficiency than at any previous time. In the nine voyages in question the ships arrived safely at their ports of destination with cargoes whose combined cost was $1,122,000. The net proceeds of the goods amounted to $1,834,000, an advance of $712,000, or 63 per cent, over the first cost. This smaller margin of profit as compared with pre-embargo days seems to indicate that greater economy in the conduct of the business was at least partially offset by the competition of European ships in the carrying trade, by declining prices in Holland, and by the imposition of differential duties upon foreign ships in the ports of Holland.

AMERICAN GOODS TO GIBRALTAR AND SOUTH AMERICA

Closely meshed with the tea and coffee trade was a traffic across the Atlantic in American produce that, when sold in Europe, helped to purchase the Spanish dollars so essential to the conduct of business in the East Indies. Occasionally, of course, a ship bound for the Pacific called at a European port with flour or cotton, the proceeds from which would augment her supply of specie. But the more usual procedure was to employ in this business the slower and smaller vessels not suited to the traffic around the Cape of Good Hope. Typical of these were the ships *Charlotte* and *General Hamilton*. Between 1816 and 1821 the former made five voyages to Gibraltar, while the latter made three to the same port and three to Amsterdam and the Baltic.

In 1816 Brown and Ives dispatched *Charlotte* to Gibraltar with flour and rice. Also converging on the Rock at that moment was their brig *Hector,* with tobacco from New Orleans, and their brig *Merchants Array*. The proceeds of the three cargoes were to be invested in Spanish dollars to be picked up by one of their ships en route to the Pacific. In the same year *General Hamilton* loaded rice, tobacco, and cotton at Wilmington, North Carolina. This cargo she carried to Amsterdam, where Crommelin and Sons sold the goods and provided Captain Page with a letter of credit for part of the proceeds. Armed with this, the captain sailed for Stockholm to purchase iron. The balance in the hands of Crommelin and Sons was available for the purchase of Spanish dollars.

Why was this traffic in American staples centered at the ports of Gibraltar and Amsterdam? In part the answer lies in their location with respect to the general currents of trade. The one was strategically located in relation to southern Europe and the Mediterranean world; the other was equally well placed with reference to northern Europe and the Baltic. Another reason of equal, if not greater, importance was the comparative ease with which Spanish dollars were to be procured at the two ports. Engaged in a business demanding heavy supplies of specie, Brown and Ives were at pains to concentrate their traffic in American produce at the principal European marts of hard money. It must be remarked, however, that the sale of American staples at the two ports by no means sufficed to procure all the Spanish dollars needed by Brown and Ives. Thus they could advise the captain of *Ann & Hope* en route to Canton via Gibraltar that Hill and Blodgett at the latter place would have for him 100,000 hard dollars for which they had authorized them to draw on Dickason and Company of London. A favorable balance in the hands of Dickason and Company or Crommelin and Sons was always available to meet a financial need in any port of the commercial world.

Gibraltar was an essential link in yet another trade in which Brown and Ives were concerned—traffic to South America. Although their ships visited neither the east nor the west coast of South America with regularity, they nevertheless made a dozen voyages to that part of the world in the twenty years following Waterloo. In so far as it is possible to discover a pattern in this traffic, it involved the shipment of American staples for sale at Gibraltar, the purchase there of wines and brandies for the South American market, and the procurement in the latter of return cargoes of hides, horns, horsehair, coffee, sugar, and jerked beef.

The voyage of the ship *Charlotte* in 1818/19 is fairly typical of this business. As they prepared this vessel for the sea, the partners advised Dickason and Company in London that they had authorized Captain Samuel Young to draw on them for any sum not exceeding £4,500 sterling.[49] Upon arrival at Gibraltar the captain was to deliver his tobacco and bread to Hill and Blodgett, who would pay him the estimated proceeds. By the brig *Francis,* Brown and Ives were shipping to Gibraltar tobacco and flour whose proceeds would materially increase the funds at the disposal of Captain Young. Should the price of Catalonian wine be reasonable, he might invest as much as $6,000 in that article, receiving the balance of his funds in specie. Portuguese gold would be best, but johannes might be "difficult to find of a proper weight." In that event he would procure Spanish dollars.

From Gibraltar, Captain Young was to sail for Rio de Janeiro. Although speculators had run coffee up to a fantastic price, the partners thought it probably would not remain high. They deemed it safe to pay $0.18 to $0.20 for coffee in Brazil. But should coffee be too high, he was to load with hides and tallow for Providence or with jerked beef for Havana, to be exchanged there for sugar, molasses, and good bills.[50]

Charlotte's cargo from Gibraltar consisted of 150 pipes of Catalonian wine, which at Rio de Janeiro found a ready sale at a good price. As coffee at $0.23 was too high, Captain Young invested some $20,000 in 430 bags of brown sugar, 30 bags of white sugar, and 5,960 hides. Having a balance remaining in his hands, he invested it in English guineas and Spanish doubloons. With this cargo he returned to Providence. It had not been necessary to draw on Dickason and Company from Brazil. The funds involved in this venture, as in the partners' South American voyages generally, were quite insignificant in comparison with those invested in the trade to China and Batavia.[51]

In their comparative neglect of South America, Brown and Ives were not typical of Providence merchants of the time. Through the years from 1800 to 1830 Latin America bulked larger than any other part of the world in the commerce of the town.[52] As trade to that area could be conducted in smaller ships and with more slender means than the East India business, it attracted chiefly the merchants of more limited resources.[53] To Brown and Ives, South America was of secondary importance. Perhaps the ill-fated voyage of *Mary Ann* to the Río de la Plata in 1802, combined with the unfortunate experience of *Eliza* in the same river in 1807, had dampened their ardor for trade to that continent. Slender profits from their occasional ventures to that part of the world doubtless also served as a deterrent to a more vigorous prosecution of the business. But a more likely explanation is that they were an important mercantile house, engaged in large-scale trade to Europe, China, and the Indies long before the Spanish monopoly in South America was broken sufficiently to allow important and regular traffic to that region. Preoccupation with these long-established types of business left the partners neither the time nor the resources to engage in a new one in any large and consistent manner.

THE DECLINE OF THE CANTON TRADE

In the maritime history of Brown and Ives the year 1821 is something of a watershed. The scale and profits of their sea-borne trade had reached a crest on the eve of the embargo. In the years immediately after Waterloo they conducted their East India trade with increased efficiency, with substantial profit, and with only a slight diminution in the scale of operations. But in 1821 there began a gradual, unbroken decline of their maritime fortunes. Diminishing profits and frequent financial losses henceforth characterized their shipping business. References to the reverses suffered by them fairly dot their correspondence in these years.

The plaintive note first appeared conspicuously in June, 1821. To Captain Kelly of *Ann & Hope* the partners wrote: ". . . how it was possible . . . to pay so much Money for a Cargo of tea, we cannot account." They ventured the opinion that the captain would have "the Character, hereafter of paying more money for a Cargo of Tea in an American Ship than was *ever* paid before." What was worse, "the loss thereon" would be "as great, as the China Cost exceeded any Cargo before."[54] When Captain Martin Page selected for the ship *Washington* the best teas shipped from Canton that season, Brown and Ives were disappointed that the vessel was not sent directly home with goods suited for the American market.[55] The prospect in Europe for tea bought in China at high cost was discouraging. Not only were prices in Holland low but the differential in duties recently imposed in that country conferred such an advantage upon Dutch ships that foreign bottoms were finding it difficult to compete in the tea trade at Amsterdam.[56] Summarizing their run of bad luck, Brown and Ives wrote: "The last Cargo [on *Washington*] did bad enough, not producing even the China invoice. This [cargo] we hope may sell to cover Cost and expences etc. Commerce is so discouraging that we Know not how to employ our Ships ... The Voyage of the *Patterson* with Coffee will be bad, and all the Tea Voyages we are concerned in will be worse—so that we have reason to be discouraged." From all their advices from Holland there was "no reason to flatter ourselves that your Cargo [in *Washington*] will sell for much more than the Canton Cost. The East India business is quite discouraging..."[57]

Six years later the situation had not changed for the better. To Captain William Salisbury they wrote: "We lost so much by Your last Cargo of Tea [in *Washington*] & by that of the *Ann & Hope,* that we are desirous of avoiding another . . . on her present voyage. . . . we have not received the account sales of *Washington*'s Cargo, but do not expect the proceeds will equal the Canton Cost."[58] Doubtless the situation of Brown and Ives was less bad than their pessimistic letters seemed to indicate; otherwise they could not have waited seventeen years before finally liquidating their maritime interests. But that their trade to the Indies had fallen upon evil times there can be no doubt.

Brown and Ives would hardly have been human had they not tried to diagnose the cause of the ills from which their East India business was suffering. If they paid attention to their ship captains, they must have fixed some of the blame at Canton. For five or six years after Waterloo the partners maintained Philip Ammidon as their agent there, arranging with him to procure cargoes for their ships. But after 1821 they had no resident agent at Canton. Instead, they shared the services of an agent with other merchants. When the partners complained bitterly about the price paid for a cargo of teas, one of their captains expressed the belief that if they had "a good man" in Canton who had their "Interest at heart," teas could be purchased on terms much more advantageous to them. The captain thought Samuel Russell "a very Good Man," but unfortunately he had "too much business to do in Credit to Employ a Cash Capital to advantage." In other words he was serving too many mercantile houses. As the captain remarked, "one man Cannot do Business for two houses to [the] advantage" of either. In the opinion of the captain, Perkins and Company was the only house "that can Carry on the Tea Trade to advantage in the present times."[59] He neglected only to say that the house of Perkins and Company had in John D. Cushing an able agent whose time and talents were devoted exclusively to the interests of his principals.

Apparently after 1821 most American merchants trading to China found a full-time agent of their own a luxury that the traffic could not bear. But where several firms shared the services of a common agent, the lack of personal attention to the interests of a particular house resulted frequently in the uneconomical procurement of cargoes; and the loss suffered in the sale of the goods in Amsterdam more than offset the savings allegedly achieved by the joint agency in Canton. It was the irony of the situation that at the moment when Brown and Ives, in the interest of real economy, were conducting at Canton a cash business with hard dollars, they were, in the name of a false economy, dispensing with the services of their own agent in the spending of these dollars.

Conduct of trade at Canton was made even more difficult by the increasingly high premium on Spanish dollars. Brown and Ives thought to alleviate this burden somewhat by resorting once more to the purchase of teas on credit. Although teas bought in this manner had always been higher in price and lower in quality than in a cash purchase, the disadvantage had in part been offset by the readiness of the hong merchants to grant a credit of twenty months, interest free. Remembering those good old days, Brown and Ives in 1824 instructed Russell and Company in Canton to purchase teas for them on credit. Great was the disappointment of the partners, therefore, when informed by Russell and Company that they had "taken up a Credit of Mr. Houqua, payable on demand with Interest, at the rate of ten per cent per Annum."[60] Two years later the same firm wrote regretfully that it "is quite impossible to Serve you in the way of credit . . . as could formerly be done." Houqua's money was always at one's service but only at a price and that a high one. As for the other hong merchants, credit could no longer be obtained from them, "at least without paying for it."[61] Finding credit a luxury they could ill afford, Brown and Ives sought in other ways to procure funds adequate to their needs. Although they continued to employ hard dollars in the trade, Spanish quicksilver and pig lead, both obtainable at Gibraltar, came increasingly into use, sometimes to the exclusion of dollars.

In seeking the cause of their trouble, Brown and Ives and their shipmasters did not overlook the Amsterdam end of the business. Captain Kelly sounded a new note when he wrote to his owners: "...the manner that the Mess Crommelins is Managing the present Cargo [of *Ann & Hope*] Makes Me Sick. Our Cargo Might have been all Sold by this time at a handsom freight. . . . it provoicts Me Very Much after having a Good Voyage in our Grasp—to Loose it by bad management."[62] It is to be doubted that anyone connected with Brown and Ives had ever spoken before in such unqualified disapproval of the Amsterdam house. At times the returns may have been disappointing, but never before had the reason been laid to the procrastination and faulty judgment of Crommelin and Sons.

Nor did Crommelin and Sons escape criticism for too great haste in the sale of goods consigned to them. When in Europe in 1824, Robert H. Ives, son of the junior partner, Thomas P. Ives, spent a considerable time at Amsterdam, where he had ample opportunity to observe the practices of the Dutch house. He thought Crommelin and Sons had shown "an undue anxiety to precipitate the sale of the black teas, the present prices of which will not produce the cost & charges."[63]

Still another complaint was that Crommelin and Sons were too much influenced by the opinion and advice of their tea broker. In 1818 Moses Brown Ives, another son of Thomas P. Ives, was serving his commercial apprenticeship in Europe; and in the course of it he confided to Brown and Ives his belief that "It is too true—that the Brokers at Amsterdam have too much influence on the markets—in all sorts of goods. . . . Messrs Crommelin never sells a chest of tea or bag of coffee —nor in fact any thing else, without first consulting their broker for that article. And I am informed it is the same with all the Amsterdam Merchants. Now how easy it is, for the head brokers in Tea—or any other article to combine & regulate the price. It is a fact the great brokers grow rich."[64]

Concurring in this severe stricture on the tea broker was Robert H. Ives, who remarked that too frequently at Amsterdam the quality of tea "turns out different here from what it was considered to be" at Canton. He thought that should Amsterdam dealers "persist in being so fastidious we shall be compelled to go more frequently to their neighbors [in Rotterdam] who certainly do not seem to be so difficult."[65]

This adverse opinion of the tea broker was shared by Brown and Ives themselves. They were convinced "from long hearsay" that Crommelin and Sons were "too much governed by the Opinion" of their tea broker. Agents visiting Providence had "verbally stated" that his influence in the tea market at Amsterdam was beyond "all bounds or reason." They accordingly argued in favor of Rotterdam "for the Sale of Tea in Holland."[66] But whatever their views and however much they may have wished to transfer their business to Rotterdam, Brown and Ives continued to the end to depend on the house of Crommelin and Sons for the sale of their cargoes in Europe. Habit, inertia, and the problem of finding a trustworthy correspondent in the other port all worked in favor of the Amsterdam house.

It was doubtless true that improper attention to their interests at both Canton and Amsterdam was affecting adversely the trade of Brown and Ives. But the real source of the malady from which their East India business was suffering lay far deeper. The partners themselves had remarked that discriminatory duties in Holland were making it difficult for American ships to compete in the tea trade. American vessels now largely brought their cargoes to the United States, where the port of New York was establishing its supremacy in the import of tea, as of other items. Not only did New York ships dominate the tea trade but vessels owned in other ports carried their cargoes to that city for sale. The ships of Edward Carrington were owned in Providence, but they discharged their tea at New York. Even James and Thomas H. Perkins of Boston acknowledged commercial allegiance to New York by dispatching their tea cargoes there. Although Brown and Ives never made this formal bow to Manhattan, they indirectly recognized the economic facts of life by the progressive reduction of the scale of their trade to Canton.

THE DECLINE OF THE BATAVIA TRADE

If trade to Canton was now less profitable than it had once been, that was no less true of traffic to Batavia. During the years of the embargo and war, when American trade to the great Javan port all but disappeared, British merchants had been quick to avail themselves of the new opportunity. In 1820 Captain Nathaniel Pearce of the ship *Patterson* wrote Brown and Ives that the "Trade of this Island is almost entirely Ingrossed by British Merchants who have their agents all over the Island." He added that the "low Rate of freight in their Returning botany bay Ships gives them a great advantage over us." Their funds were derived from "their manufactures which are introduced in great amounts." American traders could make no contracts with the British merchants, "and no Security nor dependance [was to be had] on Contracts with the natives."[67] What was worse, the agents of the British merchants became citizens of Netherlands India after a residence of six months, which entitled them to all trading privileges. Savings thus effected were in many cases sufficient to pay the expenses of the voyage. The agents, plentifully supplied with Spanish dollars, were able to buy when coffee was plentiful and cheap and to sell when it was scarce and dear.

Realizing the handicap that this situation imposed on Americans trading to Batavia, Crommelin and Sons advised Brown and Ives to join with others to form an association capable of meeting the British merchants upon their own terms. Specifically, they suggested that the Providence house join "some of your Neighbours in your Town & in Boston, to send out a proper Person with a view to contract the necessary quantity of Produce, chiefly Coffee, in order to have always a sufficiency for such a number of Vessels as may be agreed upon & as may continually be employed in navigating between this Place [Amsterdam] & the Island." In this manner "the necessary Specie could be sent out," and "much benefit could be reaped . . . if a proper experienced person could be found . . ."[68] In short, the Americans should counter British agents on Java with an agency of their own.

Failing to implement the interesting plan suggested by Crommelin and Sons, Brown and Ives within a few years found themselves caught in the cross fire between the British and Dutch on the island of Java. Displeased with the preponderance of English ships at Batavia, the Dutch government sought to redress the balance through a system of differential duties in favor of Dutch ships. Finding this unavailing, the government organized in 1824 the Netherlands Trading Company, sometimes referred to as the Grand Company, which enjoyed the blessing and financial support of William I, king of the Netherlands. At the time this enterprise was launched, John Carter Brown and Robert H. Ives, sons of the senior partners in Brown and Ives, were in Europe. Writing from Antwerp, young Ives remarked that the Grand Trading Company, with a capital of 35,000,000 guilders, backed by royal patronage "will most probably for a while drive individuals from the trade." He thought that "the share which the king has taken in the affair makes it not unlikely that a direct or indirect advantage will be enjoyed by the concern over foreign individual enterprises." No one could doubt that "every million of Dollars" that the company may throw into trade "must force one million out now employed by the individual trader."[69]

Subsequent events were to prove the fears of Robert H. Ives not unwarranted. Most of the Javan coffee and sugar was henceforth carried to Holland by ships belonging to the company. Between 1825 and 1828 Dutch ships at Batavia increased from 57 to 110. In the same period British vessels declined in number from 53 to 44, while those flying the American flag dwindled from 38 to 13.[70] After 1830 by agreement between the government and the Netherlands Company all Javan produce belonging to the government was consigned to company ships. This development placed American traders, including Brown and Ives, at a further disadvantage.

But this is not the whole story of the declining maritime fortunes of Brown and Ives. Long since, they had developed a number of other business interests, including banking, insurance, turnpikes, canal building, land investment, and cotton manufacturing. So satisfying were the results of their original investment in the Blackstone Manufacturing Company in 1808 that they were induced to divert additional funds from commerce to cotton textiles. By 1831 they had become manufacturers rather than shipowners. Once the leading mercantile firm of their state, Brown and Ives would one day take the lead in the manufacture of cotton.

The indifferent success attending their maritime trade after 1821 is reflected in the merchant fleet of Brown and Ives. By 1832 it had shrunk to three ships and two brigs. A year later *Ann & Hope* and *Hanover* were the only vessels flying their flag. In the eighteen years ending in 1838 their ships made only eighteen voyages to China and the Indies, an average of only one a year, compared with more than three a year for the six years ending in 1820.

Hand in hand with the declining volume of their shipping went a change in its pattern. No longer did certain of their ships specialize in carrying to Gibraltar American staples, whose proceeds helped to purchase the hard dollars taken on board there by their larger vessels bound for Canton or Batavia. American produce still moved to Gibraltar but in smaller amounts and chiefly in ships en route to the Pacific. At Gibraltar the sale of the flour and rice produced a return that was pitifully small in comparison with the funds required for the purchase of a cargo of teas at Canton. Because of this disparity, Brown and Ives's correspondent at Gibraltar drew heavily on Crommelin and Sons or Dickason and Company in order to provide the funds necessary for the voyage.

The changed aspect of the trade to Canton is well illustrated by the voyage of the ship *New Jersey,* which in the year 1829 carried to Gibraltar tobacco, cotton, rice, and flour. When Hill and Blodgett had sold the goods, they found the proceeds but a trifling sum in comparison with the cost of the quicksilver and pig lead they had provided for the voyage. Heavy drafts on Amsterdam were necessary, therefore, to cover the difference. *New Jersey* then proceeded to Canton where she loaded with teas.

In 1833 *New Jersey* once more sailed from Providence, commanded by Captain Solomon S. Williams. Again she called at Gibraltar, where the captain disposed of his small cargo of merchandise and took on board quicksilver and pig lead costing $64,000 and $17,000 respectively. The ship also carried from Gibraltar 40,946 Spanish dollars packed in boxes and then for security put into flour barrels, as if in anticipation of a disaster at sea.[71] Sailing from Gibraltar bound for Canton, *New Jersey* had an uneventful voyage until she struck on the Louisa Shoal in the China Sea. Making it his chief concern to save as much of the hard money as possible, Captain Williams succeeded in saving 13,000 of the Spanish dollars before he was forced to abandon his ship. With seventeen of his men in the longboat, he arrived at Singapore eleven days after the wreck.[72]

Brown and Ives appear to have been quite philosophical about the loss of the ship, but they were shocked to find that the valuable property on board was improperly abandoned by the captain. And to compound the injury, Captain Williams talked so indiscreetly about the wreck that a full account of it appeared in the Singapore *Chronicle*. This so excited the cupidity of some of the citizens of Singapore that four separate salvage expeditions were there fitted out for the purpose of working the "Quicksilver Mine," as the wreck came to be called. Two of these recovered 1,450 bottles of quicksilver, two boxes of "Treasure" (evidently Spanish dollars), and 350 piculs of pig lead.[73]

The Providence firm would have been spared no end of trouble had Captain Williams, upon arrival at Singapore, quietly organized a salvage operation on his own account. They could then have arranged a settlement with their insurance underwriters without involvement with the salvors as third parties. Instead, they and the underwriters were obliged to send an agent to Singapore, who by a combination of negotiation and litigation obtained 35 per cent of the net proceeds of the salvaged property. This sum, together with the Spanish dollars the captain had removed from the wreck and the amount paid by the insurance companies, enabled the partners to recover approximately $100,000. Their loss they reckoned in excess of $40,000.[74]

If the ill-fated voyage of *New Jersey* shows the increasing use of quicksilver and pig lead in the China trade, the voyage of *Ann & Hope* in 1831 indicates another change in that trade. On this occasion the ship called at neither Amsterdam nor Gibraltar for funds. Instead, she sailed from Providence with 60,000 hard dollars procured in the United States. Included in the small invoice of merchandise she carried were ten bales of "Brown Domestic Sheetings," the product of the Blackstone Manufacturing Company, owned by Brown and Ives.[75] Captain Page was to dispose of the cotton goods with a view to opening in the Pacific a market for the cloth woven on the looms of Rhode Island. The parting injunction of the owners to Captain Page was to "preserve Order & Strict dicipline" among the crew.[76] Read in retrospect, this appears as something of a foreboding of evil. From Batavia the captain wrote that the men were "rather Turbulant at Commencing the voyage," but he had taught them to obey orders.[77] The worst was yet to come.

At Batavia no coffee was to be had. But rice offered a prospect of profit at Canton because "the Locust Hurricane" had destroyed the crop in the Philippines. Accordingly, Captain Page set sail for Soerabaja, "a fine safe harbour," where rice was to be had and where he could scour and caulk plank. His carpenter, whom he could neither "discharge nor git rid of," was ill with consumption and "a hard bargain." The remainder of the crew were all well and "a great sett of Villains."[78] Just how great the captain would one day discover.

In March, 1832, *Ann & Hope* sailed for Canton with 7,566 piculs of rice on board. The elements being kind, she enjoyed a "Calm Smooth Passage." But on board the situation was rather less placid. Seven of the crew—five native-born Americans, one Prussian, and one Englishman—made use of their leisure time to plan a mutiny. The plot was to have been staged on the night of April 21, when the ship was in the Bangka Strait. The conspirators planned to call the second mate during his watch, to seize and heave him overboard, and to pin the crew below by securing the fore hatch. Entering the cabin, they would kill the captain and the first officer, take possession of the ship, place one of their number in command, sail the vessel to a remote spot, remove the Spanish dollars, and seek safety in flight. As the cargo of rice had not been costly, there remained on board 40,000 hard dollars of the ship's original fund. It obviously was the prospect of sharing this loot that excited the avarice of the seven conspirators.

At the appointed hour courage failed the plotters, and their design came to nothing. With proper discretion, however, they might have carried the secret with them to the grave. But after his ship's arrival at Canton, Captain Page chanced to hear the steward say to a sailor, with great feeling, that "if Justice [were] done him he would be hung." Surprised to hear "so rough language," the captain inquired as to its meaning; and he was even more amazed to hear from the lips of the steward the story of the diabolical plan as told him by one of the conspirators. The U.S. frigate *Potomac* being in port, Captain Page repaired to her to invoke the aid of Commodore J. W. Downs. An investigation was instituted; and depositions taken in the presence of the naval officer fully exposed the design of the plot. Commodore Downs received on board his ship five of the mutineers—the five who were

American-born citizens—and in exchange supplied Captain Page with men from the *Potomac*. The two foreign-born plotters were simply "landed" on Chinese soil.[79]

Ann & Hope made two more voyages to the Pacific. In neither case did she call at a European port to augment her funds. Instead she carried in each instance 40,000 hard dollars procured in the United States.

THE LAST MERCHANT VESSEL

Meanwhile, Brown and Ives had purchased in New York the ship *Hanover*, which for a period of two years enjoyed the distinction of being the one vessel remaining in their possession. *Hanover* made three visits to the East, the first by way of Gibraltar for quicksilver and pig lead. On her last voyage she carried from Providence only 30,000 hard dollars, an accurate index of the dwindling proportions of the trade to the Indies. On none of the ventures did she take her cargo to Amsterdam.

In their East India trade Brown and Ives had come full circle. In the declining stages of the business they reverted to the pattern employed in the early years of the traffic. The voyages were made direct from Providence to the Pacific. Spanish dollars, procured in the United States, were used on a small scale. Cargoes of oriental goods were brought to Providence—not sent to Amsterdam—and the wares were sold in the home market. No longer did Amsterdam or Gibraltar or even London enter the picture. The names of Dickason and Crommelin vanished from the record. Had the partners dispensed entirely with hard dollars, they would have turned the clock back to 1787, when *General Washington* sailed on her first voyage to Canton.

When *Hanover* arrived at Providence from Canton in 1838, her owners soon disposed of her. Thus ended for the Browns the East India trade begun by them fifty-one years before. But the sale of Hanover marked something more; it brought to an end the maritime history of the Brown family, which had begun in 1721 when Captain James Brown put to sea from Providence in the sloop *Four Bachelors,* bound for some of the Leeward Islands in the West Indies.

An unexpected windfall had in some small measure served as a counterweight to the decline of the maritime fortunes of Brown and Ives. On March 28, 1830, the United States and Denmark signed a convention providing for a mixed commission to pass upon claims of American merchants and shipowners who had suffered losses at the hands of Denmark in the course of the Napoleonic Wars. On July 4, 1831, the United States and France signed a treaty providing for the adjudication of the "spoilation claims" of Americans who had experienced losses from French seizures of ships and cargoes during the same Napoleonic Wars. Brown and Ives were claimants against both Denmark and France. In 1833 the commissioners under the Danish-American convention awarded Brown and Ives damages to the amount of $27,225 for the seizure of their ship *Hope* and her cargo in 1810 as she was en route home from St. Petersburg. At the same time, the commissioners awarded Thomas P. Ives, assignee of J. S. Martin, the sum of $5,981 for damages to the brig *Canton,* not the property of Brown and Ives.[80]

In 1836 the commissioners under the treaty with France made an award to Brown and Ives of $110,136 for the seizure and confiscation of the cargo of the ship *Robert Hale* in 1809, of $46,963 for the sinking of their ship *Isis* by a French naval squadron as she was en route to Gibraltar in 1812, and of $3,463.67 for the brig *Argus* seized in 1812.[81] Brown and Ives also received $10,100.35 on account of the ship *Union* of which they were not the owners but in which they had held an interest, probably as a charter party.[82] Covering losses long since written off the books, the award of $203,869.02 from these sources gave them a nest egg just at the time when they were turning their attention to a variety of new forms of investment.

CHAPTER 8

A Half-Century of
Cotton Manufacturing

ALTHOUGH the United States gained its political independence in 1783, the country's economy remained in the Colonial stage, the distinguishing feature of which was the paramount importance of exporting the products of agriculture and the extractive industries in exchange for other forms of wealth, particularly manufactured goods. Domestic manufacturing had made some progress in the course of the War for Independence because of the obstructions to maritime commerce. But when peace returned, most Americans assumed that they could once more procure their manufactured goods from England and pay for these wares by exporting the products of field and forest. After merchants had placed large orders for British goods, they began to realize that serious dislocations in the accustomed channels of maritime trade would make it hard for them to obtain the means of paying for the goods imported. Soon they found themselves heavily in debt to their British creditors. A deep depression settled upon the land.

It is a truism that in a young country the forces tending to stimulate the growth of commerce have the effect of retarding the development of manufacturing. On the contrary, the forces hampering and restricting maritime trade tend to turn men's thoughts to manufacturing. This was precisely the effect of the depression of the 1780's. With foreign commerce demoralized, the incentive for Americans to develop their own manufacturing was greatly strengthened. This was particularly true in New England, always short of natural resources and never able to produce a staple for export. And nowhere was it more true than in Rhode Island, the deficiency of whose natural produce had been stressed in the famous Rhode Island Remonstrance of 1764. Rhode Island had been compelled to import in order to export; and the majority of its articles of export had come from beyond its own borders.[1] Nowhere else was the postwar paralysis of commerce more catastrophic; nowhere else were the merchants more overwhelmed by debt. It was inevitable, therefore, that in Rhode Island serious thought should be given to manufacturing; and the most earnest advocate of manufacturing was one of the Browns, a family conspicuous in that field in Colonial times.

SOME EARLY EFFORTS

Since the most distinctive feature of the Industrial Revolution in England had been the transformation of cotton manufacturing by machine process, it was natural that when men in New England turned to manufacturing, their first concern was cotton textiles. The chief obstacle to be overcome was the inability to produce a cotton yarn of sufficient strength for use as warp in making cloth. Because of this it was necessary to use linen yarn for warp, which substantially increased costs. In England this problem had been solved by Richard Arkwright's invention of the water frame, which spun cotton yarn strong enough to be used as warp. As the British government forbade the export of the machine and of the mechanics who could make it work, the first task of aspiring cotton manufacturers in New England was to reproduce the water frame. In Massachusetts the state legislature had subsidized the building of machines called "States Models" at the works of Colonel Hugh Orr in East Bridgewater. The States Models were Arkwright water frames of sixty spindles constructed from a description by Thomas Somers, who had visited England for the express purpose of viewing the Arkwright machine. Unfortunately they proved to be unworkable. A more ambitious experiment was that of the Beverly Cotton Manufacturing Company, begun at Beverly, Massachusetts, in 1787. It was controlled by an imposing number of men of substance in Boston and Beverly. They were supplied with ample capital and were granted exemption from taxation. This, too, proved to be a dismal failure. Inadequate machines and lack of knowledge were declared to be the chief impediment to the success of the undertaking.[2]

Probably no one in Rhode Island viewed these unsuccessful experiments with greater interest than did Moses Brown. He was greatly concerned over the deteriorating economic situation in the state, particularly as it affected the Quakers. Since their moral code forbade them to engage in certain types of business, Moses was sincerely interested in developing enterprises that would afford them an opportunity to improve their lot. Along with his desire to help his coreligionists went an equally strong wish that his country achieve economic independence. He had been distressed by the swiftness with which his brothers Nicholas and John had become deeply indebted to their London correspondents through excessive importations of British goods, and he was convinced that Americans must develop their own manufacturing as a means of lessening their economic dependence on England. To Moses it seemed that cotton manufacturing would, at one and the same time, improve the lot of the Friends and contribute to the greater economic independence of his country.[3]

In 1787 Moses Brown began to apply his talents to learning all that was known in the United States about cotton manufacturing. In that year he visited the States Models at East Bridgewater, the cotton manufactories at Beverly and Worcester, and the woolen manufactory at Hartford. For two years he gathered all possible information by personal visit and inspection, by conversation, and by letter. Early in 1789 he decided to undertake the business of manufacturing cotton. His decision had been hastened by the approaching marriage of his daughter, Sarah, to William Almy, whose desire to go into cotton manufacturing had the whole-hearted support of Moses. Since he was unwilling to ask for state financial support, given freely to experiments in the business in other states, he mobilized his own somewhat scattered financial resources, formed a partnership with his new son-in-law under the name of Brown and Almy, and purchased a spinning jenny and a carding machine that he installed in the Market House in Providence.

He placed other machines in various houses and shops in Providence. He purchased crude water frames, which he installed in the barn on his farm. So that the frames could be driven by water he purchased a building on the riverbank in Pawtucket, where he placed the machines in operation only to see them fail. Although Moses had learned all that was to be known about the business in America, his venture into cotton manufacturing seemed doomed by inadequate machines and unskilled mechanics. He accepted defeat and decided to abandon his experiments until he could procure the services of someone who had acquired the necessary skill and experience in England. When at this stage Moses withdrew from his partnership with William Almy, the firm of Brown and Almy became Almy and Brown, with Smith Brown, a cousin of Moses, taking the place of the latter.[4]

The retirement of Moses from active participation in the firm in no way diminished his interest in cotton manufacturing. Before long the problem of finding a man who could build a workable Arkwright water frame solved itself. A young Englishman who had completely mastered the art of cotton manufacturing was about to set sail for America.

In 1783 Samuel Slater of Belper, Derbyshire, had been apprenticed to

Jedediah Strutt, sometime business associate of Richard Arkwright. Although only thirteen years of age when he began his term of service at the cotton mill in Milford, the youth, according to his father, "wrote well, was good at figures," and was "of a decided mechanical genius." His combination of "industry, fidelity and mechanical skill" so greatly impressed his master that after three years he was made an overseer. With unusual awareness for his years he soon became convinced that cotton manufacturing in England would be overextended. But he was led to believe that the infant cotton textile industry in the young American republic would afford limitless opportunity to a young man of his talent and experience. While in this frame of mind, he read in an English newspaper of the inducements offered by the legislatures of Pennsylvania and other states for the development of workable machinery for cotton manufacturing. He decided to emigrate to America. Knowing of the British ban upon the emigration of men of mechanical skill as well as the prohibition upon the removal from England of models and patterns of drawings of machines, he was careful to perfect his knowledge of the machinery. This would enable him, once he was in the new country, to use his memory, mathematics, and mechanical skill to build the machines involved in the Arkwright system. Disguised as a farm laborer, he sailed from London on September 1, 1789, and arrived at New York sixty-six days later.[5]

Within a few days Slater found employment with the New York Manufacturing Society, then trying to operate a cotton mill on Vesey Street in New York City. After three weeks he became convinced that the enterprise had slight chance of success, partly because of the defective machines in the mill, partly because of the lack of water power within the vicinity. He had about decided to try his fortunes in Philadelphia when the captain of a sloop plying between Providence and New York told him of the experiments being carried on in Pawtucket, Rhode Island, in the spinning of cotton yarn by water power. On December 2, 1789, Slater addressed a letter to Moses Brown, the instigator and the financial supporter of this experiment. Although this letter and the answer to it have been frequently published, they are sufficiently important, both to the history of the Brown family and to cotton manufacturing, to justify one more printing:

NEW YORK, December 2d, 1789

SIR,—A few days ago I was informed that you wanted a manager of *cotton spinning,* &c. in which business I flatter myself that I can give the greatest satisfaction, in making machinery, making good yarn, either for *stockings* or *twist,* as any that is made in England; as I have had opportunity, and an oversight, of Sir Richard Arkwright's works, and in Mr. Strutt's mill upwards of eight years. If you are not provided for, should be glad to serve you; though

I am in the New York manufactory, and have been for three weeks since I arrived from England. But we have but *one card, two machines,* two spinning jennies, which I think are not worth using. My encouragement is pretty good, but should much rather have the care of the perpetual carding and spinning. *My intention* is to erect a *perpetual card and spinning.* If you please to drop a line respecting the amount of encouragement you wish to give, by favour of Captain Brown, you will much oblige, sir, your most obedient humble servant,

SAMUEL SLATER

N. B.—Please to direct to me at No. 37, Golden Hill, New York.
Mr. Brown, Providence.

PROVIDENCE, 10th 12th month, 1789

Friend,—

I received thine of 2d inst. and observe its contents. I, or rather Almy & Brown, who has the business in the cotton line, which I began, one being my son-in-law, and the other a kinsman, want the assistance of a person skilled in the frame or water spinning. An experiment has been made, which has failed, no person being acquainted with the business, and the frames imperfect.

We are destitute of a person acquainted with water-frame spinning; thy being already engaged in a factory with many able proprietors, we can hardly suppose we can give the encouragement adequate to leaving thy present employ. As the frame we have is the first attempt of the kind that has been made in America, it is too imperfect to afford much encouragement; we hardly know what to say to thee, but if thou thought thou couldst perfect and conduct them to profit, if thou wilt come and do it, thou shalt have all the profits made of them over and above the interest of the money they cost, and the wear and tear of them. We will find stock and be repaid in yarn as we may agree, for six months. And this we do for the information thou can give, if fully acquainted with the business. After this, if we find the business profitable, we can enlarge it, or before, if sufficient proof of it be had on trial, and can make any further agreement that may appear best or agreeable on all sides. We have secured only a temporary water convenience, but if we find the business profitable, can perpetuate one that is convenient. If thy prospects should be better, and thou should know of any other person unengaged, should be obliged to thee to mention us to him. In the mean time, shall be glad to be informed whether thou come or not. If thy present situation does not come up to what thou wishest, and, from thy knowledge of the business, can be ascertained of the advantages of the mills, so as to induce thee to come and work ours, and have the *credit* as well as advantage of perfecting the first water-mill in America, we should be glad to engage thy care so long as they can be made profitable to both, and we can agree.

I am, for myself and Almy & Brown, thy friend,

MOSES BROWN

Samuel Slater, at 37, Golden Hill, New York.[6]

Moses' reply was a model of restraint. By stating frankly that he had neither the machines that would work nor the men who could make them work, he was admitting that his efforts thus far had led only to failure. He was by no means certain that even Slater could succeed where he himself had failed. He held out no false hopes of fame or fortune; the strongest inducement he could offer the young Englishman was the possible "*credit* as well as advantage of perfecting the first water-mill in America."

Without writing a reply, Slater packed his bags and boarded the packet for Providence. Years later Moses Brown told Slater's biographer that when Slater saw the machines in the mill in Pawtucket, he was extremely downcast. Shaking his head, he said, "These will not do; they are good for nothing in their present condition, nor can they be made to answer." They were worth nothing more than so much "old iron."[7] Moses therefore contracted with Slater "to direct and make a mill in his own way ..."[8] This Slater refused to do until he was promised a man to work in wood, who was to be put under "bonds not to steal the patterns, or disclose the nature of the works." When this demand had been acceded to, Slater remarked, "if I do not make as good yarn, as they do in England, I will have nothing for my services, but will throw the whole of what I have attempted over the bridge."[9]

While constructing the machinery for perpetual spinning known as the Arkwright system, Slater was to be paid by Almy and Brown one dollar a day. The "man to work in wood," for whom he had asked, was Sylvanus Brown (not related to Moses), while the necessary iron work was done by Oziel Wilkinson, whose daughter Slater soon married. Slater was to discover that the information assembled by Moses and Smith Brown and William Almy in the course of their unsuccessful experiments in cotton manufacturing, was to stand him in good stead. These men, somehow, were always able to put him in touch with the most approved sources of talent and materials whether in Rhode Island or in other parts of the country.

In April, 1790, Almy and Brown entered into a business partnership with Slater. By the terms of the agreement Slater was to build the machinery for the Arkwright system of cotton spinning and to manage the factory in Pawtucket, once it was in operation. William Almy and Smith Brown would provide the stock of raw cotton and market the machine-spun yarn through their mercantile establishment. Slater would share the profits equally with Almy and Brown.[10]

ESTABLISHING THE COTTON INDUSTRY

On December 20, 1790, almost one year from his first arrival in Providence, Samuel Slater set in motion the power-driven machinery he had made, which was then housed in the old fulling mill in Pawtucket in which Moses had earlier installed the imperfect water frames. Thus was born cotton manufacturing in America, which marked the entrance of the young country into the first stage of the Industrial Revolution.

Once Samuel Slater had brought his great skill and mechanical ability to the United States, it was inevitable that he should somewhere in the country establish the Arkwright system of the perpetual spinning of cotton. That he chanced to introduce it in Rhode Island was chiefly because of Moses Brown. Had the experiments of Moses not been known to a ship captain, Slater probably would have gone to Philadelphia, which might well have been the immediate beneficiary of his talents. But he came to Rhode Island, where he benefited not only from the experience and knowledge Moses Brown had accumulated but also from the "money, faith, and confidence" that Moses freely gave him.[11] Without these the way of Samuel Slater to glory and affluence might have been a good deal harder than it was.

There is irony in the fact that Moses Brown, a great humanitarian, should have unwittingly and indirectly, through his connection with cotton manufacturing, contributed to the perpetuation of two great evils. The English cotton manufacturing system, which Slater had brought to America, had always relied heavily upon child labor. Once established in Rhode Island, the business continued to employ children. Alexander Hamilton had frankly advocated the development of manufacturing as a means of making the labor of women and children more useful. Moses had merely believed that children as a potential labor force would be useful in the development of manufacturing. He had evidently not foreseen the unfortunate results that would issue from the exploitation of this source of labor. By the same token, he could not have realized that cotton manufacturing (which he hoped would prove beneficial to the Friends by affording them much-needed employment), once firmly established, would by its insatiable demand for raw cotton be the means of giving chattel slavery, which he strongly opposed, a new lease on life.

Though Moses Brown retained a financial interest in Almy, Brown, and Slater for many years, his active participation in the business came to an end once Slater had placed it on a successful basis. When Smith Brown retired from the partnership in 1791, his place was taken by Obadiah Brown, the son of Moses; the change required no change in the name of the firm.[12]

To Almy and Brown belongs the distinction of forming the original firm of cotton manufacturers in the United States. But they did more than that. They trained a new generation of manufacturers; mechanics with a background of service with Almy and Brown went into the business on their own account. Samuel Slater built a mill for himself in Pawtucket in 1799, operating it on his own while continuing the oversight of Almy and Brown's factory. Other men with financial support from farmers and merchants in the Providence area built spinning mills similar to that of Almy and Brown. These new ventures into the business of cotton spinning were to be found at Pomfret, Connecticut; at Scituate, Warwick, Coventry, and Cumberland, Rhode Island; at New Ipswich, New Hampshire; and at Greenwich and Whitestown, New York. In the words of a careful student, "The old Providence firm [of Almy and Brown] was indeed the parent of the American cotton industry, for it was responsible, directly or indirectly, for the erection of most of the twenty-seven mills which the Secretary of the Treasury discovered in operation in Rhode Island, southern Massachusetts and eastern Connecticut in 1809."[13]

The cotton yarn produced in the mills was sometimes blocked and dyed by women in their homes but more often by skilled artisans operating their own shops. In other instances the manufacturers built dye houses that they operated in connection with their spinning mills.[14]

As the name suggests, spinning mills before 1809 were seldom concerned with weaving, either directly or indirectly. Although Almy and Brown had put some yarn out for weaving, they pronounced the experiment a failure. They were unable to get the work done on terms favorable to themselves. Most of the yarn from the mills, therefore, was purchased at the retail stores supplied by the factory owners and woven into cloth on hand looms in the weavers' homes. Master weavers, largely in the vicinity of Philadelphia, purchased at wholesale from the mills the yarn that they worked into cloth. Merchant weavers, who put yarn out for home weaving, were not conspicuous in the business until after 1812. The woven cloth was finished either by outsiders or in a separate plant belonging to the millowner.[15] Only with the introduction of the power loom was finishing brought together under one roof with the other processes.

Workers in the spinning mills were principally children drawn from farms within the vicinity. When the supply of child workers in a given area was exhausted, resort was taken to one of two procedures: advertisements offering employment to large families of children; or the building of mills in districts where the supply of child workers was as yet untapped. The wages of the children ranged from thirty-three to sixty-seven cents a week, payable in part or entirely in goods at the company store. Frequently, the fathers of the child workers were the skilled mechanics or overseers in the mills.[16]

As provided by their agreement with Samuel Slater, the principal task of Almy and Brown was to sell the cotton yarn produced in the spinning mill in Pawtucket. It was their job to develop a market for the yarn at a time when market conditions appeared to be most unpropitious for this new article of trade. Because of a series of business failures in England and Ireland, cotton goods were being sent to America to be sold for whatever price they would bring. To make matters worse, British agents combined low prices with very large credits, "doubtless for the Discouragement of the Manufactury here," as Moses Brown remarked. "This bate," he said, had "been too Eagerly taken by Our Merchants," with the result that "the Quantities of Brittish Goods . . . on hand Exceeding the Markett Obstruct the sale of Our Own Manufacturys . . ." Moses charged that this dumping of cotton goods on the American market resulted from a deliberate plan on the part of the British to destroy the infant American cotton industry as they had tried earlier to choke off cotton manufacturing in Ireland. Moses believed that only government intervention in the form of a protective tariff would prevent the success of the British design.[17]

Actually, the British menace was more apparent than real. It was cotton cloth, not yarn, that was flooding the American market. The real problem of Almy and Brown was not to induce the public to purchase American instead of British cotton cloth. Rather, their task was to develop a demand for a product new to the American market, namely, cotton yarn. They must induce householders to accept this yarn in place of, or in addition to, the wool and flax that their hand looms had woven into woolen or linen fabrics.

Almy and Brown in 1791, their first full year of operation, sold most of their yarn to weavers in Rhode Island, though some was shipped to Norwich, Connecticut. For the two years that followed they were largely content with essentially the same customers, but they did extend their trade as far to the north as Charlestown, Massachusetts. In 1793 with their new mill in operation they felt compelled to seek a wider distribution of their yarn; this they achieved by selling to shopkeepers in the mercantile and commercial centers. Within a few years they had a large number of small accounts with such dealers. By 1801 they were supplying yarn on consignment to storekeepers in Portland, Maine; Newburyport, Marblehead, Salem, Boston, New Bedford, and Nantucket, Massachusetts; Newport, Rhode Island; and various towns in Connecticut. Much of their yarn was sent to New York City, whence it was shipped up the Hudson to the towns of Albany and Hudson.

Substantial amounts of their product they sent to dealers in Philadelphia and Baltimore. From these towns the yarn was distributed through the rural areas, where in farm homes it was woven into cotton cloth, thus supplanting wool. The cotton yarn was also extensively used in the knitting of stockings and for embroidery, fringes, and hat frames. In New York City the demand for yarn was so great that a stocking maker, unable to obtain it direct from Providence and finding none in the city's stores, purchased Almy and Brown yarn in Philadelphia at an advance in price.[18]

Almy and Brown were surprisingly successful in the development of a market for a product new to the American public. In a decade they had made their yarn a familiar article of trade in the coastal towns from Portland to Baltimore, as well as in the hinterland of each of these commercial centers. Early in its history, therefore, cotton manufacturing began to assume that nationwide aspect that was to make it an important factor in strengthening the bonds of national feeling. The finished product of an industry centered in New England, using a raw material grown in the South, was marketed over a wide segment of the nation. In this respect, the cotton manufactories differed markedly from the woolen and linen manufactories of the Colonial era. Based on wool or flax that was locally grown, spun, and woven and making products designed primarily for wear in the immediate neighborhood, these were purely local industries. In the cotton manufactories only the capital and the labor came from local sources.

The relatively wide distribution of Almy and Brown yarn had in the first decade of the business been achieved by consigning the article to merchants in the coastal towns for sale on commission. Once their yarn was well known, they hoped to replace consignment with outright sale of the yarn to the merchants. To their surprise and disappointment, however, they were not only unable to make the change but in some instances were forced to increase the rate of commission. Where the prospects warranted it, they granted liberal terms of credit. This was notably true of their dealings with master weavers who gave promise of more than ordinary success.[19]

The years from 1800 to the embargo, which brought such marked prosperity to commercial interests in the towns, brought equally good times to cotton manufacturing, whose principal market for machine-spun yarn was in the centers of maritime commerce. In these years numerous additional spinning mills were built, including new ones by Almy and Brown in 1806 and 1807. To maintain the price of yarn and to resist the demand for reduction in price to meet increasing competition, it became necessary for the manufacturers to seek an expansion of the market. As early as 1803 Obadiah Brown, junior partner of Almy and Brown, visited New York City, Philadelphia, Baltimore, and Alexandria, as well as the towns in the environs of each of these, and sought to induce merchants to take consignments of yarn on trial, to be sold on commission. With a view to an extension of their southern market, Almy and Brown asked their cotton buyer in Charleston to call their yarn to the attention of weavers in South Carolina, hoping in this way to use the yarn as a "valuable remittance for the raw material of which it is made."[20]

The fact that thirteen of the twenty cotton spinning mills in operation in southern New England before 1807 were still in business in 1832 seems to support the view that prior to the embargo the development of cotton manufacturing had been an altogether sound and conservative one. A substantial part of the credit must go to Almy and Brown, who as the pioneers in the business so largely set the tone and pace that other millowners were prepared to accept.

In December, 1807, came the Embargo Act, which by interdicting trade of the young country with the rest of the world precipitated an economic crisis of major proportions. Paralysis descended upon maritime centers within the country. Ships rotted at their wharves. Federalists denounced Jefferson and all his works. The Constitution, they said, had given the federal government the power to regulate commerce with other nations but not to destroy it. There was one segment of the economy, however, that appeared to be a beneficiary of the embargo. To cotton manufacturing it seemed to bring a period of notable expansion that was to continue virtually unchecked to the end of the war in 1814. In the popular mind the explanation for the expansion was simple. The ban on foreign trade had cut off the supply of cotton goods imported from England. To fill the void it became necessary for American cotton manufacturers to supply a market hitherto stocked with British cotton goods.

One difficulty with this interpretation is that it overlooks the fact that while the imports of English goods consisted of cotton cloth, the product of the American cotton mills was cotton yarn. For cotton cloth from England yarn could not serve as a direct substitute. In addition, the initial impact of the embargo upon cotton manufacturing in Rhode Island was exactly the opposite of the popular belief. Instead of giving the business an immediate fillip, the embargo destroyed the market that Almy and Brown had so carefully built over a period of some fifteen or more years. The partners had sold most of their yarns in the towns that dotted the coast from Portland to New York City, in the Hudson Valley, and in Philadelphia and Baltimore. They had sent almost half of their goods to Boston or the towns to the north.[21] The immediate effect of the embargo was to bring economic collapse to the port towns of New England and to destroy the ability of the populace to purchase the cotton yarn that Almy and Brown had placed in the hands of the shopkeepers. In 1808, the first full year of the embargo, the proportion of yarn distributed through these same channels declined to 17 per cent.[22] This statistical evidence of the demoralized state of the market is abundantly corroborated by the letters written by Almy and Brown to their northern agents, appealing to them not to allow much yarn to be had on credit in view of existing conditions.

Prospects for the business appeared doubtful, even though the embargo had served to reduce the price of raw cotton. This last circumstance had been more than offset by the decline in sales of yarn. Almy and Brown were disturbed by the stock of unsold goods accumulating in their warehouse. As conditions grew worse, they decided, late in 1808, that it was wise to dismiss one of their workmen. The following year it was necessary to dismiss additional workers at the expiration of the terms for which they had been employed. Because of an increasing number of bank failures in New England, the partners instructed their agents in the northern towns to refuse notes of country banks and to accept payment only in specie or in the notes of banks located in the larger commercial centers.

In a variety of ways they worked to maintain the demand for their goods. They extended more favorable terms of trade to their established customers. They endeavored to win new customers in areas not previously familiar with their goods. They gave encouragement to master weavers and tried to extend the knowledge of the art of weaving in the cottages. They instructed their agents to advertise the superior quality of the yarn spun in their mills. And they were prepared to abandon their long-established practice of selling for cash only, in favor of payment in produce. By these and by numerous other means Almy and Brown tried to hold their trade in the face of the adverse conditions that had descended upon the New England market areas. All available evidence indicates that, far from prospering, they were struggling desperately to keep their heads above water. Given the pre-eminence of this firm in cotton manufacturing in Rhode Island at that time, there is every reason to suppose that their situation was no worse than, if as bad as, that of other firms engaged in the business.

Strange as it may seem, however, the years 1808 and 1809, in which the prospects of cotton manufacturing appeared unpromising to the leading firm in the business, witnessed the building of numerous new spinning mills, all apparently in the belief that it was a highly profitable industry. Almy and Brown wrote that "The business of cotton spinning looks likely to be very much overdone."[23] Albert Gallatin, Secretary of the Treasury, thought the number of new spindles under construction in 1809 equal to the number then in operation in southern New England. This multiplication of mills was long thought by students of the period to have resulted from the need for domestic cotton goods in a market that, until the embargo, had been supplied with English cotton cloth. Since the actual effect of the embargo was to destroy much of the existing market for domestic yarn, the simple, traditional explanation of the spurt in mill construction is no longer adequate. The question still remains: Why were so many new mills built during the period of the embargo?

A possible answer is that men of capital, prevented by the embargo from the investment of their funds in maritime trade, turned their attention to cotton manufacturing, known to have been prospering at the time the embargo was imposed and to be an enterprise not directly affected by the Embargo Act. Regardless of who provided the capital, however, the practice established by the millowners of fixing the price of yarn probably served to give to the business an appearance of greater potential profit than was actually the case. Almy and Brown, as the original price-setters, had found little difficulty in persuading other millowners to maintain the stated price. The manufacturers "were apparently of one accord in the conviction that agreement was a better method of securing maximum profits than competition."[24] When millowners deviated from the fixed price, Almy and Brown urged them to reconsider, usually with success. When under the stress of the embargo some firms were disposed to lower the price of yarn to conform with the lower price of raw cotton, Almy and Brown argued successfully for adherence to the fixed price. They were sure that once the embargo was taken off, raw cotton would rise "nearly double its present price," and should the millowners now lower the price of yarn, "it would not be an easy matter to again raise it . . ."[25]

Those who built the new mills in 1808 and 1809 knew that the business, prosperous before the embargo, now enjoyed the benefit of a decline in the price of raw cotton at a time when the price of yarn remained constant. They must have concluded, therefore, that under conditions imposed by the embargo cotton manufacturing was showing unusually high profits. This fictitious appearance of abnormal prosperity probably induced mechanics to build spinning mills on their own account, and it may have persuaded merchants whose trade was adversely affected by the embargo to make small investments in the cotton manufacturing industry. The newcomers, of course, were unaware of the fact that the Almy and Brown warehouse was filled with unsold yarn. Nor did they realize that the high price of yarn was the result of price fixing rather than the operation of the law of supply and demand.

Nevertheless, it appears that many of the new mills, built under the illusion of prosperity (though the business was actually in deep depression), were able to surmount the problems posed by the embargo, nonintercourse, Macon's Bill No. 2, and war itself. While no categorical answer to the question of how success was achieved can be given for the industry generally, the manner in which Almy and Brown eventually met the crisis confronting them when the embargo destroyed the principal market they had developed for their cotton yarn is a matter of record; and since their leadership had been accepted in other respects, it seems likely that they also pointed the way in this instance. What they did was to develop a new market and to venture into the production of cotton cloth on a large scale, in addition to yarn.

COTTON CLOTH FOR THE WESTERN MARKET

Although before the embargo the principal market for their products had been the region east of the Hudson, Almy and Brown had sent substantial amounts of yarn to their agents in Philadelphia and Baltimore. In 1806 they had sold through Philadelphia some 16 per cent of the total product, with 8 per cent going to Baltimore. In 1808 they disposed of 30 per cent through Philadelphia and 14 per cent through Baltimore. Each year thereafter the proportion shipped to Philadelphia increased. In 1814 they sold 67 per cent of their total output in the Quaker City; in 1819 the proportion increased to 82 per cent. Almy and Brown thought that their entire production for the year would not provide "half the amount that may be sold" in that city. So largely did the Philadelphia market absorb their product that when the New England demand began to revive in 1814, they were unable to meet it.[26]

Unlike coastal towns in New England, Philadelphia did not suffer economic paralysis as a result of the embargo. On the contrary, the city enjoyed a period of economic expansion characterized by the construction of new buildings and the launching of new business enterprises. Though an important center of maritime trade, it was also, in the days before the Erie Canal, the leading distributing point for trade to the rapidly growing population of the trans-Allegheny region. In this period of prosperity the city itself provided an expanding outlet for the cotton goods of Almy and Brown. It is apparent that by far the greater part of the goods shipped by Almy and Brown to Philadelphia were sent over the mountains to supply the people living in the Ohio Valley.

The expanding market for their wares that Almy and Brown found in the West occasioned an important change in the organization of their business. Originally, they had been mere spinners of cotton yarn, giving only the slightest attention to the weaving of the yarn into cloth. But a demand for cotton cloth that quickly developed in the West—whether the consequence of the unavailability of British cottons or of purely native causes—forced them to combine weaving with the spinning of yarn. "Our shirtings," said Almy and Brown, "when they become known by wearing them are preferred to the India or English, being so much more durable."[27]

Since weaving in the United States was still done on hand looms, it was well suited to household production, as spinning with the Arkwright water frame was not. It was in this way that the "putting-out" system entered the industry. The mills put out their yarn to weavers working in their homes, some mills having several workers. Because of faulty organization, however, the yarn was given out at irregular intervals and returned in an even less systematic fashion. Displeased with the irregularities of the putting-out system, Almy and Brown established hand looms in their mill. They were convinced that a hundred weavers working in their homes would not weave as much cloth as ten "constantly employed under the immediate inspection of a workman." In 1809 they limited their production of cloth to the amount their own workers could weave, spinning in one mill only as much yarn as could be woven on the hand looms of another mill. Thus the development of the western market not only changed the end product of Almy and Brown from yarn to cotton cloth but it also required an increase in the scale of their operations.[28]

The era of mill building ushered in by the embargo reached new heights with the war that began in 1812. In February, 1812, Almy and Brown's agent in Georgetown in the District of Columbia had reported cotton shirting and sheetings as "very unsaleable." A month later he wrote that the "alarm" of war with England had increased the demand for domestic goods. Those mills like Almy and Brown's that bought upland cotton at bargain prices just prior to the war made enormous profits when their cloth sold in Philadelphia at high prices, thanks to the continued demand of the western market. It has long since been pointed out that the mills built during the war years were better able to survive the postwar depression than those erected during the time of the embargo. Although this fact has occasioned much speculation, the explanation seems to be the actual profits of wartime as contrasted with the illusion of profits during the embargo.[29]

The peak of mill building came in the early part of 1814. By then the price of raw cotton had fallen, the western market was still insatiable, and Almy and Brown's product was engaged well into the future. At this juncture the partners directed their agents to sell their stock at lower prices if necessary. In late August banks in Philadelphia suspended payments, followed the next day by those in New York. In December, 1814, came the Treaty of Ghent, bringing the war to an official conclusion.

What were the prospects of cotton manufacturing in time of peace? In reply to this question Almy and Brown expressed their belief that the profits of the business would be greatly diminished, not by the mere fact of peace but because of the multiplication of mills all over the country. The business, however, would be "like all others, it will regulate itself . . ." Some by virtue of their superior knowledge and experience would make a profit, "when others must be losing money."[30]

The continuing growth of the western market, served through Philadelphia and Baltimore, necessitated a change in the technique of marketing cotton goods. In the early days of the industry, when the principal market was in the coastal towns of New England, it had been the practice of Almy and Brown to place their product on consignment in the hands of retail storekeepers, who sold the yarn on a commission. When, however, the West became the chief outlet for their wares, they found it difficult, if not impossible, to discover local shopkeepers of known repute to whom they could ship consignments. They were compelled, therefore, to use wholesale commission houses located in Philadelphia and Baltimore, the two chief distributing centers for western trade. In Philadelphia their commission agent was Elijah Waring, who owned a "domestic warehouse" and dealt only in "domestic" or American goods. He distributed their yarn and cloth to the city's retail stores, to merchant weavers in the vicinity, to shopkeepers in the small towns of the area, and to the expanding market over the mountains. Almy and Brown found it more convenient, more economical in time and money, and safer to channel their shipments through this one house than to deal with numerous retail traders who were likely to be delinquent in making remittance for goods consigned to them.[31]

Philadelphia retained her pre-eminence as distributor of cotton goods as long as her superior contact with the western market remained unchallenged. After 1820 Baltimore increasingly shared with her the trade to the Southwest. With the opening of the Erie Canal in 1825 Philadelphia was destined to lose the trade of the Northwest to New York.

Among those in Rhode Island who turned their attention to cotton manufacturing because of the dislocations in maritime trade occasioned by the embargo was the firm of Brown and Ives. So absorbed had Nicholas Brown and Thomas P. Ives been in commercial ventures and so successful had they been in their trade with Batavia and Canton that they had never been tempted to invest any of their funds in the new industry that for years had engrossed the time and energy of Moses Brown, his son Obadiah, and his son-in-law William Almy. Once Samuel Slater had perfected the water frame of Arkwright, the firm of Almy and Brown had made themselves the recognized leaders of the cotton spinning business of Rhode Island, even of southern New England. To the year 1808 Brown and Ives had been a living proof of the dictum that success in maritime commerce tends to discourage an interest in manufacturing. Beginning with the embargo, however, their behavior was evidence that the forces that disrupt sea-borne trade turn men's thoughts in the direction of manufacturing. Writing early in 1809 with respect to a young cotton manufacturing company in the Blackstone Valley, Brown and Ives remarked that "the increasing embarrassments attending Commerce" were their "only motive for taking an Interest in this New Establishment."[32]

The new establishment was the Blackstone Manufacturing Company, organized in 1808 and located on the Blackstone River in the town of Minden in Worcester County, Massachusetts. The company was a copartnership of Samuel Butler and Son; Samuel Butler, Jr.; Seth Wheaton; and Brown and Ives, all of Providence. With a capital of $150,000, representing 200 shares assessed at $750 a share, it may well have been the most heavily capitalized cotton spinning company yet organized in the country. Samuel Butler and Son and Brown and Ives each subscribed $50,000, while the other two partners each invested $25,000.[33] Brown and Ives paid $30,000 of their share in cash, most of it between September, 1808, and April, 1811, in fifty installments of $500 each at the rate of two or three payments a month. Their method of contributing capital to be invested in the new company illustrates the manner in which funds accumulated in the maritime trade were usually transferred to manufacturing.[34]

Although the mill when it began operations in November, 1809, was equipped to drive but 5,000 of the 10,000 spindles originally planned for, its capacity was exceeded by only one other New England mill—that of Almy, Brown, and Slater at Slatersville, Rhode Island.[35] The initial product of the Blackstone Manufacturing Company mill was cotton yarn. But emulating the example of Almy and Brown, the proprietors of the new company increasingly sought to funnel their goods into the western market through a wholesale distributor in Philadelphia. Just as the demands of the western trade had forced Almy and Brown to arrange for the weaving of the yarn into cloth, so the same western demand compelled the Blackstone Manufacturing Company proprietors to concern themselves with weaving. Brown and Ives therefore became the instrument for the establishment in Philadelphia of a wholesale commission house that would, it was hoped, sell the goods of the company and of other new Rhode Island cotton mills to the people residing beyond the mountains.

On December 11, 1813, there appeared a printed circular announcing the formation of the firm of Gilman and Ammidon, a commercial house in Philadelphia, whose purpose was to vend "Domestic Manufactures" and to transact business on commission. Benjamin Ives Gilman, cousin of Thomas P. Ives, had been one of the shareholders in the Ohio Company and one of the original settlers at Marietta, Ohio, where he had succeeded in business, among his interests being shipbuilding. Otis Ammidon, once a business associate of Jonathan Russell, soon became one of the commissioners to negotiate the Treaty of Ghent. The circular announcing the new house was at pains to remark upon Gilman's many years of residence at Marietta, which had enabled him to acquire a "general knowledge" of the "wants of the people of the Western Country" that would prove "highly important" to the young firm. For proof of their standing in the world of business the two partners referred interested parties to the great Boston mercantile house of James and Thomas H. Perkins, to Loomis and Bethune of New York, and to Brown and Ives of Providence.[36] The last-named firm lost no time in telling other business houses that the new establishment had their support and confidence. The partners had gone into business not only with the moral support and encouragement of Brown and Ives but, perhaps, with their financial assistance as well.

Just as Brown and Ives were instrumental in the establishment of the house of Gilman and Ammidon, so did they use their influence to secure patronage for the new firm. Writing to millowners in Taunton, Massachusetts, they expressed the hope that the firm "may have your patronage & any facilities in our power will cheerfully be given."[37] It was not simply fortuitous that within a few weeks Gilman and Ammidon had received consignments, some of them very large, from eighteen of the new cotton mills in Rhode Island, including, of course, the Blackstone Manufacturing Company.[38] This was clearly the result of exertion on the part of Brown and Ives, who of their own volition inserted in all Rhode Island newspapers advertisements of Gilman and Ammidon's firm, an act that the latter characterized as "very satisfactory, and . . . in unison with [your] every other act towards us."[39]

Before Gilman and Ammidon were able to sell and collect the

money for the cotton goods consigned to them, the manufacturers in Rhode Island, in order to maintain liquid assets, were in need of a certain amount of cash on account of their consignments. The partners in Philadelphia found remittance difficult, partly because the suspension of specie payments early in the war by banks outside of New England had made money scarce over much of the country. When the millowners began to press for advances, Brown and Ives were in a difficult situation. While helping their protegés in Philadelphia, they could not be insensible of the fact that their own urging had prompted the millowners to consign their goods to Gilman and Ammidon. Brown and Ives had to advance to the manufacturers the funds that the Philadelphia firm itself was unable to remit. Writing to Gilman and Ammidon, they offered "to pay to your corrispondants on account of their consignments, such sums as they may require" to the extent of "ten or fifteen thousand Dollars." They knew no more effectual way of helping their friends than by "making advances at this time when money is becoming scarce & the difficulty of drawing it from the Southward increases."[40]

Accordingly, Brown and Ives advised Gilman and Ammidon that Caleb Greene, agent of the Manchester Company, "called on us this day to inform us of his intention to send forward to you . . . 12 Cases of Goods, amounting to about Eight Thousand Dollars, on which he asks an advance of Four Thousand Dollars . . . which we have promised to give him . . ."[41] This is fairly typical of the manner in which Brown and Ives in trying and uncertain times helped both Rhode Island millowners and their wholesale commission house in Philadelphia to remain in business.

Gilman and Ammidon developed a wide market for Rhode Island cotton goods in the West, but their ability to sell to their customers in that area always outran their ability to collect from them. They continued, therefore, to receive financial assistance from Brown and Ives, not only of the sort outlined above but also in more direct ways. As credit became tighter in 1818, they asked the Providence house to "lend us your acceptance for Ten thousand dollars at Ninety days," a request that was readily granted.[42] They received from Brown and Ives a credit of another $10,000 at the Bank of North America in Philadelphia.[43] For Benjamin Ives Gilman, Jr., Brown and Ives negotiated bills for $10,000, which they forwarded to him in checks on New York and Philadelphia banks. When suspension of payment by banks in Ohio and Kentucky became imminent later in 1818, increasing the doubt that Gilman and Ammidon would ever be able to collect from their debtors, Nicholas Brown made a special visit to Philadelphia, where he agreed to furnish $20,000 to relieve the pressure on the wholesale house.[44] Such measures, however, could only postpone the inevitable. The truth was that Gilman and Ammidon had greatly overextended themselves in the western market. As of October 15, 1821, 138 individuals and firms in Ohio, Kentucky, Indiana, Tennessee, Missouri, and Alabama owed them $141,000 on account of domestic goods.[45] They were irretrievably ruined. In referring to their appalling debt to Brown and Ives, Benjamin Ives Gilman expressed the vain hope that the principal and simple interest could somehow be paid ultimately. Aside from his assigning to them some ten shares of stock and a small tract of land in Marietta, Ohio, nothing seems to have been done to extinguish the debt.

Great as the debt of Gilman and Ammidon to Brown and Ives was, their obligations to the other Rhode Island cotton millowners, whose goods they had sold on consignment in the country beyond the mountains, were even greater. The number of mills that closed in the crisis brought about by the failure of the Philadelphia house is unknown, of course. It appears not unlikely, however, that advances of Brown and Ives, amounting to more than $75,000, whether made directly to the manufacturers or indirectly through Gilman and Ammidon, meant the difference between ruin and survival for some of the Rhode Island millowners.

The wholesale house of Gilman and Ammidon was not the only medium through which domestic goods from Rhode Island mills entered the trans-Allegheny market. In 1816 Brown and Ives sent Ray Clarke of East Greenwich, Rhode Island, to Kentucky, where he was to purchase tobacco for shipment to New Orleans, to be shipped on board their vessels to various ports in Europe. Since the buying of the tobacco was a seasonal occupation, it occurred to Brown and Ives and the other owners of the Blackstone Manufacturing Company that Clarke might utilize some of his time to place the cotton goods of the company in the hands of merchants who would sell them on commission. In this way Clarke secured the services of mercantile houses in Louisville, Shelbyville, Lexington, and Frankfort, which not only sold the goods but succeeded in collecting the proceeds. Once the funds were in his hands, however, Clarke had to face the problem of remitting to his principals in Providence. He was authorized to invest the Blackstone Manufacturing Company funds in tobacco for shipment to New Orleans, from which place remittance could be made in several different ways.[46] When John Corlis, who was then living in Bourbon County, Kentucky, succeeded Clarke as tobacco buyer for Brown and Ives in that state, he also inherited the job of selling the wares of the Blackstone Manufacturing Company and investing the proceeds in tobacco for shipment down the Mississippi River.[47]

The spinning mills, which were the distinguishing feature of Rhode Island cotton manufacturing, not only multiplied in the state after the imposition of the embargo in 1807 but spread into southern Massachusetts, eastern Connecticut, and the Mohawk Valley of New York. These new mills were established sometimes by the millowners of Rhode Island, sometimes by mechanics who had learned the business in Rhode Island mills. As early as 1818 Brown and Ives, together with Ephraim and William Bowen of Providence, were the owners of a cotton "factory" at Newport, in Herkimer County, New York. The building of the mill had cost $8,465.27. In 1824 the owners valued the establishment at $10,000. The property included a building of stone with 765 spindles, a stone store, a blacksmith shop, twenty acres of land, and a water privilege capable of enlargement.[48]

INTEGRATING THE COTTON-MANUFACTURING SYSTEM

The first twenty-four years of cotton manufacturing in the United States constitute what is properly known as the Rhode Island phase of the industry. The business had not only begun in the state but its expansion, by means of multiplication of the spinning mill, had been confined to the state, the adjacent areas of Massachusetts and Connecticut, and the Mohawk Valley. In this development the Brown family had played a conspicuous role. The work of Moses Brown had come to the attention of Samuel Slater, who with the patronage of Moses, built the Arkwright water frame so necessary for successful spinning of cotton. It was Almy and Brown who developed the first market for cotton yarn and became the recognized leaders of the business. It was they again who pioneered in new markets beyond the Alleghenies. Prominent among the new millowners during the period of the embargo were Brown and Ives, who sponsored the Philadelphia house of Gilman and Ammidon. This firm in turn had made the domestic goods of Rhode Island a familiar article of trade in the West and Southwest. Ironical though it was, Gilman and Ammidon suffered bankruptcy because they had been so successful in the sale of cotton goods in the trans-Appalachian region.

Throughout its Rhode Island phase cotton manufacturing had remained true to its prototype, the original spinning mill of Almy, Brown, and Slater. A small unit requiring no great outlay of capital, the spinning mill was concerned with but two of the stages in the manufacture of cotton cloth—carding and spinning. For years the millowners had paid no attention to weaving. Only reluctantly had they put yarn out for weaving or installed hand looms in their mills. Only with the western demand for cloth, rather than mere yarn, had weaving become a primary concern of the manufacturers. Even then the business was still unintegrated in the absence of the power loom. American cotton manufacturing remained a faithful reproduction of the English system that Samuel Slater had brought to Rhode Island.

After Slater's departure from England the perfecting of the power loom made weaving in that country a factory process; but spinning, weaving, and finishing were done in separate factories, usually under separate ownership and management. It remained, therefore, for an American to conceive the idea of integrating cotton manufacturing by bringing the successive operations together under one roof and one management. This concept was the brain child of Francis Cabot Lowell of Boston. Having amassed a comfortable fortune in trade while still a comparatively young man, he was of the opinion that the lucrative maritime commerce of pre-embargo days would now return to England. In 1810 he went to England, where for a season he was privileged to indulge the supposedly innocent curiosity of a successful Boston merchant in the intricacies of cotton manufacturing, including the workings of the power loom. As with the water frame, British law forbade the export of the power loom and of the men who could build it. But the law did not cover the case of a gentleman visitor from another country, capable of carrying home in his brain a blueprint of the loom.

Once back in Boston, Lowell proceeded to implement his plan for integrated cotton manufacturing. This, in turn, involved two principal problems: raising a sufficient capital and finding a mechanic who could build a power loom. Many men of means hesitated to risk their money in so hazardous an undertaking. Even Lowell's Cabot relatives, their fingers singed in the unsuccessful experiment at Beverly in 1787, refused to invest in another venture in cotton manufacturing. Only with some difficulty did Lowell procure the subscription of the first $100,000 of the capital stock of the Boston Manufacturing Company, through the medium of which he hoped to introduce the integrated system of cotton manufacturing.[49] Even when he had the necessary funds in hand, the success of the venture depended upon Lowell's ability to produce a power loom; and this, in turn, depended upon the skill of the Yankee mechanic Paul Moody in translating Lowell's drawings of the English loom into a workable machine. But the new power loom was a success, and the new system of manufacturing began at Waltham on the Charles in 1814. At one stroke Lowell had scored a mechanical triumph and founded a profitable business enterprise. Within some seven years the young company paid in dividends to its shareholders a sum in excess of its original capital stock.

The financial success of the new establishment dispelled all lingering doubts of the Boston mercantile community in regard to the future of this new type of manufacturing. Their eagerness to invest guaranteed

ample funds for expansion of the business. The result was the building
of a new town named Lowell near the falls of the Merrimack, north of
Boston. Here those who had achieved success at Waltham established
the Merrimack Company to carry on the integrated form of cotton manufacturing. Joined by other mercantile families of Boston, they had
organized at Lowell by 1831 the Hamilton, Appleton, Lowell, Lawrence, Suffolk, Tremont, and Middlesex companies, each with capital
ranging from $600,000 to $1,000,000. Representing for that time an
enormous transfer of capital from sea-borne trade to manufacturing,
these new companies were closely patterned after the original model
at Waltham, and all employed the type of machinery used there; and
since the rights to this machinery were protected by patents, the owners of the new plants built their own textile machinery at their Saco-
Lowell shops. This small, compact, interrelated group of men thus became town builders, owners and dispensers of water-power rights, real
estate promoters and operators, builders of machinery, and manufacturers of cotton goods. When their mills had outgrown the water-power
potential of the Merrimack at Lowell, they promoted the new town of
Lawrence, where more mills were to be built.[50]

For more than twenty years these great companies continued to be
owned and controlled by the small group of men who had founded them.
In this period the business was enormously profitable, paying dividends that averaged about 16 per cent a year. After 1846, however, the
ownership of the stock became more dispersed, and a decline in the
dividend rate followed. The new stockholders charged that although
ownership was now more decentralized, control and management remained in the hands of the original group, who contrived to milk
off the profits by appointing their sons and sons-in-law to highly paid
executive posts in the various companies. Whatever the facts may have
been on this disputed point, there can be no doubt that Francis Cabot
Lowell's idea of integrated cotton manufacturing had achieved a notable success. The concentration of capital in the great companies at
the town of Lowell was unprecedented for that time; and few types of
enterprise yielded greater profits over a span of years. Lowell was a man
with a big idea, an innovator, who had conceived a new and better
way of manufacturing cotton cloth.

The introduction of the power loom protected by patent right, first
at Waltham, then at Lowell, enabled the cotton textile industry in the
Boston area to get off to a fast start; and in a short time Massachusetts
supplanted Rhode Island as the leader in this field of manufacturing.
Without the power loom the long-term prospects of the millowners in
Rhode Island would have been well-nigh hopeless. The greater economy
of large-scale production of cotton goods in the integrated mills would

surely have doomed the cotton-spinning mill to extinction. From this fate the millowners could be saved in one of two ways: either a Rhode Islander with a mechanical bent could visit England, there to master the intricacies of the power loom; or an immigrant from Britain could carry the secret of the loom in his head to Rhode Island shores.

In 1815 William Gilmore, a machinist from Glasgow, arrived in Boston. He had acquired a knowledge of the power loom and dressing machine in Scotland. On a visit to Rhode Island, Gilmore was taken to the town of Smithfield, where ten years before Almy and Brown and Samuel Slater had built a new mill. Located in the village of Slatersville, this mill was under the superintendence of John Slater, the younger brother of Samuel. Gilmore offered to build looms for power weaving at Slatersville, stipulating that he would demand no compensation for his time and labor if his looms should prove a failure. John Slater is said to have looked with favor upon the proposal but was overruled by Samuel, who thought it unwise to make an investment in the power loom at a time when the outlook was so unpromising. A similar proposal made to the Lyman Cotton Manufacturing Company in Rhode Island elicited a more favorable response. Daniel Lyman immediately entered into a contract with Gilmore for the building of a power loom. The machine constructed by Gilmore was essentially the same as that invented and first put into successful operation by William Horrocks of Stockport, England. Although at first called the "Scotch" loom because the builder had come from Scotland, the machine is known historically as the Gilmore loom. Refusing to patent the loom, Judge Lyman made its secrets freely known to other millowners, thereby earning for himself an admirable place in the history of cotton manufacturing. The manufacturers in turn expressed their appreciation of the services of William Gilmore through subscriptions to a fund of $1,500 for his benefit in the spring of 1817.[51]

The chief difference between the Gilmore and the Waltham loom was that the former used a crank, the latter a cam to effect the rise and fall of the harness. Although the cam conferred an advantage upon the Waltham loom, Gilmore's machine offered the countervailing advantage of greater simplicity and lower cost. It sold at $70, whereas the cost of the Waltham loom was near $300.[52]

In the words of Samuel Batchelder, "There was thus established two different systems or *schools* of manufacturing, one of which might be denominated the *Rhode Island,* and the other the *Waltham* system." One employed the live spindle, the other the dead spindle, one the "Scotch dresser, the other the Waltham dresser; one the crank-loom, the other the cam-loom."[53]

The refusal of Judge Daniel Lyman to take out a patent for the power loom of William Gilmore made it freely available to all Rhode Island millowners. The latter took advantage of the opportunity thus offered them with varying degrees of alacrity. Ten years after the appearance of the new loom only a third of the Rhode Island mills had adopted power weaving. Of the others, some had integrated the business but used hand looms in their mills, while others continued as mere spinners of yarn. The comparative slowness of the mill proprietors to adopt the new machine has been made the occasion for some rather severe strictures upon the Rhode Island businessman of the day. "This cautiousness," says one writer, "represented a weakening of the daring sense of risk taking which had characterized the entrepreneurial spirit" so evident in privateering and slave trading, in the opening of the East Indian trade of the Browns in 1787, and in the "establishment of cotton manufacturing itself," also with the aid of the Browns.[54] The author of these critical comments, however, takes some of the sting out of them by remarking that the millowners, in the absence of the power loom, had developed the putting-out system, under which they placed their yarn in the hands of cottagers who wove it on hand looms in their homes. The putting-out system thus led to a vested interest in the *status quo* and to resistance to change to the power loom. This probably explains a good deal of the caution of the mill proprietors, but one may well doubt that it tells the whole story.

Among the cotton manufacturers of Rhode Island at this time, of course, were Brown and Ives, co-owners of the Blackstone Manufacturing Company. They had not been attracted to the business by the illusion of unusually high profits prevailing at the time of the embargo, which had induced many men to build spinning mills. They had stated with the utmost frankness that only the embarrassment to maritime trade had led them to invest $50,000 in the new venture. Then and for years thereafter they regarded sea-borne commerce as their first concern. They were venturing but a small capital in a cotton mill. They confidently expected their commerce to revive, once world conditions had returned to normal. Before the Treaty of Ghent officially ended the war between the United States and England, they returned to the China trade. Until 1821 they pursued their traffic with Canton and Batavia on a scale and with a degree of success only slightly inferior to the flush times of 1800–1807. True, they invested a few thousand dollars in a cotton mill at Newport, New York, but they still were not committed to manufacturing. They were merchants and traders with only an incidental interest in cotton textiles. Well might they therefore hesitate to invest a substantial sum in power looms.

The turning point in the East India trade of Brown and Ives came in 1821. From that time the danger signals were increasingly apparent. For another fifteen years they would continue as merchants and traders but on a smaller scale and with diminishing success. The long term of their maritime decline and decay would run parallel to their gradually increasing concern with cotton manufacturing. In 1822 they were using power looms of the best construction in their mill at Newport, New York. A short time later, they and their merchant associates in the Blackstone Manufacturing Company installed power looms in the mills of that enterprise. In the case of the proprietors of the Blackstone Manufacturing Company, therefore, it was a prior commitment to maritime trade, not a vested interest in the putting-out system, that delayed their adoption of the Gilmore power loom.

The Blackstone Manufacturing Company appears to have been a financial success from the beginning. In 1813 Edward Carrington purchased a small interest at a figure indicating an increase of some 46 per cent in the estimated worth of the company. The following year the original investment had more than doubled in value.[55] Although shares declined in value in the depression of 1816, they nevertheless continued to sell at a figure substantially above their original cost. In July, 1821, the company paid a dividend equivalent to 13 per cent on the original investment of $150,000; and the proprietors now estimated the value of the business at $380,000.[56] In 1831 the company declared a dividend of $250 a share, a figure that they doubled the following year. For 1832, therefore, Brown and Ives received a payment of $40,833.33, representing a return of 80 per cent on their original investment of $50,000, or of 67 per cent on the shares they then held.[57] The profits of the company in these years more than held their own with those of the great companies at Lowell.

The high rate of return on their investment in the Blackstone Manufacturing Company not only proved satisfying to Brown and Ives but it encouraged them to extend their holdings in the field of cotton textiles. They and Holden Borden rented a mill building in Fall River, Massachusetts, which they proceeded to equip with the necessary machinery.[58] For a number of years the two parties shared equally the operation of this enterprise, known as the Massasoit Manufacturing Company.

More indicative, however, of the growing interest of Brown and Ives in cotton manufacturing was their decision in 1831 to organize a new company. Acquiring land on Scott Pond, in the town of Smithfield, Rhode Island, they planned to establish there the Lonsdale Water Power Company. From August, 1831, to June, 1833, they paid out some $65,000 in more than sixty separate payments ranging from $100 to $6,000, as the building of the new mills went forward. In January, 1834, the General Assembly of Rhode Island granted a charter to a corporation to be known as the Lonsdale Company. Stock of the company was to be divided into 500 shares, each with a value of $500, owned in the following manner: Nicholas Brown, 125 shares; Thomas P. Ives, 125 shares; Moses B. Ives, 41 2/3 shares; John Carter Brown, 41 2/3 shares; Robert H. Ives, 41 2/3 shares; Walter Kelly, 41 2/3 shares; and Edward Carrington, 83 1/3 shares.[59] Edward Carrington soon sold his stock to other shareholders, leaving Walter Kelly as the one proprietor not a member of the Brown and Ives families. Long closely associated with the Browns and one-time master of the second *Ann & Hope,* Kelly became the first agent of the Lonsdale Company.

Meanwhile, Brown and Ives through financial assistance extended to other cotton millowners, found themselves in possession of a minority interest in two other cotton manufacturing companies. One of the mills built in Rhode Island in the period of the embargo was that of the Providence Manufacturing Company. Brown and Ives and others had endorsed notes of this company. Because of the postwar depression of 1816 the company had been unable to pay the notes, which amounted to some $25,000. By an agreement of January 15, 1819, the property of the company was divided among the Roger Williams Bank, John K. Pitman, and Brown and Ives, the interests of the last-named firm amounting to $5,530.[60] Brown and Ives had also made a loan to Mark Collet, one of the owners of the Hamilton Manufacturing Company in Paterson, New Jersey.[61] Before the debtor was able to liquidate the loan, a deep depression settled upon cotton manufacturing in the New Jersey city. By dint of great effort Collet managed to make a substantial payment on the loan in March, 1834; he apologized for his inability to pay more. In 1840 Brown and Ives were listed as the owners of 763 of the 4,075 shares of stock of the Hamilton Manufacturing Company, which then operated two mills, named Hope and Hamilton.[62] It is a reasonable conjecture that Collet, unable to extinguish his debt to the Providence partners, had found it necessary to assign his stock to them.

Cotton manufacturing in the United States was half a century old in 1840. One member of the Brown family, Moses, had been instrumental in the successful beginning of the industry in 1790; and his son and son-in-law, in the partnership of Almy and Brown, had largely dominated the business during its first twenty-four years. Nicholas Brown and Thomas P. Ives, representing another branch of the family, had entered the field in 1808; and by 1840 the firm of Brown and Ives was well on its way to becoming the leading cotton manufacturer in Rhode Island and indeed one of the most important in all New England.

CHAPTER 9

Private Enterprises in the Public Interest

IN the period when the Browns were expanding their maritime commerce to the Indies and to Europe, they were also directing their attention to various new enterprises in their home state and town. In these private businesses the profit motive was always present, but in each case it was complemented by the desire of the promoters to be of service to the community. Each new undertaking, into banking and insurance, into turnpike, bridge, and canal building, was to a degree in the public interest.

BANKING

Banks made their appearance in the colonies before the close of the War for Independence. The nation's first bank was the Bank of North America, which opened its doors in Philadelphia in 1781. By 1784 banks were established in both Boston and New York. These first banks were regarded as a sort of "public utility, as public blessings." Officers of the Bank of North America soon pointed with pride to its loans to the government, its aid to the Commonwealth of Pennsylvania, its part in the restoration of a sound currency, and its "support of trade and commerce." Promoters of the Massachusetts Bank thought "the proven usefulness" of the Bank of North America a convincing argument in support of their own bank project. Their bank would afford protection against usury, provide a safe place of deposit for the assets of men of means, promote the habit of punctuality among debtors, and augment the circulating medium—all in the public interest. The Bank of New York asserted that one of the essential objects of banks was that of "affording financial aid to governments in exigencies."[1]

In 1784 the *Providence Gazette* suggested that Providence should emulate the example of her larger sister cities by establishing a bank.[2]

A prime mover in this direction was John Brown.[3] But it was obvious to others that Rhode Island was not yet prepared for such a step. It was only after another experiment with paper money that the little state became ready for a sound currency. By 1791 conditions had become far more propitious for a bank. In the interim the legislature had repealed the Legal Tender Act, the state had ratified the federal Constitution, and Congress had in February, 1791, chartered the Bank of the United States.

On June 3, 1791, there appeared over the name of Brown and Francis a public notice addressed to Colonel Zephaniah Andrews, setting forth the desire of the subscribers to promote the "Interests of this town by the Establishment of a Bank." Like the promoters of the earlier banks, John Brown and his partner were stressing the public utility of a bank, although the common weal for which they were speaking was circumscribed by the boundaries of their own home town. It was the hope of John Brown that the good citizens of Providence would be so impressed with the utility of such an institution that "a Considerable Meeting of the Gentlemen" of the town would convene the following day in the courthouse "to digest a Plan the most eligible" for the formation of a bank.[4] Two weeks later the town newspaper announced that "A Bank is about to be established in this Town" with a capital of $40,000.[5]

Later in the summer of 1791 John Brown wrote to his brother Moses that "now is the Time to Finance a Bank hear." It was obvious that John's ideas were growing with every passing day. He now planned a capital of $120,000 for the bank, half in specie and half in the 6 per cent funded debt of the United States. He had gathered information on banks and banking and was forwarding to Moses the charters of the Baltimore Bank and the Bank of the United States, together with the plan of the Boston Bank. John thought that making the bank as nearly like the national bank as possible would make it more popular than any other plan. He was convinced that nothing would so greatly enhance Providence's chances of securing a branch of the national bank as the founding of "one of our own." Should Providence remain sluggish, he wrote, thereby creating the impression that the town was "of No Suffitient Consiquenc" to be entitled to a branch, it would surely be passed by.[6]

Knowing that Moses was one of the executors of the estate of Nicholas Brown, which included more than $200,000 in public securities alone, John asked how could a "Considerable part of our Worthey Deceased Brothers Securitys be put to a Better Use then in a Bank of our own." If part of the securities were sold at an advance of 12 to 15 per cent and put in a bank that would yield 10 to 12 per cent, it would be an "Object Worthy" of Moses' attention. Providence might be "Insignifficant" and "Mizarable in point of Welth" compared with the other towns having banks, but by "our Exurtions" and by "Forming a Good & Substantial Foundation for the Commertial, Manufactoral, & Macanical, Riseing Generation it may in time become no Inconsiderable Cappetell but without a Spring to promote Our Young Men in Buissiness, hear they must & will Continue to go to Such places as will Aid them with the Means of Buissiness." As a result, "all our Welth I mean the Welth as fast as Acquired in this State must be Transferd to those Other States who by their Banks promote all the Valuable Arts of Mankind."[7]

It would be hard to find a more forthright statement of the concept of the intermingling of public and private advantage to be derived from banks, even though the public with which John was concerned was limited to his own town or state. John Brown concluded his letter by suggesting that if Moses would outline the best plan that could be devised for the bank's constitution, John had no doubt that the General Assembly in its October meeting would incorporate the proprietors of the bank. Acting upon John's suggestion, Moses did formulate a plan for the bank, a plan that was to undergo substantial revision in the course of the next several weeks.

Once the bank's constitution was drafted, Moses had planned to avoid all further connection with the project. His prime concern with the bank had been the improvement of the moral tone of the business community by the promotion of "integrity and punctuality in dealing" on the part of both the debtor and creditor elements of the community. He found, however, that he could not completely dissociate himself from this important undertaking. The bank needed the support of all those who commanded the confidence of the public. Since Moses yielded to no one in the community in this respect, he was importuned to continue to lend his name and influence to the enterprise. This, with some misgiving, Moses continued to do.[8]

On August 13, 1791, the *Providence Gazette* announced that the "Scarcity of Specie for a Medium of Trade and Commerce in this Town" required the speedy "Establishment of a Bank." And it requested all those desirous of promoting the "public Welfare" in this way to meet at the courthouse for the purpose of determining the "most eligible Method" of obtaining a branch of the national bank or of establishing "an individual State Bank." On September 1 John Brown wrote to Moses that "time is Roleing on," that "Fall is Now Come," and that the "Bank . . . ought to be Soone in Motion." His ideas still expanding, John began to think in terms of a capital of $150,000, payable half in "Silver & Goald," and half in the 6 and 3 per cent funded debt of the United States. New York and Boston, John had reason to believe, would "afford Some Subscribers" if they liked the plan and had sufficient notice thereof.[9]

The *Providence Gazette* spoke out again on September 3, 1791, stating that the experience of Philadelphia, New York, Boston, and Baltimore showed the utility of well-regulated banks as instruments for the promotion of commerce and the mechanic arts. Since it was generally supposed that the town of Providence was as largely concerned with navigation as any town in the United States, considering its "numbers and wealth," it had been determined by a number of public-spirited men to open a subscription for a bank to be established in Providence with a capital of $150,000 in 500 shares of $300 each. Within a week the proposed capital had been increased to $160,000, consisting of 400 shares of $400 each.

The actual organization of the Providence Bank took place at a meeting hall on October 3, 1791, when about one hundred "Gentlemen met at the Court-House and "Choice [was] made of WELCOME ARNOLD," well-known Providence merchant, as chairman. A "Plan of a Constitution" was there presented, discussed paragraph by paragraph, altered in some minor particulars, and then unanimously adopted.[10] The preamble to the constitution affords a striking illustration of the prevailing concept of banks as public utilities: "TAUGHT by the experience of Europe and America, that well-regulated *BANKS*" were highly useful to society, "by promoting punctuality in the performance of contracts, increasing the medium of trade, facilitating the payment of taxes, preventing the exportation of specie, furnishing for it a safe deposit, and by discount rendering easy and expeditious the anticipation of funds on lawful interest," while "advancing . . . the interest of the proprietors," the subscribers engaged to take the number of shares "set against" their names.[11]

The capital stock was fixed at $250,000, consisting of 625 shares, each with a value of $400. Of this number, however, 125 shares were reserved for the United States and 50 shares for the state of Rhode Island, should either choose to avail itself of the opportunity to buy.[12] The remaining 450 shares were declared open to private subscription. So eagerly were these shares sought after that they were greatly oversubscribed. An influx of investors from Philadelphia, New York, Massachusetts, and various parts of Rhode Island subscribed a total of 1,324 shares.

The stock subscription settled, the stockholders turned their attention to the election of officers. Chosen as directors were John Brown, John Innes Clark, Jabez Bowen, Moses Brown, Welcome Arnold, Nicholas Brown, Samuel Butler, Andrew Dexter, and Thomas Lloyd Halsey. Thus John and Moses Brown, joint instigators of the movement for the bank, were now joined by their nephew Nicholas Brown, Jr., member of the house of Brown and Benson, soon to become the firm of Brown and Ives.[13] The following day the directors offered the presidency of the bank to Moses Brown. When he declined the honor, John Brown was unanimously named to the post.[14] The first payment of specie was made the next day, and five days later the bank was to be ready to receive proposals for discount. The first office of the bank was in the two rooms on the second floor of the house on the south side of the street called "Bank Lane," later to be known as Hopkins Street.

On the day of the formal organization of the bank the General Assembly of Rhode Island granted to the proprietors a charter incorporating them as the Providence Bank. As one writer has put it, "practically without amendment" the lawmakers "ratified the charter the Browns and their allies, the Ives, submitted."[15] Except in the most routine matters the charter imposed no hampering restrictions. On the other hand, certain features of the document were distinctly beneficial to the bank. The provision for limited liability induced small and cautious investors to subscribe. More significant was the privilege known as "bank process," conferred upon the bank in return for its guarantee to redeem its own notes in hard money upon demand. In its formative stage at least, the bank would need to conserve its working capital by promptly collecting all debts owed to it. Bank process was designed to enable the bank to recover its debts without recourse to litigation. When an obligation became due, officers of the bank were to notify the debtor, at the same time swearing under oath to the truth of the notice. The court then rendered judgment against the debtor, demanding payment without trial in ten days. Should the debtor disclaim the debt, however, he was entitled to the privilege of a trial. Once the debt was ten days overdue, the bank was entitled to a writ of attachment of real property upon presenting evidence of the unpaid debt.[16] In the words of a competent student of the question, "Since realty was a prerequisite for admission to the rank of freeman in Rhode Island, a status conferring both political and legal rights, the bank's ability to go directly to real property without first attaching personalty represented an important safeguard" for the bank.[17] Bank process became even more effective when in 1807 the General Assembly removed the ten-day period of waiting, thus allowing immediate attachment of real property.

Bank process, an institution peculiar to Rhode Island, has attracted considerable attention from those who have concerned themselves with the history of early American banking. Until recently, such writers have regarded bank process as a device intended solely to safeguard the interests of the bank as a private business enterprise. A recent writer, however, has interpreted the process as a "legal institution . . . predicated on the conceptions of banks as public affairs, of punctuality as a virtue, needing special protection, and of bank directors as semi-public officials."[18] Thus construed, the theory of bank process becomes part and parcel of the philosophy that conceived of early American banks as public utilities, designed quite as much for the welfare of the community, national, state, or local, as for the profit and advantage of those who owned and controlled them.

Although ownership of the bank's stock was in the hands of some 138 subscribers with average holdings of $4,000 each, neither this fact nor the enjoyment by small shareholders of voting rights out of all proportion to their ownership threatened the control of the small group of original promoters. On July 7, 1792, Nicholas Brown made the last quarterly payment of 6 per cent stock on ninety-seven shares amounting to $38,800, somewhat more than 20 per cent of the total capital of $180,000.[19] Assuming that John Brown, Moses Brown, Welcome Arnold, and one or two others had subscribed in roughly the same proportion as Nicholas, this handful of men must have owned a large majority of the stock.

It was still the hope of the bank's promoters that a branch of the Bank of the United States might be established in Providence, in which case the bank they had just organized might be merged with it. To this end John Brown had urged Benjamin Bourne, congressman from Rhode Island, to try to persuade the directors to locate the branch in Providence. While awaiting a decision on the branch bank, John Brown devised a plan that promised to be of substantial benefit to the Providence Bank. Through Representative Bourne, Alexander Hamilton, Secretary of the Treasury, was induced to direct customs collectors in Rhode Island to deposit in the bank all customs receipts collected in the state and to accept the notes of the bank in payment of tariff duties, the bank being subject to the payment of all government drafts on sight. The importance of this measure, which was instituted but a few weeks after the bank had opened its doors, before stock subscriptions had been paid and when deposits had not had time to grow, is apparent. It is small wonder that the *Providence Gazette* regarded this as merely the most recent example of the "Wisdom and Patriotism" of Alexander Hamilton. And how could this manifestation of the great man's blessing upon the Providence Bank venture fail to inspire confidence in that enterprise?

The *Gazette* thought "This Arrangement of the Secretary," besides aid-ing "mercantile and other Business," must give "the Notes [of the Bank] a general Circulation."[20]

Nevertheless, this arrangement within a year involved the bank's president, John Brown, in a somewhat difficult situation. In late Octo-ber, 1792, customs officers, including William Channing of Newport, appeared at John's counting house, saying that the Secretary of the Treas-ury had asked them to "apply to the Directors of the Bank" to ascertain "the State it was in, and weither the publick Deposits" were safe, which John admitted gave him a "Little Alarm." When John asked his visi-tors if they wished to know whether the bank's vault was secure against thieves and robbers, he was told that "Some Melishus Information" had been given to the Secretary, thus giving him some concern as to whether the public money was secure against mishandling by bank officials. John thereupon assembled the bank directors and invited his visitors to be present at the meeting. At the meeting Mr. Channing "Intro-duced the Buissiness by Reading a paragraph of Mr. Hambletons Letter" in reference to "Information of the Deranged State" of the bank com-ing from "Such a Respectable Quarter" that he felt it his "Duty to have the Matter . . . Inquired into by the Gentlemen aforesaid," who were to withdraw the public deposits if they were found unsafe in the bank. Channing refused to let the bank directors present read "Mr. Hamble-ton's" letter, but John thought that he would allow Moses Brown to see it. From this point Channing and his associates dealt with Moses, "in whose impartiality and honesty they apparently had the utmost confi-dence."[21] Although there is no record of the discussion that Moses had with the visitors, he evidently dispelled doubts they may have had as to the soundness of the bank, since Hamilton later acknowledged that he had been incorrectly informed as to its allegedly "Deranged State."[22] The first Bank of the United States, however, did not see fit to establish a branch at either Providence or Newport, and the directors' hope of a merger with that institution was not realized.

John Brown's refusal to allow his visitors to examine the books of the bank, coupled with his remark that their request had given him a little alarm, could be taken to mean that perhaps he felt the affairs of the bank could not stand close scrutiny. Yet Hamilton's admission that his inquiry was occasioned by misinformation would seem to indi-cate that John knew he had nothing to conceal.

This incident assumes a larger significance when it is considered in the light of John Brown's own belief as to the source of the malicious information that had come to Hamilton's attention. In writing to Moses about the visiting delegates from the Secretary of the Treasury,

John refers to the designs of gentlemen at Newport against the Providence Bank that made it impossible for him to allow the business of the bank to be fully laid open to Mr. Channing. In these words John appears to imply that the inquiry stemmed from jealousy of the Providence Bank on the part of the business and mercantile community at Newport, of which William Channing was a prominent member. At another point in the same letter to Moses, John became more direct and more explicit, saying that "the Information to the Secretary" most likely went from some place not more than thirty miles distant. This pointed and obvious reference to Newport indicates that in the mind of John Brown the "malicious and slanderous attack" upon the Providence Bank was merely another episode in the long-standing rivalry between Newport and Providence.[23] Once far more important than Providence, Newport had consistently resented the fact that her rival, largely upon the initiative of the Browns, had become the fifth town in the United States to establish a local bank. If by planting the seed of doubt and suspicion in the mind of Alexander Hamilton there could be set in motion a chain of developments leading to the collapse of the bank in Providence, Newport would not only settle a score with her rival but also improve her chances of securing a bank of her own.

With this crisis behind it, the Providence Bank quickly became an institution of importance in the expanding business life of Providence. Although John Brown, in promoting it, had stressed its public utility rather than the profit motive of the founders, the bank was profitable from the first. Stock soon sold at a premium, and dividends during the first decade ranged from 6 to 10 per cent. But while the bank was returning a satisfactory profit to its shareholders, John Brown, its president, did not allow the citizens of Providence to forget the benefits he believed it had brought to the community. The *Providence Gazette* for December 5, 1795, carried a statement over his name, pointing out that the bank had supported its "Credit equal to any Bank whatever," fostered punctuality in the payment of debts, increased public confidence in its note issues through prompt redemption in specie, regenerated all business transactions from "Barter Traffic" to a more "agreeable Cash Trade," and hastened the day when the laborer could be paid his "just Due" in specie or bank paper, which was always redeemable in specie upon demand. The bank, together with the "present general Government," had been the means of the "rapid Increase of this Town" and the revenue of the port of Providence to the point where "the last Quarter's Impost has nearly equalled three Times that of the whole Year, when the Bank was established." To extend the benefits of the institution the directors, finding "the present Capital insufficient," had decided to increase the capital fund from $180,000 to $250,000. One week later the paper reported that the increase had been formally voted.

For the next half-century and more the Browns and Iveses wielded great influence in the affairs of the bank and operated it in close co-operation with their far-flung business enterprises. In the 1820's Thomas P. Ives was president of the bank; in the next decade his son Moses Brown Ives also occupied the post.

As banks in Rhode Island increased in number and as profits continued to be large with high discount rates on commercial and industrial paper, the popular suspicion of financial corporations began to express itself in the form of a demand that the legislature impose a tax upon the capital stock of banks. Such a tax had been levied in 1805 only to be repealed in the face of general noncompliance. In 1822, however, a new and higher tax was imposed.[24] Coming shortly after the decision in the Dartmouth College case in which John Marshall had declared a charter to be a contract whose obligation a state could not impair, banks in Rhode Island contended that the tax was unconstitutional. The charter of the Providence Bank contained no stipulation on the part of the state that it would not impose such a tax nor any reservation of the right to do so. Probably as a result of an opinion by Chancellor James Kent, legal and constitutional luminary, the Providence Bank brought suit to test the validity of the tax. Before the Supreme Court of the United States the bank argued that if the state could impose a tax, it might tax so heavily as to render the franchise of no value, thereby destroying the institution. The bank further contended that the tax was inconsistent with the charter and was implicitly renounced in granting it. The Supreme Court in its decision, however, held that the taxing power was essential to the existence of government and that the relinquishment of this power was not to be assumed.[25]

Between 1820 and 1836, when the overseas trade of the state was shrinking and when manufacturing was stabilizing after its earlier expansion, the number of banks in Rhode Island doubled, while capital, loans, and circulation increased threefold. Various local banking crises revealed the speculative character of many banking enterprises. In the early 1830's popular hostility to banks in Rhode Island, together with the controversy over the second Bank of the United States and the agitation for "free banking," combined to destroy the generally privileged position of banks.

In Rhode Island popular suspicion of banks led in 1836 to the appointment of a commission to investigate complaints of excessive interest charges by the banks. The best known of the commission members was Thomas Wilson Dorr, soon to be the leader of Dorr's Rebellion.

Although the commission members revealed no conspicuous weakness in the structure of banking within the state, they were able to document the charge of usury. By a combination of devices banks were able to exact interest payments as high as 18 per cent. So profitable had banking become that only four of some sixty banks in the state paid dividends of less than 6 per cent.

Notwithstanding the basic soundness of Rhode Island banks, the commissioners recommended reforms that were incorporated in the Bank Act enacted by the General Assembly in its June session of 1836. The "Act to regulate process against Banks" and to fix the legal rate of interest to be charged by banks became the first comprehensive American banking statute. The act stipulated in detail conditions governing the organization and conduct of banks, established the maximum interest rate at 6 per cent with forfeiture of the charter as penalty for violation, fixed a scale of exchange rates for all localities within the United States, and provided for permanent state regulation of banking by the creation of a commission of three members. A rather novel feature of the act was found in Section 8, saying that no person should serve as an officer of a bank unless he had been "sworn or affirmed" to discharge the duties of his office according to law and to "support the laws regulating the interest of money." Any officer failing to comply with this section was liable to the forfeiture of $1,000.[26]

How would the banks of Rhode Island in general and the Providence Bank in particular react to this effort of the state to bring banking under strict public control? Since the comparatively mild and moderate act of 1822 imposing a tax upon banks had been contested by the Providence Bank, what would be the attitude of that institution toward this more stringent measure? Moses Brown Ives, president of the bank, lost no time before asking the opinion of legal counsel. On July 4, 1836, Peter Pratt submitted an opinion that filled eight pages of foolscap paper. The learned counsel deemed the Bank Act a violation of the Bill of Rights of Rhode Island, of the principles of the common law, of common justice, and of the Constitution of the United States. Section 8, requiring that bank officers be sworn or affirmed to obey the laws and to forego usury, he thought particularly obnoxious. Some of the principles of the act, "if carried to their full extent would be subversive of a free Government" and were therefore "ill suited to the sentiments genius or Institutions of a free people."

Peter Pratt thought the Bank Act unconstitutional. But he remarked that "constituted as our State Courts are I am inclined to the Opinion that they will support the law . . ." How the question of constitutionality would be decided by the Supreme Court of the United States he would not presume to say, since John Marshall, who had so long dominated the tribunal, had died the previous year. He then added that "If this Court was constituted of the member which it once was . . . they would declare the law to be unconstitutional . . ." Pratt obviously recognized that Chief Justice Robert Brooke Taney and his court might be disposed to allow the states rather more freedom in corporate matters than they had enjoyed in the days of Marshall.

Shifting his attention from the question of law to that of expediency, the counsel was "inclined to the opinion that the Directors of the Bank had better," if they could bring their feelings to it, "Submit to the law with the hope that [if] it should prove in practice what it appears to be in principle . . . the General Assembly would repeal it."[27]

Nicholas Brown, in behalf of the bank, sought legal advice and opinion from no less an authority than Daniel Webster, who had argued the case of Dartmouth College before the Supreme Court bench in 1819. In the papers of Brown and Ives, under date of July 21, 1836, in Webster's own hand, is his opinion. The Bank Act "in several respects . . . does materially change and alter the terms of the Original Charter," which was a contract whose obligation no state could constitutionally impair. The act "transcends, in these particulars, the Constitutional power of the General Assembly." Webster made no allusion to any possible change of attitude of the Supreme Court in consequence of Taney's succession to Marshall's post. Like Peter Pratt, however, he did raise the question of the expediency of the bank's compliance with the act, which he said must be "left to the discretion of others."[28]

The board of directors of the Providence Bank was quick to react to the Bank Act. Fortified with the opinions of Peter Pratt and Daniel Webster, the directors resolved on July 25, 1836, that it was "not advisable" for the officers of the institution to take the oath required by Section 8 of the law. Whether they anticipated similar action by other banks within the state is not known. In any event it was soon "understood" that the directors of "all the other Banks" in the state had taken the oath. Popular feeling against the Providence board ran high. The directors soon realized that because they stood alone in their opposition to the oath, "or from other causes," their motives in refusing to be sworn had been misunderstood by the public. People believed that they had been influenced by personal feelings of contempt for the legislature. They were charged with arrogating to themselves "peculiar privileges" beyond the control of law. To the dismay of the directors they found arrayed against them "a powerful excitement which pervades the community." This excitement, they feared, might reach "even to the halls of legislation," since a government "founded upon

... popular opinion must necessarily partake of every feeling which deeply agitates the public mind."

Under these circumstances the board thought that "the pursuit of justice" through the courts must be undertaken at the "hazard of sacrificing interests of paramount importance." In other words, resort to litigation over the Bank Act would merely invite legislative action adverse to the bank. Rather than make the bank "the victim of an unhappy excitement," it was better to suffer wrong in the hope that when the "agitation of feeling" had subsided, the "corrective power of an enlightened public opinion" would demand the repeal of the Bank Act of 1836.[29]

The board had found, as Peter Pratt had suggested they might, that it was expedient to comply with the Bank Act. On December 21, 1836, they formally resolved it was "advisable that the Directors and Cashier of the Providence Bank" should take the oath or affirmation required by the act. They were disappointed, however, in their hope that an enlightened public opinion would soon demand the repeal of the law.[30]

Another banking institution that engaged the attention of the Browns was the Rhode Island branch of the second Bank of the United States. President James Madison, who had allowed the first Bank of the United States to die a natural death in 1811, found it desirable five years later to recommend to Congress the chartering of an institution similar to the one lately expired. Congress promptly complied and the second national bank was established in Philadelphia. Its charter provided that its directors might establish branch offices of discount and deposit in various parts of the United States.

If such an office were to be established in Rhode Island, every consideration of reason and logic dictated that it should be located at Providence. The town was now the undisputed center of commerce and manufacturing within the state. Newport not only had not recovered from wounds suffered during the War for Independence but gave every indication of continuing indefinitely in its lethargic state. As for other towns in the state, none had half the population of Providence, and none could remotely compare with it as a center of trade and industry.

In the autumn of 1816 Brown and Ives informed James Lloyd, a director of the mother bank in Philadelphia, that they were forwarding to him a paper signed by twenty-eight Providence stockholders of the Bank of the United States that set forth the town's claims to the branch bank and urged that it be located there. In the same letter Brown and Ives advised Lloyd that James De Wolf of Bristol, Rhode Island, had set out for Philadelphia, "to make exertions" for the location of the branch bank in that town. They considered it "idle to think of such a thing," but since "party politicks" might well influence some of the directors, they wished to make known the relative importance of the two places.[31] For the moment, at least, hard cold facts triumphed over politics. Within a short time, Brown and Ives received from James Lloyd a letter saying that upon a motion made by him, the board of directors had voted to locate the branch bank in Providence.[32]

But James De Wolf was one of those men who become the more resolute in the face of a momentary reverse. He was capable of bringing great pressure upon the directors to change their vote. Ownership of $200,000 of the stock of the mother bank gave him tremendous leverage. In his favor, too, was the fact that one of the Bristol banks had subscribed its entire capital stock to the Bank of the United States. Not the least of his assets was his own conversion to Jeffersonian Republicanism, a fact that might weigh heavily with an institution chartered by the administration of Madison.[33]

Brown and Ives therefore could not have been greatly surprised to learn from James Lloyd that the bank directors had received a memorial asking for the removal of the branch bank from Providence to Bristol. If Brown and Ives considered it important "to retain the Branch at Providence," they were advised to prepare an exhibit to be laid before the directors stating the superior claims of Providence arising from "her wealth, tonnage, commerce, population, manufactures—Revenues— central Situation, connexion . . . with other places, etc." The fuller the facts were stated the better. This exhibit should be sent on to Philadelphia by a delegation of "two or three respectable intelligent Inhabitants, zealous in the wish to have the Branch located" at Providence. As a counterpoise to the Republicanism of James De Wolf, Lloyd advised that a majority of the delegation "should be in the Republican interest in politics," a reminder to the Federalist firm of Brown and Ives that the management of the second Bank of the United States was not entirely divorced from politics.[34]

While Brown and Ives were engaged in the preparation of the exhibit in support of the claims of Providence, they arranged with Samuel Aborn, then in New York on business, to visit Philadelphia, where he was personally to plead the case of Providence with certain of the directors. Reporting upon his mission, Aborn expressed his confident belief that the location of the branch would not be changed. Directors Thomas Willing, Robert Ralston, Henry Bohlen, and Thomas Lieper were decidedly in favor of Providence. As for William Jones, president of the bank, Aborn found it "difficult to discover his opinion," though he felt that gentleman seemed to lean "in favor of Mr. D. Woolf."[35] To a query from one of the directors as to how James De Wolf had accumulated so much property Aborn replied that he had been in the African trade and from that source alone had drawn the principal part of his wealth. De Wolf, "in defiance of the laws of his country & of humanity," still pursued "that trade in an indirect manner even to this day." At the conclusion of the conversation Aborn was sure that Lieper's "mind is fixed."[36]

On January 3, 1817, Brown and Ives advised Thomas Willing that they were forwarding to him the memorial, which "with the Table annexed to it" showed in "a Striking Manner the Superior Claims of Providence" to the branch bank. If located in Providence, the branch would be "prudently & economically Conducted [by] independent Men from both Political parties." Brown and Ives flattered themselves that they would have Willing's vote to retain the branch in Providence.[37] Three days later, they forwarded to Willing a petition signed by persons in Providence and other towns in the state who belonged to both political parties, asking that the location of the branch not be changed. It was the hope of Brown and Ives that James Burrill, one of the committee appointed by the stockholders, might "be prevailed upon to proceed to Philadelphia to advocate their Memorial before the board."[38]

Not content to rely solely upon the good offices of James Lloyd and Thomas Willing, Brown and Ives were at pains to present their case to several other members of the board of directors of the second Bank of the United States. Urging upon Robert Ralston the great advantages offered by Providence, they remarked that "Should the location be removed to Bristol it must be attributed to Party Considerations entirely. that Town never would have been thought of—but for the accidental Circumstance of its being the residence of a large proprietor of Bank Stock & of Several of his family connexions."[39]

Nor did Brown and Ives neglect other possible means of influencing the board of directors in Philadelphia. In that city was located the commission house of Gilman and Ammidon, whose senior partner was a first cousin of Thomas P. Ives. Enjoying the friendly blessing and patronage of Brown and Ives, the members of this house were on such good terms with several of the directors as to be able to plead the cause of Providence effectively. Brown and Ives therefore bombarded Gilman and Ammidon with letters advising them of ways in which they could shape the views of the directors.[40] Hearing that Jonathan Russell, a member of Madison's own party, would soon visit Philadelphia, they had asked him to "make such representations" to the bank directors as "to convince them of the propriety" of retaining the branch bank in Providence.[41]

Meanwhile, James De Wolf was not inactive. One of his arguments was that politically independent directors could not be found in Providence. Having supplied Gilman and Ammidon with the names of potential directors, Brown and Ives requested them to use these names to convince the board of the falsity of De Wolf's assertion. Another of De Wolf's charges against Providence was that its citizens had made no loans to the federal government in the War of 1812. Writing to Samuel Aborn and Edward Carrington, then in Philadelphia, Brown and Ives asked them to remind the bank board that "some of our names" were affixed to "the first Loan made to the General Gov't"; that the "Banks in this Town & a great number of Individuals advanced a considerable Sum to the Gov't, to prosecute measures of defense . . ." Nor should they fail to point out that "the zeal manifested in preparations to repel invaders, by throwing up works in the vicinity of this Town, all by the voluntary Labour of our Citizens . . . obtained the strongest marks of approbation from the Engineers & other Officers employed by the War department to visit the different districts." In conclusion, Brown and Ives remarked that "If Patriotism be the test, certainly we deserve the Branch in this Town."[42]

Brown and Ives believed that De Wolf had enlisted the aid of the Roger Williams Bank of Providence and of the bank at Newport (both repositories of federal funds) by assuring them that with the branch bank at Bristol they would "continue to be collectors of the public monies."[43]

At last Brown and Ives received from Gilman the glad tidings that the bank board in Philadelphia had unanimously decided not to reconsider their vote locating an office of discount and deposit in Providence.[44] There remained to be decided, however, the membership of the board of directors of the Providence branch bank. Stockholders of the second Bank of the United States residing in Providence could reasonably expect a major voice in the decision on this question, subject, of course, to the approval of the board of the mother bank. Brown and Ives had already submitted to the board in Philadelphia a list of thirteen names, all from Providence with the exception of Samuel Vernon of Newport and Charles De Wolf of Bristol.[45] They would appease Bristol by including Charles De Wolf, whom they deemed preferable to his brother James. But, much as they would have liked to keep James De Wolf off the board, they realized on second thought that his heavy stake in the capital stock of the second national bank entitled him to a voice in the management of the branch in Providence.[46] They were "extremely anxious" that a respectable board be chosen composed of men who would "harmonize & act for the best interest of the Institution" as well as for the accommodation of the community. Nor could they conceal their apprehension that "if the Democratic Party in Bristol & Providence Should be gratified in the Selection Made . . . the Bank may not be judiciously Conducted."[47]

Their fears of undue political influence in the affairs of the branch bank were strengthened when within a few days Brown and Ives received from Benjamin Ives Gilman of Philadelphia a letter marked private advising them of a Democratic caucus in Providence that had proposed a list of names of directors for the branch in Providence. Although the name of Nicholas Brown headed the list, which included other Federalists, the slate unquestionably had a Democratic Republican cast to it, which may have prompted Gilman to add that "From some symptoms which have recently appeared," he was inclined to believe that party considerations would govern the choice of the Rhode Island directors.[48]

For some months the board of the mother bank, in determining the composition of the board for the branch in Providence, was subjected to influence and counterinfluence, most of it of a political nature. Brown and Ives, both directly and through Gilman and Ammidon, submitted new names for appointment to the board. But eventually Gilman and Ammidon received from one of the bank officers in Philadelphia a list of the directors of the Providence branch. The name of Nicholas Brown headed this list, which also included both James and George De Wolf. Meanwhile, an official list had been sent to Seth Wheaton, whose name stood at the top. Brown and Ives thought that "possibly there was some management on the part of the President & Cashier . . . after the Election was over." The cause of the difference in the two lists "it would be Satisfactory to Know." The board, Brown and Ives wrote, was not made up exactly as they could wish, but to that they "must acquiesce for the present."[49] If they had not achieved complete victory in the contest with De Wolf and Bristol, they had none the less won on the essential point, the retention of the branch bank in Providence.

One other question involving the second Bank of the United States was of concern to Brown and Ives, namely, their belief that one of the members of the house of Gilman and Ammidon in Philadelphia should seek election to the board of directors of the mother bank. Preferably, they thought, it should be Otis Ammidon, since Benjamin Ives Gilman had recently received a high honor from the city of Philadelphia. They considered Ammidon's election to the board quite important to the Philadelphia house. Among both Boston and Providence stockholders of the bank Brown and Ives were active in enlisting support for Ammidon, who found in Philadelphia "strong jealousy against

New England." After the election, in which he was not elected to the board, Ammidon wrote to Providence that William Jones (president of the bank) did not say that he "would not have a Yankee among them, He is too polite for that, but I have no doubt that was thought of . . ."[50]

As businessmen of substance, interested both in the welfare of their country and in profitable investment of their funds, Brown and Ives purchased not less than 520 shares of stock of the second Bank of the United States.[51] This considerable financial stake in a semipublic institution nicely complemented their holdings of the funded debt of the United States, which in 1806 amounted to about $100,000.[52]

Brown and Ives were soon to become concerned in yet another banking enterprise. Savings banks, first organized in Switzerland and Germany in the eighteenth century for the benefit of the poorer classes, had spread to England in the form of Friendly Societies, these being insurance plans for the poor rather than sources of credit for them. From these remote beginnings came the first self-supporting modern savings bank, established in Scotland in 1810. The idea spread quickly to America, and savings banks were soon organized in Philadelphia, Boston, and New York in the order named. Scarcely were they in business before savings banks appeared in Baltimore, Salem, Hartford, Newport, Providence, and Albany, all prior to 1821.[53] In Providence the plan for a savings institution was sponsored by Moses Brown, Nicholas Brown, Thomas P. Ives, and Samuel G. Arnold, among others. The Providence Institution for Savings, now known as the Old Stone Bank, received its charter from the General Assembly in 1819.[54] Presided over in its early years by Thomas P. Ives, it has remained the oldest and largest mutual savings bank in Rhode Island.

INSURANCE

In a commercial community such as that prevailing in Rhode Island in pre-Revolutionary days, the writing of marine insurance was a matter of importance to men of business. Until after the winning of independence, the writing of this type of insurance remained in the hands of individual underwriters. There were no insurance companies. For such men insurance was not their sole concern in business. It was merely one more way of making a shilling, and it often represented merely one facet of a many-sided business. An early insurance underwriter in Providence was Obadiah Brown, whose underwriting occupied but a small part of his time and capital not employed in distilling rum, manufacturing nails and spermaceti candles, operating a retail store, conducting an active trade to the Caribbean, and pursuing a coastwide traffic to the North Atlantic ports of America.

The first stock company in the United States devoted to the writing of insurance was the Insurance Company of North America, organized by a group of Philadelphia merchants in 1792. This was followed in 1794 by the Insurance Company of the State of Pennsylvania, of which Thomas Willing of the firm of Willing and Francis was one of the founders. Given the close relations existing between Willing and Francis and Brown and Francis of Providence, merchants of Rhode Island soon became familiar with the insurance business in the Quaker City. The *Providence Gazette* of July 12, 1794, carried the announcement that John Mason of Providence was opening an insurance office upon the principles and regulations established by the leading merchants of the town at a recent meeting.[55] From this it appears that Mason was acting for merchants who would one day formalize the business under the auspices of a chartered company.

A significant step in this direction is found in the notice in the *United States Chronicle* of January 3, 1799, of a "Subscription for . . . an Insurance Company" under the superintendence of Moses Lippitt, John Rogers, John Corlis, Thomas P. Ives, Amos M. Atwell, and James Burrill. John Brown was not a direct participant in the movement to form this insurance company, but he could not remain indifferent to any proposal that promised to further the interests of the business community in his home town. Upon seeing the notice in the paper, therefore, he wrote to the men supervising the stock subscription, giving his blessing to the undertaking. John would have been acting out of character, however, had he not been disposed "Just to hint a Few Observations." He would be glad to be "Considderablely Concerned in the adventure," provided he could "bring in to the Funds" 6 per cent stock of the United States, which he thought "Most Proper for the Whole Fund to be Invested In." If subscriptions were to be paid in money, the money would "Lay Dead" until the stock of the United States could be purchased. He favored low salaries for officers of the insurance company, believing that if the salaries were too high, it would have a bad effect on other institutions already established. He was referring to the Providence Bank, of which he was president.[56]

Formal organization of the Providence Insurance Company took place on January 5, 1799. Capital stock was fixed at $150,000 in 2,000 shares of $75 each. No shareholder, individual or corporate, was to hold more than 50 shares. The townspeople showed their confidence in the young company by subscribing 2,623 shares. Management of the company was entrusted to a board of directors that included some of the outstanding merchants of the town, among them Thomas P. Ives, junior partner of Brown and Ives.[57] Although 142 persons held stock in the company, the bulk of it was controlled by the Brown, Lippitt, Butler, Ives, Halsey, Clark, and Allen families, the very group that also controlled the destinies of the Providence Bank.[58] Through these families the policies of the two institutions were closely harmonized.

Twenty-four stockholders, acting upon John Brown's advice, had paid their subscriptions wholly in 6 per cent funded stock of the United States. A committee, of which Thomas P. Ives was a member, was appointed to confer with the directors of the Providence Bank in regard to a further purchase of 6 per cent funded stock and an investment of $60,000 in 150 shares of the bank. Knowing it was a safe, short-term investment, the directors of the Providence Insurance Company authorized a loan of $18,000 for six months to Brown and Ives, the first of a long succession of such loans to business houses. At the end of the first year of business the company declared a dividend of $15 a share on stock costing $75. The enterprise was off to a good start.

There was not room in one insurance company for all the businessmen in Providence who were seeking a profitable investment of their funds. Aware of the bright prospects of the Providence Insurance Company, these outsiders soon moved to form a company of their own. In January, 1800, they organized the Washington Insurance Company, and their influence in the General Assembly was sufficient to procure a charter, despite the fact that many of the legislators were friends of the Providence Insurance Company.

But the newcomers received no friendly greeting from the Providence Insurance Company. Writing to John Brown, then in Congress, Brown and Ives advised him that "a new Insurance Co. by the Stile of Washington Insurance Compy. has been established in this Town. Capital D. 110,000 . . . this we consider a very unfortunate circumstance as it will tend to create a party spirit." Besides, they said, "the Office in which you & ourselves are concerned could safely do three times the business that is offered there. If we all become Insurers, where are we to look for business."[59]

Events of the year 1800 did not justify this pessimism on the part of Brown and Ives. The Providence Insurance Company declared dividends in March and September. In its first twenty-one months the company had paid a dividend of $37.50 a share on stock whose par value was $75.00. Realizing the profitable relationship existing between the Providence Insurance Company and the Providence Bank, the Washington Insurance Company resolved that it too should have a bank and a double profit. It was the plan of the Washington Insurance Company to apply for a charter for the Providence Exchange Bank at the February, 1801, session of the General Assembly. News of this intention came to John Brown in Washington via a letter from Brown and Ives. A second insurance company in Providence had not greatly alarmed him, but the very thought of a second bank in the town brought terror to his heart.

Writing to Brown and Ives, John suggested that a committee from the board of directors of the bank meet with the directors of the Washington Insurance Company to "taulk the Buissiness over Friendly and Fairly," stressing that the disadvantage of multiplying the number of banks was the lessening of the dividends of each. One bank at Providence could circulate as much paper as two. ". . . from the Increesed Number of Banks their Certinly will be a Graiter probibillity that Some one May Fail," destroying all confidence in banks.

Should this argument fail to dissuade them, John would "offer them a Concern with us in our Bank on the Same terms and in the Same propotion as their Stock is to the Stock of the Providence Insurence Compy." If they "Declined an Accommodation," John would "put up the Standard and Join the other Banks of the State in a Sperited & Joint Opposition." He would point out to the General Assembly that "their is allredy Double the Number of Banks in our State than in Aney Other Considering its Biggness Nay three times as Maney, Compaired Either to our Extent or Welth . . ." In his letter John Brown predicted that should the Washington Insurance Company secure a charter for its bank, insurance companies in other Rhode Island towns would also organize their own banks.[60] That this forecast was correct is indicated by the fact that the nine banks operating in the state between 1799 and 1807 were closely connected with a like number of insurance companies. Thus the interlocking interest between banking and insurance had become an accepted aspect of business in Rhode Island.

But the founders of the Washington Insurance Company were not to be diverted from their course. They sold their stock, chose their officers, and organized the Providence Exchange Bank, needing only a charter in order to open their doors. John Brown's one last hope of blocking the plan was to play upon the fears of the General Assembly members and of the bank promoters. He proposed to circularize the assemblymen with data designed to show the dangers inherent in a multiplicity of banks in the state. He appears to have suggested that financial pressure be brought upon the promoters of the proposed bank by calling in "all our money [owed to the Providence Bank] from the Gentlemen" who were sponsoring the new bank. John's proposals were to no avail. The Providence Exchange Bank received its charter at the February, 1801, session of the Assembly.[61]

The bitter rivalry between the two insurance companies was not destined to last. By the close of the War of 1812 influential persons in each company had come to see that their mutual advantage would be best served by a union of the two. The first gesture was probably made by the Providence Insurance Company, which appointed Thomas P. Ives and James Burrill, Jr., a committee to carry into execution the uniting of the two companies, subsequently to be known as the Providence Washington Insurance Company. In the new company Thomas P. Ives and his eldest son, Moses Brown Ives, were conspicuous. In 1818 some of the directors of the new company petitioned for and received a charter for the Providence Fire Insurance Company, which proved to be the first step in the ultimate entrance of the Providence Washington Insurance Company into the fire insurance business, a fortunate move in the face of the declining importance of the marine insurance business.[62]

TURNPIKE AND BRIDGE BUILDING

In the history of transportation in the United States one of the recognized and well-defined stages was that known as the turnpike era, which began in the last decade of the eighteenth century and extended well into the nineteenth. (Overlapping the turnpike era was the canal era, which was in turn overlapped by the railway era.) States granted to men of capital and enterprise charters authorizing them to expend their capital in the improvement of existing arteries of trade and travel on the condition that they be permitted to recoup their expenses by charging tolls for the use of the roads.

At the beginning of the period of turnpike building in Rhode Island, promoters thought of themselves primarily as public benefactors rather than investors seeking financial gain. When later the profit motive became more prominent, merchants and manufacturers who sponsored the toll roads expected their monetary return to come from expanding markets and from lower costs of transporting materials, raw and finished, to and from the factories. They hoped, of course, that the turnpike companies would pay good dividends, but this consideration was a secondary one.[63]

Although a total of forty-six toll road companies were incorporated in Rhode Island, many of the proposed roads remained unbuilt. Quite naturally, Providence was the center from which most of these arteries, actual or proposed, radiated. Some led to Pawtucket, where connection was made with the Boston turnpike; others led into Massachusetts by way of Cumberland and Smithfield; and still others fanned out to the west and southwest toward the Connecticut line.

The Browns first participated in the movement to build turnpikes in 1794, when John Brown, Nicholas Brown, Thomas P. Ives, and other

Providence merchants incorporated as the "Providence and Norwich Society for Establishing a Turnpike Road from Providence to the Connecticut line through Johnston, Scituate, Foster, and Coventry." They were prepared to venture $600 of their own money, plus a larger amount to be obtained from a lottery. The charter stipulated that the pike was to revert to the state when its promoters had recovered the sum of $1,800 plus 12 per cent interest thereon.[64]

Eventually Brown and Ives invested in sixteen toll roads in Rhode Island and neighboring parts of Massachusetts and Connecticut. The number of shares that they purchased in a particular turnpike company varied from two in the Providence and Pawcatuck company to ten in the Providence and Pawtucket company, twenty in the Norfolk and Bristol company, and forty-two in the Smithfield company. Their comparatively large investment in the Norfolk and Bristol company is somewhat puzzling. When the Smithfield pike was projected in 1806, they bought only six shares. In 1808 they, with others, organized the Blackstone Manufacturing Company, their first venture in cotton manufacturing. Located on the Blackstone River in the town of Smithfield, the factory stood to benefit from the Blackstone toll road. This doubtless explains the subsequent increase in their holdings of Smithfield stock.

Except for the Providence and Norwich company, Brown and Ives appear to have taken no very active part in the management of any of the turnpike companies. The companies paying them the most substantial dividends were the Providence and Norwich and the Providence and Pawtucket. The high profits of the latter company led the state to take it over in 1833.[65] In 1814, a year of exceptionally heavy traffic on the Providence and Norwich turnpike, that company paid a dividend of 27 per cent. In 1831 it paid 15 per cent, but from 1837 to 1852 it paid an annual dividend of from 6 to 8 per cent.[66]

Brown and Ives held stock in two turnpike companies at a distance from Providence. In 1809 they purchased five shares in the Pasumpsick turnpike in Vermont, a step prompted undoubtedly by the fact that they then owned several thousand acres of wild land in that area. Two years later they invested in ten shares of a turnpike extending from Milford, Pennsylvania, on the Delaware River, to Owego in southern New York State. This investment was dictated by the fact that they owned some 13,000 acres of land in northeastern Pennsylvania in close proximity to the Milford and Owego pike. It had been the original hope of Brown and Ives that the pike would bisect their tract of land, in which event they would have been disposed to invest more heavily in the road.

Investment by the Brown and the Ives families in turnpikes was modest compared with their purchases of stock in banks, insurance companies, canals, railways, and other enterprises. Their total investment in toll roads could not have exceeded $15,000, a modest sum when compared with the $40,000 that Samuel Slater, pioneer cotton manufacturer, is supposed to have put into turnpikes. This disparity is easily explained. Slater's career as a manufacturer coincided closely with the turnpike era, and he evidently believed these roads were an important aid to his textile interests. Brown and Ives, however, until the day when turnpike building had passed its zenith, were primarily merchants concerned in maritime trade, upon which the turnpike could have no direct or immediate effect.

Closely connected with the turnpikes radiating from Providence was the interest in the improvement of the approaches to the town from the east and south. Although two ferries, one near the site of the present Red Bridge, the other at Fox Point, had long provided service across the Seekonk River, no one could deny that a bridge over the river was much to be preferred. Initially, Moses Brown appears to have been the most active proponent of a bridge. Public-spirited citizen that he was, Moses would naturally have favored such a project on its merits alone. But he could not have been unmindful of the fact that if the river were spanned at the site of the present Red Bridge, it would be necessary to build a road through his farm, located to the east of Providence, to establish the most direct route from the bridge to the business section of the town. Private as well as public interest would thus be served by the bridge. Moses persuaded his son, Obadiah, and Thomas P. Ives to join him as proprietors and promoters of the Providence Central Bridge Society.

But another member of the Brown family had yet to be heard from. John Brown had lately carried out extensive improvements in the water front near the south ferry. He had transformed a high hill into level ground, constructed a fine wharf where his Indiamen could dock, and built a large distillery. His business interests clearly dictated the building of the bridge at India Point, in close proximity to his improvements. He, along with his nephew Nicholas, partner in the firm of Brown, Benson, and Ives; Joseph Nightingale; John Innes Clark; and Welcome Arnold became proprietors and promoters of the Providence South Bridge Society. With the Brown family divided, the obvious course was to persuade the General Assembly of Rhode Island to charter both bridge societies. In June, 1792, the Assembly did grant charters to both societies, with the stipulation that the bridges be drawbridges, for the benefit and convenience of the merchants and shipowners of Pawtucket.[67]

Turnpikes, generally speaking, were not a lucrative form of business enterprise. Profits were seldom as great as expected; costs frequently were in excess of the estimates of their promoters. Uncertain financial returns combined with competing forms of transportation to render the turnpike largely obsolete. The railway, of course, was the prime competitor. But the canal also played its part in the passing of the toll road.

CANAL BUILDING

When canal construction in the United States was still in its infancy, John Brown in 1796 had conceived the idea of extending the economic hinterland of his home town by diverting to Providence the trade of northwestern Massachusetts from Springfield and of Worcester County from Boston. This ambitious design was to be realized by means of a "navigable Canal" from Providence "thro' the County of Worcester to some part of Connecticut River." Influenced by "the profitable Experience of Europe," John was convinced of the undoubted advantage that such a waterway would confer on the areas tributary to it. Farmers of central Massachusetts would benefit from the reduced cost of shipping the products of their farms and forests to market, manufacturing would develop along the canal route; employment would increase; the seaport towns of Rhode Island would obtain firewood and lumber at lower prices; the lime manufacturers of Smithfield, Rhode Island, would produce at reduced cost in proportion to the "greater Plenty of Wood"; consumers of lime would enjoy lower prices; and the owners of "the Rocks & Kilns" would see their profits increase. Providence would become the emporium of trade of this large area.[68]

An engineer employed by John Brown to survey the route of the proposed canal reported it both feasible and easy to execute.[69] John himself was prepared to invest $40,000 in the enterprise. The mercantile elite of Providence—including Moses Brown, his son Obadiah, Nicholas Brown, and Thomas P. Ives—expressed their concurrence in John's judgment by joining with him in a petition to the General Assembly asking incorporation of the Providence Plantations Canal.[70] Although the Assembly voted to defer action until the next session, a second petition with additional names induced the legislature to recede from that vote. The following day the *Providence Gazette* announced the passage of an act to incorporate "JOHN BROWN, Esq.; and others" as the Providence Plantations Canal.[71] The estimated cost of the canal was $400,000 to be divided into 4,000 shares of $100 each. In consequence of a resolution adopted by a conference committee of citizens of Rhode Island and of Worcester County, subscription was opened in both Providence and Worcester on April 21, 1796.

Not all of Massachusetts shared the interest of Worcester in the proposed canal. Although the "western counties" were reported to be "almost entirely in favor of the plan," Springfield and Boston merchants, as well as the proprietors of the Middlesex Canal, threw the weight of their influence against the project. Some said the canal would ruin Boston; others thought that unless the plan were blocked, "Boston will be in a few years reduced to a *Fishing Town*."[72] Sentiments such as these were sufficient to defeat any and all efforts to wrest a charter for the canal from the General Court of Massachusetts.

A quarter of a century passed before meetings were held in both Providence and Worcester to consider anew the question of a canal. Committees appointed in the two towns engaged Benjamin Wright, chief engineer for the middle section of the Erie Canal, to make a topographical survey of the route, to examine the character of the soil, to ascertain whether the volume of water was sufficient, and to estimate the cost of construction. Wright found the project altogether feasible and believed such a canal would pay the stockholders fair and increasing interest on their money.[73] Companies were organized in the two towns that applied to their respective state legislatures for charters. Believing the canal no longer posed a threat to them, Boston and other interests placed no obstacles to incorporation by the General Court of Massachusetts early in 1823. At its June session of the same year the General Assembly of Rhode Island incorporated the Providence proprietors as the Blackstone Canal Company. Stock in the company was to be $100 a share, and both it and the tangible property of the corporation were to be exempt from any "species of taxation" for a period of eight years.[74]

Conspicuous among the promoters of the Blackstone Canal Company were Nicholas Brown, Thomas P. Ives, Edward Carrington, Moses Brown Ives, Cyrus Butler, and Sullivan Dorr. The elder Ives was a member of the committee to supervise the stock subscription, while Moses Brown Ives was one of the commissioners charged with arrangements for construction of the canal. So great was the confidence of the business community of Providence in the project that the 4,000 shares of stock at $100 a share stipulated by the charter were quickly subscribed, leaving many prospective investors to be turned away, an unfortunate circumstance since conversion of the Blackstone River into a navigable canal was to be a far more costly undertaking than it would have been thirty years earlier. In the years since the canal had first been proposed the mill privileges upon the river had been largely occupied by cotton manufacturing companies. Their presence had greatly enhanced the value of the land, but the factories constituted a vested interest not always in harmony with the plans of the canal proprietors. Nevertheless, the Blackstone Canal Company was able to push ahead with construction and bring the canal to completion.

The formal opening of the canal occurred on July 1, 1828, and by autumn of that year canal boats seventy feet in length and nine feet in beam with a capacity of twenty to thirty tons were making the run to Worcester. A score of these freight barges and one passenger packet constituted the fleet of the Blackstone Canal Company.

But even before the waterway was completed, the company's financial condition began to deteriorate, thus emphasizing the initial folly of turning away investors who eagerly desired to subscribe to the capital stock. In July, 1828, the original stock subscription had been spent, and it was evident that substantial additional funds would be needed. Thomas P. Ives, Sullivan Dorr, and Benjamin Hoppin were accordingly constituted a committee to raise the money either by borrowing or by issuing new stock. They were authorized to pledge the faith and credit of the company, the canal with all its appurtenances, and the income and tolls for the repayment of loans they might negotiate.[75]

The first move of the committee in the execution of their commission was to plan the issuance of loan certificates of $1,000 each. Believing that purchasers of the certificates would require security beyond the faith and credit of the Blackstone Canal Company with its property, income, and tolls, they asked men of substance in Providence to be guarantors for one or more of the certificates. Within a short time the energetic committeemen had secured the signatures of forty-nine businessmen or firms guaranteeing from one to ten of the certificates, the total amounting to $100,000.[76] Brown and Ives pledged security for ten of the certificates, Edward Carrington for ten, Sullivan Dorr for five, Moses Brown Ives for two, and Robert H. Ives for two. Armed with this security, the committee applied to several Providence banks for loans ranging from $2,000 to $10,000.[77] For whatever reasons, most of the banks refused to purchase the certificates.

Foiled in this plan, the committee spent the next six months in an effort to find purchasers of the certificates. On March 6, 1829, they reported that they had negotiated eighty of them for a total of $80,000. Strangely enough, most of those who had signed as guarantors of one or more of the certificates had declined to lend their money. Brown and Ives purchased thirty certificates; the Providence Bank, in which the partners were so heavily involved, took twenty; and the Providence Institution for Savings, of which Thomas P. Ives was president, bought five.[78] These three subscribers accounted for $55,000 of the $80,000 the committee had been able to raise.

On the report of the committee there appears this notation: "It may be asked why Mr. [Cyrus] Butler, who is known as a Capitalist, has not taken any Part of this Loan. Mr. Butler is a Stockholder in the Canal Company, but in the course of its construction he was disappointed of the indemnity anticipated for its Location thro' the Blackstone Manufacturing Company's Village & some little difficulty took place in consequence between him & the Commissioners—which induced him to decline all further aid."[79] Cyrus Butler's financial stake in two companies not entirely in agreement was thus caught in a conflict of interest in which he seemed to give priority to his concern in manufacturing. Brown and Ives were in precisely the same situation. They were original heavy investors in both companies. Yet, in spite of their concern in the Blackstone Manufacturing Company, they were the largest subscriber to the loan to the Blackstone Canal Company.

If Cyrus Butler was conspicuous by the absence of his name from the list of subscribers, the absence of the name of Edward Carrington is even more surprising in view of the fact that he was then the president of the canal company and had been a guarantor of the loan certificates in the sum of $10,000. Also absent from the subscribers to the loan were Sullivan Dorr and Benjamin Hoppin, who with Thomas P. Ives constituted the committee that had issued the loan certificates.

The committee had not been neglectful of other sources that might be tapped. One of these sources was the second Bank of the United States. Accordingly, Thomas P. Ives, in behalf of the committee, wrote to Philip Allen, president of the Providence Exchange Bank, asking him to submit to Nicholas Biddle their application for a loan of $20,000. He explained to Allen that the committee had issued loan certificates "founded on the authority of the Company," and to "give entire Confidence in the security" they had had them guaranteed by "Individuals of responsibility." Ives enclosed certificates for $20,000 with the names of the guarantors.[80] Allen promptly dispatched the application to Nicholas Biddle with a covering letter in which he noted in particular the added security afforded by the certificates, whose guarantors he considered "good security" for the sums indicated. As for Ives and his associates on the committee, Allen remarked, "with us they are consedered of the first respectibility." Although Allen was not a stockholder in the canal, he was satisfied that its affairs had been managed with economy.[81]

In his reply Nicholas Biddle observed that the respectability of the Blackstone Canal Company and "the solidity of the parties offering the additional guarantee of their names" would render the loan secure. It was the settled policy of the bank, however, to employ its funds in short business loans and to avoid "permanent loans" and "generally all loans to corporate bodies especially those engaged in enterprizes the success of which may be in any degree contingent." These views of the subject had "constrained the board" of the bank to "decline the application of the Blackstone Canal Company."[82] Biddle seemed to be saying that while the security for the loan was beyond question, the success of the canal was by no means certain; and it was not the policy of the bank to aid corporate enterprise of a dubious character.

Thomas P. Ives and his associates next sought to obtain a loan in New York City. Knowing that Samuel Wetmore, president of the Marine Insurance Company of Providence, was planning to spend several days in Manhattan, they asked him to try his hand at negotiating a loan for them. They accordingly placed in Wetmore's hand forty-four of the loan certificates, thirty-two with, and twelve without, guarantors. Although Wetmore would use his own discretion as to the best mode of effecting the loan, Ives did suggest that either Prime, Ward, King, and Company, American agents of Baring Brothers, or John Jacob Astor might "readily avail themselves of making so favourable an investment." But should those gentlemen decline, their extensive knowledge of financial affairs would enable them to give Wetmore sound advice as to the procedure he should adopt in order to achieve his objective.[83]

Coming at a time when the money market was very tight, Wetmore's mission was a failure. Obviously, the prospects of the Blackstone Canal Company inspired no great confidence in the financial circles of New York.

Thus the finance committee of Ives, Dorr, and Hoppin had raised only $80,000 by means of loans. Meanwhile, by exercising another power delegated to them by the stockholders, they had issued new stock that had brought into the treasury something in excess of $200,000. By this time, however, the estimated cost of the canal had risen to $700,000. Additional funds were urgently needed. Not yet at their wits' end, the committee recommended an expedient that had become standard practice in American business. Experience had shown that one way of financing an enterprise too large for the resources immediately at hand was to tie it to a so-called improvement bank. In this way canal, gas-light, industrial, and other projects had been successfully promoted. The improvement bank created new capital for the desired enterprise by the issue of purchasing power in the form of bank notes. The finance committee therefore recommended to the stockholders the organization of an improvement bank. In turn, in March, 1829, the stockholders authorized the committee to apply to the General Assembly for a bank charter.[84] At its January session in 1831 the Assembly incorporated the Blackstone Canal Bank, which was formally organized in the following month. It was capitalized at $250,000 with shares of $25 each. Stockholders in the Blackstone Canal Company were at liberty to subscribe for as many shares in the bank as they had shares in the canal. If this provision were carried into effect, the proprietors "in both Institutions" would be the same. The bank was to purchase of the canal company new stock to the value of $150,000. The funds thus provided, together with other assets then in the possession of the canal company, would be sufficient, it was hoped, to discharge all claims against it. Stockholders in the canal would "see their interest promoted" by taking their proportion of the stock of the bank, which would give them double profit.[85]

Members of the Brown and Ives families promptly availed themselves of the opportunity offered to them as shareholders in the Blackstone Canal Company. Brown and Ives subscribed 800 shares with a par value of $25, John Carter Brown took 200 shares, and Moses Brown Ives and Robert H. Ives each took a like number. The group thus owned 1,400 shares of the bank stock with a par value of $35,000.[86] Meanwhile, Brown and Ives had rendered to the young bank a service that banks ordinarily perform for their clientele. At a time when the doors of the institution had scarcely been opened for business, they had loaned it $30,000 at 6 per cent for four months and an equal sum at 5 per cent for twelve months.[87]

Within limits the Blackstone Canal Bank brought aid and comfort to its rather halting partner. Its purchase of new canal stock enabled the canal company to repay the $80,000 that Thomas P. Ives and his associates had negotiated in loans. The canal company enjoyed a short lease on life, which was reflected in small dividend payments in 1832, 1834, and 1835. Nevertheless, it soon became clear that the canal was doomed. Reading the signs of the time correctly, the bank officials decided it was better to sever all connection with the canal than to wait to be pulled down by it. They accordingly obtained an amendment to their charter authorizing them "to divide out" the canal stock owned by the bank, after which the stock so divided out would cease to constitute any part of the stock of the bank.[88] In this way the Blackstone Canal Bank disposed of its interest in the Blackstone Canal. Its capital stock in 1834 was increased by a provision that gave to every current shareholder the right to purchase five additional shares for every one he then held. Taking advantage of this opportunity, Brown and Ives made one purchase of 1,060 shares for $9,060 and another of 3,550 shares for $30,175, while Nicholas Brown subscribed 125 shares for $1,062.50, a total of 4,735 shares at a cost of $40,297.50.[89] The combined interest of the various members of the two families in the Blackstone Canal Bank was thereby increased to more than $75,000.

From this point the bank entered upon a period of success that was to continue until its merger with the Providence National Bank in 1945. For the Blackstone Canal Company, however, the end was only a question of time. In 1849 the General Assembly authorized the formal dissolution of the corporation, which had been moribund for several years.

There has been much discussion of the reasons for the failure of the Blackstone Canal. The proprietors have been charged with "lack of foresight, [and] inefficiency." In the opinion of one writer the promoters should have acquired full riparian rights instead of being content with joint use. "This embroiled the company in disputes over its management of water resources, deprived it of revenues from the sale of water to manufacturers, and aggravated problems of slack water navigation."[90] Other difficulties stemmed from spring freshets that "broke through the embankments. Summer droughts sometimes lowered the water to a point that prevented passage of the canal boats; ice in winter had a similar effect. Additional trouble was caused by millowners, who, convinced that the canal was drawing off their water supply, ordered their workmen to damage locks and place impediments in the channel..."[91]

That the cost of the canal was initially underestimated was the fault of the engineer. The acquisition of full riparian rights was impossible because the canal was constructed through a river valley dotted with cotton mills, whose mill privileges seemed to be threatened by the canal. The other difficulties would not have been insoluble had conditions otherwise been propitious. The tragedy of the Blackstone Canal was that it was not built in 1796, when the cotton mills in the Blackstone Valley were nonexistent. Then the questions over riparian rights and water use would not have arisen, and much of the difficulty would have been obviated. A careful weighing of all the evidence would indicate that the fundamental mistake of the promoters was bad timing. This error in judgment not only led to all the troubles over water rights but it made the canal obsolete before a shovelful of earth had been turned. In 1828 when the canal was completed, the railway era was at hand, and railway tracks were soon to parallel the canal between Providence and Worcester.

The Brown and Ives families had a heavy stake in, and commitment to, the Blackstone Canal. It is evident that the house of Brown and Ives had made a very substantial original investment in canal stock, though it is not possible to determine the firm's precise holdings. These, however, were increased by investment in further stock issues. As of February 2, 1835, Brown and Ives, together with individual members of the two families, owned a total of 2,827 shares of canal company stock. Of this the firm of Brown and Ives owned 1,435 shares, John Carter Brown 266 shares, Hope Brown Ives (wife of Thomas P. Ives) 66 shares, Moses Brown Ives 522 shares, and Robert Hale Ives 522 shares, while Moses Brown Ives and Robert H. Ives owned jointly 16 shares.[92] It is impossible to determine the par value of the shares, since the stock had been purchased at the various figures of $100, $25, $15, and $10 a share. The total stock issues of the company come to at least $700,000, represented by some 23,000 shares, of which the two families owned about 12 per cent. If one may assume that they purchased that proportion of every issue, their holdings would have represented an investment of $84,000.

Perhaps their heavy financial interest in the Blackstone Canal Company explains the steadfast manner in which Brown and Ives supported the enterprise throughout its existence. In comparison with the investments of other monied men and institutions, their subscription of $30,000 to the loan of 1828/29 was especially notable. The many documents of the financial committee of Ives, Dorr, and Hoppin, chiefly in the handwriting of Thomas P. Ives, attest to the thought and energy given by him to the interests of the project. At a time when certain cotton mill owners in the Blackstone Valley were inclined to look askance at the canal, Brown and Ives, as heavily concerned as any in cotton manufacturing, were able to maintain a nice balance between their interest in the canal on the one hand and their concern in the Blackstone Manufacturing Company on the other. The canal was not one of their wisest business ventures. In their own interest and that of their town they helped launch an enterprise foredoomed to failure but one on which they staked a considerable capital, great energy, and genuine devotion.

CHAPTER 10

Speculation on New Frontiers

THROUGHOUT the early history of the United States speculation in wild lands was a constant attraction to men possessed of fluid capital. In the days when industrial enterprises were comparatively few, when the corporation was in its infancy, and when the stock exchange was either nonexistent or in its formative stage, the land seemed to offer unusual opportunity for investment. The legion of land companies organized for speculative purposes attest to that fact. Of the countless individuals and families indulging in this form of speculation, there were few who bought and sold land on as many frontiers or over as long a period of time as the Browns of Providence.

Speculative land companies were notably active in the years before and during the War for Independence, sometimes exerting a marked influence upon the course of politics both in America and in England. Land speculators were the cause of delay in the ratification of the Articles of Confederation and also in the creation of the national domain. Although the interest of the Browns in virgin lands cannot be said to have had political repercussions, this does not in any substantial degree detract from the historical importance of their ventures into this form of speculative activity. So complete is the record of their land investments that it offers a prime opportunity for a study of the whole process of land speculation in divers times and places.

VERMONT

The War for Independence had not yet run its course when the elder Nicholas Brown made the first of the speculative purchases that were to engage the time and attention of the Brown family for more than a hundred years. In the summer of 1781 Rufus Hopkins and twelve other men of Rhode Island origin executed a quitclaim deed in favor of Nicholas Brown, to whom they bargained and sold the rights and titles to thirteen undivided tracts of land in the township of Random in what was to be the state of Vermont. The area sold amounted to 7,288 acres for which the consideration was £9 15s. lawful money of Rhode Island paid to each of the men making the sale.[1] Nicholas Brown's investment, therefore, was approximately £127, or slightly less than $0.06 an acre.

As economic conditions in the young country were greatly depressed and unsettled during the next few years, there was little, if any, opportunity to dispose of any part of the land. Besides, the very slender investment he had made in the land relieved Nicholas of any feeling of urgency or compulsion in regard to the sale of his holdings. In consequence, for some years there apparently was no mention of Vermont lands in the records of the Browns. In 1789 Nicholas and other Rhode Islanders owning lands in Vermont appointed Jonathan Arnold as their joint agent in the management of their lands.[2] But there is no evidence that Arnold sold any land. After several more years had elapsed, Brown and Ives appointed a new agent who agreed to redeem the land from sale for nonpayment of the one cent tax and to give timely information of any future tax that might be imposed. The assessor returned the land at $0.50 an acre, which the agent thought to be about its full worth considering that it lay "pretty high and uneven," and was some six miles from the nearest settlement.[3] Once more complete silence settled upon the Brown acres in Vermont.

In 1824, more than forty years after the purchase of the land, not one acre had been sold, probably because the owners had demanded too high a price. In any event, Brown and Ives were now of the opinion that absentee owners should sell "cheap at first" with a view to forming a nucleus of settlement. Then as the density of population increased, sales could be made at higher prices.[4]

Soon this new policy began to show results. The agent sold several lots and sold them well. The purchasers were to pay $0.50 an acre in four annual installments.[5] While not a handsome price, it was tolerable for land that had cost so little and upon which the taxes had been negligible. In 1834 the agent sold 760 acres in the town of Brighton (the new name of Random) at $0.50 an acre.[6] A year later he recommended the sale of some 3,900 acres at $0.50 to $0.60 an acre. Although Brown and Ives thought these figures unreasonably low, they were nevertheless prepared to offer the land at a modest figure, provided they could make "an entire sale of the whole" of their holdings. They divided the land into three categories, to be offered at $0.70, $0.60, and $0.50 an acre.[7] Although unable to dispose of the entire tract on those terms, they soon were able to sell 1,200 acres of the better land at the comparatively high price of $1.00 an acre.

In the early 1850's the town clerk of Brighton valued the better of the unsold land as high as $3.76 an acre.[8] Brown and Ives, by making the first sales at $0.50 an acre, had succeeded in attracting some hardy spirits to the land whose labor and capital expenditures had brought a sharp appreciation in the value of the adjacent areas. An inventory taken in 1853 showed that 4,000 acres had been sold, leaving something more than 3,000 acres unsold.[9] These, of course, were the inferior lands, deemed by the agent to be utterly unfit for settlement. Owners less hard-headed than Brown and Ives might well have abandoned the land as the easy and economical way out. But they waited, and after 1860 land that the agent had thought unfit for any purpose sold at prices ranging from $4.60 to $6.58 an acre.[10] By 1875 there remained but 500 of the 7,288 acres comprising the original purchase. In 1881, a hundred years after the purchase, the last acre was sold and the account closed.

It is clear that the Vermont lands were no gold mine. Nevertheless, the returns could not have been anything other than substantial. True, some of the land sold at $0.50 an acre, but by far the greater part brought from $1.00 to $6.58 an acre.[11] Land purchased at $0.06 an acre on which the taxes had been extremely moderate and on which the owners had incurred no other expense could not fail to show a good profit when sold at $1.00 an acre and above.

NEW YORK

Even before making the purchase of lands in Vermont, Nicholas Brown had shown an interest in the fertile lands in the Mohawk Valley, an interest that was quickened when lands of the Loyalists, which had been confiscated by the state of New York, came on the market.[12] In the autumn of 1786 he and John Innes Clark and Joseph Nightingale, Providence merchants, were negotiating with James Caldwell and John Van Rensselaer, merchants in Albany, in regard to the purchase of land in Kingsland, on the large tract of land granted by the British Crown to the late Sir William Johnson, who had been superintendent of Indian affairs north of the Ohio River under the British imperial policy inaugurated in 1763. The land in question had formed part of the great estate in the Mohawk Valley over which Sir William presided. When in the War of Independence the Johnson family remained Loyalists, their holdings had been declared forfeit to the state. Caldwell and Van Rensselaer had purchased certain of the sequestered lands as a speculative investment. They, in turn, were prepared to resell the land to other speculative investors.

On October 16, 1786, Nicholas Brown placed in the state treasury office in the city of New York twenty-one loan office certificates issued by the Continental loan officer of the state amounting to the nominal sum of $13,000 but with a specie value of only $4,174.[13] The certificates were exchanged for 116 final settlement notes issued to the officers and soldiers of the New York line, whose nominal value with interest was $13,403. Nicholas then used the final settlement notes to finance two purchases of lands. On November 8, 1786, he bought from James Caldwell and John Van Rensselaer 1,680 acres in Kingsland, two thirds for himself and one third for Clark and Nightingale. On the same day Joseph Nightingale purchased 2,814 acres from Henry Oothoudt and Jeremiah Van Rensselaer, who were serving as commissioners of forfeitures for the western district of New York State, one third for Clark and Nightingale and two thirds for Nicholas Brown.[14] These lands, also situated in Kingsland, were thus acquired directly from men charged with the responsibility of administering and selling the Mohawk Valley land that had been forfeited by Loyalists. By these two transactions Nicholas Brown became the owner of "two equal, and undivided third parts" of 4,494 acres of Mohawk Valley land, which had cost him $1.30 an acre in specie.[15]

The land acquired by Nicholas was located in Montgomery County, New York, north of the Mohawk, in close proximity to the river. Indeed the land was so well situated that it should probably have been classed as semi-improved rather than as wild land. This presumption is strengthened by the readiness with which the land was sold at good prices. Some of the land may well have been cultivated by tenants of Sir William Johnson. Within a decade much of the land had been disposed of at $6 and $7 an acre.[16]

These speculative purchases of lands once owned by Sir William cast a ray of light upon the controverted question as to the degree to which confiscation of Loyalist estates in New York fostered the democratization of land ownership in the state. Once it had been believed that confiscation had led to a devaluation of land ownership, but a measure of doubt has since been cast on that view by the discovery that in the southern district of the state the Loyalist holdings frequently passed into the hands of speculators or other owners of large tracts of land.[17] The two purchases here discussed cast further doubt on the older view.

In one of the purchases the land had been passed from speculator to speculator; in the other the commissioners of forfeitures had sold the confiscated land to two merchant speculators. Ultimately, of course, the land came into the possession of farmers but only at a profit to the speculator, and in one instance, at a profit to successive speculators.

While Nicholas Brown and others were thus buying and selling on a small scale lands in the lower Mohawk Valley, buyers in western and northern New York were making speculative investments of massive proportions.[18] The area lying west of a line drawn from Sodus Bay on Lake Ontario to the New York–Pennsylvania boundary, 6,000,000 acres in all, first came into possession of Oliver Phelps and Nathaniel Gorham, two Massachusetts speculators, who disposed of it to Robert Morris, the so-called financier of the American Revolution. Morris in turn sold the eastern third of the tract to a group of British capitalists led by Sir William Pulteney at a profit of £45,000. The western two-thirds attracted the attention of four Amsterdam business houses then speculating in American securities in the wake of Alexander Hamilton's funding plan. They were joined by two Amsterdam banking houses in the formation of the Holland Land Company. By late 1792 they had purchased from Morris 2,500,000 acres in western New York, and within a few months they had acquired from other sources an additional 1,500,000 acres in western Pennsylvania. Thus most of western New York and Pennsylvania had rapidly passed into the hands of European speculators, British and Dutch. Since both groups possessed ample capital, they could easily afford to develop their lands, something that American speculators with limited funds had not attempted.

In 1792 Charles Williamson, agent of the Pulteney Estates, arrived in western New York. Knowing the large resources of his principals, Williamson planned to force the settlement of their lands by building roads, improving navigation on the rivers, and constructing stores, taverns, sawmills, gristmills, distilleries, and places of amusement— all designed to provide in advance some of the amenities of life to the farmers who were expected to purchase and settle upon the land. At the town of Bath, whose name attests to Williamson's British origins, he built houses, farm buildings, a theater, a race track, two sawmills, a gristmill, and a tavern. On Sodus Bay he improved the harbor and built an elaborate wharf. He built roads connecting the Pulteney lands with Williamsport on the Susquehanna River in Pennsylvania, whence there was connection with the markets of Philadelphia and Baltimore. He persuaded the legislature of New York to extend the Mohawk turnpike westward through Geneva and Canandaigua, both on Pulteney lands. In pursuance of this "hothouse" method of promoting settlement, Williamson spent $1,000,000 in ten years; in the same period receipts for land sales amounted to only $146,000. In 1801 Williamson was superseded by a new agent more concerned with earning money for his principals than spending it. Nevertheless, Williamson's improvements on the land had accelerated settlement.[19]

At the same time the Holland Land Company was also trying out the hothouse system of promoting settlements on some of its vast holdings. Their agent in New York State, Theophile Cazenove, had ideas no less grandiose than those of Charles Williamson. In a five-year period he spent $128,000 on a small tract of land in the vicinity of the town of Cazenovia, where he built a distillery, a brewery, sawmills, gristmills, two stores, a potash works, and a tavern. North of the Mohawk, Cazenove spent $15,000 on an abortive experiment in the production of maple sugar. In this area he planned model farms, purchased additional land on which to build the market town of Utica, and spent $15,000 annually for five years in an effort to make the land more attractive to purchasers. By 1798 his principals in Amsterdam had had enough. They replaced Cazenove with a more practical agent.[20]

The methods of Williamson and Cazenove, however unrealistic they may have been, attracted wide attention and became part of the general fund of American experience in the sale and settlement of wild lands. It is not surprising, therefore, that speculators of smaller means were sometimes tempted to emulate their example.

The speculative fervor of the 1790's was not confined to western New York; the wilderness areas of northern New York also attracted investors in land. In 1787 a fertile tract known as the St. Lawrence Ten Towns, adjacent to the river of the same name, was auctioned off to a group of speculators headed by Alexander Macomb. His appetite for land still unsated, Macomb laid his plans to acquire the vast acreage adjoining his purchase. In 1791 his ambition was realized when he purchased all the remaining unpatented land in northern New York, some 4,000,000 acres, at the price of $0.08 an acre. Macomb immediately divided the bulk of his purchase into six tracts, each with a frontage either on the St. Lawrence River or on Lake Ontario, and sold them to lesser speculators for development. Most notable of these buyers was William Constable, a bold manipulator from New York City. Constable in turn sold part of his holdings to Belgian capitalists; part to a group of refugees from Revolutionary France; and part to Samuel Ward of New York, with whom Aaron Burr was said to be associated. But when Burr sought release from his part of the bargain, Ward completed the purchase on his own. In 1794 Constable sold 210,000 acres to James Greenleaf, who soon mortgaged the tract to Philip Livingston for $38,000.[21]

It was through this tract of land that the Brown family became fortuitously concerned in land speculation in the Adirondacks. To understand their involvement it is necessary to take a look at John Brown's family. His daughter Abby had married John Francis, scion of a prominent Philadelphia family long business correspondents of the Browns. Although young Francis had neither an interest in nor an aptitude for business, he possessed a pleasing manner, a good edu-

cation, a taste for literature and the arts, a fondness for the pursuits
of leisure, and an inclination toward gracious living. John Brown
is said to have made him his partner in the house of Brown and Francis partly because of his desire to keep his daughter near him and
partly because of his disappointment that his own son, James, had developed tastes "which were emphatically uncommercial." The firm of
Brown and Francis prospered in spite of the junior partner. Not only
were they the Rhode Island pioneers in the China trade but they pursued the trade on a large scale.

But there came a fateful day when one of their ships was to arrive at
New York with a cargo that had been sold en route for the sum of
$210,000. John Brown sent his young partner to New York to meet the
vessel and to attend to the details of the transaction. Unable to determine the precise time of the ship's arrival, John Francis found himself in the city with several days to kill. His convivial nature was
instrumental in bringing him into association with James Greenleaf, Philip Livingston, Aaron Burr, and one of the Morris family, all
of whom happened to be interested in the Adirondack wilderness.
The details of the following events are lacking, but it appears that
while John Francis was in his cups, his friends and associates succeeded in stimulating his interest in lands in the Adirondacks.
They said they had discovered, by a strange coincidence, that the
number of dollars Francis was to receive for the ship's cargo exactly
equaled the number of acres of land, 210,000, that Greenleaf had mortgaged to Philip Livingston. The result was that John Francis returned
to Providence, not with $210,000, but with an imperfect claim to
210,000 acres of wild land in the Adirondacks. It was under these circumstances that John Brown found in 1794 that he possessed a rather
dubious title to a portion of the Adirondack wilderness, henceforth
to be known as the John Brown Tract. It is easy to believe the report that
John, when told what his partner and son-in-law had done, "dropped his
head into his hands and wept bitter tears . . ."

The imperfect title to the land that John Brown received was evidently either a second mortgage or a quitclaim deed, since he succeeded in perfecting his title to the land only after foreclosure proceedings that required him to cover the first mortgage. Four years later,
on December 5, 1798, he received a deed carrying the signature of
Thomas Cooper, master in chancery of New York. By this time the
total cost of the tract had increased to $250,000. Meanwhile, John Fran-
cis, the cause of his partner's woes, had died in 1796.

John Brown's new acquisition was situated on the southwest slope
of the Adirondack Mountains. Some 46,000 acres of the tract were lo-

cated in Lewis County, 3,000 acres were in Hamilton County, and the remaining 161,000 acres in Herkimer County comprised one sixth of the county's total area. After he had spent $40,000 to perfect his title to this isolated block of land cursed with a frigid climate and a barren soil, John's pertinacity (which he shared in abundance with other members of the Brown family) would not permit him to leave well enough alone. In an effort to retrieve something from the mistake of his late partner, he began to send good money after bad. He had heard, no doubt, of the hothouse methods employed during the decade by the agents of the Pulteney Estates and the Holland Land Company in an effort to promote the sale and settlement of their lands. One of the principal acts of folly of Theophile Cazenove, agent of the Holland Land Company, had been the new village of Utica, which would now be the gateway to the John Brown wilderness. Although John was a wealthy man by the standards of his day, his resources were nevertheless limited when compared with those of the numerous companies combined in the Holland Land Company or of the several men of wealth represented in the Pulteney group; he could ill afford to emulate the example of these men, who had allowed their own large capital fund to be endangered by the reckless expenditures of their agents. Nor should John have overlooked the basic fact that capital expenditures appropriate to lands that were fertile and accessible might be wholly unrealistic on a barren and isolated tract such as his own.

But resolved at any cost to develop and sell his Adirondack holdings, John Brown visited the tract in 1799 and had the land surveyed and carefully divided into eight townships. As if to rebuke the heedless extravagance of the late John Francis, he named the townships not Brownsville or New Providence or for any persons or places of Rhode Island but for the acquisitive virtues: Industry, Enterprise, Perseverance, Unanimity, Frugality, Sobriety, Economy, and Regularity. John then built a road through the forest from Remsen in Oneida County to Township 7, a distance of twenty-five miles. The construction of this thoroughfare, which crossed two rivers of considerable size, was an extremely ambitious and a very costly venture for one person. He started two settlements on the tract, one in Township 1, Industry, the other in Township 7, Economy. At what is now the village of Old Forge in the latter township he built a sawmill, a gristmill, several houses, and a frontier store. To provide water power for his mills, he built a dam across the mouth of the middle branch of Moose River. His objective was to establish permanent settlements on the tract, to convert the wilderness into farms. John succeeded in attracting to the land a few settlers who with his assistance managed to subsist as long as he lived but who were quickly overwhelmed by the "wintry blasts," the inhospitable soil, and the stark isolation once he was gone. There was irony in the fact that this shrewd businessman, in a vain effort to salvage something from a misadventure not of his making, should have wasted thousands of dollars in the township that bore the name Economy.[22]

Although John had spent money freely on the tract in the hope that the improvements would attract settlers and enhance the value of his holdings, he appears to have believed that the aggregate worth of the land remained unchanged. In his last will and testament he valued the 210,000 acres, of which the original cost was a like number of dollars, at $210,065. Township 7, Economy, on whose 23,180 acres he had spent money so freely, he valued at $29,180. In bequeathing this township to his favorite grandson, John Brown Francis, he referred to the "good improvements"—among them the cleared land, the house, the barn, the sawmill, and the gristmill—and the fact that on the tract was "plenty of the best pine timber."[23]

With the benefit of hindsight it is easy to condemn John Brown's handling of this piece of wilderness, which had come into his hands through no fault of his. It is clear that he and his family would have been ahead financially had he made no effort to perfect his title to the land, allowing it to revert to the state. But in clearing his title, John was acting in a realistic manner. He ceased to be a realist, however, when after visiting the land, he failed to accept it for what it was—a mountain waste to be disposed of as quickly and easily as possible. His great mistake was his costly attempt to convert this forbidding and inaccessible bit of terrain into a prosperous colony of arable farms. So the name of one of the shrewdest men of business of his time is inseparably connected with one of the most ludicrous and fantastic ventures of the day.

Following the death of John Brown in 1803, the tract that continued to bear his name reverted to a state of nature as one by one the settlers he had worked so hard to attract acknowledged their defeat by abandoning the land. His costly improvements steadily deteriorated through exposure to the elements. Not until the year 1811 was another effort made to establish on the land a viable way of life; this time the attempt was made by Charles Frederick Herreshoff, son-in-law of John Brown.[24] Born at Minden, Prussia, in 1763, Herreshoff was the son of an officer in the famous Potsdam Guards. From the father the lad inherited his magnificent physique (he was 6 feet 4 inches tall), while to his mother he owed his charm of manner as well as his undoubted artistic leanings. He received a good liberal education, was equipped with "the accomplishments of a cultured gentleman," and possessed "a well-trained voice and the ability to play the flute with taste and skill." Finished with his formal education, young Herreshoff traveled in Europe for a time, came to New York about 1786, entered into a partnership with a fellow German, and engaged in the importation of German goods. He quickly built up a successful business, while rounding out his accomplishments by acquiring an excellent command of his adopted tongue.

In 1793 a business engagement brought the young man to Providence, armed with a letter of introduction to John Brown, then at the pinnacle of his success in the world of business. Properly impressed by the "cultured" visitor, John extended to him every courtesy, including an invitation to his home. John's daughter Sarah, then twenty, a young woman of grace and charm with a hobby of calculating eclipses and a fondness and aptitude for music, so completely captivated Herreshoff that henceforth he found all manner of pretexts for visiting Providence. Disappointed that his daughter had fallen in love with a foreigner, although a cultivated one, John Brown finally made a virtue of necessity, and on July 1, 1801, staged a wedding in "royal style" for the young couple at his mansion on Power Street in Providence. Taking his bride to New York, Herreshoff rented a house in Westchester County and resumed the business he had neglected during his long courtship; but the damage was so far beyond repair that it failed and was dissolved within a year.

The unemployed Herreshoff and his wife then returned to the Providence mansion of John Brown, where their first child was born. Upon John's death they took up residence at the farm at Point Pleasant, Bristol, Rhode Island, where John and his family had spent much of their time in summer. Here young Herreshoff began the congenial task of trying to improve his wife's property. With an unquestioned love of, and some understanding for, agriculture, he remodeled the house, changed the driveway, and laid out beautiful gardens filled with exotic plants, vines, and flowers acquired at substantial cost. Not content with this, he then built a new house of stone, tried to drain a fifty-acre swamp, and bought an additional farm. Although his improvements made the farm a more beautiful and pleasant place to live, they yielded no monetary return at a time when his wife's income was beginning to decline. Unfortunately, although John Brown had left a large estate, there was no one to hold together his business structure, which had been the source of the family's wealth. His son, James, was not interested in business; his grandson John Brown Francis was too young; one son-in-law, James Brown Mason, was unreliable; and the other son-in-law, Charles Frederick Herreshoff, was a gentleman farmer, apparently unsuited to the ways of the counting house.

It is not unlikely that various members of the family reproved Herreshoff for spending their money too freely and that now, in time of adversity, they challenged him to show results from the farm on which he had made such costly improvements. Herreshoff, to escape the reproaches of the family and to buttress his own self-respect, apparently suggested that he go to the John Brown Tract, there to retrieve the fallen fortunes of the family. The family offered no objections, and in 1811 Charles Frederick Herreshoff, who had failed to make a success of a good farm in a well-settled area, headed for the Adirondacks, where he would attempt to wrest a fortune from an inhospitable wilderness. John Brown Francis, to whom Herreshoff had been a second father after John Francis' untimely death, considered going with Herreshoff (he had inherited Township 7, the most improved part of the tract), but he abandoned the idea. The young man did, however, pay two or three visits to the area during Herreshoff's sojourn there.

Learning nothing from the earlier failure of his father-in-law, Herreshoff planned to offer strong inducements to men to settle the tract and convert it into prosperous farms. This nucleus of settlement would then serve to attract other persons who would purchase the land at good prices. But about 1815 the tide of settlement on the land was at a low ebb, and Herreshoff decided that the tract would be well suited to pastoral farming. After making costly improvements to this end, including building a great shed some 300 feet long, he purchased and assembled at Providence a large herd of sheep to be driven all the way to the Adirondacks by a family retainer named Adrian Thresher. Although the sheep arrived safely after a trek of six weeks, the experiment in raising sheep on the tract did not succeed.

The attempt at pastoral farming was scarcely at an end when Herreshoff became convinced that he had discovered another way to make a fortune from the tract. In August, 1816, he addressed a seventeen-page letter to Brown and Ives, reviewing the disappointments of the preceding five years and setting forth his hopes for the future. "Our soil though rough" would eventually make the settlement one of the most "flourishing" in the state. The one thing needed to provide the "spring" to permanent prosperity was "a safe and regular branch of business" that could be pursued to advantage. He had conceived a business combining "safety & simplicity," which had received the approbation of several leading citizens of Utica with whom he had consulted. This business promised to replenish his fallen fortunes, if he could only procure the means of launching the enterprise. It was his hope that Brown and Ives would advance the necessary funds.

This latest scheme of Herreshoff was a slitting and rolling mill "in connection with the manufactory of cut nails." The nail was not only a product of great and regular consumption generally but it was more "peculiarly important and lucrative" in his part of the world because of certain local circumstances. He claimed that the supply of nails in the interior of New York State was "irregular and deficient," the demand always great and ever increasing, and the price often extravagant. Nails always commanded cash without discount. Their manufacture had been much neglected in the state. The John Brown Tract, he maintained, was ideally situated to "monopolize the whole custom of this northern county." It was equidistant from the Black River road on the west and the new road connecting Albany with Ogdensburg on the east, the two great thoroughfares to northern New York. Nails used to the northward were made in Utica. He concluded that a nailery located to the north of Utica would capture the nail market of northern and western New York.

His plan, in theory at least, would have been more practical had it contemplated the use of iron ore from the John Brown Tract. But Herreshoff described this ore as of such low grade as to be unsuited to his purposes. His scheme, therefore, was to purchase bar iron in New York City, pay the high costs of transportation to Utica and thence to his mill, convert the bar iron into iron hoops from which to cut the nails, undersell the manufacturers in Utica by twenty-nine dollars a ton, and make a net profit of ninety dollars a ton. Included in his letter to Brown and Ives were the figures proving to his own satisfaction that the use of power-driven machinery would give him a marked advantage over all competitors.

Having convinced himself of the feasibility of the proposed nailery, he revealed to Brown and Ives that funds, of which he was chronically deficient, were required for its implementation. He estimated that he would need $5,000 with which to provide "a large building for the works, a small dwelling house, the water works & running gear, machinery for rolling & slitting, cutting & heading machines, and all necessary implements & tools, for the working of 100 tons a year..." If Brown and Ives would make this amount available to him, Herreshoff would offer as security "a deed of the establishment and all belonging to it, and of 5000 acres of land in this same township (all I have to dispose of in my own right)." Both deeds were to remain in the hands of Brown and Ives until the debt was canceled with interest. Herreshoff would further engage to "apply 3/4 of the neat proceeds of the business" to the liquidation of the debt.[25]

For three and a half months Brown and Ives were silent on the proposal made by Herreshoff. When they eventually replied, they partly explained the delay in terms of "the difficulty we found in Complying with your request," an allusion, no doubt, to the fact that Herreshoff was already in debt to them. The more important reason for their hesitation, however, was their "conviction that the business in which you propose employing a capital in the interior of New York cannot possibly succeed." Nails were made in the vicinity of Providence and in "various other places" by large manufacturing establishments at the rate of two or three tons a day, thus completely dwarfing the scale of operations envisioned by Herreshoff. They were not only made at low cost but the expense of shipping them was "quite light." When he was next in Providence, they would be glad to have conversations with him "on this & other subjects connected with your Black River" project. Should there be a reasonable prospect of furthering his interests, they would be pleased "to contribute towards it."[26]

Though direct evidence is lacking, circumstances indicate that such conversations did take place. Brown and Ives held a mortgage from Herreshoff, and they became the owners of 5,000 acres once belonging to the John Brown Tract, which Herreshoff had offered as security for the proposed loan of $5,000. Thus they seem to have in some degree succumbed again to the charm and plausibility of Herreshoff. But the complete absence of any further reference in the records to nails creates a rather strong presumption that Brown and Ives agreed to the $5,000 loan on condition that Herreshoff abandon the idea of a nailery in the wilderness. Whether they stipulated the precise use to which the money must be put is not known.

Within less than a year Herreshoff informed Brown and Ives that he had drawn on them for $400 in payment for forge iron from Salisbury, Connecticut. In the same letter he said, "My forge is in considerable forwardness, and will probably be ready to work about 1st November." He assured them that "Our ores are now beyond all doubt inexhaustible, and of the very richest quality," in reference to ore that he had previously considered unfit for making nails. It remained "only to ascertain whether those same ores will yield a good iron here, as they do in other countries." There was "every possible prospect not only of a successful experiment, but of an opportunity for the most lucrative business on an extensive Scale."[27]

In April, 1818, Herreshoff wrote that he had "pursued the mining business with redoubled vigour through the whole of this severe season," and he had "exposed to full view, that Nature in forming this body of ore, has worked on a vast and magnificent scale." Thousands of tons of ore were "now as it were in plain sight." He claimed that the ore was without defect and answered "every purpose of the best imported iron" with the added virtue of "perfect uniformity." These qualities would ensure an extensive and permanent market in the vast area north and west of Albany. The price of "foreign iron" had never been less than $130 a ton in Utica. He would not only be able to sell at a lower figure but he would make a profit of 100 per cent on materials and labor.[28]

These two letters from Herreshoff do not reveal the precise nature of the iron business he planned to carry on. An inexhaustible store of iron ore of the finest quality would ordinarily be processed into pig iron in a blast furnace, of which he makes no mention. Instead, he refers repeatedly to his forge, in which iron pigs are commonly converted into bar iron. But, whatever his plan, he needed more money at a time when he admitted "transgressing the limits" of his credit with Brown and Ives. Nevertheless, he was sure they would approve his conduct under the circumstances. The project was one "which to part with, One hundred thousand Drs. could be no temptation to a man with the means and inclination to pursue this business . . ."[29] (He had already spent not only the $5,000 advanced by Brown and Ives but also an unknown sum of money obtained by drawing frequently on them for amounts ranging from $300 to $400.) He now wished to lay in a stock of material sufficient for "10 months of uninterrupted work," including a large supply of coal and 300 tons of ore. In addition, it would be necessary to built a coal house, one dwelling for the workmen at the forge, and a depot at the head of "our river navigation" for the shipment of the "iron coming from the works." Funds were required, too, for "working cattle," boats, wages, etc. This would necessitate an added $5,000. Of this, he expected to obtain $2,000 from the sale of iron. The remaining $3,000 he asked Brown and Ives to provide. With this added assistance the works would become self-sustaining.[30]

To this request Brown and Ives replied that they had already paid "a larger Sum, than was contemplated & agreed upon when the Mortgage was executed." It was very inconvenient for them to continue to advance funds "for carrying on your Iron Manufactury." They hoped his family friends, all interested in his future prosperity, would give him "proportionable aid." Specifically, they said they would provide additional funds "if either Mr. James Brown, Mr. Mason, or the Female branches of the Family will undertake & engage to us in a written stipulation to make us safe by a collateral security."[31]

The absence of further reference to this proposal would seem to indicate that the members of the John Brown family were unwilling to risk anything more on what was apparently a losing proposition. Of Herreshoff's estrangement from his wife's family there is little doubt. His visits to Providence were more and more infrequent. Finally they ceased entirely. He lived in the wilderness; his wife and children remained in Providence.

Failing to procure a direct advance from Brown and Ives, Herreshoff reverted to his earlier practice of drawing on them and then advising them of the fact. Within a period of two months his drafts on them amounted to $1,512. Brown and Ives thereupon directed him not to draw upon them again until he was authorized to do so.[32] Within a few months he advised them that although success was assured, he had been "compelled to draw" upon them once more to the extent of $550, which he hoped they would not view as "in defiance of your injunction."[33]

At about this time it must have become apparent to Herreshoff that he was a ruined man. Iron ore that he had termed of "the very richest quality" yielded a finished product at a cost of $1 a pound—$2,000 a ton on the spot, far removed from a market and without facilities for reaching one. On Sunday morning, December 19, 1819, he picked up a pistol and shot himself.

After Herreshoff's death, his nephew John Brown Francis, owner of Township 7, tried vainly to hold together the little community his uncle had established. But, unable to cope with the harsh environment, the settlers one by one vanished from the land, as their property steadily deteriorated.[34]

A third and final effort was made to settle Township 7 in the years 1834–37. Silas Thompson, an agent of the John Brown family, took up residence in the Herreshoff house with instructions to offer 160 acres of land, a cow, and 10 sheep to the first ten families who would settle on the tract and remain for two years. Once again the controlling theory was that of liberal inducements designed to attract a nucleus of settlement, after which the adjacent lands could be sold at good prices. Once again the theory worked, up to a point. The ten families came, a school was built, the gristmill was reconditioned for the benefit of the settlers, and other forms of encouragement were provided. But again man proved unequal to his stern surroundings, and this settlement went the way of its predecessors.[35]

From the Herreshoff tragedy in the wilds of the Adirondacks, Brown and Ives emerged as the owners of 5,000 acres once belonging to the John Brown Tract, while John Brown Francis, who had inherited Township 7 from his grandfather, ultimately found himself the owner of virtually all the remaining acres, as other members of the John Brown family died. In 1850 Asa Hogins of Boston, who was interested in the promotion of a railway in northern New York and labored under the mistaken idea that Brown and Ives were the owners of the John Brown Tract, asked them to make a grant of land to the railway.[36] In reply, Brown and Ives advised him that they had owned a small area in the tract, but through remissness of agents in payment of taxes part of the land had been sold by New York State. They further informed Hogins that John Brown Francis had recently contracted for the sale of the John Brown Tract.[37] Thus ended the one wholly disastrous venture of the Browns in their long history of land speculation on many frontiers.

OHIO

Probably no land speculation in American annals was of greater historical significance than that of the Ohio Company of Associates. The Ohio land purchase grew out of the desire of the Continental Congress to obtain a larger revenue from the sale of public lands and a plan of certain New Englanders who had been officers in the Continental army, for the speculative purchase of a large tract in the public domain suitable for the planting of a colony. Specifically, the idea was conceived by General Rufus Putnam, who enjoyed the support of General Benjamin Tupper and General Samuel Holden Parsons. Knowing that the soldiers of General Washington's army had been paid off in certificates of indebtedness acceptable in payment of public land rather than in cash, Putnam proposed to form a company, sell stock to veterans in exchange for these depreciated certificates, and then use the same certificates to pay the government for a large tract of land on the Ohio River. Through the Massachusetts newspapers Putnam and his associates invited Revolutionary veterans who were interested to meet at the Bunch of Grapes Tavern in Boston on March 1, 1786. Those who attended this meeting organized the Ohio Company, engaged to sell stock in the company to the amount of $1,000,000 in exchange for Continental certificates, and pledged themselves to emigrate to lands on the Ohio to be purchased with the same certificates. Although a year later only $250,000 worth of stock had been sold, they decided to purchase as much land as they could with the funds at hand, believing they could enlarge their purchase when the success of their venture had attracted new investors. To sell this plan to the Congress, Putnam and his associates obtained the services of the Reverend Menassah Cutler of Ipswich, Massachusetts.[38]

In early July, 1787, Cutler arrived in New York, where the Congress was in session. He proposed that the Congress abandon the plan of selling public lands in small tracts, as contemplated in the Land Ordinance of 1785, in favor of the sale of 1,000,000 acres or more to the Ohio Company at $1 an acre. The impecunious government probably would have jumped at the chance to obtain $1,000,000 in sound money by the sale of a large block of land at $1 an acre. But when Cutler suggested that the Congress allow a rebate of one third for badlands that would inevitably be included in a large purchase, the ardor of Congress was somewhat dampened. And when Cutler further proposed that payment be made in depreciated government securities, the Congress seemed to lose all interest. Discouraged, Cutler was about to pack his bags for the homeward journey when he received a call from Colonel William Duer, Secretary of the Board of Treasury, with jurisdiction over all land sales. "A 'number of the principal characters in the city,'" Duer said, were well disposed toward the sale to the Ohio Company but only on condition that they be permitted to share secretly in the profits. Duer spoke for members of the Congress, government officials, business-men, and others eager to purchase Ohio lands, whose official status made it improper for them to do so. Duer and Cutler agreed that the latter should apply to the Congress for two separate tracts of land. One of 1,500,000 acres would go to the Ohio Company; the other, of 5,000,000 acres was for Duer and his associates, organized as the Scioto Company. Cutler and one of his associates, Winthrop Sargent, would receive thir-teen shares in the Scioto Company, Duer and his friends would keep thirteen, and six shares were to be sold in Europe; everyone involved in the agreement would benefit financially.[39]

Duer, his agreement with Cutler signed and sealed, promptly pushed the scheme through the Congress, which authorized Duer's Board of Treasury to sell large tracts of land to companies. After waiting for three days, to give the impression of due deliberation, the board agreed to the sale on Cutler's terms of $0.666 an acre, payable in depreciated Continental certificates. For about $0.08 an acre in hard money, the Ohio Company received title to 1,781,760 acres situated immediately to the south and west of the confluence of the Ohio and Muskingum rivers.[40]

The Ohio Company was principally a New England concern, although certain New Yorkers, including Alexander Hamilton, were shareholders. The guiding spirits in organizing and launching the enterprise were from Connecticut and Massachusetts. Although Rhode Islanders had no part in the conception or implementation of the plan, they were conspicuous among the stockholders. And prominent among these were various members of the Brown family. Nicholas Brown held five shares; John, five; Moses, three; and Nicholas, Jr., three. Together with women of the family the Browns had a total of twenty-two shares, more than were held by any other family group.[41] A share entitled the owner to a house lot plus 1,173 acres of land divided into lots of 3, 8, 100, 160, 262, and 640 acres. Through Nicholas, Sr., and Nicholas, Jr., Brown and Ives owned eight shares amounting to 9,384 acres. By 1820 their holdings had increased to almost 18,000 acres as a result of their acquisition of land originally belonging to other proprietors in the company.[42]

Share owners who continued to live in Rhode Island found it necessary to have an agent residing in Marietta (the new town established by the Ohio Company), whose function it was to pay the taxes on the land, keep a watchful eye on trespassers, and handle land sales. In the early years the agent of Brown and Ives and other Rhode Island share owners was Benjamin Ives Gilman, a cousin of Thomas P. Ives, a shareholder of the company, and one of the first band of settlers to move to Marietta.[43] He had been a pioneer in the building of ocean-going ships at Marietta, had established wide connections in the new territory, and was a delegate to the convention that framed the first state constitution of Ohio.

For the first dozen or more years of his residence at Marietta, Gilman's time as agent was chiefly occupied not with selling land but in explaining to his principals in Providence the territorial tax on their lands. Although his residence was in Ohio, Gilman faithfully reflected in his letters the absentee-owner point of view of the men he served. He wrote that the tax for the year 1800 was "unreasonably high," but it could not be prevented. What was worse, he added, the money raised by the tax was "principally expended" at the seat of government in the territory, and it would be "equally beneficial" to Washington County (in which Marietta was located) "to have the money distributed at Boston." The shareholders, said Gilman, were sufferers from "Representative Government." Had the people of the territory been content with the first stage of territorial government (in which a governor and judges governed), they might have been spared the cost of a legislature (required in the second stage of territorial government). And not satisfied with this extravagance, a considerable party in the territory was "striving to push us forward to a State Government," whose greater costs would require even higher taxes. It was to the advantage of the people to rest quietly in their present stage, applying existing revenues to the building of roads and other internal improvements. But ambitious and unprincipled men were beguiling well-disposed but ignorant citizens into believing that statehood would bring them innumerable blessings. These selfish men had two objects in view: to create and fill state jobs and to strengthen the "Democratic Principles" of Jeffersonian Republicanism.[44]

Until 1820 neither Gilman nor Paul Fearing, who succeeded him as agent for the Providence proprietors, was able to make sales, either in the good times prevailing from 1793 to 1807 or in the years of commercial obstruction that began with the Embargo Act. A conspicuous exception was the sale of two 100-acre lots at $8 and $5 an acre.[45] This lack of demand for lands in the Ohio purchase resulted in part from overpricing at a time when the government, under the Land Act of 1800, was selling lands in the public domain at $2 an acre on a credit of four years. These liberal terms, which encouraged men to overpurchase, made it difficult for private owners to compete.

Another deterrent to the sale of the land had been the drive on the part of certain proprietors, including Brown and Ives, to sell land in whole shares of 1,173 acres, in the erroneous belief that there was a "close connexion or dependence between the lots of a share." Actually, many shares had lots "more than 100 miles asunder" with no greater natural relationship than "a farm in Connecticut, has with one in the new State of Maine."[46] Insofar as this system of scattered lots guaranteed to the proprietor lands of varying quality in different parts of the purchase, it was thoroughly equitable. But it nevertheless embodied features that created problems for the owner. When the Ohio Company surveyed the land in the purchase, no provision was made for subdividing the 262- and the 640-acre lots, which accounted for 902 of the 1,173 acres belonging to a share. Since those lots were far too large for an impecunious pioneer farmer in a wooded country, not much land could be sold until provision was made for the division of these lots. Small wonder, wrote the agent of Brown and Ives at Marietta, that the land values in the Ohio Company purchase were not rising in proportion to those in the western part of Ohio and in the states farther to the west, "where the principal part of the emigrants go." He reminded his principals that if they wished to sell their land, they should have it "run into quarter sections" of 160 acres, which would enable him to determine the proper pricing of the different tracts.[47]

On January 1, 1820, the firm of Putnam and Turner became the resident agents at Marietta for Brown and Ives and the other Providence proprietors. In a circular letter of that date they remarked upon certain circumstances that had previously retarded the sale of the lands of the Ohio Company, and they had pertinent suggestions to make with respect to changes designed to promote sales in the future. The first step to be taken was to gather data providing a full description of each of the widely scattered lots of Brown and Ives. Only if this were done would judicious pricing of the lands be possible. Then the larger lots should be divided, preparatory to the sale of the land "in detail," which was far to be preferred to sale by entire shares. Selling lands in detail would pay all costs of surveying, exploring, subdividing, and selling and would yield "from twenty-five to fifty per cent. advance on any amount, for which they would have sold by shares entire."[48]

Accepting much of the advice of their agents, Brown and Ives agreed to the survey and exploration of their land and to the division of the 640-acre sections into half and quarter sections and even into parcels of 80 and 40 acres. There is no evidence, however, that the 262-acre lots were divided, perhaps because they comprised awkward units incapable of being fitted into the rectangular system of survey.

The agents were greatly alarmed by the Land Act of 1820, which abolished the credit system, reduced the price of land to $1.25 an acre payable at time of entry, and reduced the minimum salable unit to 80 acres. This, they thought, would retard the sale of privately owned lands for many years, by which time the price of government land would again be reduced and proprietors in the Ohio purchase subjected to heavy taxes on land altogether unproductive. The interests of all land owners in the Marietta area were being sacrificed to replenish the Treasury at Washington. Few tracts of wild land in Ohio could "continue to ... pay taxes & advance anything in value." Brown and Ives were thus advised by Putnam and Turner to "encounter the Government— on their own ground" by resurveying their land, dividing it into tracts of a size suitable for farms, and offering it for sale at $1.25— "cash down." Land not sold on these terms and in this way should "be exchanged to persons at the east," who would emigrate to Ohio, giving good property or other security for the land. Mr. Schieffelin of New York disposed of his land in this manner to the benefit of himself and the settlers. He was reported to have sent out twenty to twenty-five families in this way.[49]

Putnam and Turner reported that many of the smaller lots owned by Brown and Ives would sell readily if it were possible to dispose of the produce of the country at a profit. But because of the depression wheat worth $1.25 a bushel three years earlier was selling at $0.25; corn had declined from $0.75 to $0.125 a bushel. Immigration had previously brought large sums of money into the territory, but the tide had turned. From 1812 to 1818 land values had risen at the rate of 10 per cent a year, but for three years the price had steadily declined, reflecting the diminishing demand for private land. Sales could be made only at a sacrifice, which the agents were sure the owners should not make. Some of the land was so poor that it would never repay the sums spent in trying to sell it, and barring the introduction of a more equitable kind of taxation in Ohio, Brown and Ives should abandon it.[50]

On this occasion, as on many others, Brown and Ives accepted no part of the counsel of despair offered them by their agents. They neither reduced the price of their land to $1.25 an acre in an effort to compete with government land nor did they adopt the policy of exchanging lands with persons in the East. The idea of abandoning their inferior lands in the Ohio purchase would have been entirely out of character for the Brown family, who never abandoned anything.

Far from arbitrarily reducing the price of their Ohio lands with a view to a quick sale, Brown and Ives continued their conservative policy of charging all the traffic would bear—a realistic policy for the sale of land costing $0.08 an acre on which the taxes (despite the groans of the agents) were not especially onerous. Judged by its fruits, the policy was a success. The record reveals no sales at less than $2.00 an acre.[51] The maximum price received was $25.00 an acre.[52]

On December 31, 1819, Brown and Ives paid a tax of $159.26 on 15,725 acres of land in the Ohio Company purchase. By 1845 their holdings had shrunk to 8,499 acres, assessed for tax purposes at $7,117. Nine years later, the 6,573 acres then unsold were assessed at $21,926. In February, 1858, there remained 5,724 acres assessed at $19,221 but believed by the agent to be worth $28,528. It is evident that the steady appreciation in value of the land far outran the increase in taxes.[53]

Not until 1881, more than ninety years after the original purchase, was the last acre sold and the account closed. Available data do not permit us to draw a balance sheet of the Ohio Company investment of the Brown family. By their system of accounting, in which interest on the original capital investment and on taxes paid, compounded annually, was reckoned as a cost, their profit on the transaction was greatly reduced. But their steadfast rejection of the agents' advice to reduce prices for the sake of quick sales or to abandon the inferior lands indicated their confident expectation of a profit, even by their ultraconservative bookkeeping methods. That their correspondence about the Ohio lands makes no mention of regret or disappointment indicates reasonable satisfaction with the investment. Brown and Ives realized no fortune from these lands. But their returns were enough to make their first venture in land speculation in the West a moderate success.

YAZOO LANDS

Most notorious of all ventures in land speculation in America were the celebrated Yazoo companies. Insisting on her claims to western lands after other states had ceded their claims, Georgia in 1789 sold more than 25,000,000 acres west of the Chattahoochee River for the trifling sum of $207,580. The purchasers were the Virginia Yazoo Company, the South Carolina Yazoo Company, and the Tennessee Company, which offered payment mainly in depreciated South Carolina and Continental notes. These the state of Georgia refused to accept and declared the bargain of no force.[54] The region being an attractive one, four new land companies were quickly formed: the Georgia, the Georgia Mississippi, the Upper Mississippi, and the Tennessee. On January 7, 1795, these companies became the beneficiaries of a most notorious piece of legislation. Thirty-five million acres, comprising most of present-day Alabama and Mississippi, were sold to the companies for $500,000. The law authorized them to take 2,000,000 additional acres for the benefit of such citizens of Georgia as might later be taken into the scheme. Among those admitted to one or more of the companies either before or after the passage of the act were all save one of the legislators who had voted for it.[55] When the facts leaked out, the irate citizens of Georgia turned out the malefactors and elected a new legislature, most of whose members were pledged to the repeal of the act of sale. On February 13, 1796, the new legislature declared the sale unconstitutional, null, and void.[56]

Prior to the rescinding act, however, the companies had sold some of their land to purchasers who were ignorant of the fact that the legislature had been bribed. When Georgia in 1802 ceded her claims to western lands to the federal government, these buyers hoped that Congressional action would compensate them for the losses they suffered by the repeal. For a season the Yazoo frauds became a bone of bitter contention in legislative halls. Meanwhile, certain of the injured persons, all based in New England, had instituted litigation designed to test the legality of the Georgia Repeal Act of 1796. Ultimately the question reached the Supreme Court of the United States, which in 1810, in the famous case of *Fletcher* v. *Peck,* declared the sale by the legislature, though conceived in fraud, to be a contract that the federal Constitution forbade the legislature of Georgia to impair. Thus the fraudulent sale of 1795 was legal and constitutional.

Although *Fletcher* v. *Peck* established a great constitutional principle, it did not immediately bring financial relief to those persons who had purchased land from the four companies that were parties to the fraud. Among these buyers were Brown and Ives. In 1796 they had purchased from the directors of the Georgia Mississippi Company two certificates for land, estimated at 56,000 acres, for which they paid the sum of $4,480, or $0.08 an acre.[57] After the Georgia legislature rescinded the grant, this property appeared to be virtually worthless. The Georgia Mississippi Company had sold their entire claim to a group of gentlemen resident in Boston, with the stipulation that the certificates previously issued were to be receivable at a specified rate. Brown and Ives, however, were never able to get a sufficient offer for their certificates. After *Fletcher* v. *Peck* the way to indemnification became clear, but it was not until March 26, 1814, that Congress finally voted $5,000,000 in land scrip to quiet the claims for compensation.[58] After three more years of waiting, Brown and Ives, in March, 1817, received stock certificates for $3,490.25 by way of indemnification.[59]

PENNSYLVANIA

Among public figures of his day, one of the most persistent of land speculators was James Wilson of Pennsylvania. Born in Scotland, an eminent member of the legal profession, outstanding among the delegates to the federal Constitutional Convention, and a justice of the Supreme Court of the United States, he takes high rank among the Founding Fathers. Although there is no mention in the one reference made to Wilson in the papers of Brown and Ives of the circumstances that brought him in touch with the Providence firm, on January 26, 1796, Brown and Ives bought from James Wilson 13,491 acres of land situated in Luzerne County, Pennsylvania, for a consideration of $25,892.[60] The land in question, lying between the Susquehanna and the Delaware rivers, was part of a larger area later detached from Luzerne County to form the new counties of Bradford and Susquehanna. These were wild lands, rough and broken and covered with a dense growth of hemlock and other forest trees, and the price of roughly $1.92 an acre was much the highest that Brown and Ives had yet paid for raw and unimproved land.

For the sale of their lands in Vermont, in the Mohawk Valley, and in Ohio, Brown and Ives had depended on local agents residing in the area. In Pennsylvania, however, their lands were so remote from established settlements that such agents were not to be had. Accordingly, they were forced in the beginning to recruit in Rhode Island the first settlers who were to make the long, difficult journey to their Luzerne lands. Once they had succeeded in persuading a few families to make the move, they selected Caleb Jenks, not as agent to sell the land, but as a sort of local overseer, who would give aid and counsel to new settlers arriving from Rhode Island. They requested Jenks to "encourage all the Settlers on our Land & tell them to *persevere* & be *industrious,* & they will in a short time acquire an easy livlihood."[61]

Only by dint of great industry did Brown and Ives succeed in establishing a small settlement on their purchase. The remoteness and inaccessibility of the land from Providence made it an uphill battle. The problem was made yet more difficult by the high price they felt obliged to ask for the land. Since it had cost them almost $2 an acre, they felt they had to charge $3 an acre, a figure few were able or willing to pay for land wholly unimproved. To induce sales and recruit settlers they resorted to devices they had spurned in selling their other lands. Thus they agreed to sell to Samuel Mason of Providence 400 acres of Luzerne land at $3 an acre. As "inducement of said Mason to make the . . . purchase," Brown and Ives agreed to purchase his dwelling house and lot in Providence for $1,800, making payment of $600 in cash and $1,200 in Luzerne land (400 acres at $3 an acre).[62] Later they sold Richard Burke of Providence 200 acres at $3 an acre by taking his house, lot, and workshop in exchange.[63] Both Mason and Burke agreed to move to the Luzerne lands.

In their other purchases Brown and Ives had steadfastly refused to adopt the hothouse system of making improvements upon the land in order to entice purchasers and settlers. When John Brown and Charles Herreshoff had yielded on this point, Brown and Ives had remained adamant. But in Pennsylvania they relented and built a sawmill and a gristmill for the settlement at a considerable outlay of funds and provided the cost of keeping them in repair; they also forwarded potash kettles for the benefit of the settlement. For the accommodation and use of a settler they sent goods, and for the transport of his family they gave money.[64] They frequently sent sums ranging from thirty to sixty dollars to be divided among individual settlers in small amounts, for which they asked their notes or their labor on the mill or dam.[65] The one form of assistance at which they balked was the building of a distillery. To the request for this they replied that it would not be useful at present. The "too frequent use of Whiskey, must injure, and perhaps might lead some to intemperance."[66]

While eager to sell their land and to promote its settlement, Brown and Ives were not guilty of encouraging a false optimism or of minimizing the hardship awaiting the settler. To a Rhode Islander who contemplated immigration they wrote that two of their settlers had described their poverty in "such a manner, that we cannot recommend any person's going there without some *property*"; they added that for all their efforts the settlers had had a hard winter and appeared much discouraged.[67] When Brown and Ives heard that some of the settlers were in a destitute condition, "not having the means of procuring Bread," they sent fifteen dollars to one and twenty dollars to others in the hope of relieving their distress. They allowed men who had engaged to purchase land to remain on the land for years without making payments, either on principal or interest. Their patience wore thin only when the delinquent, upon leaving the land, proposed to sell his "improvement" to another. Brown and Ives pointed out that the purchaser of the improvement might "again sell to another," leaving them, the rightful owners, "without any indemnity."[68]

Even with outright financial assistance and with the most lenient and indulgent treatment by Brown and Ives, only the most hardy souls were able to survive in their struggle with the land. After twenty years of effort by the owners and the settlers, there were but twenty families on the land in Bradford County and only nine in Susquehanna County.[69] By this time the earlier inaccessibility of the land had been partially overcome by the construction of a turnpike from Milford on the Delaware to the town of Owego on the Susquehanna in southern New York State. Had this pike bisected their lands, as Brown and Ives had hoped, they were prepared to make a handsome investment in shares of the company. But since it was finally located some distance from their tract, they purchased only ten shares at $25 a share.[70]

A new era in the history of the lands was inaugurated when in 1823 Parly Coburn, a resident of the area and a justice of the peace, became the agent of Brown and Ives.[71] Continuing in this capacity for almost forty years, Coburn's understanding of Brown and Ives and of the settlers was so complete that the rapport between owners and settlers was always of an unusually friendly character.

Before a month had passed, he had printed hand-bills advertising "Land in Pennsylvania for sale." A "VALUABLE tract" of 10,000 acres was offered for sale to actual settlers at $3.00 an acre interest free for two years, to be payable in eight annual installments secured by mortgage on the premises. Farmers disposed to move with their families onto the land might "have an opportunity of exchanging their farms for new land, on advantageous terms."[72] The remission of interest for two years as well as the provision for payment in eight annual installments reflected a desire of the owners to sell on terms advantageous to buyers. So, too, did the offer to exchange land in the tract for farms elsewhere. But the fact remained that $3.00 an acre was too high a price for heavily forested land, even though this figure appeared to be almost imperative because of the $1.92 an acre paid for the land.

Coburn's advertising was largely void of results as far as increased sales were concerned. In 1828 he strongly urged Brown and Ives to reduce the price of their lands with a view to making them more competitive with other land in the vicinity.[73] Two owners in the area who had slashed prices seemed to be reaping the benefit thereof. Although direct evidence as to the nature of the reply given by Brown and Ives to Coburn's suggestion is lacking, circumstances seem to indicate that they followed his advice. A document bearing the date of 1834 contains a statement of lots under contract, the name of the occupant, the acreage of each lot, the price an acre, the amount paid to date, and the state of the improvements on the land.[74] Seventy names appear in the list, mostly of men whose contracts were entered into between 1829 and 1833. Those who had purchased prior to 1829 were to pay $3 an acre. Those buying their land in 1829 and after had agreed to pay $2 an acre, indicating a price reduction in that year. The same document lists twenty-six men whose lots were paid for and the deeds delivered. A total of ninety-six men had either bought and paid for, or were under contract to purchase, land in the Brown and Ives tract. This was the measure of accomplishment, against heavy odds, over the period of thirty-eight years that had elapsed since the original purchase in 1796.

While the reduction in the price of land had clearly led to an increase in the number of men disposed to purchase, it still was very hard for the settler to earn a living from the soil and at the same time make payments on his land. A schedule of April, 1836, showed that of the original tract 2,770 acres had been sold and paid for, that 1,969 acres had been sold and paid for in part, and that 4,069 acres had been sold but were wholly unpaid for.[75] This discouraging revelation of the state of affairs on the tract prompted Brown and Ives to send John Tillinghast of Providence to the Luzerne land with instructions to gather all pertinent facts with respect to the situation. A six-day sojourn on the tract enabled Tillinghast to visit virtually all parts of it and to talk with "nearly all, if not all of the settlers." He found the country hilly and so covered with hemlock and other forest trees as to be very difficult to clear. Once the trees were removed, the soil was fertile and well suited to forage and pastoral purposes. The settlers were generally very poor, hard-working men with young families, living in log houses or in small frame dwellings. With few exceptions the appearance of their land, homes, and families seemed to confirm their own statements that at the moment they were unable to pay for their land. The quantity of cleared land varied greatly. Some had just made a beginning; others had cleared ten acres; still others, thirty, forty, and fifty acres. The cleared land was valued at $8 to $12 an acre.

Tillinghast attended meetings in different parts of the tract with twenty to thirty settlers present at each. Most of them protested their inability to pay anything at the moment, and all agreed that they would never be able to pay unless they were granted remission of interest from the time their occupancy of the land began. All expressed a strong desire that Brown and Ives should retain possession of the tract. Although equally good land in the neighborhood had been available at $1.25 to $1.50 an acre, lands of Brown and Ives had been taken at $2.00 an acre in preference, "in the expectation of a Continuance of the lenity with which you have always treated" the settlers.[76]

The precise reaction and reply of Brown and Ives to Tillinghast's report is not known. But circumstantial evidence indicates that while they declined to grant a formal remission of interest, they continued to be lenient with the delinquent settlers. On May 15, 1846, twenty-eight of these men formally petitioned Brown and Ives to "Relinquish the Interest up to this time," but expressed their gratitude for the "Lenity you have Shown us."[77] Ten years later thirty-two of the settlers, alarmed by rumors that Brown and Ives might sell the tract, addressed to the owners a letter affirming their belief that "it would be injurious to us to have the tract conveyed into other mens hands" and requesting that it be kept in the hands of the present owners. If Brown and Ives would agree "to throw off the back Interest," the settlers would undertake to pay within two years for all land for which they had contracted. Reminding Brown and Ives that they had "endured much hardship in the settlement of this new country," they acknowledged "the past favours" they had received from the Providence house.[78]

Again direct evidence of the reaction of Brown and Ives to this request is lacking, but the circumstances point strongly to concessions on some of the points at issue. Events on the Brown and Ives tract began to unfold at an unaccustomed tempo. The whole process of land sale and settlement was accelerated. Within four years the last acre had been sold and all accounts closed. Surely nothing short of a generous gesture by Brown and Ives could have changed the gloom to sunshine in so short a period of time.

Parly Coburn's death on September 20, 1860, coincided almost exactly with the completion of the task he had undertaken almost forty years before. His son, C. R. Coburn, thought it almost unique that such a large tract of land had been sold and paid for with so little trouble to the settlers, most of whom had not one cent when they took possession of their lands. They had literally dug the pay out of the land itself by the sweat of their brows. Much of the credit belonged to the agent, Parly Coburn, regarded by the settlers as their friend. No settler had ever "been driven from his lot because he was not able to pay."

But while much was "due to the agent," it was not to be forgotten that it was the owners "from whom the favors . . . must come." Parly Coburn "has never asked a favor for the settles, and he has asked many, that had not been most freely and most cheerfully granted" by Brown and Ives. His appeals to them for aid to the distressed pioneers had never been in vain. "No principals could be kinder to an agent, no landlords more indulgent to settles."[79]

In relation to their Pennsylvania land Brown and Ives found themselves cast in the paternalistic role of colonizers rather than mere land sellers. In no other purchase were they so closely identified with, or so concerned in, the welfare of those who occupied the land. If this was something less than their most successful business venture, it nevertheless revealed them as men of great patience, of broad understanding, and of humane feeling toward pioneer farmers hard pressed in their efforts to make a living on the forest-clad hills of northeastern Pennsylvania.

Brown and Ives had bought the tract of land in Luzerne County at too high a figure. For years, therefore, they had overpriced the land to settlers, thereby retarding the sale of the land. Once they had reduced the price to $2.00 an acre, the land sold with greater ease. But this figure was too low for land that had cost them $1.92 an acre. At best, they may have broken even on the land. It is more probable that they lost, but not heavily. They clearly were disappointed at the failure of these lands to appreciate in value. In 1835 John Carter Brown remarked that these lands seemed unlikely "to rise as lands in Maine have." At that time he would have welcomed an offer for the entire tract at "a lump sum." If the offer ever came, it was not accepted, perhaps because of the petitions from the settlers praying that Brown and Ives would keep the title in their own hands. "What a pity," John Carter Brown ruefully observed, that "the sums paid for these Penna Lands had not been laid out in purchasing 'the widow Rogers' farm' . . . on Manhattan 30 or 40 years ago." The widow's farm had sold lately for "6 or 700 *m* Dlls."[80]

MAINE

Not all Maine lands had appreciated in value in the manner suggested by John Carter Brown in the remark quoted above. Within a few months Brown and Ives were to consider it their good fortune to be able to divest themselves of lands in that state without serious difficulty.

In 1820 they and John Whipple of Providence had purchased at auction sundry lots in the town of Embden, Maine, one third for Whipple, two thirds for Brown and Ives. The area involved amounted to 2,347 acres for which they paid $986.02, or a fraction in excess of $0.42 an acre.[81] Of the circumstances leading to this investment, the record is completely silent. Nor is there any evidence of efforts made by the owners to use or to dispose of the land during the decade that followed. But sometime before 1831 Joseph N. Greene and Elizabeth Nightingale succeeded Whipple as co-owners with Brown and Ives. On August 20 of that year the new owners entered into an agreement with Brown and Ives for a division of the notes received for the land sold, indicating that some of the land had been disposed of.[82] In 1836 in consideration of $989.37 Brown and Ives sold to Joseph N. Greene nineteen lots or parcels of land containing 1,790.5 acres.[83]

This speculation was not a brilliant success. But since Brown and Ives had incurred little expense during the comparatively brief period of their ownership, they could have suffered no substantial loss. Of all their ventures in land speculation, this was the least known, the least significant, and the least interesting.

ILLINOIS

In the meantime the Browns had become interested in lands in the newer West, where the young state of Illinois was fast becoming a mecca for land speculators. In the western part of that State, situated between the Illinois and Mississippi rivers, was a large stretch known as the Military Tract, comprising 3,500,000 acres reserved under the military bounty land acts of 1811 and 1812 for the purpose of satisfying the claims of soldiers of the War of 1812 and of earlier wars. Many of the men eligible to receive the warrants pursuant to this legislation were unable to move to the Military Tract to locate them, and later these warrants largely passed into the hands of high officers of the Army, members of Congress, and other speculators, rich and poor. The national legislators, through speculative purchase of the warrants, became the owners of 840,000 acres within the tract.[84]

Although the first land the Browns acquired in Illinois was located in the Military Tract, this was entirely by chance rather than by design. In 1835 the law firm of Davis and Krum of Alton, Illinois, acting for Nicholas Brown, brought suit against William Elliott for the recovery of a debt of unknown origin and amount. Before the law had run its course, however, Nicholas Brown agreed to accept from Elliott a warranty deed of 1,920 acres of land in satisfaction of the debt. This land was located in Knox, Peoria, Putnam, Hancock, and Fulton counties, Illinois, all in the area between the Illinois and Mississippi rivers.[85]

Once fortuitous circumstances had placed him in possession of the land, Nicholas Brown had the benefit of experienced counsel. Then in business in Alton was Winthrop S. Gilman, son of Benjamin Ives Gilman. Gilman assured Nicholas that he could readily sell the land for a sum more than sufficient to cover the amount of the debt and the cost of the suit, plus interest and all other expenses incurred. On the other hand, he was sure that lands throughout Illinois would advance rapidly in price because of the great tide of immigration from the East and South that was pouring in upon the state. He was of the opinion, therefore, that it would be a good investment for Nicholas to take the lands "at their present value & await the rise."[86]

Choosing the latter course, Nicholas and his heirs for the next twenty-five years gradually sold their holdings at prices that steadily advanced. So promising seemed the prospect of steady profit that in

May, 1836, Brown and Ives purchased from the federal government 5,900.86 acres of land in Henry County, Illinois, at the currently minimum price of $1.25 an acre. This in turn was followed by a purchase of 1,931 acres in Tazewell County; of somewhat more than 1,300 acres in Bureau County; of 320 acres in Stark County; and of various amounts of land in Madison, Rock Island, and Joe Davies counties. Not the least of their acquisitions was 789 acres purchased at tax sales at a total cost of $24.20, or slightly more than $0.03 an acre. In 1843 the Brown and Ives families owned not less than 14,881 acres of land in Illinois.[87]

(In the meantime, Nicholas Brown came into possession of a mortgage on land in the vicinity of Terre Haute, Indiana, the title to which was in the name of Joseph S. Jenckes. In satisfaction of his claim upon this property the Brown family in 1853 became the full owners of 640 acres of this land, half of which was then valued at $35 an acre.)[88]

Among the interesting documents relating to the earlier ventures of the Browns in land speculation in Illinois is one dated August, 1854, entitled "Memorandum Relative to Henry County Lands in Illinois." This memorandum presents a clear and concise statement on the 5,900.86 acres in land in Henry County from the day of purchase on May 14, 1836, to the sale of the last acre on August 1, 1854. Although the land had cost $1.25 an acre, 1,000 acres of it were sold by Brown and Ives at prices ranging from $0.25 to $1.00 an acre. Another 440 acres sold at $1.50 to $3.50 an acre. More than half the total acreage, 3,260.86 acres, yielded $4.00 an acre, while the remaining 1,200 acres sold at $5.00 to $20.00 an acre. Following the procedure they had employed in other land investments, Brown and Ives had made the first sales at low prices—actually below the first cost of the land. As demand increased with the settlement of adjacent lands, they had steadily increased the price asked for the land. The memorandum shows that the area that had cost $7,376.08 had brought a return of $29,307.44, an increase of $21,931.36. This last amount, however, was not clear profit, for the taxes paid on the land, plus the compound interest thereon, brought the total outlay to $10,215.62. Deducting this last sum from the total proceeds of $29,307.44, the profit on the venture by one system of accounting was $19,091.82, or 187 per cent of the total cost of the land, a very handsome return indeed.

Calculated by the ultraconservative accounting methods so long employed by the Browns, however, the profit was much more modest. In reckoning the profit or loss on a maritime venture, they had always included as a cost the compound interest on the capital investment in a ship and her cargo for the duration of the voyage. When later they began to invest in wild lands, they charged themselves compound interest on the first cost of the land from the time of purchase to the day of sale of the last acre. Thinking in terms of what the economist calls "opportunity cost," they reasoned that their capital, if not tied up in land, could be otherwise invested at 6 per cent. So they regarded the compound interest on the original investment as a cost. In the case of the purchase in Henry County, Illinois, more than eighteen years elapsed between the time of purchase and the final sale. The principal item of cost, therefore, was not the $7,376.08 originally paid for the land but the compound interest on that sum over a period of eighteen years, amounting to $13,947.92. In this way the total cost of the land was increased to $24,163.54, while the profit was reduced to a mere $5,143.90, or less than 18 per cent of the proceeds. By whatever method it was reckoned, the profit was sufficient to encourage a new generation of the Brown, Ives, and Goddard families to make further and larger investments in land in Illinois and neighboring states.[89]

CHAPTER 11

A New Generation
of Businessmen

IN the history of the Browns the years from 1835 to 1841 must
be regarded as an era of transition. This brief span of time
witnessed the passing of the third and the advent of the fourth generation of the family in business. The year 1835 was marked by the death
of Thomas P. Ives, whose initiative, energy, and sagacity had helped
to make Brown and Ives one of the foremost American houses trading
to China and the Indies. In the words of his long-time friend Francis
Wayland, president of Brown University, Ives "for the greater part of
his life" had been "the acknowledged head of the mercantile interest
in Providence."[1] Six years later came the death of Nicholas Brown, Jr.,
who, though he brought to Brown and Ives talents somewhat less brilliant than those of his colleague, had supplied the qualities of integrity,
industry, economy, and deliberate judgment and caution.

The four children of the second Nicholas Brown were Nicholas,
Moses, Ann Carter, and John Carter Brown. Nicholas III appears to have
had no interest in business, and Moses died in infancy. Therefore the
duty and the responsibility of carrying on the family business for the
fourth generation fell upon John Carter Brown. Born in 1797, he graduated from Brown University in 1816 and entered the counting house
of Brown and Ives, where his duties gave him an opportunity to travel
extensively. In 1818 he visited Kentucky, where he assisted in the purchase of tobacco on account of his principals. In 1822 he was supercargo of their ship *General Hamilton,* bound for Gibraltar with a
cargo of tobacco. In 1832 he became a junior member of the house of
Brown and Ives. Upon the death of his father in 1841, he inherited a
large estate that elevated him to a position near the summit of business
leadership in New England.

Representing the new generation of the Ives family in business was

Moses Brown Ives. Born in 1794, he was the second child and oldest son of Thomas P. Ives. Marked early in life for a mercantile career, he had been carefully trained for business in accordance with the belief of his father that no one could "attain to eminence" in trade without "large knowledge and a thoroughly disciplined mind." Entering Brown University in 1808, he graduated with the class of 1812. He then entered the law school at Litchfield, Connecticut, where such notables as Aaron Burr and John C. Calhoun had received their legal education. Upon finishing the prescribed course, he made a tour of Europe and traveled in his own country. While in Europe his purpose seemed to be less to see the sights than to "acquaint himself with the habits and manners of merchants of distinction."[2] Actually, however, the sojourn of Moses Brown Ives in Europe was not confined to the mere observation of men and manners. His many letters to Brown and Ives, covering the period from June 4, 1818, to July 30, 1819, written from Amsterdam, Antwerp, Le Havre, London, and Paris, reveal his close acquaintance with every facet of the commercial system of Brown and Ives when trade to Canton and Batavia was yet in its prime.[3] At Amsterdam, especially, he enjoyed a ringside seat for the study of the traffic in tea and coffee. In the year 1832 Moses Brown Ives became a junior member of the firm of Brown and Ives. From 1840 to his death in 1857 he was "looked upon as the head of the house, and, by general consent, the leading merchant" of Providence.[4]

Meanwhile, his younger brother Robert Hale Ives, born in 1798, had served his apprenticeship in business, including an extended stay at Amsterdam in the year 1824. Here he had observed at first hand the methods employed by Daniel Crommelin and Sons in marketing the tea and coffee consigned to them in ships owned by Brown and Ives. Surviving his older brother by almost twenty years, he shared with John Carter Brown the control of the house of Brown and Ives in the eventful years of the Civil War.

Charlotte Rhoda Ives, older sister of the brothers Ives, was married in 1821 to William Goddard, later a member of the faculty of Brown University. As Charlotte R. Goddard she had an active business career in her own right, sharing in cotton manufacturing, in land investments, and in other enterprises of the Brown and Ives families. She is best known, perhaps, as the mother of William, Thomas P. Ives, Moses B. Ives, Francis Wayland, and Robert Hale Ives Goddard, who formed Goddard Brothers, the agency for all the cotton manufacturing companies controlled by Brown and Ives. The house of Brown and Ives continued in all its accustomed vigor, but after 1830 there was to develop a Brown-Ives-Goddard business complex. The Brown-Ives and the Ives-

Goddard marriages had resulted in a closely knit group through which the Brown-Ives-Goddard families exercised a far-reaching influence in the business councils of the day.

Along with the appearance of new faces went new policies. Brown and Ives for many years had been both merchants and manufacturers but were still thought of only as merchants by their contemporaries. The sale of their last ship in 1838, terminating their long history of maritime trade, changed all this. Henceforth, they were to be known as manufacturers but with ancillary enterprises in which they would invest the profits of their cotton textile business.

The course that Brown and Ives were to pursue was, perhaps unwittingly, charted by John Carter Brown in a letter to young Robert H. Ives in July, 1835. Fond of mingling socially with people of affluence, John Carter Brown was luxuriating at Saratoga Springs during the hot summer weeks. Remarking upon the fact that the "company appear . . . not as fashionable as formerly," he reported, nevertheless, a "considerable gathering of politicians," including Martin Van Buren, the heir apparent to the Presidency. Politics, however, had little charm for John Carter Brown. "Only let me have a cool million," he observed, "and others may have the Offices . . ." He was convinced that "cash & cash alone" gave a man "credit and substantial consequence" in the United States, that "mankind & womankind too" were prone to "rate an individual according to his rent-roll." John Carter Brown was declaring his intention to become a man of wealth. But how was one to accumulate great wealth? John Jacob Astor had become a multimillionaire by investing the profits of the fur trade in land on the island of Manhattan. With Astor obviously in mind John Carter expressed regret that Brown and Ives had not thirty or forty years before bought " 'the widow Rogers' farm' " on Manhattan instead of the land purchased by them in northeastern Pennsylvania. But the family experiences in land speculation did not encourage John Carter to emulate Astor by undertaking further adventures in land. Their fathers having missed the golden opportunity on Manhattan, John Carter Brown and Robert H. Ives, whose "lot" was "fixed in Rhode Island, where real estate" was *almost valueless,*" must either "thrive & 'go ahead' by means of manufacturing & Banking" or content themselves to sink to "a level with the common herd."[5]

STRENGTHENING THE COTTON BUSINESS

Given this choice of alternatives, the Brown and Ives families moved to strengthen their position in cotton manufacturing. In January, 1841, a few months prior to the death of Nicholas Brown, the Blackstone Manufacturing Company, since 1808 a partnership whose control Brown and Ives had shared with the Butlers, Wheatons, and Carringtons, became by act of the General Assembly of Rhode Island a "body corporate and politic" with an authorized capital of $500,000.[6] The incorporators included Nicholas Brown, Hope Ives (widow of Thomas P. Ives), Charlotte R. Goddard, William Goddard, Moses Brown Ives, John Carter Brown, and Robert H. Ives. Before a score of years had passed, the holdings of this group were to become concentrated in the hands of John Carter Brown, Robert H. Ives, and Charlotte R. Goddard. Other incorporators were Cyrus Butler, Alexander Duncan, and Sarah Duncan, who were not only the owners of the original Butler-Wheaton interest in the Blackstone Manufacturing Company but were to hold the majority of the stock to the end of the Civil War, when the company finally became the exclusive property of the Brown-Ives-Goddard interests.

Soon this same group acquired a controlling interest in still another cotton manufacturing enterprise. In 1806 the owners of Hope Furnace, which the four Brown brothers had established and operated successfully in the years from 1765 to the end of the War for Independence, had conveyed the property to a group of five Providence men organized for the purpose of carrying on cotton manufacturing, first under the name of the Hope Cotton Factory Company and later as the Hope Cotton Manufacturing Company. There is every reason to believe that the young establishment, like other ventures of a similar nature, prospered in the period from 1807 to 1815 only to fall upon evil days in the postwar depression of 1816. About 1821 the company was acquired by Ephraim Talbot, a Providence merchant and one-time ship captain of Brown and Ives, and by John Whipple, an eminent lawyer of Providence. They operated the mills jointly until 1833, when Talbot became the sole owner. When the mills burned in 1844, he conveyed the property as it then stood to Charles N. Talbot of New York City, who within a few days sold it to John Carter Brown, Moses Brown Ives, Robert H. Ives, and Charlotte R. Goddard, already the owners of the Blackstone Manufacturing Company and the Lonsdale Company.[7] In 1847, once the mills had been rebuilt and placed in operation, these four people together with Samuel Aborn of Providence procured from the General Assembly of Rhode Island a charter making them a "body corporate and politic."[8] Before many years had passed, the Brown-Ives-Goddard clan became the sole owners of the Hope Company. At a time when the ownership of the great companies at Lowell was becoming dispersed, the stock of the Rhode Island enterprises was becoming concentrated in the hands of a half-dozen members of three families closely allied by marriage. This small, select group had become one of the largest cotton manufacturers in New England.

With the benefit of hindsight one can now see that common ownership of the Blackstone, Lonsdale, and Hope companies called for common policies on the procurement of items such as raw cotton, coal, and machinery as well as agreement in the marketing of the finished product. In these respects, however, the owners until 1851 managed the three companies as if they were under separate ownership and control. From its very inception they had employed for the Blackstone Manufacturing Company an agent to whom they entrusted the purchase of the baled cotton and the sale of the yarn and cloth that came from the mill. Over a period of years the agent had developed certain clearly defined methods and policies in the marketing of goods. When Brown and Ives organized the Lonsdale Company, they employed their long-time friend and former ship captain Wilbur Kelly as agent for the sale of the cotton goods. The purchase of the baled cotton, however, they entrusted not to Kelly but to Thomas P. Bancroft, who was a nephew of Thomas P. Ives and was engaged in a general commission business in New Orleans. The first agent of the Hope Company when it began operations in 1847 was Thomas P. Ives Goddard, one of the five Goddard brothers. With procurement and marketing in the hands of different men, each pursuing different policies, the small group who owned the three companies had become their own competitors, endeavoring to sell their goods to the same set of buyers. The difficulty appeared to be further compounded by the practice that had developed of consigning the same kinds of cotton goods to several houses in the same city, which then sought to sell the wares on commission.

In 1850 the owners of the three companies took steps to correct the practices that were causing them to compete with each other. First they appointed Goddard Brothers as the salaried agents of the Blackstone, Lonsdale, and Hope companies and charged the agents with the responsibility of purchasing raw cotton, coal, machinery, and other items necessary to the operation of the mills and of finding markets for the finished goods produced in the mills. Next the owners, in conjunction with Goddard Brothers, adopted the general policy "of confining the sale of the same goods to one agency, in every city, where sold." The reasons for this new policy were explained by Robert H. Ives in a letter to a New York dealer who was thus forced to forego the sale of goods produced by the Lonsdale Company. After trying for a period of years the plan of dividing the sale of Lonsdale goods among different houses in the same city, the owners had decided that this method, "though occasionally beneficial in extending sales," was in the long run disadvantageous to the manufacturer by making "him his own competitor." It was open to the further objection that it led to "embarrassing relations" among the different dealers in which the manufacturer became "unpleasantly involved."[9] Goddard Brothers remained the agents for all the Brown-Ives-Goddard cotton manufacturing companies, but the resolve to sell goods through only one house in a given city was adhered to in certain cities and disregarded in others, depending upon the circumstances of time and place.

Until the middle 1870's Goddard Brothers shipped the goods produced by the three companies principally to Boston, Hartford, New York, Philadelphia, and Baltimore. The bulk of it went on consignment to houses who sold on commission and rendered accounts of their sales at more or less regular intervals. Although these marketing centers were all located east of the Alleghenies, this does not mean that the ultimate purchasers of the wares were confined to this area. From the three cities last named a large volume of goods undoubtedly moved into the Old Northwest, the Ohio Valley, and the South. At times consignments went to only one house in a given city, but at other times there were multiple dealers in the same metropolis. Even when goods were being shipped on consignment to only one dealer in a particular city, Goddard Brothers frequently were selling outright to merchants in the same places. Thus in 1855 when the sole consignee in New York for Blackstone, Lonsdale, and Hope company goods was the house of Lawrence, Clapp, and Company, sales were made outright to Tefts, Griswold, and Kellogg; to Trowbridge, Dwight, and Company; and to Claflin, Miller, and Company, all in the same city. The house receiving the goods on consignment was a wholesale outlet, probably serving the western market, while the three firms making outright purchases were local retailers.

As soon as Goddard Brothers became the agency for the three manufacturing companies, one finds evidence of product differentiation. No longer were the mills merely producing cotton goods blindly for the same market. Instead they were making a particular kind of cotton cloth to meet a specific need or to serve a particular purpose. The Lonsdale Company was making umbrella cloth on a large scale. On May 8, 1853, Isaac Smith's Sons and Company of New York and Wright Brothers and Company of Philadelphia entered into a contract with Goddard Brothers for the purchase of all the umbrella cloth made by the Lonsdale Company. Justly proud of their product, the three contracting parties inserted in the press a "cautionary" notice informing the world that they had a monopoly of all umbrella cloth bearing the Lonsdale label. They were therefore warning all dealers and manufacturers that selling or causing to be sold "any Umbrella Cloths, or Umbrellas made from cloths under the name of Lonsdale," except when purchased from Smith's Sons and Company or Wright Brothers and Company would result in prosecution according to law.[10]

Specialities of the Blackstone Manufacturing Company were Blackstone "A" thirty-nine-inch Brown sheeting and Blackstone print cloths. In 1867 the principal office for the sale of these two products of the Blackstone Manufacturing Company was the house of Rice, Chase, and Company at 4 Worth Street, New York City. Hearing that A. I. Stewart and Company, the great New York dry goods house, was advertising for sale some of the wares of the Blackstone Manufacturing Company, Goddard Brothers asked of Rice, Chase, and Company, "Were the Blackstones offered by A. I. Stewart & Co. purchased from you or elsewhere?" A. I. Stewart, though not a consignee, became a considerable outright purchaser of Blackstone wares. Five shipments to the firm of bleached goods and print cloths between June 1, 1867, and November 16, 1869, amounted to more than $40,000. The Blackstone Manufacturing Company announced that their print cloths went primarily to print works or were used for printing into calicos.[11]

Conspicuously absent from the marketing system of Brown and Ives was the selling house, which played a prominent role in the sale of the cotton goods of the large companies at Lowell, Massachusetts. The first of the selling houses was J. W. Paige and Company, formed in 1828 by some of the leading stockholders in the Waltham, Merrimack, Hamilton, and Appleton companies to sell on commission all the goods of these establishments. Previously, the companies had sold their wares through general commission houses in the different cities, which devoted only part of their time to cotton goods. By contrast, Paige and Company gave its full and undivided attention to the product of the four companies that created it. It relieved the manufacturers of all responsibility in the area of marketing, including the burden of bad debts. The selling house charged the manufacturer a commission for selling, plus a fee ranging from 2 to 4 per cent as a guarantee against bad debts. In good times and with proper care the guarantee fee provided the selling house with a considerable part of its income while relieving the manufacturer of all risk. Besides being his merchant, therefore, the selling house served the manufacturer as a sort of insurance agent.[12]

The selling house rendered to the manufacturer yet another service of prime importance. At a time when business obligations were paid mainly by promissory notes due six or eight months from date and when many banks either refused to discount such paper or would do so only at exorbitant rates of interest, the selling house became the manu-

facturer's banker. By virtue of the advances that it made to the manufacturer on goods received for sale, the selling house became his chief
source of credit. Extending funds to the manufacturer in sums of $5,000
to $10,000, the selling house was often his creditor to the extent of
$100,000, reimbursing itself from the sale of his goods when completed.
There were years when the interest on funds thus advanced provided
the selling house with nearly 20 per cent of its total income.[13]

If the selling house was advantageous to the companies whose goods
it sold, it was no less attractive to the men who owned and controlled it.
Requiring virtually no expenditure for plant and equipment, the commission and interest on its services represented almost clear profit. The
selling house came to play a most important role in relation to the great
manufacturing companies at Lowell. It set prices, named the terms of
payment, determined discounts, dictated styles, and exercised a large
influence upon the general production and marketing procedures of the
manufacturers in Lowell.[14]

Once Goddard Brothers had become the agents for the Blackstone,
Lonsdale, and Hope companies, they performed most of the same func-
tions that the selling house at Lowell did. They made outright sales
of goods to many purchasers, and they consigned goods to numerous
houses, which received from the manufacturing companies a commission for selling as well as a guarantee fee against bad debts. At Providence, as at Lowell, the manufacturer was relieved of all responsibility
for the marketing of goods. The agents, like the selling house, largely
dictated prices, discounts, credit, and styles. But there was one service
rendered by the selling house to the Lowell manufacturers that Goddard
Brothers were utterly incapable of performing for the companies whose
goods they sold. As mere salaried employees of the companies, they were
in no position to provide credit for them or to play the role of bankers
to them.

How, then, were the cotton manufacturing companies owned and
controlled by Brown and Ives maintained in a financially liquid state
during the long months that must elapse before consignees were able to
make remittance for the goods sold by them? Conceivably, the Providence Bank, organized by the Browns in 1791 and controlled by them
for a century thereafter, could have served as banker for the companies.
Failing this, the Blackstone Canal Bank, which Brown and Ives had
been largely instrumental in founding, might have served in this
capacity. For whatever reason, however, neither of these two banks nor
any other formal banking institution served as banker to the companies.

It remained for the partnership of Brown and Ives, owner of the three cotton manufacturing corporations, to provide the credit so much needed by them. The house of Brown and Ives had long been known for its exceptional liquidity. Unlike so many business concerns, it had always conducted business with its own capital. This had enabled it to withstand with comparative ease a loss such as that of the ship *Mary Ann* and cargo in 1803, which amounted to $450,000; or the loss of *Ann & Hope* and the capture of *John Jay* in 1806, which amounted to $500,000. No longer subject to the risks involved in maritime trade, the house appeared to have more cash assets than ever. As early as 1837 Brown and Ives were caring for the credit needs of the Blackstone and Lonsdale companies. In the Brown papers are some two dozen books for the years 1837–50 containing literally thousands of receipts for funds "received from Brown and Ives." The great majority were signed by representatives of the two companies in acknowledgment of sums of money from $100 to $50,000 advanced by Brown and Ives to pay for raw cotton, machinery, coal, or the wages at the mills.

Brown and Ives also extended credit to the companies by discounting for them commercial paper, payable in six to nine months, received in payment of cotton goods. For the year 1842 the Lonsdale Company received advances from Brown and Ives to the amount of $152,135, and the Blackstone Manufacturing Company received $244,964, a total of $397,099. In 1849 the Blackstone Manufacturing Company received $301,817, largely in the form of discount by Brown and Ives of short-term commercial paper. On February 27, 1850, Brown and Ives advanced to the Blackstone Manufacturing Company the sum of $118,687, representing the "proceeds" of notes discounted by them. On July 10 of the same year the company received from Brown and Ives $159,230, representing again the "proceeds" of commercial paper discounted. In the month of December, 1859, Brown and Ives advanced to the Blackstone, Lonsdale, and Hope companies a total of $153,180 in sums ranging from $3,000 to $20,000.[15]

Thus Brown and Ives, not bankers in any formal or legal sense of the term, were performing an essentially banking function on a scale that would have done credit to many institutions properly designated as banks, providing evidence of both the efficiency and the liquidity of the Providence house. The interest payments that the Lowell manufacturers made to the selling house were made by the Blackstone, Lonsdale, and Hope companies to their owners, Brown and Ives. While it is impossible to determine the amount of interest that the partners in Brown and Ives received annually from themselves as owners of the manufacturing companies, it represented a substantial sum, all retained within the close family circle. Even the salaries paid after 1850 to Goddard

Brothers as agents for all the companies remained within the select Brown-Ives-Goddard group.

Writers have often remarked upon the slowness of Rhode Island cotton manufacturers to adopt the completely integrated system of manufacturing first introduced at Waltham in 1814, the system under which the baled cotton taken in at one end of the mill emerged from the other end as finished cotton cloth, with the successive processes of carding, spinning, weaving, bleaching, dyeing, and finishing all combined under one roof. Content to be mere cotton spinners, many Rhode Island millowners adopted the power loom with some reluctance. Once they had combined carding, spinning, and weaving in one plant, many of the owners were still willing to have other companies do their bleaching, dyeing, and finishing. Brown and Ives belonged to this latter group. Cotton cloth woven in the mills of the Blackstone and Lonsdale companies was, for many years, sent to local bleachhouses and dyehouses specializing in the finishing processes of cotton manufacturing. Thus on December 31, 1841, the Lonsdale Company had goods in the hands of the Providence Dyeing, Bleaching, and Coloring Company; the Providence Canal Bleaching Company; and the Rhode Island Bleaching Works.[16] Within a few years, however, Brown and Ives were to build at the Lonsdale mills a bleachery, where cloth from the Blackstone and Hope companies, as well as Lonsdale, was put through the finishing processes. The annual statement of the Lonsdale Company for 1850 is dotted with such terms as bleach house, dye house, dyeing and bleaching works, calender room, mangle room, and finishing and packing room. At long last Brown and Ives had developed a completely integrated system of cotton manufacturing. That this came some forty years after their entrance into the business and only when they had emerged as one of the great cotton manufacturing houses in New England is evidence of the essentially conservative ways so characteristic of the Browns, with the single exception of John. Such men were not likely to startle the world with their innovations in business; but by the same token, they would never take substantial losses through undue risk-taking.

HIGH PROFITS

The owners of the Blackstone, Lonsdale, and Hope companies found cotton manufacturing enormously profitable. The Blackstone Manufacturing Company paid Brown and Ives dividends of $26,700, $55,625, and $26,900 in the years 1841, 1846, and 1847, representing returns of 10 to 20 per cent on the value of the stock they then owned.[17] The Lonsdale Company paid a dividend of $60,000 in 1843, the equivalent of 24 per cent on a capital of $250,000. In the decade of the 1850's total dividend payments of the company amounted to $680,000. This annual average of $68,000 for ten years was 27 per cent of the capital stock with which the Lonsdale Company began the decade and some 13.6 per cent of the $500,000 outstanding after 1855. In the same period the company added $500,000 to its undivided earnings.[18] The Hope Company made in 1853 a payment of $65,000, or 32.5 per cent, on a capital of $200,000. Although the figure declined to $15,000 in the panic year of 1857, the payment for 1859 was $60,000, or 30 per cent.[19]

Wartime conditions appear to have affected the Hope and Blackstone companies in about the same degree, as a comparison of the dividends for the war years will indicate:

HOPE COMPANY		BLACKSTONE COMPANY	
1860	$ 30,000	1860	$100,000
1861	16,000	1861	50,000
1862	12,000	1862	100,000
1863	30,000	1863	50,000
1864	55,000	1864	95,000
1865	80,000	1865	150,000
1866	105,000	1866	175,000
TOTAL	$328,000	TOTAL	$720,000.

Dividend payments by the Hope Company ranged from 6 per cent to 52 per cent on a capital of $200,000, while those of the Blackstone Manufacturing Company varied from 10 per cent to 35 per cent on a capital of $500,000.[20]

For the years leading to the panic that occurred in 1873, the Blackstone Manufacturing Company seems to have done less well than either the Hope or Lonsdale companies. After omitting dividends from 1867 to 1871, Blackstone paid $40,000 in February, 1872.[21] On the other hand, the Hope Company made dividend payments annually from 1867 to 1872 ranging from $50,000 to $150,000 and amounting to a total of $543,600.[22] As for the Lonsdale Company, in the three and one-half years from May 1, 1868, to November 1, 1871, it made payments to John Carter Brown, Robert H. Ives, and Charlotte R. Goddard for a total of $765,800, the first named of these receiving $385,900.[23] Small wonder John Carter Brown was able to indulge himself in the luxury of collecting rare Americana. The large earnings of Lonsdale and their concentration in the hands of three persons are even more impressive when it is realized that from November 1, 1871, to the same day in 1872 the dividend payments of the company amounted to $653,000, or 65 per cent on its $1,000,000 capitalization.[24]

So satisfactory were the profits of cotton manufacturing in the years immediately following Appomattox that Brown and Ives were encouraged to make a further investment in the business. In May, 1863, the General Assembly of Rhode Island had granted to Amos D. Smith, Charles M. Smith, and William S. Smith a charter incorporating them as the Melrose Company for the purpose of manufacturing, dyeing, bleaching, printing, and finishing cotton and other kinds of cloth.[25] The authorized capital stock was $50,000 divided into shares of $1,000 each, a figure that the company might increase to $300,000. The annual meeting, the counting house, and the place of business were all to be located in Providence. In May, 1872, the General Assembly amended the original act of incorporation by changing the name to the Berkeley Company and by authorizing an increase of the capital stock to a figure not exceeding $600,000.[26] The mailing address of the new company was listed as 50 South Main Street, Providence, indicating that the company was now controlled by Brown and Ives, whose counting house had long carried that same street number.

Stock of the new company was divided into 600 shares, each with a value of $1,000. The Lonsdale Company, itself the property of Brown and Ives, owned 300 shares, while various members of the Brown, Ives, and Goddard families held 190 shares, leaving 110 shares in the hands of outsiders.[27] As the Brown-Ives-Goddard group had just acquired exclusive ownership of the Blackstone Manufacturing Company, they now had the exclusive ownership and control of three cotton manufacturing companies while controlling a fourth company, whose ownership they shared with others. With the acquisition of the Berkeley Company they came one step nearer the pinnacle of that particular form of business activity within the United States.

In cotton manufacturing, size has long been measured in terms of spindles. In 1897 Brown and Ives were estimated to own and operate more than 225,000 spindles, exclusive of the Berkeley Company.[28] As a matter of fact, the Blackstone, Lonsdale, and Hope companies at maximum capacity housed more than 280,000 spindles. It is clear, however, that this maximum had not been achieved in 1872, when the Berkeley Company was acquired. A total of 240,000 spindles is a more realistic figure for the three companies as of that date. Assuming, however, that the Berkeley Company, whose capitalization exceeded that of the Hope Company and whose dividends surpassed those of the Blackstone, had a spindle capacity equal to the 44,000 of these companies, the total spindles of the four companies as of 1872 would have been some 284,000.[29] Some years later, the total number of spindles operated by them would have been somewhat in excess of 320,000, which would have placed them near the top in New England cotton manufacturing.

In the remainder of this chapter the author intended to discuss the rivalry of Brown and Ives with the A. and W. Sprague Manufacturing Company. In the 1850's and 1860's the Spragues had become the most powerful family in Rhode Island. They owned factories of various kinds, including a series of vertically integrated textile plants that covered all operations from the purchase of raw cotton to the marketing of finished cloth. They owned timber in Maine and water power in South Carolina. In Providence they owned or controlled a street railway, an iron works, a mowing machine factory, a horseshoe company, a horseshoe nail company, and five banks. They employed 12,000 people and did not hesitate to tell them how to vote.

An early head of the dynasty, William Sprague, had been the governor of Rhode Island and a United States Senator. His nephew, also named William Sprague, emulated his career and served as governor of Rhode Island from 1860 to 1863 and as United States Senator from 1863 to 1875. The second Senator Sprague had a reputation for erratic and sometimes violent behavior, especially when in his cups. The fortunes of the family nevertheless continued to prosper until 1873. The panic of that year found the Spragues with assets of some $19,000,000 but also with debts that could not be met without throwing the companies they controlled into bankruptcy. They were obliged to appoint a trustee to operate their textile and other mills; and as the panic turned into a long depression, they were unable to recover either their economic or their political power.[30]

The Browns' rivalry with the Spragues during the period of the latters' ascendancy was undoubtedly acute. The correspondence of Thomas Allen Jenckes, Republican congressman from Rhode Island (1863-71), shows that Brown and Ives were gathering their forces against the Spragues as early as 1869. Copies of letters written to Jenckes in that year were received by Professor Hedges just before his death.[31] Among them are several by William Goddard, who had emerged as the leading figure in Brown and Ives. Goddard thought that Senator Sprague was "half crazy" and that his financial condition was extremely shaky. "The fact is," wrote Goddard on March 8, 1869, "his house owe an *enormous* amount of money. . . . I think they owe largely for *fixed instruments* and that is not a safe position for a great house to occupy." Ten days later Goddard told Jenckes that he would prevent the Providence Bank from accepting Sprague's notes. "I do not want them to fail," he said, "but it would be a blessing to Rhode Island if they should come so near breaking up, that their malign influence in this poor little state could be forever destroyed." By the end of the year Charles Adams, a Providence merchant, reported to Jenckes that "There is a very queer feeling here about Spragues credit and my opinion is that Brown and Ives (that means William Goddard) are trying all they know how to fail Sprague. Mr. G. is certainly using all his influence to damage their credit. They will hardly go over, there are too many interested to let them fail."

But fail they did in 1873. Whether the reason lay in the competitive assiduity of Brown and Ives or in poor management by the Spragues awaits the investigation of another historian.

E. S. M.

CHAPTER 12

Investing Capital in the West

COTTON manufacturing, once a capital-consuming industry, became after 1850 a capital-producing form of economic activity. So great were the profits that the manufacturers were no longer able to invest their earnings in further expansion of the business. New areas of investment had therefore to be found. One possibility was a fresh speculation in wild lands. Having achieved no glittering success in their previous ventures of this sort, it is doubtful that Brown and Ives of their own volition would have again invested in land.

In 1850 Winthrop S. Gilman, a relative of the Ives family, had established himself in the banking business in New York.[1] To this new field of endeavor Gilman brought many years of business experience, first at Alton, Illinois, later in St. Louis. Frankly acknowledging that his prosperity in business was "fairly attributable" to the kind aid he had received from Brown and Ives, Gilman was eager both to benefit himself and to be of service to Brown and Ives by directing their attention to profitable fields for the investment of some of their surplus capital. In the course of his years of residence in the West he had been much impressed by the potentialities for growth and development of the state of Illinois. He therefore suggested an arrangement with Brown and Ives by which the firm was to advance the funds for an investment in Internal Improvement Bonds and unregistered Canal Bonds of Illinois. The Providence house would receive a 12 per cent return on all capital thus advanced, after which all profits would be shared equally by them and Gilman. Gilman on his part was to arrange for the purchase of the bonds, to collect the interest thereon, and to attend to all other details involved in the investment.[2] With no apparent enthusiasm, Brown and Ives gave their approval to this plan, and within a few months they found themselves the owners of Illinois bonds to the value of more than $52,000.[3]

With the trunk-line railway from the Atlantic seaboard to Chicago just completed and with 1,200 miles of railway projected within the state, Gilman remarked on the prevailing belief that "these rich lands . . . will be greatly enhanced in price" by "these vast improvements in a country so capable of rapid cultivation."[4] Most important of the railways then under construction was the Illinois Central, extending southward from Chicago across the prairie of Illinois. Thanks largely to the persistent effort of Stephen A. Douglas, this was the first land-grant railway in the United States. Endowed with a land subsidy of 2,595,-000 acres, the Illinois Central company was already in the process of becoming a vast agency interested not merely in the sale and settlement of its own lands but also in the sale and occupation of government lands tributary to its lines.

After 1850 Illinois became the center of a new wave of land speculation that was to dwarf the earlier one, which after 1815 had engrossed so much of the fertile domain situated between the Illinois and Mississippi rivers in the so-called Military Tract. Limited to no single part of the state, the speculative fever was especially virulent, of course, in those areas in reasonable proximity to projected railway lines; and it reached its apogee in the fertile prairie lands traversed by the Illinois Central.

It has been estimated that between 1849 and 1856 no less than 6,000,000 acres of public domain in Illinois passed into the hands of speculators. Four types of speculators active in the state within these years have been identified. The first type was the farmer-speculator, who bought lands in excess of his capacity to cultivate in the hope of disposing of his surplus holdings at greatly increased prices. In the second category were businessmen operating on a small scale, bankers, editors, judges, lawyers, politicians, and government officials who purchased land usually as a speculative investment. In this group was to be found virtually every leading politician in Illinois, Abraham Lincoln excepted. A third type was the professional speculator, a man capable of purchasing land in large acreage who identified himself with the Illinois environment, advertised his holdings, and made the management of his landed domain his chief, if not his sole, concern. Finally, there was the Easterner of capital and enterprise who made speculative investments in the lands of Illinois. To this last category belonged Brown and Ives.[5]

LAND SPECULATION IN ILLINOIS

Left to their own devices, the partners probably would not have made a new land investment in Illinois. Still in their hands was a substantial part of 19,000 acres in that state acquired partly by outright purchase, partly in satisfaction of debts owing them. They were convinced that they had suffered severely "by the hasty & ill advised" selection of the lands purchased by them in 1836.[6] Winthrop Gilman, however, had other ideas. Convinced of the opportunity for a profitable speculation in the prairie lands of Illinois, he suggested to Brown and Ives a plan for such an investment. They were to provide the funds with which to purchase the lands, while Gilman would bear the comparatively negligible cost of selecting them. He would manage the lands and share the profits equally with Brown and Ives. When the latter house protested that the party supplying the capital should have a guarantee of a 9 per cent return on the outlay (to cover the risk involved) before sharing the profits, Gilman readily consented.[7] Still cautious and unenthusiastic, Brown and Ives limited the initial investment to $18,000.

On June 30, 1852, Gilman reported his first purchase of land warrants issued to soldiers under the various military bounty land acts of Congress. Since most of the veterans receiving these warrants were not in a position to locate them on land in the West, they disposed of them to speculators. The result was that the warrants, mostly depreciated, were bought and sold by brokerage houses in financial centers as freely as other kinds of securities; and the prices of warrants were quoted daily on the financial pages of metropolitan newspapers. Buying 216 warrants covering 22,080 acres at a cost of $18,034.85, Gilman had slightly exceeded the limit imposed by his principals on the initial purchase. But since the warrants had cost not quite $0.82 an acre, Brown and Ives were not averse to a further investment. By May 30, 1853, Gilman had made five separate purchases of warrants totaling 82,400 acres at a cost of $77,296.65, or an average cost of almost $0.94 an acre.[8]

If Brown and Ives depended on Gilman to purchase the land warrants, they were no less dependent on him for locating them on land in the West. Since Gilman's business engagement in New York would not permit him to select the lands in person, everything depended on his ability to choose the right man to make the selections. For this important task his first choice was J. S. Hayward of Hillsboro, Illinois. Over a long period of years, Gilman had found Hayward to be "a cautious, sagacious and withal a very responsible agent," with great experience and wide acquaintance with conditions in Illinois. His "standing and influence" in Illinois gave him a decided advantage over those less accustomed to the land business and over those less intimately associated with the officials of the land offices in the state. Another person might make as good selections, but he would be less likely to secure the lands selected. At this point, Hayward's acquaintance with the officials would be of prime importance; and to make doubly certain that Hayward would secure the land he selected, Gilman gave his authority to pay the officials, at his discretion, a small sum of money on each tract of land selected.[9]

The lands thus selected by Hayward were located in the counties of Champaign, Moultrie, Piatt, Macon, Christian, Shelby, Coles, and Clay, in east-central Illinois. Much of the land was within fifteen miles of the Illinois Central lines and equally close to the town of Decatur. Almost exactly 5,000 acres lay within the limits of the Illinois Central's land grant, where the minimum price of the sections retained by the government was $2.50 an acre. For these lands, of course, the land warrants (worth $1.25 an acre at the land office) had to be supplemented by a cash outlay; but since the depreciated warrants had cost less than $1.00 an acre, the total cost of these lands was only about $2.30 an acre instead of $2.50.[10]

Since the policy of homestead (under which 160 acres of land were to be given to the actual settler) was then being agitated and discussed in Congress and since a prime argument in support of homestead was that it would foil the land speculator by depriving him of all incentive to engross the public lands, speculators should have been opposed to the very idea of homestead. When Brown and Ives raised the question as to the impact of homestead upon lands held by them and other speculators, Gilman's reply was that for a few years the effect would be unfavorable, tending to depress land values; but that, as homestead brought settlers into Illinois, it would within a few years bring about an appreciation in the price of land.[11] This seems to have been the view of eastern land speculators generally. Their initial doubts thus dispelled, Brown and Ives in 1860 were able to give their support to Lincoln, who was running for the Presidency on a platform in which homestead was a principal plank.

Months before the purchase of land warrants was complete, Gilman as well as Brown and Ives gave careful thought to the formulation of a policy governing the sale of the lands they were about to acquire. Past experience with land in Vermont, in Pennsylvania, and in the Ohio Company purchase should have disposed Brown and Ives to favor a quick sale of their lands. At that very moment they were burdened with lands acquired from fifty-five to seventy years before. Gilman appears to have been of two minds on the question. His first suggestion was that if settlers wished to purchase and improve small tracts, thereby enhancing the value of adjoining lands, sales should be made to them at low prices. He would sell none of the land at less than $2.50 an acre; and he would hold all the land (except the small parcels for actual settlers) until all the railways then building in the vicinity of the land were nearly completed.[12] A month later, however, he proposed that they sell at $2.50

an acre "if by *one Sale* we could close the whole."[13] And midway through the purchase of land warrants he agreed with Brown and Ives that the lands yet to be located by them in Illinois should be sold within three years.[14]

Actually, all this discussion was largely academic. What Brown and Ives as well as Gilman had not perceived was that the prairie lands of central Illinois were about to become the object of a speculative craze. The lands would sell themselves at good prices. Large speculative purchases such as those of Brown and Ives soon attracted smaller speculators eager to reap their share of the profits. Between May 31, 1853, and October 18, 1855, Gilman negotiated nine separate sales ranging from 1,400 acres to 32,717 acres, thereby disposing of 76,394 of the 82,400 acres purchased in Illinois. On paper these sales appeared to be highly advantageous to Brown and Ives, bringing them a sevenfold return upon their original investment.

The first of these sales was to M. L. Sullivant of Columbus, Ohio, who bought 1,841 acres at $2.50 an acre, payable within three years with interest, making a total return of somewhat less than $5,100. The second sale of 2,240 acres at $3.00 an acre was also to Sullivant, whose total payments over a period of four years amounted to $7,929.60. Next came a purchase by Robert Smith of Alton, Illinois, long a member of the lower house of Congress, who contracted for 7,168 acres with total payments of $29,195.38. J. A. Freeland of Sullivan, Illinois, was the purchaser of 1,400 acres for total payments of $4,900.84, while two Chicago gentlemen named Dow and Staples bought 2,412 acres for a total of $10,854.50 One of the most colorful of the speculative purchasers was Isaac Shelby of Chicago, grandson of the first governor of Kentucky, who had borne the same name. He was reputed to be very rich and a very daring businessman. His purchase amounted to 5,449 acres for $37,247.60. Much of this land had been sold through the Chicago commission house of D'Wolf, Maclay, and Quimby. In September, 1855, D'Wolf, in behalf of himself, Isaac Shelby, and others, purchased 19,191 acres for which the total payments were to be $99,114.77.[15]

By this time the Illinois lands of Brown and Ives were known as far east as Philadelphia. E. R. Helmbold, secretary of the Farmers and Mechanics Insurance Company of that city, visited Chicago as the representative of a land company desirous of placing 150 German families upon the land, with a view to purchasing from the Illinois Central. While in Chicago, however, he called upon D'Wolf, Maclay, and Quimby, which had plats of the lands of Brown and Ives. Through the Chicago house, Helmbold made contact with Winthrop Gilman in New York, with whom he began negotiations for some 30,000 acres of land. In the end a sale was made to the Philadelphia company represented by Helmbold, although the contract was signed by Stephen S. Remak. As a result, the transaction came to be referred to as the "Remak sale."[16] By the terms of the agreement Remak, in behalf of the Philadelphia company, purchased 32,717 acres for $156,834.46. Interest on the unpaid balance over a period of five years brought the total payments to $180,897.28.[17]

Among the numerous railways projected in Illinois in the middle 1850's was the Indiana and Illinois Central (not to be confused with the Illinois Central) which planned to build an air-line railroad between Decatur, Illinois, and Indianapolis. Its promoters hoped that this line would become a link in a direct rail chain extending from St. Joseph, Missouri, to the Atlantic seaboard. Knowledge of this projected railway had influenced both Gilman and Hayward in the selection of land for Brown and Ives in Illinois. Actually, some 30,000 acres of their land lay within three miles of this proposed line. Like so many western railways of the time, the enterprise required financial resources that outran the ambition of its promoters. But the company appeared to take a new lease on life when Judge Roach resigned his seat in the Indiana Supreme Court to become president of the railroad. Roach promptly approached Gilman in New York, requesting him to secure a generous stock subscription from Brown and Ives, whose lands would be so greatly benefited by the completion of the railroad. It was Gilman who conceived the idea of a subscription by Brown and Ives to be paid half in cash, half in land. In short, they should use a small portion of the land they owned in close proximity to the railway in order to enjoy the benefit of the enhanced value that the completed railway line would bring to their remaining land. If it could be assumed that the railway would be completed and would remain in a sound financial condition, Gilman had negotiated an agreement entirely to the advantage of Brown and Ives. In return for 5,001 acres of land, they were to receive $40,000 worth of stock of the Indiana and Illinois Central Railroad.[18]

It appeared that Winthrop Gilman had achieved a phenomenal success in the disposition of the lands of Brown and Ives in Illinois. Within a period of three years he had, by means of nine separate transactions, sold some 76,394 acres of land that had cost about $65,000 for a consideration of about $420,000. The returns, therefore, were more than six times the first cost of the land; and since Brown and Ives had owned the land for only a short period of time, their outlay for taxes, interest, and other expenses was very light. The profit seemed to be unexpectedly great.

While these sales of large tracts of land were being made, a limited acreage was being sold in small units of 40 to 160 acres. Of the 82,400 acres that Gilman had purchased for Brown and Ives there remained only about 4,200 acres within the limits of the Illinois Central land grant. The lands were too valuable to sell in bulk. Brown and Ives reserved these lands for sale at $15 an acre.[19]

None of the nine large sales was made for cash. Although a down payment was made in every instance, the bulk of the purchase money was paid in installments over a period of three to five years with 6 per cent interest on the unpaid balance. Amply protected by mortgages on the land, Brown and Ives were not greatly concerned should the purchaser default on his contract. In such a case the land reverted to Brown and Ives, sometimes at the sacrifice of the money paid by the purchaser. All the sales had been made in the years 1853–55, when confidence was running high. In certain cases the buyer probably overreached himself to the point where he might well have encountered difficulty even with a continuance of good times. In any event, though, the onset of depression in 1857 hastened the coming of the day of doom for some of the purchasers. Before the 1857 panic had run its course, Brown and Ives had discovered the fact that while men were eager to enter into contracts for the purchase of large tracts of land, they were likely to be something less than punctual in making payments on the land.

The first of the purchasers to default was Stephen Remak, whose contract bore the date of October 8, 1855. On July 3, 1856, Gilman reported that he had no "intelligence" from Remak relative to the payment due from him on July 1, 1856, of $26,923.[20]

Professor Hedges had written thus far in his final chapter at the time of his death in 1965. He left behind eighty-seven pages of closely written notes on the voluminous correspondence of Brown and Ives and Winthrop S. Gilman and later with Gilman, Son, and Company, in relation to the purchase and sale of western lands. It is impossible to reconstruct what Professor Hedges intended to say in the remainder of the chapter. The loss is the greater because he was an authority on the settlement of the West, and his treatment of this part of the history of the Browns would have been especially valuable. But from his notes it is possible at least to sketch the course of some of the Browns' investments in the lands of Illinois, Iowa, and Nebraska, where their main holdings were located.

Brown and Ives met with difficulties in the sale of their Illinois lands in the 1850's, when the initial purchasers failed to make payments. In 1869 they still held some of these lands and were selling lots in Piatt and Moultrie counties at $14 an acre, a considerable advance on the $5 or $6 an acre they had hoped to get in 1855. In 1873, after another land boom, their lands in Piatt County were selling for as much as $50 an acre. The Browns' Illinois speculation seems to have been a highly successful one in the end.

Meanwhile, between 1869 and 1873, again on the advice of Winthrop S.

Gilman, Brown and Ives purchased extensive tracts of land in Nebraska and Iowa for various members of the family. The prices ranged from a little over $1 an acre to somewhat over $4, sometimes in cash, sometimes in land warrants. The total amount of land purchased at this time is not entirely clear, but it was evidently close to 100,000 acres. The family may already have been in possession of other Iowa lands. Their holdings in that state were located in the counties of Adair, Adams, Audubon, Boone, Cass, Crawford, Dickinson, Emmett, Fremont, Greene, Harrison, Humboldt, Ida, Kossuth, Lyon, Monona, Monroe, Osceola, Palo Alto, Plymouth, Pocahontas, Potta-wottamie, Shelby, Sioux, Tyler, and Woodbury; in Nebraska the Browns' lands were mainly in the counties of Cedar, Dixon, Pierce, and Wayne.

Iowa and Nebraska lands proved also to be a sound investment. Brown and Ives began selling to settlers at once, through the agency of the Gilmans, usually in lots ranging from 80 to 160 acres. Their policy was to require a payment of one fifth of the purchase price in cash and to give a mortgage for the remainder, with interest rates at first as high as 12 per cent, later reduced to 10 per cent and in 1880 to 8 per cent. By that date the Iowa lands were bringing from $6 to $12 an acre, the Nebraska lands somewhat less. Prices about doubled during the next decade and in 1891 underwent a spectacular rise.

Some notion of the profits involved may be gained from a letter of 1883 in which Gilman, Son, and Company computed that the lands in Cedar County, Nebraska, selling then at $8 an acre, were paying 250 per cent on the first outlay after deducting the original cost and taxes, with interest compounded annually at 7 per cent (the Browns continued to compute profits in this conservative manner). At the same time, lands in Wayne County, selling at $12 an acre, were paying 500 per cent. By 1891 Cedar County lands were selling at $15 an acre and Wayne County lands at $20. Four years later Wayne County lands went for $30 an acre. In 1896 the boom collapsed momentarily, but in 1902 the Browns refused $50 an acre for Wayne County lands. By that time they were selling lands in Lyon and Boone counties in Iowa at $55 and $60 an acre.[21]

Brown and Ives did not rely entirely on the natural advance of settlement to increase the value of their lands. By loans and by exchange of lands they assisted the building of railroads near their holdings, and they occasionally offered lands at less than cost to colonizing groups of settlers, whose presence in a new area could be expected to enhance the value of adjoining lands. In addition, Gilman, Son, and Company persuaded them to try another method of improving their holdings. Beginning in 1887, they leased lands for five-year periods, at first for $1 a year an acre, later in the early 1890's for $2 and even $3.

Initially they leased lands as a means of achieving an income to defray taxes. But it soon became apparent that lands leased to farmers who brought them under cultivation increased in value much more rapidly than lands that simply lay idle. On November 21, 1892, Gilman, Son, and Company assured Brown and Ives:

Our observation leads us to say without hesitation that Iowa lands that are properly cultivated improve in price by leasing. The danger in this direction is in obtaining careless or indifferent lessees, who may either not cultivate thoroughly, & with a proper regard to rotation of crops, or who may allow brush to increase without any attempt to remove same either by the grazing of animals, or otherwise. We believe that all these lands might be advantageously leased for at least two five year terms, if not longer, to men who will cultivate for crop in good fashion. At the end of the leases, if not sold earlier, the property will have ordinarily advanced in value, faster than if left idle.[22]

Following this advice, Brown and Ives leased and rented more and more of their lands. The usual agreement provided for a very small rental the first year, when the tenant would be heavily engaged in breaking the sod. In succeeding years the rents would rise, to average out over the five-year period to the agreed yearly figure. At the end of the lease, provided he had paid in full, the tenant was entitled to remove any buildings or fences he had erected. If he failed to remove them or if he failed to pay his lease in full, he forfeited them. It was not the policy of Brown and Ives to purchase them from him (though they occasionally did so in order to make the land more attractive to a new tenant).

After the depression of 1896 it became difficult to lease lands for much more than $1 an acre yearly. But Gilman, Son, and Company continued to lease as many lands as possible for Brown and Ives in order to bring them into, or keep them in, a state of cultivation. It was better, they repeated, in September, 1901, "to rent at $ 1. than to allow land to lie idle."[23]

Some measure of the amounts of land that Gilman, Son, and Company leased for Brown and Ives in this manner is suggested by the fact that rentals for the year 1900 amounted to about $40,000. The taxes on the lands at this time probably came to about $8,000. The commission paid to Gilman, Son, and Company was 2.5 per cent on sales, 2.5 per cent on collection of interest, and 2 per cent on collection of rents. Before 1891 the commission had been larger, but the Gilmans had themselves reduced it as the value of the lands rose.

It is scarcely to be doubted that the venture of the Browns in western lands was a financial success or that Gilman, Son, and Company served them well. Although the first experiments of the family with this form of investment had not all been fortunate, the men who guided the family business had, as usual, learned from experience.

By the end of the nineteenth century the Browns could look back on more than 150 years of economic achievement. In a small colony without extensive natural resources, by energy and patience and occasionally by daring, they had created opportunities for themselves and their community. The family had built the trade of Providence to rival that of Newport and the trade of Rhode Island to rival that of areas more favorably endowed by nature. Their candles had lit the balls and assemblies of America's Colonial gentry. The cannon they cast had armed American ships in the War for Independence. Their trading vessels had carried the American flag to Canton and Batavia and St. Petersburg. Their cottons were worn in every state of the union. In pursuit of their own interests they had often served the interests of the community and even of the nation. Among their services was the preservation of their papers. By keeping their records in such detail, they not only helped to insure the family's long-range success but they made possible the reconstruction in these pages of a remarkable case history of American economic growth.

E. S. M.

Afterword

AFTERWORD

For a period of five years it was my privilege to work closely with James B. Hedges, a very warm friend and a man whose eminence as an American economic historian spanned three decades. We were researching similar sources relating to the eighteenth- and nineteenth-century business enterprise of Rhode Island in general and of Providence in particular. Because we shared adjoining alcoves in the library vault, there was daily opportunity to discuss our work at length, and as the months went by each grew familiar with what the other was doing and freely shared information. It is in light of this association that I have been asked to set down a few recollections that might shed light on those intentions of Professor Hedges that are not reflected in the preceding pages.

The Brown Papers, housed in the John Carter Brown Library of Brown University, consist of well over a quarter of a million documents touching upon nearly every important phase of American economic development from 1750 to 1920; and over the last twenty-five years Professor Hedges had made himself the master of this vast source. He possessed a remarkable memory, repeatedly demonstrated by the recall of a particular manuscript, its details, and its location, though he might not have worked with it for a decade. His was a mind capable of encompassing the whole, able not only to fit the individual manuscript into his own special understanding of the Browns of Providence, but to relate it to the total sweep of American economic history. Coupled with his erudition was the disciplined drive of a man a third his age.

The first volume of Professor Hedges' study of the business enterprises of the Brown family, published in 1952, carried the story to 1789. It was his original plan to complete the work in two additional volumes. He gradually became convinced, however, that the years from 1789 to the twentieth century should be treated in a single, comprehensive volume. With this decision made, he began to rewrite old chapters while he continued writing new ones. That some chapters of the draft would require editing, others division and regrouping, he fully realized; had he lived, the finished volume would most certainly have appeared in a different form. Yet, as any who knew him will recognize, the rhetoric remains that of the meticulous and vigorous scholar he was.

If we are to judge by the standards of the author, the manuscript, both in its discrete parts and as a whole, was unfinished. The excellence that Hedges as a teacher required from his students he exacted in increased measure from himself as a historian. He never considered a manuscript to be approaching final form until he had reworked it through three drafts; upon completing a first draft he set it aside for at least a year to permit the work of time to verify or to show need for modification. Approximately two-thirds of the existing manuscript for this volume had been through a second draft; a third was in first draft; and another part, equal perhaps to a fourth of the existing manuscript, remained largely uncast.

Two chapters—Chapter 11, the second of two chapters detailing the role that Brown and Ives had played in the later development of the Rhode Island textile industry, and Chapter 12, the second of two chapters covering their speculations in western lands—were only partially finished. The chapter on the textile industry was to have carried the discussion of the activities of Brown and Ives into the twentieth century, when the firm divested itself of all its textile holdings. This chapter was also to have included an analysis of a celebrated business and political feud. The history of southern New England cotton manufacturing in the post-Civil War years centered mainly in the activities of two Rhode Island families in the textile business: the Brown-Ives-Goddard family and the Sprague family. The bitter rivalry that developed between the two houses erupted into a struggle on the part of the Browns to purge the state of the political control of the Spragues, and verbal manifestations of the fight were heard in the United States Senate as well as in the General Assembly of Rhode Island. Indeed, on the floor of the Senate William Sprague accused Brown and Ives of forcing his business combine into bankruptcy. Before he could complete this chapter, Professor Hedges needed copies of material from the Library of Congress. Because the Sprague business papers had been destroyed by judicial decree, he was attempting to evaluate Senator Sprague's accusation through the use of collateral evidence. This collateral information, as it turned out, was highly pertinent; but, unfortunately, it arrived during the week of Professor Hedges' death.

No aspect of American history captured the imagination and interest of Professor Hedges as did the settlement of western lands. At the time of his death he was working on the chapter dealing with Brown and Ives's trans-Mississippi lands (Iowa, Missouri, Kansas, and Nebraska), concerning which an extensive correspondence exists. He wished to carry his discussion of the acquisition of lands by Brown and Ives into the twentieth century and to learn more about the present disposition of lands held by the firm.

Two chapters that were to have been included in this volume were those on the Brown family's so-called United Fund and on the Civil War commodity speculations by the Browns. By the middle 1840's, the Browns, the Iveses, and later the Goddards formed what would now be called a mutual fund, which they called the United Fund. Each of the three families owned shares in the fund, which in turn held assets worth over $2,000,000 in long-term business papers and in stocks and bonds in the public institutions and industries of the nation. Profits were used to increase the portfolio of the fund and to pay large annual dividends to the shareholders. This was the by-product of an advanced and vigorous business mentality of a new generation.

Economic historians, in treating the Civil War period, mention the fact that large profits were to be had by those willing to speculate in commodities needed to carry on the conflict. Specific documents illustrative of this practice are few. The Brown Papers, however, contain the source material for what Professor Hedges called a "complete-type study" of this subject.

The manuscript as it exists is therefore but a part of what—if the excellence of all Professor Hedges' earlier work is a valid criterion—would have been a great work in American economic history. But even unfinished, what appears here is a vital contribution to the knowledge of past American economic life. As a true scholar James B. Hedges was always more interested in opening subjects than in closing them. Thus, for those who want to pursue further what he has treated here, the work should serve as an invaluable guide to the abundant and detailed sources he discovered and explored.

F. S. C.

Notes

The manuscript materials cited in the Notes are to be found in the Brown Papers in the John Carter Brown Library of Brown University unless otherwise indicated. The abbreviation RIHS refers to the Library of the Rhode Island Historical Society.

NOTES

CHAPTER 1. A VARIETY OF EXPERIMENTS

1. Brown & Benson to Hewes & Anthony (Philadelphia), January 24, 1785, P H4.

2. For data on the codfishing fleet of John Brown see Book of Manifests, 1785–1789, Rhode Island State Archives.

3. John Brown to Moses Brown, November 27, 1786, Peck Collection, Box VIII, 1786–92, RIHS.

4. Elisha Perkins (1741-99) is best known as a physician. He was termed by one of his biographers a "celebrity par excellence in the quack line." He is said to have studied at Yale, and received the education necessary for medical practice from his father, an "eminent practitioner." In 1792 he became one of the incorporators of the Connecticut Medical Society, from which he was expelled in 1797 because he was "a patentee and user of nostrums" (see Herbert Thoms *s.v.* "Elisha Perkins," *Dictionary of American Biography,* ed. Allen Johnson, *et al.* [22 vols.; New York, 1928–36], XIV, 466–67). The *DAB* article on Perkins makes no mention of his business activities. For his early business dealings with Brown & Benson see the many letters that passed between them, May 29, 1785–October 16, 1789, P P45.

On November 25, 1786, Brown & Benson entered into a contract with Dr. Perkins by which he agreed to purchase as many as sixty jackasses, should their brig *Harmony* return with that number. He was to make payment in "Sixty Thousand weight of good ox beef" and "Twenty Thousand five Hundred & seventy One pounds and a half pound of Pork" (for the contract see P P45). *Harmony* returned to Providence with a freight of fifty-four jackasses, which Perkins presumably distributed among farmers in Connecticut. On February 25, 1788, Brown & Benson ordered from Dr. Perkins "twenty good Mules to be Delivered here in

the Month of March perhaps you may think it advisable to ride down and make a bargain . . ." For the next several years ships of Brown & Benson frequently carried mules to Surinam in lots of ten to forty.

5. Brown & Benson to Hewes & Anthony, March 9, 1789, P H4.

6. Typical of the tales of woe of the shipmasters are the following: "Find it the most difficult times to Collect money I ever knew, you must either give away your Cargo . . . for a Trifle, or retail it & then you find it the hardest work ever done to even get your money" (Capt. John B. Hopkins [at Surinam] to Brown & Benson, November 6, 1788, V H2); "Molasses is very scarce and on the whole my prospects are very poor." "I do not think it possible to Sell it [tobacco] as the Markets is glutted . . . Mollasses is very scarce . . . not a drop on board as yet . . . Markets are dull and glutted with every kind of American produce" (Capt. Seth Wheaton [at Surinam] to Brown & Benson, July 1 and August 2, 1790, V H2); " . . . it is the Dulles Times hear I Ever Saw" (Capt. Thomas Jackson [at Paramaribo] to Brown & Benson, September 4, 1791, V H2).

7. Brown & Benson to Capt. Seth Wheaton, November 14 and December 19, 1789, and May 17, 1790, V H2.

8. Brown & Benson to Capt. Seth Wheaton, February 22 and 23, 1790, V H2.

9. Capt. Simon Smith (at Surinam) to Brown & Benson, May 25, 1787, V C6.

10. Samuel Brandon (Surinam) to Brown & Benson, December 8, 1786, V C6; Brandon was a resident merchant in Surinam.

11. Capt. Simon Smith (at Surinam) to Brown & Benson, May 25, 1787, V C6.

12. Brown & Benson to Capt. Seth Wheaton, December 19, 1789, V H2.

13. Instructions of Brown & Benson to Capt. Seth Wheaton, November 3, 1791, V H6.

14. Brown & Benson to Capt. Christopher Perry, March 12, 1790, V C6.

15. Capt. Seth Wheaton (at Surinam) to Brown & Benson, March 30, 1793, V H6.

16. Brown & Benson to Capt. Seth Wheaton, January 6, 1790, V H2.

17. Brown & Benson to Capt. Seth Wheaton, February 20, 1790, V H2.

18. Instructions of Brown & Benson to Capt. Seth Wheaton, October 8, 1788, V C6.

19. Brown & Benson to Capt. William Reed, March 7, 1791, V C6.

20. John B. McMaster, in his *History of the People of the United States,* ed. Louis Filler (2 vols.; New York, 1964), II, 27, 28, 42, 43, 189, 190–203, discusses the opposition to the excise in other areas of the country but makes no mention of the protests from New England and New York.

21. Welcome Arnold to Benjamin Bourne, January 4, 1791, Welcome Arnold Letter Book, January, 1787–March, 1791.

22. Welcome Arnold, John Innes Clark, Thomas Lloyd Halsey, and George Benson (all of Providence) to Joseph Stanton and Theodore Foster, U.S. senators from Rhode Island, and to Benjamin Bourne, U.S. representative from Rhode Island, January 27, 1791, V Misc., Vol. VII.

23. "The Petition of the Merchants and Traders of the Town of Providence to the Senate and House of Representatives of the United States in Congress assembled," January 28, 1791, P P6.

24. Mungo Mackey and Henry Hill, committee of the distillers of Boston, to Welcome Arnold, John Innes Clark, Thomas

Lloyd Halsey, and George Benson, January 30, 1791, V Misc., Vol. VII.

25. For the provisions of the Excise Act see *Acts Passed at the Third Session of the Congress of the United States of America* (Philadelphia, 1791), pp. 241–60; see also *The Public Statutes at Large of the United States of America,* ed. Richard Peters (Boston, 1848—), I, 199–214.

26. Isaac Clason, P. Hamilton, and Theodore Van Wyck to the Distillers in the State of Rhode Island, July 16, 1791, V Misc., Vol. VII.

27. Hewes & Anthony to Brown & Benson, April 9 and July 7, 1791, and March 23, 1792, P H4.

28. George Sears (Baltimore) to Brown & Benson, March 4, 1792, P S4.

29. Brown & Benson to Capt. Seth Wheaton, May 13 and 15, 1793, V C6.

30. *Ibid.*

31. Brown & Benson to Capt. Nicholas Cooke, May 24, 1794, V C6.

32. W. B. Weeden, *Economic and Social History of New England, 1620–1789* (2 vols.; Boston, 1890), II, 902, refers to domestic gin in a table of prices for 1784. He makes no mention of it in Colonial times. I have seen no reference to it in mercantile papers before 1794.

33. *Providence Gazette,* February 6, 1796.

34. John Brown to Hezekiah Sabin, January 17, 1800, Peck Collection, Box XI, 1798–1801, RIHS.

35. John Brown to Hezekiah Sabin, March 19 and 30 and December 8, 1800, and February 3, 1801, Peck Collection, Box XI, 1798–1801, RIHS.

36. *Ibid.,* February 3, 1801.

37. The investment in the rum distillery of Welcome Arnold and Brown & Benson, supposedly one of the most costly in America, was $25,000.

CHAPTER 2. TO THE EAST INDIES

1. Clarence L. Ver Steeg, *Robert Morris, Revolutionary Financier, with an Analysis of His Earlier Career* (Philadelphia, 1954), p. 189.

2. John Brown to Moses Brown, August 18, 1787, Moses Brown Papers, Vol. VI, 1787–89, RIHS.

3. John Brown to Brown & Benson and to Welcome Arnold, September 29, 1787,

V G35. This letter indicates clearly that these men at some earlier time had held a conference at John Brown's house on the subject of an East India voyage. It also shows that John was becoming rather impatient at the delay.

4. The bond is in the Rhode Island State Archives.

5. *Providence Gazette,* October 9, 1784.

6. John Brown to Brown & Benson and to Welcome Arnold, undated; *ca.* 1789, V G35.

7. John Brown to Brown & Benson, undated; 1789, V G35.

8. John Brown to Brown & Benson and to Welcome Arnold, May 12, 1788, V G35.

9. See the invoice, December 22, 1787, V G35.

10. Ibid.

11. William F. Megee, "A Journal of Passage from Newport to Madeira in the Good Ship *Gen'l Washington,* Jonathan Donnison Commander, and from thence to the heither Indies and Canton," entry for December 27, 1787.

12. Ibid., entries for December 27, 1787, and March 7, 1788.

13. Samuel Ward, "Memorandum of the First Voyage of *General Washington,*" RIHS. See also extracts from his letters, May, 1788, in V G35.

14. See the notation in the handwriting of George Benson on the invoice of the cargo, December 22, 1787, V G35.

15. Megee, "Journal," entries for March 7, 21, and 22, 1788.

16. Ibid., entry for May 8, 1788.

17. Ibid., entry for May 21, 1788.

18. Ibid., entry for July 18, 1788.

19. Ibid., entries for July 21 and 25, 1788.

20. Ibid., entries for July 29 and August 15, 19, and 23, 1788.

21. Ibid., entry for August 24, 1788.

22. Ibid., entries for September 7 and 26, 1788.

23. Ibid., entries for October 4 and 5, 1788.

24. Ibid., entries for October 27 and 29, 1788.

25. In preparing this summary of the organization of foreign trade at Canton, I have derived great benefit from a reading of the careful study by Jacques M. Downes, "The American Community in Canton, 1784–1841" (unpublished Ph.D. dissertation; Georgetown University, 1961), especially pp. 81–93 and 124–38. I have also had the privilege of discussing the subject with Dr. Downes on several different occasions.

26. Megee, "Journal," entries for February 13, 16, and 17 and April 4 and 29, 1789.

27. See the invoice of goods shipped on *General Washington* from Pondicherry and Madras, August 23, 1788; and the invoice of goods shipped on her from Canton, January 27, 1789, both in V G35.

28. Maritime Papers: Manifests—Import Cargoes, Vol. VII (1788–89), Rhode Island State Archives.

29. See the account current of profit or loss on the voyage, undated, V G35.

30. Major Samuel Shaw, *The Journals of Major Samuel Shaw, the First American Consul at Canton* (Boston, 1847), pp. 301–4.

31. Brown & Francis to Brown & Benson and to Welcome Arnold, October 15, 1789, V G35.

32. See the agreement, December 26, 1789, V G35.

33. Joseph Rogers, Memo Book, V Misc., 1789; Rogers was supercargo aboard *Providence.*

34. There is a statement of the cargo sold at Bombay, July 16, 1790, V G35, but it does not indicate either the invoice price or the figure at which the various items were sold.

35. Megee, "Journal," entry for December 30, 1789.

36. William F. Megee (at Bombay) to Brown & Francis, June 9, 1790, V G35.

37. William F. Megee (at Bombay) to Brown & Francis, June 13, 1790, V G35.

38. Ibid.

39. William F. Megee (at Bombay) to Brown & Francis, July 16, 1790, V G35.

40. Joseph Rogers (at Madras) to Brown & Francis, August 25, 1790, V G35.

41. Megee, "Journal," entry for October 4, 1790.

42. U.S. Custom House Papers, Providence and Bristol, 1791, RIHS.

43. Ibid.

44. See the agreement, November 30, 1791, V R55.

45. John Rogers to Nicholas Brown, December 11, 1791, V R55.

46. Instructions of Brown & Benson to John Rogers, January 7, 1792, V R55.

47. See the invoice of the cargo, January 10, 1792, V R55.

48. John Rogers (at sea) to Brown & Benson, March 2, 1792, V R55.

49. John Rogers (at Bombay) to Brown & Benson, July 14, 1792, V R55.

50. Ibid.

51. John Rogers (at Bombay) to Brown

& Benson, July 21, 1792, V R55.

52. Ibid.

53. John Rogers (at Canton) to Brown & Benson, December 10, 1792, V R55; he took on board 272 whole chests, 86 half-chests, and 112 quarter-chests of bohea tea.

54. Ibid.

55. Brown, Benson, & Ives to John Rogers, April 4, 1793, V R55.

56. Brown, Benson, & Ives to John Rogers, April 25, 1793, V R55.

57. Ibid.

58. Brown, Benson, & Ives to John Rogers, May 2, 1793, V R55.

59. Brown, Benson, & Ives to John Rogers, May 7, 1793, V R55.

60. See "Estimate of Ship *RS* journey to Canton," January 6, 1794, V R55.

CHAPTER 3. A REJUVENATED FIRM

1. See the agreement, V J6.

2. The agreement is dated March 31, 1792, V J6.

3. John and Joseph Sheldon's agreement with Brown, Benson, & Ives, April 4, 1792, Miscellaneous Letters.

4. Instructions of Brown, Benson, & Ives to Lemuel Bishop, April 5, 1792, V Misc., Vol. VI.

5. Brown, Benson, & Ives to Capt. William Rodman, June 7, 1792, V H15.

6. Providence Association of Mechanics and Manufacturers, *Mechanics Festival: An Account of the Seventy-first Anniversary of the Providence Association of Mechanics and Manufacturers,* comp. Edwin M. Stone, *et al.* (Providence, 1860), pp. 68–69.

7. See the agreement, December 3, 1793, V Misc., Vol. VI.

8. Col. Benjamin Tallman to Brown, Benson, & Ives, July 19, 1794, V J6.

9. John Brown (for Brown & Francis) to Brown, Benson, & Ives, December 4, 1793, P B72.

10. "Coppy Questions asked Capt. Clarke respecting a Voyage up the Baltic," January, 1788, V Misc., Vol. V.

11. George Benson to William Gray, January 12, 1788, Miscellaneous Letters.

12. Instructions of Brown & Benson to Capt. Jacob Westcot, May 31, 1788, V H6.

13. In 1791 Brown & Benson dispatched their ship *Hamilton* on a voyage to France, a country that their vessels had visited on occasion in the preceding several years. *Hamilton*'s visit was to Bordeaux, where Capt. William Rodman wrote that "Charges, Duties, Pilotage, and many other Enormous Charges Makes me Almost Blast Bordeaux." He thoroughly disliked the place with its "Old Houses, Narrow Dirty Streets full of Poor Beggers that Acosts you Every five Yards thro the City." It was filled with "Jews without Number, and Indeed they are all Jews In trade if not by Profession." But for one thing he would give the city credit—its "Play House," a notable building, "the 2nd in Europe for Elegance and Size." But he thought it a pity "they have not some other Amusements Except always to the Play" (Capt. William Rodman [at Bordeaux] to Nicholas Brown, October 30, 1791, V H15).

In 1792 Brown & Benson fitted the sloop *Nancy* for a voyage to the Mediterranean, where the Brown flag had never flown before. They ordered her to Gibraltar, where the captain was to sell his rum at the best possible price and also his coffee, if he could obtain one shilling sterling a pound for it, taking the proceeds in good bills on Málaga. The remainder of his cargo he was to take to Málaga. He was to be at pains to obtain all possible information regarding trade to the Mediterranean, "how far up we may go to advantage & without hazard," the best articles to carry, and the goods to be had from there, as they might "go larger in this business in future" (Instructions of Brown & Benson to Capt. Jacob Westcot, August 9, 1792, V N22).

Nancy arrived at Gibraltar on September 22, 1792. Although eager to make all possible dispatch, Capt. Westcot lost the day because it was the Jewish Sabbath in a place where "they are Mostly Jews . . ." There he found his rum would not bring its first cost; nor would the coffee "fetch the price Limited." When he sold the rum, it fell short in gauge as well as in price. At Málaga flour and coffee sold at a low price, but his total proceeds were sufficient to load the sloop with mountain wine, sherry, figs, grapes, China oranges, raisins, almonds, and anchovies (Capt. Jacob Westcot [at Gibraltar] to Brown & Benson, September 23,

1792, V N22). The sloop returned safely to Providence, but from their first venture to the Mediterranean the partners reaped more of experience than of profit. They reckoned their loss on the voyage at £609 lawful money of Rhode Island (see the calculation, November 9, 1792, V N22).

14. See the calculation, September 23, 1792, V H15.

15. Capt. William Rodman (at Boston) to Brown, Benson, & Ives, November 21, 1792, V H15.

16. Brown, Benson, & Ives to Capt. William Rodman, November 23, 1792, V H15.

17. Capt. William Rodman (at Boston) to Brown, Benson, & Ives, December 5, 1792, V H15.

18. Brown, Benson, & Ives to Capt. William Rodman, December 7, 1792, V H15.

19. Capt. William Rodman (at Boston) to Brown, Benson, & Ives, January 4, 1793, V H15.

20. Brown, Benson, & Ives to John Bulkeley & Son (Lisbon), January 1, 1793, V H15.

21. Capt. William Rodman (at Lisbon) to Brown, Benson, & Ives, February 8, 1793; and John Bulkeley & Son to Brown, Benson, & Ives, February 16, 1793, both in V H15.

22. Brown, Benson, & Ives to Capt. William Rodman, March 2, 1793, V H15.

23. Capt. William Rodman (at Lisbon) to Brown, Benson, & Ives, March 26, 1793, V H15.

24. John Bulkeley & Son to Brown, Benson, & Ives, March 30, 1793, V H15.

25. Brown, Benson, & Ives to Joseph Fenwick (Bordeaux), December 14, 1793, V H15.

26. Brown, Benson, & Ives to Thomas Jefferson, December 16, 1793; Thomas Auldjo (Cowes) to Brown, Benson, & Ives, March 28, 1794; and Aaron Vail (Lorient) to Brown, Benson, & Ives, July 3, 1793, all in V H15.

27. Brown, Benson, & Ives to Capt. William Rodman, March 11, 1793, V H15.

28. See the calculation, December 12, 1793, V H15.

29. Instructions of Brown, Benson, & Ives to Capt. William Rodman, December 14, 1793, V H15.

30. Upon orders from Paris an embargo on all neutral shipping was instituted at Bordeaux, August 11, 1794. According to Capt. James Bentley, master of Welcome Arnold's brigantine *Harriot,* then anchored

at that port, only those vessels left that were "got away by Brabery" (Capt. James Bentley [at Bordeaux] to Welcome Arnold, January 4, 1794, Arnold-Green Correspondence, Box VII).

31. Capt. William Rodman (at St. Martin's Roads, France) to Brown, Benson, & Ives, February 3, 1794, V H15.

32. Capt. William Rodman (at Bordeaux) to Brown, Benson, & Ives, May 20, 1794, V H15.

33. Capt. William Rodman (at Marstrand, Sweden) to Brown, Benson, & Ives, July 15, 1794, V H15.

34. See the calculation, July, 1795, V H15.

35. Instructions of Brown, Benson, & Ives to Capt. John Warner, August 31, 1793, V T45.

36. See Capt. John Warner's protest of the wreck of *Three Friends,* February 5, 1794, V T45.

37. See the calculation, undated, V T45.

38. For a brief but adequate treatment of the alignment of European powers and their diplomacy during the Anglo-French wars in the years 1793–1815 and how this influenced American trade, see Samuel Flagg Bemis, *A Diplomatic History of the United States* (5th ed.; New York, 1965), chaps. vi, vii, and ix.

39. Instructions of Brown, Benson, & Ives to Capt. Daniel Olney, June 12, 1793, V R55.

40. Capt. Daniel Olney (at Baltimore) to Brown, Benson, & Ives, June 28, 1793, V R55.

41. Ibid.

42. Brown, Benson, & Ives to George Sears, June 15, 1793, V R55.

43. See the invoice, August 1, 1793, V R55.

44. Capt. Daniel Olney (at Baltimore) to Brown, Benson, & Ives, July 21, 1793, V R55.

45. See "Certificate that the passengers of the *Rising Sun* are refugees of Cape Francois . . ." attested by a citizens' committee of Baltimore, August 3, 1793, V R55.

46. Capt. Daniel Olney (at Baltimore) to Brown, Benson, & Ives, July 1, 1793, V R55.

47. Brown, Benson, & Ives to Capt. Daniel Olney, August 27 and September 26, 1793, V R55.

48. See Capt. Daniel Olney's protest entered at Jersey, October 2, 1793, V R55.

49. Capt. Daniel Olney (at London) to Brown, Benson, & Ives, November 10, 1793, V R55.

50. See "Thomas Dickason & Company's account of the Money received from the Admiralty in *Rising Sun* Case," June 1, 1796; see also Brown, Benson, & Ives's claim for the ship *Rising Sun,* January 26, 1798, both in V R55.

51. Capt. Daniel Olney (at London) to Brown, Benson, & Ives, November 10, 1793, V R55.

52. Capt. Daniel Olney (at Jersey) to Brown, Benson, & Ives, December 20, 1793, V R55.

53. Seth Wheaton to Capt. Charles Sheldon, June 8, 1793, V H6.

54. Brown, Benson, & Ives to Capt. Charles Sheldon, July 20, 1793, V H6.

55. Capt. Charles Sheldon (at Lisbon) to Brown, Benson, & Ives, February 11, 1794, V H6.

56. Instructions of Brown, Benson, & Ives to Capt. John Warner, August 5, 1793, V H25.

57. Capt. John Crumby (at Curaçao) to Brown, Benson, & Ives, October 5, 1793, V H25; it will be observed that Capt. Warner, to whom the preceding letter was addressed, did not make the voyage in *Harmony.*

58. Capt. John Crumby (at Curaçao) to Brown, Benson, & Ives, December 23, 1793, V H25.

59. Capt. John Crumby (at Curaçao) to Brown, Benson, & Ives, January 10, 1794, V H25.

60. Capt. John Crumby (at Hamburg) to Brown, Benson, & Ives, April 16, 1794, V H25.

61. Capt. John Crumby (at Hamburg) to Brown, Benson, & Ives, May 1, 1794, V H25.

62. Brown, Benson, & Ives to Caspar Voight, May 24, 1795, V H25.

63. Agreement between Capt. John Crumby and Head & Amory (Boston), October 22, 1795, V H25.

64. See the invoice of the cargo, February 14, 1795, V A62.

65. Instructions of Brown, Benson, & Ives to George Page, February 14, 1795, V A62.

66. George Page (at Bordeaux) to Brown, Benson, & Ives, April 13, 16, 20, and 22 and May 26, 1795, V A62.

67. See the calculation, November 5, 1795, V A62.

68. See the charter agreement, June 29, 1795, V R15.

69. Instructions of Brown, Benson, & Ives to Capt. Jacob Westcot, July 2, 1795, V R15.

70. Capt. Jacob Westcot (at London) to Brown, Benson, & Ives, August 18, 1795, V R15.

71. Thomas Dickason & Co. (London) to Brown, Benson, & Ives, December 21, 1795, V R15.

72. Instructions of Brown, Benson, & Ives to Capt. George Tyler, June 13, 1795, V C52.

73. See "Protest against the Captors of [the] Ship *Charlotte,* entered at Plymouth," August 4, 1795, V C52.

74. Thomas Dickason & Co. to Brown, Benson, & Ives, December 27, 1795, V C52.

75. Instructions of Brown, Benson, & Ives to Ebenezer Thompson, March 18, 1795, V H6.

76. Ebenezer Thompson (at Brest) to Brown, Benson, & Ives, May 24, 1795, V H6.

77. Ebenezer Thompson (at Copenhagen) to Brown, Benson, & Ives, August, 1795, V H6.

78. Ebenezer Thompson (at Orkney Islands) to Brown, Benson, & Ives, December, 1795, and February 4 and (at Leith, Scotland) June 7, 1796, concerning the wreck and repairs at Leith, V H6.

79. See the calculation of the voyage, November 8, 1797, V F7.

80. Instructions of Brown, Benson, & Ives to George Page, December 24, 1795, V F7.

81. Instructions of Brown, Benson, & Ives to Capt. Henry Olney, December 25, 1795; and Brown, Benson, & Ives to George Page, December 25, 1795, both in V F7.

82. George Page (at Le Havre) to Brown, Benson, & Ives, April 11, 1796, V F7.

83. Instructions of Brown, Benson, & Ives to Ephraim Talbot, January 12, 1796, V E5.

84. Brown, Benson, & Ives to Capt. Whipple Andrews, January 1, 1796, V H27.

85. George Page (at Copenhagen) to Brown, Benson, & Ives, June 3, 1796, V H27.

86. See the calculation, October 26, 1797, V H27.

87. George Tyler (at Dunkirk) to Brown, Benson, & Ives, May 2, 1796, V C52.

88. George Tyler (at Copenhagen) to Brown, Benson, & Ives, May 29, 1796, V C52.

89. See the calculation of the voyage, settled May 30, 1797, V C52 (1796).

90. Instructions of Brown, Benson, & Ives to Ephraim Talbot, January 14, 1796, V E5.

91. Ephraim Talbot (at Charleston, S.C.) to Brown, Benson, & Ives, February 24, 1796, V E5.

92. Brown, Benson, & Ives to Ephraim Talbot, January 26, 1796, V E5.

93. Ephraim Talbot (at Charleston, S.C.) to Brown, Benson, & Ives, February 9, 1796, V E5.

94. Brown, Benson, & Ives to Ephraim Talbot, February 13, 1796, V E5.

95. George Tyler and Ephraim Talbot (at Charleston, S.C.) to Brown, Benson, & Ives, February 25, 1796; and Ephraim Talbot (at Charleston, S.C.) to Brown, Benson, & Ives, March 1 and 10, 1796, all in V E5.

96. Brown, Benson, & Ives to Ephraim Talbot, March 30, 1796, V E5.

97. Brown, Benson, & Ives to Ephraim Talbot, April 1, 1796, V E5.

98. Ephraim Talbot (at Amsterdam) to Brown, Benson, & Ives, May 24, 1796, V E5.

99. Elizabeth carried from Charleston 765 whole barrels and 95 half-barrels of rice, which cost $32,315.15. The rice at Amsterdam netted 54,898 guilders, or $21,-959.20; see the invoice and the account of sales, July, 1796, V E5.

100. Ephraim Talbot (at Amsterdam) to Brown, Benson, & Ives, July 14, 1796, V E5.

101. Ephraim Talbot (at Cadiz) to Brown, Benson, & Ives, September 7, 1796, V E5.

102. Ephraim Talbot (at Castletownshend, Ireland) to Brown, Benson, & Ives, December 30, 1796, and January 1, 1797, V E5.

103. Ephraim Talbot (at London) to Brown, Benson, & Ives, May 3, 1796, V E5.

104. Contract between Brown, Benson,

& Ives and Chace, Walker, & Eddy (Providence), February 20, 1796, V H5.

105. See the invoice and sales of flour, March 23, 1796, V H5; the freight of the flour was $2.50 a barrel from Baltimore to Le Havre and £135 sterling from there to London.

106. Ephraim Talbot (at London) to Brown, Benson, & Ives, May 3, 1796, V E5.

107. V E5.

108. See the agreement between Brown, Benson, & Ives and Daniel Olney, December 22, 1794, V J6.

109. Brown, Benson, & Ives to Samuel Snow, August 29 and September 8 and 13, 1791; and Samuel Snow (Canton) to Brown, Benson, & Ives, September 4, 7, 9, 10, and 13, 1791, all in P S57.

110. See the invoice of the cargo, December 22, 1794, V J6.

111. Nicholas Brown and Thomas P. Ives to Daniel Olney and Samuel Snow, December 24, 1794, V J6.

112. Instructions of Brown, Benson, & Ives to Samuel Snow and Daniel Olney, December 24, 1794, V J6.

113. Samuel Snow and Daniel Olney (at Cape Verde Islands) to Brown, Benson & Ives, January 31 and (at sea) April 6, 1795, V J6.

114. Samuel Snow and Daniel Olney (at Bombay) to Brown, Benson, & Ives, June 27, 1795, V J6.

115. Samuel Snow and Daniel Olney (at Bombay) to Brown, Benson, & Ives, July 2, 1795, V J6.

116. Ibid.

117. Samuel Snow and Daniel Olney (at Bombay) to Brown, Benson, & Ives, July 22, 1795, V J6.

118. Samuel Snow and Daniel Olney (at Canton) to Brown, Benson, & Ives, November 6, 1795, V J6.

119. Samuel Snow and Daniel Olney (at Canton) to Brown, Benson, & Ives, November 6 and 19, 1795, V J6.

120. See the account current, January 6, 1796, V J6.

121. According to the U.S. Custom House manifest, the value of that portion of the cargo on which an ad valorem duty was paid was $75,406.48. The specific duties paid on the other portions of the cargo amounted to $60,296.96. At the time specific duties averaged about a third of the value of the goods. If one assumes that this ratio applies in this instance, the value of that part of the cargo was $180,891. The total of this figure plus the $75,406.48, the declared value of goods on which the ad valorem duty was paid, is $256,297.48; see Gertrude S. Kimball, "The East India Trade of Providence from 1787 to 1807," *Papers from the Historical Seminary of Brown University* (Providence, 1896), p. 17.

122. Instructions of Brown, Benson, & Ives to Capt. William Rodman, January 17, 1795, V H15.

123. Capt. William Rodman (at Madeira) to Brown, Benson, & Ives, March 3 and 19, 1795, V H15.

124. Capt. William Rodman (at Madeira) to Brown, Benson, & Ives, March 19, 1795, V H15.

125. Ibid.

126. Capt. William Rodman (at Calcutta) to Brown, Benson, & Ives, November 4, 1795, V H15.

127. Capt. William Rodman (at Calcutta) to Brown, Benson, & Ives, November 4, 20, and 30, 1795, V H15.

128. Capt. William Rodman (at Calcutta) to Brown, Benson, & Ives, January 20, 1796, V H15.

129. Ibid.

130. Capt. William Rodman (at Boston) to Brown, Benson, & Ives, July 13 and 14, 1796, V H15.

131. See the calculation of the voyage, July, 1796, V H15.

132. See the statement in Miscellaneous Letters, 1796, Vol. I. The paper bears no specific date, but it is clearly contemporaneous with the reorganization of the firm, which occurred in October, 1796.

133. Memorandum from Benjamin Dexter (Providence) to John Bowers, undated (*ca.* 1797), V J6.

134. Jeremiah Jenkins to John Bowers, April 8, 1797, V J6.

135. Joseph Rogers to John Bowers, March 14, 1797, V J6.

136. See the estimation of costs of the cargo, undated, V J6; in this document is set forth a detailed plan for providing the necessary funds.

137. Daniel Olney and John Bowers (at sea) to Brown & Ives, June 2, 1797, V J6.

138. Daniel Olney and John Bowers (at Canton) to Brown & Ives, November 6 and 11, 1797, V J6.

139. See the agreement, October 13, 1797; see also Daniel Olney and John Bowers (at Canton) to Brown & Ives, November 6, 1797, both in V J6.

140. Daniel Olney and John Bowers (at Hamburg) to Brown & Ives, June 28 and July 16, 1798, V J6.

141. See the protest entered by officers of *John Jay* at Lisbon, November 23, 1798, V J6.

142. See the agreement between Capt. Benjamin Page and Brown & Ives, April 2, 1798, V A65.

143. See the agreement between Samuel Snow and Brown & Ives, July 7, 1798, V A65.

144. Instructions of Brown & Ives to Samuel Snow, July 7, 1798, V A65.

145. Ibid.; for this first voyage of *Ann & Hope* see Robert W. Kenny, "The Maiden Voyage of *Ann & Hope* of Providence to Botany Bay and Canton, 1798–1799," *American Neptune,* XVIII, No. 2 (April, 1958), 105–36.

146. Brown & Ives to Samuel Snow, July 7, 1798, V A65.

147. Ibid.

148. Benjamin Carter, "Journal of a Voyage to Canton in the Ship *Ann & Hope,*" RIHS.

149. Instructions of Brown & Ives to Capt. Benjamin Page, July 7, 1798, V A65.

150. See Timothy Pickering, Secretary of State, to Brown & Ives, August 29, 1798, Miscellaneous Letters; in this letter Pickering says he has sent "a commission for the private armed Ship *Ann and Hope* . . ." The ship was equipped with twelve 9-pounders, while the crew had pikes, cutlasses, nets to intercept boarding parties, and a store of small arms.

151. Instructions of Brown & Ives to Capt. Benjamin Page, July 7, 1798, V A65.

152. See the Steward's Book, October 12, 1798, V A65.

153. Capt. Benjamin Page (at Canton) to Brown & Ives, December 18, 1798, V A65.

154. See the Steward's Book, December 7, 1798, V A65.

155. See the invoice of the cargo, February 5, 1799, V A65.

156. Samuel Snow (at Canton) to Brown & Ives, January 16 and 28, 1799, P S57.

157. Samuel Snow (at Canton) to Brown & Ives, February 5 and 14, 1799, P S57.

158. Samuel Snow (at Canton) to Brown & Ives, November 9, 1799, P S57.

159. Samuel Snow (at Canton) to Brown & Ives, January 26, 1800, P S57, in which he writes that he is "much pleased to hear the *Ann & Hopes* cargo turned out so good," and that he was "happy to hear the Cargo generally has come to so good a market & so ready sale." Evidently Brown & Ives had written Snow the good tidings; see the invoice of the cargo at Canton, February 5, 1799, V A65; see also Kimball, "The East India Trade of Providence," p. 28, for the estimated value of the cargo at Providence.

160. See the agreement between Brown & Ives and Daniel Olney, George Page, and Ephraim Talbot, May 15, 1799, V J6.

161. Instructions of Brown & Ives to Capt. Daniel Olney, May 16, 1799, V J6.

162. Instructions of Brown & Ives to George Page and Ephraim Talbot, May 16, 1799, V J6.

163. See the invoice of the cargo, October 19, 1799, V J6.

164. See the invoice of the cargo, April 8, 1800, V C52; the cargo was charged at $48,000.

165. See the account of sales at Amster-dam, July 26, 1800, V C52; the sales netted 138,466 guilders, or $55,386.40.

166. Secretary of the Navy to Capt. Silas Talbot, August 29, 1798, in *Naval Documents Related to the Quasi-War between the United States and France: Naval Operations from February 1797 to October 1798* (Washington, D.C., 1935), pp. 351–52; in this letter the Secretary gives John Brown's description of the ship.

167. Secretary of the Navy to John Brown, August 7, 1798, in *ibid.*, pp. 277–78.

168. Secretary of the Navy to Capt. Silas Talbot, August 29, 1798, in *ibid.*, pp. 351–52.

169. Secretary of the Navy to John Brown, September 18, 1798, in *ibid.*, p. 423.

170. Secretary of the Navy to Capt. Silas Talbot, September 20, 1798, in *ibid.*, pp. 428-29.

171. Secretary of the Navy to President John Adams, June 19, 1799, in *Naval Documents . . . Naval Operations from April 1799 to July 1799*, p. 362.

172. Gibbs & Channing (Newport) to the Secretary of the Navy, November 17, 1799, in *Naval Documents . . . Naval Operations from August 1799 to December 1799*, p. 411.

CHAPTER 4. A SOUTH AMERICAN INTERLUDE

1. American State Papers: Documents, Legislative and Executive (38 vols.; Washington, D.C., 1832–61), *Foreign Relations*, III, 262–92 *et passim;* see also Arthur Preston Whitaker, *The United States and the Independence of Latin America, 1800–1830* (Baltimore, 1941), pp. 1–39.

2. See the statement of the case of *Mary Ann* by Thomas Lloyd Halsey, Jr., undated, V M25, Vol. VIII; see also his letter [at Buenos Aires] to Brown & Ives and John Corlis, October 16, 1800, V E49.

3. Brown & Ives to Ephraim Talbot, April 22, 1800, V C52.

4. The spelling of Innes used throughout this volume appears in John Clark's will.

5. Brown & Ives to Ephraim Talbot, April 22, 1800, V C52.

6. A fine example of the failure to comprehend the real purpose of visits by American ships to Rio de Janeiro is Charles Lyon Chandler's explanation of the call of the Boston ship *Gladiator* at Rio in the year 1800. According to Chandler she sailed from Boston in May, 1800, with a cargo of dried fish, hardware, tar, etc., bound for the Cape of Good Hope. She was blown off her course and was allowed eleven days "to re-fit at Rio de Janeiro" (see Chandler, "List of United States Vessels in Brazil, 1792–1805, Inclusive," *Hispanic American Historical Review*, XXVI [1946], 608). Thomas Lloyd Halsey, Jr., close friend and associate of Brown & Ives, who was in South America at the time of *Gladiator*'s visit to Rio de Janeiro, was told by the supercargo that she was bound, not for the Cape of Good Hope, but for Rio de Janeiro and Buenos Aires; that she carried dry goods charged in the invoice at $64,000; that her owner then filled her up with tar, pitch, staves, iron hoops, and "some few trifling articles of that kind"; that the dry goods were to have been sold at Rio de Janeiro. But the arrival of a fleet of British East Indiamen loaded with dry goods so depressed the price there that it was decided to enter the goods at Buenos Aires (Thomas Lloyd Halsey, Jr. [at Buenos Aires], to Brown & Ives and John Corlis, October 16, 1800, V E49; see also Bernice A. Carroll, "The *Mary Ann,* an Illicit Adventure," *Hispanic American Historical Review,* XXXVII, No. 2 [May, 1957], 202).

7. Brown & Ives to Ephraim Talbot, April 22, 1800, V C52.

8. Ephraim Talbot (at London) to Brown & Ives, August 22, 1800, V C52.

9. Ephraim Talbot (at Buenos Aires) to Brown & Ives, January 27 and April 11, 1801, V C52.

10. Ephraim Talbot (at Buenos Aires) to Brown & Ives, April 11, 1801, V C52.

11. Ephraim Talbot (at Buenos Aires) to Brown & Ives, April 22 and (at Ensenada) June 4, 1801, V C52.

12. For the contract see V M25, Vol. I.

13. For the bills of sale see V M25, Vol. I.

14. For the agreement, May 1, 1800, see V M25, Vol. I.

15. Instructions of John Corlis, Brown & Ives, and Thomas Lloyd Halsey, Jr., to Capt. Daniel Olney, June 9, 1800, V M25, Vol. I.

16. Instructions of Brown & Ives, John Corlis, and Thomas Lloyd Halsey, Jr., to Thomas Lloyd Halsey, Jr., June 23, 1800; and instructions of Brown & Ives, John Corlis, and Thomas Lloyd Halsey, Jr., to Capt. Henry Olney, June 23, 1800, both in V E49.

17. Thomas Lloyd Halsey, Jr. (at Buenos Aires), to Brown & Ives and John Corlis, October 16, 1800, V E49.

18. See the undated deposition of Nicholas Brown and Thomas P. Ives, V E49.

19. See the copy of the "treaty," V M25, Vol. I.

20. Thomas Lloyd Halsey, Jr. (at Buenos Aires), to Brown & Ives and John Corlis, November 29 and December 6, 1800, V E49.

21. Capt. Daniel Olney (at Rio de Janeiro) to Brown & Ives and John Corlis, February 10, 1801, V M25, Vol. II.

22. Thomas Lloyd Halsey, Jr. (at Buenos Aires), to Thomas Antonio Romero and Pedro Andrés Garcia, July 2, 1801, V M25, Vol. II.

23. Thomas Lloyd Halsey, Jr. (at Buenos Aires), to Brown & Ives and John Corlis, July 4, 1801, V M25, Vol. II. See the contract and the bond, both dated July 4, 1801, V M25, Vol. II.

24. The terms of the decree are to be found in the letter of Capt. Daniel Olney (at Buenos Aires) to Thomas Lloyd Halsey, Jr., October 29, 1803, V M25, Vol. IV.

25. See the document in Spanish, with English translation, May 8, 1804, V M25, Vol. IV.

26. Capt. Daniel Olney (at Buenos Aires) to Brown & Ives, John Corlis, and Thomas Lloyd Halsey, Jr., August 14, 1804, V M25, Vol. V.

27. "Address of sundry Citizens of the United States . . . to the Vice Roy—del Pino, Buenos Aires," March 31, 1802, V M25, Vol. III.

28. "Address of sundry Citizens of the United States—restrained at Buenos Aires to the American Minister at the Court of Madrid," April 22, 1802, V M25, Vol. III.

29. Plea from U.S. Citizens at Buenos Aires to the U.S. Minister at Madrid, May 1, 1802, V M25, Vol. III.

30. See the deposition of Jonathan Russell, July 20, 1822, V M25, Vol. IX.

31. Brown & Ives to William Hunter, December 12, 1823, P H76.

32. See the undated depositions of Nicholas Brown and Thomas P. Ives, V E49.

33. Writing to John Corlis (one of the partners in the venture of *Mary Ann*) in 1822, they engaged in this line of rationalization: "that the owners here, never intended to violate the Municipal regulations of Spain, is evident from the circumstance of Insurance being made . . . without including the risk of illicit Trade. We expected to have had a regular entry & to have paid the Lawful Duties. It would have been madness to have risked so valuable a Ship & Cargo, as the *Mary Ann,* upon a Smuggling Voyage" (Brown & Ives to John Corlis [then living in Bourbon County, Kentucky], February 6, 1822, P C66). One wonders what Brown & Ives hoped to gain by writing in this fashion more than twenty years after the event to a man living in Kentucky. In retrospect they may have thought it "madness" to have risked such a ship on a smuggling voyage, but it is clear that they did not think so in the year 1800.

CHAPTER 5. DISTANT ENTERPRISES OF MAGNITUDE AND HARD MONEY

1. See the agreement, or charter party, July 27, 1799, V A65.

2. Instructions of Brown & Ives to Capt. Christopher Bentley, August 3, 1799, V A65.

3. For prices paid for sea otter skins see Sullivan Dorr to Joseph and John Dorr, September 15, 1801; Sullivan Dorr to James & Thomas H. Perkins (Boston), October 23, November 17, and December 21, 1802; and Sullivan Dorr to Henry Dorr, November 20, 1802, all in "Letters of Sullivan Dorr," ed. Howard Corning, in *Proceedings of the Massachusetts Historical Society,* LXVII (1945), 284, 333, 345, 347, and 355. See also "List of American Ships arrived at Canton from Aug. 1799 to Mar 1800, with Their Cargoes," *ca.* March, 1800, V A65.

4. Sullivan Dorr to James & Thomas H. Perkins, October 23, 1802, in "Letters of Sullivan Dorr," p. 333.

5. For the prices of sealskins at Canton see Sullivan Dorr to Joseph and John Dorr, December 28, 1801, and February 13, 1802; and Sullivan Dorr to Samuel Snow, December 28, 1801, all in "Letters of Sullivan Dorr," pp. 297, 300, and 296.

6. Sullivan Dorr to John and Joseph Dorr, December 2, 1800, in "Letters of Sullivan Dorr," p. 234.

7. Sullivan Dorr to David Sears, October 22, 1802, in "Letters of Sullivan Dorr," p. 332. On another occasion Sullivan Dorr wrote: "At all times you may expect inferior goods [in exchange for] Otter Seal or any other Skins and cargo, unless you accept the price at which they can be consolidated into money or receive goods in exchange at an extravagant price, so as to make the difference bear between the price of goods barterd with a Hong Merchant and the real cash price of teas, so that in barter one generally loses in quality what he gets in price in fact much more" (Sullivan Dorr to Andrew C. Dorr, April 10, 1801, in "Letters of Sullivan Dorr," p. 266).

8. Instructions of Brown & Ives to Capt. Christopher Bentley, August 3, 1799, V A65.

9. Thomas Thompson (at Canton) to Brown & Ives, January 25, 1800, V A65.

10. Samuel Snow (Canton) to Brown & Ives; Gibbs & Channing (Newport); John Innes Clark; and Munro, Snow, & Munro, January 26, 1800, V A65.

11. See "List of American Ships arrived at Canton from Aug. 1799 to Mar 1800, with Their Cargoes," *ca.* March, 1800, V A65.

12. Samuel Snow (Canton) to Brown & Ives, January 26, 1800, V A65.

13. Gertrude S. Kimball, "The East India Trade of Providence from 1787 to 1807," *Papers from the Historical Seminary of Brown University* (Providence, 1896), p. 28.

14. John Jay carried 99,500 hard dollars. In addition Joseph Anthony & Co. (Philadelphia) had shipped 10,000 hard dollars, Murray & Mumford (New York) had shipped 10,000 hard dollars, and Isaac Moses & Sons (New York) had shipped 20,000 hard dollars, all to Samuel Snow on account of Brown & Ives; see Brown & Ives to Samuel Snow, May 10 and 12, 1800, V J6.

15. Samuel Snow (Canton) to Brown & Ives, July 23, 1800, V J6.

16. Samuel Snow (Canton) to Brown & Ives, December 27, 1800, V J6.

17. Capt. Benjamin Dexter (at North Island) to Brown & Ives, February 18 and (at sea) March 29 and June 5, 1801, V J6.

18. See the invoice, January 28, 1801, V J6; and Kimball, "The East India Trade of Providence," p. 18.

19. Brown & Ives to Samuel Snow, December 22, 1800, V A65.

20. See the agreement between Perez Jones; William Barton, Jr.; Caleb Tuttle; and Aaron Hosford on the one part and Brown & Ives on the other regarding the ginseng to be procured by these men, December 5, 1800; see also Brown & Ives to Samuel Snow, December 22, 1800, both in V A65.

21. Sullivan Dorr to Andrew Dorr, August 1, 1802, in "Letters of Sullivan Dorr," p. 319.

22. Sullivan Dorr to Israel Munson, November 13, 1802, in "Letters of Sullivan Dorr," p. 339.

23. If Brown & Ives followed their usual practice of marking up coffee and sugar for re-export, the invoice figure was far in excess of the actual cost of the goods.

24. Thomas Thompson (at London) to Brown & Ives, January 30 (with postscript dated February 2), February 12, and April 11, 1801, V A65.

25. Thomas Thompson (at Bali Strait) to Brown & Ives, August 6 and (at Canton) September 1 and October 17, 1801, V A65.

26. See the invoice of the cargo from Canton, November 30, 1801, V A65.

27. "Memo. of American Ships at Canton," October 18, 1801, V A65.

28. This figure is an estimate based upon the following calculation: The tariff duty on tea was a specific duty. The exact amount of the specific duty paid on *Ann & Hope*'s teas is known but not the valuation on which the duty was levied. The total amount of the duty on the teas was slightly in excess of $84,000. Under the tariff of 1789 the specific duty on tea seems to have averaged about a third of its value. At this rate the teas on *Ann & Hope* were worth $252,000. On the other items in the cargo the ad valorem duties amounted to $14,016. Assuming that these duties averaged 10 per cent, the goods on which they were levied had a value of $140,000. This sum, plus the estimated value of the teas, brings the total value of the cargo to $392,-000. Even if one allows for a substantial margin of error in this estimate, it can hardly be doubted that this voyage of *Ann & Hope* returned a fine profit. This calculation is based upon "Copy of Ship *Ann & Hope*'s Entry at Customs House," April 6, 1802, V A65.

29. Arthur carried 140,000 Spanish dollars; see Brown & Ives to Samuel Aborn, May 5, 1803, V A7. *Isis* had on board 90,000 Spanish dollars; see Brown & Ives to Thomas Thompson, October 25, 1803, V I8.

30. Instructions of Brown & Ives and Gibbs & Channing to Samuel Aborn, May 5 and 6, 1803, V A7.

31. Samuel Aborn (at Soenda Strait) to Brown & Ives and Gibbs & Channing, September 2, 1803; and Samuel Aborn (at Canton) to Brown & Ives, November 2, 1803, both in V A7.

32. Samuel Aborn's list of American vessels at Canton, September 2, 1803, V A7.

33. Samuel Aborn (at Canton) to Brown & Ives, November 2, 1803, V A7.

34. Samuel Aborn (at Canton) to Brown & Ives, November 17, 1803, V A7.

35. Instructions of Brown & Ives to Capt. Benjamin Dexter, October 26, 1803, V I8.

36. Capt. Benjamin Dexter (at Soenda Strait) and Thomas Thompson (at Soenda Strait) to Brown & Ives, March 10, 1804, V I8.

37. Thomas Thompson (at Canton) to Brown & Ives, May 25, 1804, V I8.

38. Brown & Ives to Thomas Thompson, July 12, 1804, V A72.

39. A total of $100,213 was sent in the ship *Asia;* see the memorandum of dollars deposited at the Providence Bank, July 12, 1804, V A72.

40. Instructions of Brown & Ives to Thomas Thompson, July 12, 1804, V A72.

41. Ibid.

42. Instructions of Brown & Ives to Capt. Nathaniel Pearce, July 12, 1804, V A72.

43. Capt. Nathaniel Pearce (at Bali Strait) to Brown & Ives, November 1 and (at Canton) December 14, 1804, V A72.

44. Thomas Thompson (at Canton) to Brown & Ives, December 12, 1804, and January 19 and 24, 1805, V A72.

45. See the undated invoice and memorandum of cargo for *Asia;* see also the invoice dated January 19, 1805, both in V A72 (1804–5).

46. Brown & Ives to Capt. Nathaniel Pearce, June 8, 1805, V A72.

47. Capt. Nathaniel Pearce (at Texel Roads) to Brown & Ives, July 9, 1805, V A72.

48. Ships with cargoes from Batavia had gone on to Europe, but no arrivals from Canton had done so without first breaking bulk.

49. See the account current of Daniel Crommelin & Sons (Amsterdam) with Brown & Ives, covering the period from June 29, 1804, to August 14, 1809, U A; the net proceeds of the cargo of the ship *Asia* are listed as 645,935 guilders, July 16, 1806.

50. John Bulkeley & Son (Lisbon) to Brown & Ives, September 16, 1805, and Capt. Nathaniel Pearce (at Macao) to Brown & Ives, January 22, 1806, both in V A72.

51. Thomas Thompson (at Canton) to Brown & Ives, January 2 and February 4 and 6, 1806, V A72.

52. Thomas Thompson (at Canton) to Brown & Ives, February 19, 1806, V A72.

53. Capt. Nathaniel Pearce (at Guernsey) to Brown & Ives, August 11, 1806, V A72.

54. Capt. Nathaniel Pearce (at London) to Brown & Ives, September 1 and 19, 1806; see also the copy of the decree of the High Court of Admiralty, September 25, 1806, all in V A72.

55. See the account of sales, August 27 and 28, October 8, and December 22, 1807, and January 30 and June 7, 1808, U A.

56. Brown & Ives to John Bulkeley & Son, March 30, 1805; and Brown & Ives to Samuel Aborn, March 30, 1805, both in V I8.

57. Samuel Aborn (at Lisbon) to Brown & Ives, May 8, 1805; and Brown & Ives to Samuel Aborn, May 16, 1805, both in V I8.

58. Samuel Aborn (at Canton) to Brown & Ives, November 10 and 11, 1805; and Samuel Aborn and Thomas Thompson (at Canton) to Brown & Ives, November 10, 1805, all in V I8.

59. William Carter (at Canton) to Brown & Ives, February 2 and 7, 1807, V A7.

60. *Arthur* actually carried only 90,000 Spanish dollars to Canton, but by four vessels belonging to various other houses Brown & Ives had sent well over 100,000 hard dollars to be placed at the disposal of Capt. Solomon Townsend. Of this latter sum a substantial amount was employed in the liquidation of obligations previously given to hong merchants in part payment for cargoes of various ships belonging to Brown & Ives. See Brown & Ives to George Page, August 30, 1806; and Brown & Ives to William Carter, August 30, 1806, both in V A7.

61. See "List of American Vessels entered and cleared from the Port of Canton from July 1, 1804 to March, 1805," V A72; "List of American Vessels arrived at the Port of Canton May Season 1805 commencing 10," V I8; and "List of American Vessels entered and cleared at the Port of Canton in China, from January 1st, 1806 to March 20th, 1807," V A7.

62. See the charter party between Brown & Ives and Willing & Francis (Philadelphia), September 11, 1801; see also Brown & Ives to Capt. John F. Fry, September 12, 1801, both in V J6.

63. John Bowers (at Amsterdam) to Brown & Ives, December 7 and 23, 1801, V J6.

64. John Bowers (at Amsterdam) to Brown & Ives, February 9, 1802; see also the charter party between the Dutch East India Company and John Bowers for *John Jay*, March 2, 1802, both in V J6.

65. John Bowers (at Batavia) to Brown & Ives, August 18, 1802, V J6.

66. See the protest by John Bowers and Capt. John F. Fry against the condemnation of the ship as unfit to carry a cargo to Europe for the Dutch East India Company, September 25, 1802, V J6.

67. Instructions of Brown & Ives to Capt. Thomas Laing, May 15, 1802, V A65.

68. Instructions of Brown & Ives to Thomas Thompson, May 15, 1802, V A65.

69. Instructions of Brown & Ives to Capt. Thomas Laing, May 15, 1802, V A65.

70. At the current rate of exchange 136 paper rix-dollars were the equivalent of 80 Spanish dollars.

71. Thomas Thompson (at Batavia) to Brown & Ives, September 29 and October 3, 1802, V A65.

72. Thomas Thompson (at London) to Brown & Ives, January 28, 1803, V A65.

73. See Daniel Crommelin & Sons account of sales, August 18 and September 27, 1803, U A.

74. See the agreement between Ephraim Talbot and Brown & Ives, January 20, 1802, V I8.

75. Instructions of Brown & Ives to Capt. Benjamin Dexter, January 20, 1802, V I8.

76. Ephraim Talbot (at Batavia) to Brown & Ives, July 19, 1802, V I8.

77. Ephraim Talbot (at St. Helena) to Brown & Ives, December 21, 1802, V I8.

78. *Ibid.;* see the enclosed account of sales.

79. See "Account Sales of 1103 Bags Mocha Coffee per Ship *Isis*," August 19, 1803, V I8.

80. See John Bowers' agreement with Brown & Ives, November 2, 1803, V A65.

81. Instructions of Brown & Ives to John Bowers, November 5, 1803, V A65.

82. Instructions of Brown & Ives to Capt. Thomas Laing, November 5, 1803, V A65.

83. See the invoice of the cargo, April 10, 1804, V A65.

84. Daniel Tillinghast (at Batavia) to Brown & Ives, April 5, 1804, V J6.

85. See the invoice of the cargo, April 21, 1804, V J6.

86. Brown & Ives to Daniel Tillinghast, August 21, 1804, V J6.

87. See "Daniel Crommelin & Sons' Account, from our Books," 1804–5, U A.

88. See Daniel Crommelin & Sons account of sales of coffee by *Charlotte,* August 23, 1804; and their account of sales of coffee by *Polly,* August 27, 1804, both in U A.

89. In 1803 John Bowers had gone out to Batavia as supercargo of *Ann & Hope,* but he had returned on *John Jay.*

90. Instructions of Brown & Ives to John Bowers, September 18, 1804; instructions of Brown & Ives to Capt. John F. Fry, September 19, 1804; and agreement between John Bowers and J. J. Van Loffeld, March 11, 1805, all in V J6.

91. John Bowers (at Batavia) to Brown & Ives, September 24 and 26 and (at sea) November 26 and December 16, 1805, V J6.

92. John Bowers (at St. George's Island) to Brown & Ives, January 13, 1806, V J6.

93. Brown & Ives to the President and Directors of the Providence Bank, February 24, 1806, V J6.

94. Board of Directors of the Providence Bank to Samuel Ward, February 24, 1806, V J6. As security for the $60,000 that the bank made available to Ward, Brown & Ives deposited with the bank certificates of funded stock of the United States as follows:

Eight certificates of 8 per cent stock amounting to   12,800.00

Four certificates of Navy 6 per cent stock amounting to   10,000.00

Twenty-seven certificates of 3 per cent stock amounting to   72,264.12

    $95,064.12

See the statement by Olney Winsor, cashier of the bank, March 3, 1806, Miscellaneous Letters.

95. The letter is dated February 26, 1806, Moses Brown Papers, XI, 19, RIHS.

96. The letter is dated February 26, 1806, V J6.

97. See the sentence of condemnation, April 28, 1806, V J6.

98. See the certificate, V J6.

99. Brown & Ives to Thomas Dickason & Co. (London), September 3, 1804, P C5; Brown & Ives to John Bowers, November 7, 1804, V A65; Brown & Ives to Thomas Dickason & Co., November 9, 1804, and June 25, 1805, P C5; Thomas Dickason & Co. to Brown & Ives, August 5, 1805, P C5.

100. According to Nicholas Brown, the repairs at the Île de France (Mauritius) cost $20,000; Nicholas Brown to Amos T. Jenckes, June 11, 1806, V Misc., Vol. VIII.

101. A detailed account of the wreck of *Ann & Hope* is to be found in the letter of Brown & Ives to Thomas Dickason & Co., January 31, 1806, P C5.

102. Nicholas Brown to Amos T. Jenckes, June 11, 1806, Miscellaneous Letters.

103. Thomas Dickason & Co. to Brown & Ives, June 14, 1806, P C5; her cargo was invoiced at Batavia at $102,960.

104. Brown & Ives to Thomas Dickason & Co., January 16, 1806, P C5.

105. Capt. John F. Fry (at Batavia) to Brown & Ives, March 4 and 6, April 19, and May 18, 1807, V J6.

106. See Capt. John F. Fry's protest, August 24, 1807; see also Capt. John F. Fry (at Batavia) to Brown & Ives, August 30, 1807, both in V J6.

107. Gustavus Taylor (at Batavia) to Taylor & Talbot, September 6, 1807, V J6; the Providence firm had a quarter interest in the voyage.

108. Gustavus Taylor to Taylor & Talbot, September 6, 1807, V J6.

109. Writing to Brown & Ives from Batavia on July 19, 1807, exactly four weeks before the wreck, Capt. John F. Fry suggested that they secure insurance of $125,000 to $130,000 on the cargo. When he wrote, Capt. Fry had half his cargo on board; see the letter in V J6.

110. See Daniel Crommelin & Sons account of sales, August 23 and 27 and September 3 and 21, 1804, U A.

111. See Daniel Crommelin & Sons account of sales, September 13, 1803, U A.

112. Brown & Ives to Thomas Dickason & Co., July 12, 1806, P C5.

113. See Daniel Crommelin & Sons account of sales, December 12, 1806, U A.

114. Brown & Ives to Thomas Dickason & Co., July 24, 1806, P C5.

115. See the invoice, February 28, 1807; see also the account of sales by Jonathan Jones, July 1 and December 5, 1807, and February 13 and March 2, 1808; and the account of sales by John Lewis Brown &

Co. (Bordeaux) June 30 and December 2, 1807, and January 10, 1808, all in V P25.

116. For data on the trade in iron with the ironmasters of Taunton see "Memoran-dum Book, 1804–1822" and "Memorandum Book, 1823–1834." In these two books one finds the records of the many agreements relating to the purchase of the iron.

CHAPTER 6. A GROWING FLEET IN TRADE TO EUROPE

1. See the protest from the ship's carpenters to Brown & Ives, April 18, 1807, V A65; affixed to this document are the signatures of eighteen men, including that of Benjamin Tallman, Jr., son of the well-known shipbuilder at whose yard the new ship was being built.

2. Brown & Ives to Col. Benjamin Tallman, April 19, 1807, V A65.

3. Archer B. Hulbert, "Western Ship-Building," *American Historical Review,* XXI (July, 1916), 720–33.

4. See Franklin S. Coyle, "The Arnolds, Merchants of Providence" (unpublished Ph.D. thesis, Brown University, 1968), p. 256.

5. See Constance Le Neve Gilman Ames, *The Story of the Gilmans and a Genealogy of the Descendants of Edward Gilman of Hingham, England* (Yakima, Wash., 1950), p. 83.

6. Gilman owned a quarter part of the ship; see the bill of sale by Benjamin Ives Gilman to Brown & Ives, December 23, 1809, V A6.

7. See Benjamin Ives Gilman (Marietta) to Thomas P. Ives, April 5 and 27, August 8, and September 4, 1807; and Thomas P. Ives to Benjamin Ives Gilman, October 27, November 7, and December 11, 1807, all in V R6.

8. See Brown & Ives to Isaac Robbins, December 11, 1807; Brown & Ives to Benjamin Ives Gilman, December 16, 1807; instructions of Brown & Ives to Capt. Charles Holden, Jr., December 11, 1807; and Capt. Charles Holden, Jr. (at Alexandria), to Brown & Ives, January 11, 1808, all in V R6.

9. That Benjamin Ives Gilman, who arranged for and supervised the building of *Robert Hale* at Marietta, had a financial interest in the ship is also shown by the certificate of ownership contained in Brown & Ives to Benjamin Ives Gilman, May 3, 1809, V R6.

10. See the bill of sale from Oliver Kane and Ephraim Bowen, Jr., to Brown & Ives, July 14, 1809, V P3; Kane and Brown were executors of the estate of John Innes Clark; Kane resided in New York and Bowen in Warwick, R.I.

11. See the bill of sale from Amasa and William H. Mason to Brown & Ives, June 13, 1809, V H6.

12. Instructions of Brown & Ives to Samuel Aborn, April 14, 1809, V A65.

13. Samuel Aborn (at Soenda Strait) to Brown & Ives, July 18, 1809, V A65.

14. Capt. Daniel Olney (at Canton) to Brown & Ives, September 27, 1809, V A65.

15. Samuel Aborn (at Canton) to Brown & Ives, September 23 and November 25, 1809, V A65.

16. Brown & Ives to Perkins & Co. (Canton), April 27, 1811, P P46.

17. The Erskine agreement "provided that Britain would exempt American vessels from the Orders in Council in return for the United States lifting all commercial interdicts from England, and forbidding American ships to trade with France" (Samuel Eliot Morison and Henry Steele Commager, *The Growth of the American Republic* [2 vols.; New York, 1950], I, 408).

18. Brown & Ives to Capt. John H. Ormsbee, July 21 and 22, 1809, V A72.

19. Capt. John H. Ormsbee (at Cowes) to Brown & Ives, October 6, 7, and (at Tönning) 27, 1809, V A72.

20. See the account of sales by Schwartz Brothers (Hamburg), December 31, 1810, and July 10, November 10, and December 14, 1811, U A. For the current exchange rate see Samuel W. Greene (at Hamburg) to Brown & Ives, January 9, 1810, P G72; at that time Greene was a sort of roving agent of Brown & Ives in Europe.

21. Capt. John H. Ormsbee (at Setúbal) to Brown & Ives, December 17, 1809, V A72.

22. Instructions of Brown & Ives to Capt. Uriel Rea, June 14, 1809, V H6.

23. Capt. Uriel Rea (at Jade River) to Brown & Ives, July 29 and (at Rustersiel) September 8, 1809; and Saunders Malbone (at Jever) to Brown & Ives, August 18 and (at Rustersiel) September 1, 1809, all in V H6.

24. See the invoice of the cargo, June 14, 1809, V H6.

25. See Daniel Crommelin & Sons (Amsterdam) account of sales of teas by *Hope,* February 12, 1810, U A.

26. See Capt. Uriel Rea (at Amsterdam) to Brown & Ives, September 14 and (at Göteborg) October 3 and (at Kronshtadt) 24, 1809, V H6.

27. See the examination of the ship *Hope* captured and taken into Kristiansand, August 2, 1810; Capt. Uriel Rea (at Kristiansand) to Brown & Ives, August 14, 1810; and the court decree of condemnation, August 21, 1810, all in V H6.

28. Instructions of Brown & Ives to Capt. John H. Ormsbee, May 18, 1811, V A72.

29. Daniel Crommelin & Sons to Capt. John H. Ormsbee, July 4, 9, and 16, 1811, V A72.

30. Ryberg & Co. (Copenhagen) to Capt. John H. Ormsbee, July 9 and 16, 1811, V A72.

31. See the figures in Daniel Crommelin & Sons account as stated in the books of Brown & Ives, September 13, 1811–March 4, 1815, especially the item dated September 29, 1813; see also Daniel Crommelin & Sons account of sales of teas by *Asia,* October 22, 1812, all in U A.

32. See the invoice of coffee, June 14, 1811; and the account of sales of coffee, October 5, 1811, both in V H4.

33. Instructions of Brown & Ives to Capt. Martin Page, May 20, 1809, V R6.

34. Capt. Martin Page (at Cowes) to Brown & Ives, July 7, 1809, V R6.

35. Thomas Auldjo (Cowes) to Brown & Ives, July 13, 1809, V R6.

36. Capt. Martin Page (at Cowes) to Brown & Ives, August 8, 1809, V R6.

37. V R6.

38. See Thomas Dickason & Co. (London) account of sales of 50 pounds of New Orleans tobacco, net proceeds £2,549 sterling, or $11,317.56, January, 1810; and Thomas Dickason & Co. account of sales of 400 bales of cotton, net proceeds £7,015 10s., or $31,147.04, October 21, 1809, both in U A.

39. Brown & Ives to Capt. Charles Randall, December 26, 1809, V R6.

40. See Capt. Charles Randall's protest,

together with depositions of members of the crew, March 2, 1810, V R6.

41. Macon's Bill No. 2, which became law in 1810, supplanted the Nonintercourse Act of the previous year. It lifted the restrictions upon U.S. trade with both England and France, but it provided that should either of the two countries remove its restraints upon American shipping, the President might impose a ban on U.S. trade with the other. Tricked into the belief that Bonaparte had revoked his Berlin and Milan decrees, Madison in February, 1811, proclaimed anew an embargo upon American trade with England.

42. Instructions of Brown & Ives to Capt. Charles Randall, November 26, 1810, V R6.

43. Capt. Charles Randall (at Carnarvon) to Brown & Ives, December 29, 1810, V R6.

44. See their depositions, taken at Carnarvon, December 29, 1810, V R6; the four men were Henry W. Nichols, Joseph Snow, Anthony Spink, and James Leach.

45. See their "Public Instrument of Protest," January 10, 1811, V R6.

46. Instructions of Brown & Ives to Capt. Joshua Rathbun, November 6, 1809, V A7.

47. Capt. Joshua Rathbun (at London) to Brown & Ives, February 12, 1810, V A7.

48. Capt. Joshua Rathbun (at London) to Brown & Ives, February 25, 1810; see also the copy of the condemnation of the ship *Arthur,* February 20, 1810, both in V A7.

49. Brown & Ives to Capt. Charles Holden, Jr., September 25, 1809; and the invoice of goods loaded at Wilmington, December 18, 1809, both in V G34.

50. See the account current of Brown & Ives with Thomas & Adrian Cremer (St. Petersburg), July 13, 1810, V G34.

51. See the invoice, April 7, 1812, V G34.

52. Instructions of Brown & Ives to Capt. Charles Holden, Jr., April 7, 1812, V G34.

53. Brown & Ives to William Gray, December 7 and 14, 1810, Miscellaneous Letters.

54. See the account of sales by Bulkeley, Allcock, & Oxenford (Lisbon), December 15, 1809, U A.

55. See the invoice, December 28, 1811; and the account of sales, April 2, 1812, both in V C52.

56. Brown & Ives to Thomas Dickason & Co., November 4, 1812, P C5.

57. See the invoice, September 1, 1812;

and the account of sales at Cadiz, November 18, 1812, both in V H4.

58. See the decision of the Court of Vice-Admiralty at Gibraltar, December 10, 1812, V A68.

59. P C5.

60. Brown & Ives to Thomas Dickason & Co., November 4, 1812, P C5.

61. P C5.

62. Amasa and William H. Mason to Brown & Ives, January 4, 1813, Miscellaneous Letters.

63. See David Parish to Parish & Co. (Hamburg) introducing Brown & Ives to them, January 20, 1810, V G34. David Parish, together with Stephan Girard and John Jacob Astor, all foreign born, were the men who, as loan contractors, so largely aided the government of the United States in the financing of the War of 1812; see Fritz Redlich, *The Molding of American Banking* (New York, 1951), Part II, pp. 316–17.

CHAPTER 7. AN END TO THE MARITIME BUSINESS

1. Philip Ammidon to Brown & Ives, June, 1813, V R15.

2. Brown & Ives to Philip Ammidon, June 16, 1813, V R15.

3. Philip Ammidon to Brown & Ives, December 24, 1813, V R15.

4. Philip Ammidon to Brown & Ives, February 3, 1814, V R15.

5. Brown & Ives to Philip Ammidon, November 26, 1813, V R15.

6. Philip Ammidon (at Canton) to Brown & Ives, September 26, 1814, V R15.

7. Ibid.

8. See the bill for $7,000, the price paid by Brown & Ives for one-quarter interest in *Rambler,* May 10, 1814; invoice of cargo to Canton, May 1, 1814; sales of cargo at Canton, December 24, 1814; sale of prize property at Canton, November 9, 1815; disbursements at Canton, December 31, 1814; invoice of return cargo, December 23, 1814; invoice of goods shipped on the ship *Canton* for the owners of *Rambler,* November 9, 1814; sales of goods in Boston, September, 1815; sales of cargo at Boston, May 23, 1815; and disbursements at Boston, December, 1815, all in V R15.

9. Brown & Ives to Philip Ammidon, June 17, 1815, V A65.

10. Instructions of Brown & Ives to Capt. Wilbur Kelly, March 15, 1816, V A65.

11. Capt. Wilbur Kelly (at Canton) to Brown & Ives, October 12 and 28, 1815, V A65.

12. Instructions of Brown & Ives to Capt. Wilbur Kelly, March 15, 1816, V A65.

13. Capt. Wilbur Kelly (at Nieuwediep) to Brown & Ives, April 20 and May 8, 1816, V A65.

14. See the invoice at Canton, signed by Philip Ammidon, November 21, 1815, V A65.

15. See the account of sales of the teas comprising part of the cargo received from Canton by the ship *Ann & Hope,* sold at auction November 12, 1816, for the account of Brown & Ives at net proceeds of 630,671 guilders, dated January 9, 1817; the account of sales of the teas comprising part of the remainder of the cargo received from Canton by the ship *Ann & Hope* in 1816 and sold at auction May 29, 1817, for the account of Brown & Ives at net proceeds of 284,063 guilders, dated September 3, 1817; and the invoice of 264.25 chests of congou and 488.25 chests of "campoy" tea withdrawn at auction May 29, 1817, and sold for the account of Brown & Ives at net proceeds of 58,580 guilders, dated October 7, 1817, all in U A.

16. Capt. Wilbur Kelly (at Canton) to Brown & Ives, October 20, 1816, V A65.

17. Capt. Wilbur Kelly (at Canton) to Brown & Ives, November 6 and 16, 1816, V A65.

18. Capt. Wilbur Kelly (at Beachy Head) to Brown & Ives, March 5 and (at Amsterdam) 19, 1817, V A65.

19. Capt. Wilbur Kelly (at Amsterdam) to Brown & Ives, April 16, 26, and 29, 1817, V A65.

20. See the account of sales of all articles, except teas, of *Ann & Hope*'s cargo, delivered to Daniel Crommelin & Sons (Amsterdam) in April, 1817, dated October 16, 1817; see also the account of sales of the teas of *Ann & Hope*'s cargo delivered in April, 1817, dated at Amsterdam May 30, 1818, both in U A.

21. Capt. Wilbur Kelly (at Canton) to

Brown & Ives, February 23 and 25, 1818; see also the invoice at Canton, March 19, 1818, all in V A65.

22. V A65.

23. See the account of sales of the cargo of *Ann & Hope,* landed at Amsterdam in 1818, November 21, 1818, U A.

24. Brown & Ives to Capt. Wilbur Kelly, September 10, 1818, V A65.

25. Brown & Ives to Capt. Wilbur Kelly, October 14, 1818, V A65.

26. Capt. Wilbur Kelly (at Canton) to Brown & Ives, January 30, 1819, V A65.

27. See the invoice at Canton, February 9, 1819; see also Daniel Crommelin & Sons account of sales of the cargo at Amsterdam, November 27, 1819, both in V A65.

28. Brown & Ives to Truman Beckwith, March 14, 1815, V P3.

29. Nathaniel Pearce and John Rogers (at Île de France) to Brown & Ives, February 18, 1816, V P3.

30. See the invoice, June 10, 1816, V R15.

31. Nathaniel Pearce and John Rogers (at Batavia) to Brown & Ives, May 31, 1817, V P3.

32. Nathaniel Pearce and John Rogers (at Semarang) to Brown & Ives, July 11, 1817, V P3.

33. Daniel Crommelin & Sons to Brown & Ives, February 24, 1818, V P3.

34. Invoice of cargo at Batavia, November 9, 1816; and account of sales of the cargo at Amsterdam, May 19, 1818, both in V P3.

35. Nathaniel Pearce and John Rogers (at Amsterdam) to Brown & Ives, March 26, 1818, V P3.

36. Brown & Ives to Daniel Crommelin & Sons, May 18, 1818, V P3.

37. Daniel Crommelin & Sons to Brown & Ives, March 27, 1818, V P3.

38. Nathaniel Pearce and John Rogers (at Batavia) to Brown & Ives, August 24 and September 25, 1818, V P3.

39. Nathaniel Pearce and John Rogers (at Soerabaja) to Brown & Ives, October 31 and November 1, 1818, V P3.

40. Daniel Crommelin & Sons to Brown & Ives, December 28, 1818, V P3.

41. See the invoice of the cargo from Canton, February 5, 1819, V P3.

42. Instructions of Brown & Ives to Capt. Nathaniel Pearce, July 13, 1819, V P3.

43. See the account of sales at Amsterdam, dated April 29, 1820, V P3.

44. Capt. Nathaniel Pearce (at Batavia) to Brown & Ives, November 29, 1820, V P3.

45. Capt. Nathaniel Pearce (at Batavia) to Brown & Ives, January 5, 1821, V P3.

46. See the invoice of the cargo, dated June 21, 1821, V P3.

47. Capt. Nathaniel Pearce (at Batavia) to Brown & Ives, June 28 and (at Amsterdam) November 23, 1821, V P3.

48. Daniel Crommelin & Sons to Brown & Ives, November 8, 1822, V P3.

49. Brown & Ives to Thomas Dickason & Co. (London), November 6, 1818, V C52.

50. Instructions of Brown & Ives to Capt. Samuel Young, November 6, 1818, V C52.

51. Ships of Brown & Ives did make voyages (though not regularly) direct from Providence to both the east and west coasts of South America in this period. For example, the ship *Patterson* cleared from Providence on December 31, 1823, with a cargo of 2,250 barrels and 220 half-barrels of superfine flour, 8 hogsheads of Kentucky tobacco, 60 boxes of spermaceti candles, 150 barrels of prime pork, and 50 barrels of prime beef, bound for Rio de Janeiro and a market; see the bill of lading, December 31, 1823, V P3. Flour was perhaps the most important single article exported direct to South America.

In 1821 Capt. John Jennings of the brig *Nereus* (which had sailed from Providence), writing from Valparaiso on March 15, reported the sale from his cargo of 15 hogsheads of brown sugar, 77 boxes and 398 bags of Calcutta goods, 10 hogsheads of rum, and 23 hogsheads of tobacco. These, of course, were all familiar articles of export. Included in his sales, however, were 2 cherry bureaus, 5 mahogany bureaus, 2 dining tables, 24 rush-bottomed chairs, 12 yellowwood-bottomed chairs, 8 greenwood-bottomed chairs, and 8 mahogany bureaus. These articles of furniture, made in Rhode Island, were fast becoming standard items of export to South America (Capt. John Jennings to Brown & Ives, March 15, 1821, V N45).

Some time later, A. M. Vinton, supercargo of *Nereus,* sent to Brown & Ives from Valparaiso a sample cargo of goods suitable to be carried to that market in a vessel of 150 tons: 50 hogsheads of tobacco, 20 hogsheads of New England rum, 40 tons of good cordage, 20 barrels of linseed oil, 20 barrels of spirits of turpentine, some candlewick and some cotton thread, 2,000 pieces of britannia, and 500 pieces of platillas. This was to be supplemented by sheathing copper and nails, well-dried codfish, hats, shoes, "Cheap fancy Chairs & settees, Bedsteads, Tables a few Bureaux—always in Pairs" (A. M. Vinton [at Valparaiso] to Brown & Ives, June 16, 1821, V N45).

52. See Earl C. Tanner, "The Providence Federal Customhouse Papers as a Source of Maritime History since 1790," *New England Quarterly*, XXVI, No. 1 (March, 1953), 88-100. Tanner says the "impost books record 1,432 vessels arriving with dutiable cargoes" from the Caribbean and Latin America during 1800–30, compared with 459 dutiable cargoes from Europe and 86 from Asia (p. 90). The 86 from Asia are not an accurate measure of the China and East India trade of Providence since the ships from Canton or Batavia so often proceeded direct to Amsterdam; or if they called at Providence, the goods were not entered at the customhouse. If allowance is made for this, the trade with Asia was on a substantially larger scale than Tanner's figures would indicate.

53. A notable exception was Edward Carrington, who shared with Brown & Ives the East India trade carried on from Providence.

54. Brown & Ives to Capt. Wilbur Kelly, June 6, 1821, V A65.

55. Capt. Martin Page (at Whampoa) to Brown & Ives, December 7, 1821; Brown & Ives to Capt. Martin Page, February 6, 1822, V W2.

56. Brown & Ives to Capt. Wilbur Kelly, June 6 and 8, 1821, V A65.

57. Brown & Ives to Capt. Martin Page, February 6 and 15, 1822, V W2.

58. Brown & Ives to Capt. William Salisbury, October 17, 1828, V W2.

59. Capt. Wilbur Kelly (at Amsterdam) to Brown & Ives, June 14, 1821, V A65.

60. Russell & Co. (Canton) to Brown & Ives, January 28, 1824, P R8.

61. Russell & Co. to Brown & Ives, November 18, 1825, P R8.

62. Capt. Wilbur Kelly (at Cuxhaven) to Brown & Ives, July 25, 1822, V A65.

63. Robert H. Ives (at Amsterdam) to Brown & Ives, June 25, 1824, V A65. The

excessive haste of Daniel Crommelin & Sons was alleged to extend to sugar as well as tea. In 1825 the ship *Asia* arrived at Amsterdam with sugar selected with the greatest care. To the great distress of Brown & Ives, Daniel Crommelin & Sons "very injudiciously & unnecessaryly sold the Cargo soon after its arrival & at a low price, where the prospect was . . . by their own letters in favour of a rise in Sugar . . ." As a result, "it brought but a trifling freight" from its first cost. Had it been held for a time, it would have produced at least an additional "Ten Thousand Dollars." Daniel Crommelin & Sons were in too much of a hurry "to Make Sales & clear their Warehouses" (Brown & Ives to Capt. Martin Page, July 28, 1825, V A65).

64. Moses Brown Ives (at Paris) to Brown & Ives, November 13, 1818, P I9.

65. Robert H. Ives (at Amsterdam) to Brown & Ives, June 25, 1824, V A65.

66. Brown & Ives to Capt. Martin Page, July 28, 1825, V A65.

67. Capt. Nathaniel Pearce (at Batavia) to Brown & Ives, November 30, 1820, V P3.

68. Daniel Crommelin & Sons to Brown & Ives, December 3, 1817, P C7.

69. Robert H. Ives (at Antwerp) to Thomas P. Ives, July 17, 1824, V A65.

70. Sharm Ahmat, "The Rhode Island Java Trade, 1799–1836," *Rhode Island History*, XXIV (January, 1965), 10; J. S. Furnival, *Netherlands India, A Study of Plural Economy* (New York, 1944), p. 94.

71. Brown & Ives to Samuel W. Greene, August 30, 1834; see "Statement of total loss on Ship New Jersey & Cargo, wrecked on Louisa breakers, China Seas, November 10, 1833," V N53.

72. Capt. Solomon S. Williams (at Singapore) to Brown & Ives, November 26, 1833, V N53.

73. See the undated clipping, V N53.

74. See the statements of salvage from the wreck of the ship *New Jersey*, February 22, 1836, and July 14, 1838, V N53.

75. See the invoice, October 8, 1831, V A65.

76. Instructions of Brown & Ives to Capt. Martin Page, October 8, 1831, V A65.

77. Capt. Martin Page (at Batavia) to Brown & Ives, February 1, 1832, V A65.

78. Capt. Martin Page (at Soerabaja) to

Brown & Ives, February 1 and 24 and March 2, 1832, V A65.

79. See the depositions taken on board the U.S. frigate *Potomac,* then at Canton, in the presence of Commodore J. W. Downs and other officers, June 3, 1832; the depositions taken on board *Ann & Hope* in the presence of Capt. Martin Page, June 3, 1832; the undated extract from the *Providence Journal;* and Capt. Martin Page (at Lintin, China) to Brown & Ives, May 28 and June 3, 1832, all in V A65.

80. John Connell (at Washington, D.C.) to Brown & Ives, January 10, 1833, V Misc., Spoliation, Vol. III.

81. John Connell (at Washington, D.C.) to Brown & Ives, November 25, 1835; and Nicholas Brown to Lin Woodbury, Secretary of the Treasury, June 8, 1836, V Misc., Spoliation, Vol. IV.

82. George Law (Washington, D.C.) to Brown & Ives, January 8, 1836, V Misc., Spoliation, Vol. IV.

CHAPTER 8. A HALF-CENTURY OF COTTON MANUFACTURING

1. This situation prompted Nicholas Brown to write in 1785 that "Our State do the most in Coasting according to the Bizness of any State in the Union" (Nicholas Brown to David Howell, March 26, 1785, RIHS Manuscripts, XIV, 53). Only by dint of intercolonial trade had Rhode Island merchants been able to assemble cargoes suitable for export.

2. For early American efforts to establish cotton manufacturing on a sound basis see William R. Bagnall, *The Textile Industries of the United States* (Cambridge, Mass., 1893), pp. 135–65, 213–19; Samuel Batchelder, *Introduction and Early Progress of the Cotton Manufacture in the United States* (Boston, 1863), pp. 21–75; George S. White, *Memoir of Samuel Slater: The Father of American Manufactures* (Philadelphia, 1836), pp. 72–74, 76; J. Leander Bishop, *A History of American Manufactures from 1608 to 1860* (3 vols.; Philadelphia and London, 1861–68), I, 398–403; and Mack Thompson, *Moses Brown, Reluctant Reformer* (Chapel Hill, N.C., 1962), pp. 203–33.

3. Thompson, *Moses Brown,* pp. 206–7.

4. *Ibid.,* pp. 208–11, 219–20.

5. White, *Memoir of Samuel Slater,* pp. 25–36; Bagnall, *Textile Industries,* pp. 144–46.

6. See the letters in White, *Memoir of Samuel Slater,* pp. 72–73.

7. *Ibid.,* p. 74.

8. Moses Brown to John Dexter, October 15, 1791, in Batchelder, *Introduction and Early Progress of the Cotton Manufacture,* p. 48.

9. White, *Memoir of Samuel Slater,* p. 74.

10. *Ibid.,* pp. 74–75; Thompson, *Moses Brown,* pp. 228–29.

11. Thompson, *Moses Brown,* p. 231.

12. *Ibid.,* p. 233; the partnership of Almy, Brown, & Slater was concerned primarily with manufacturing cotton, while the firm of Almy & Brown was involved with marketing the mill's products.

13. Caroline Ware, *The Early New England Cotton Manufacture* (Boston and New York, 1931; reprint, New York, 1966), pp. 27–28.

14. *Ibid.,* p. 28.

15. *Ibid.,* p. 29.

16. *Ibid.,* pp. 29–30.

17. Moses Brown to John Dexter, July 22, 1791, in *Industrial and Commercial Correspondence of Alexander Hamilton,* ed. Arthur H. Cole (Chicago, 1928), pp. 75, 76.

18. Ware, *Early New England Cotton Manufacture,* pp. 32–33.

19. *Ibid.,* p. 35.

20. *Ibid.,* p. 36.

21. *Ibid.,* p. 39.

22. *Ibid.*

23. *Ibid.,* p. 42; Almy & Brown to Joseph Pope, December 2, 1808, in *ibid.,* p. 43.

24. Ware, *Early New England Cotton Manufacture,* p. 44.

25. Almy & Brown to John Wintringham, June 23, 1808, in *ibid.,* p. 46.

26. Almy & Brown to E. W. Lawton, March 11, 1814, in Ware, *Early New England Cotton Manufacture,* p. 48.

27. *Ibid.,* pp. 48–49; Almy & Brown to K. E. Townsend, February 24, 1809, in *ibid.,* p. 49.

28. Ware, *Early New England Cotton Manufacture,* pp. 50–53; Almy & Brown to John Wintringham, January 17, 1809, in *ibid.,* p. 51.

29. Ware, *Early New England Cotton Manufacture,* pp. 53–57; Morgan & Burgess

(Georgetown) to Almy & Brown, February 26, 1812, in *ibid.*, p. 53.

30. Almy & Brown to S. Penneman, April 12, 1815, in Ware, *Early New England Cotton Manufacture*, p. 59.

31. Ware, *Early New England Cotton Manufacture*, pp. 166–67.

32. Brown & Ives to Walter Channing, April 1, 1809, P G52.

33. See the accounts of the Blackstone Manufacturing Co. with the various partners, March 14, 1812; and the account of Brown & Ives with the Blackstone Manufacturing Co., March 18, 1812, all in P B522.

34. See the various receipts signed by Seth Wheaton, treasurer, all in P B522.

35. Bagnall, *Textile Industries*, p. 529.

36. See copy of the circular letter, P G57.

37. Brown & Ives to Brocker, Bush, & Richmond (Taunton), January 11, 1814, P C695.

38. Gilman & Ammidon (Philadelphia) to Brown & Ives, April 4, 1814, P G57.

39. Gilman & Ammidon to Brown & Ives, March 2, 1814, P G57.

40. Brown & Ives to Gilman & Ammidon, February 10, 1814, P G57.

41. Brown & Ives to Gilman & Ammidon, March 29, 1814, P G57.

42. Gilman & Ammidon to Brown & Ives, March 28, 1818, P G57.

43. Brown & Ives to the Bank of North America, September 24, 1818, P G57.

44. Thomas P. Ives to Benjamin Ives Gilman, November 25, 1818, P G57.

45. See "from Joseph Gilmans lists of debts [owed to Gilman and Ammidon] in the Western Country," October 15, 1821, P G57.

46. See Ray Clarke's letters from Kentucky to Brown & Ives, 1816–18, P C54.

47. See the letters of John Corlis to Brown & Ives, 1818–20, P C66.

48. "Terms proposed . . . for Cotton Fac-

tory in Newport, N.Y.," July 19, 1824, Miscellaneous Letters.

49. George S. Gibb, *The Saco-Lowell Shops, Textile Machinery Building in New England, 1813–1949* (Cambridge, Mass., 1950), p. 9.

50. Ware, *Early New England Cotton Manufacture*, pp. 121–60, and Appendix A.

51. Bagnall, *Textile Industries*, pp. 546, 547.

52. *Ibid.*, p. 549.

53. Batchelder, *Introduction and Early Progress of the Cotton Manufacture*, p. 73.

54. Peter J. Coleman, "Rhode Island Cotton Manufacturing, A Study in Economic Conservatism," *Rhode Island History*, XXIII, No. 3 (July, 1964), 67.

55. Bagnall, *Textile Industries*, pp. 529–31.

56. See the memorandum respecting the property and dividend, July 1, 1821, P B522.

57. Journal No. 11, February 14, 1831; and Journal No. 12, February 17, 1832; see also the Blackstone Manufacturing Co. Receipt Book for Dividends, February 20, 1832, RIHS.

58. See Journal No. 11, February 5 and 14, June 11, and July 30, 1831.

59. See the charter, dated January 24, 1834, in Charters, Vol. XII (1834–36), entry 8, Rhode Island State Archives; also Charters dated March 5, 1834, and October, 1838, in P C675.

60. "Memo of Division of Property on endorsed paper of the Providence Manufacturing Company," January 15, 1819, Unclassified Papers.

61. Mark A. Collet (Paterson) to Brown & Ives, March 31, 1834, Miscellaneous Letters.

62. Memorandum regarding the Hamilton Manufacturing Co. (Paterson), July 1, 1840, Miscellaneous Letters.

CHAPTER 9. PRIVATE ENTERPRISES IN THE PUBLIC INTEREST

1. For a clear and cogent discussion of the concept of the early American banks as semipublic institutions see Fritz Redlich, *The Molding of American Banking* (New York, 1947), Part I, pp. 7, 8, 31.

2. *Providence Gazette*, February 21 and March 6, 1784.

3. Hope F. Kane and William Greene

Roelker, comps., "The Founding of the Providence Bank," *Rhode Island Historical Society Collections*, XXXIV (October, 1941), 113.

4. *Ibid.*, p. 114.

5. *Providence Gazette*, June 18, 1791.

6. John Brown to Moses Brown, August 14, 1791, Moses Brown Papers, VII, 53,

RIHS; and Kane and Roelker, "The Founding of the Providence Bank," pp. 114–17.

7. John Brown to Moses Brown, August 14, 1791, Moses Brown Papers, VII, 53, RIHS; and Kane and Roelker, "The Founding of the Providence Bank," pp. 116–17.

8. Mack Thompson, *Moses Brown, Reluctant Reformer* (Chapel Hill, N.C., 1962), p. 249.

9. John Brown to Moses Brown, September 1, 1791, Moses Brown Papers, VII, 55, RIHS; Thompson, *Moses Brown,* p. 249; and Kane and Roelker, "The Founding of the Providence Bank," p. 118.

10. *Providence Gazette,* October 8, 1791.

11. For the constitution of the bank see *ibid.,* October 15, 1791.

12. Since neither the United States nor the state of Rhode Island ever exercised their options to subscribe to the stock of the bank, the actual capital stock consisted of 450 shares at $400 each, a total of $180,000.

13. *Providence Gazette,* October 8, 1791.

14. Thompson, *Moses Brown,* p. 250.

15. Peter Coleman, *The Transformation of Rhode Island, 1790–1860* (Providence, 1963), p. 187.

16. Charters, Vol. I (1790–1800), entry 6, Rhode Island State Archives.

17. Coleman, *The Transformation of Rhode Island,* p. 187.

18. Redlich, *The Molding of American Banking,* Part I, p. 232.

19. See the receipt in P B192.

20. *Providence Gazette,* November 26, 1791; and Thompson, *Moses Brown,* p. 252.

21. John Brown to Moses Brown, November 1, 1792, Moses Brown Papers, VIII, 13, RIHS; and Thompson, *Moses Brown,* pp. 253–54.

22. Thompson, *Moses Brown,* p. 254.

23. John Brown to Moses Brown, November 1, 1792, Moses Brown Papers, VIII, 13, RIHS.

24. Coleman, *The Transformation of Rhode Island,* p. 193.

25. Providence Bank v. Billings, 4 Pet., 514. In the Brown Papers is an opinion of Chancellor James Kent regarding the constitutionality of the tax upon the capital stock of the bank. Kent asserted that "A Bank Charter . . . cannot be destroyed, altered, or impaired without the consent of both parties to the compact unless there be some right to that effect reserved and

incorporated in the Grant itself. To tax Bank property equally with other property is not objectionable; but after subjecting it to ordinary taxation in the hands of the owners [of the stock], to tax it again in the gross in the Shape of a direct Assessment upon the aggregate capital in its corporate State is in my opinion a Breach of Contract, and Contrary to the Constitution of the United States" (December 12, 1827, Miscellaneous Letters).

26. See a copy of the Bank Act of 1836 in P B192.

27. See the document in P B192.

28. See his opinion in P B192.

29. See three copies of the resolution of the board of directors of the Providence Bank, December 21, 1836, P B192, in which reference is made to the decision taken on July 25, 1836, that the directors should not take the oath. Two of the three copies of the resolution are of a preliminary nature and somewhat different from the one finally voted on. Taken together the three copies clearly reveal the changes in the board's thinking upon the question of the oath in the six months between July and December, 1836, and the reasons that induced those changes.

30. *Ibid.*

31. Brown & Ives to James Lloyd, October 21, 1816; and Brown & Ives to "the President & Directors of the Bank of the United States," October 22, 1816, both in Miscellaneous Letters.

32. James Lloyd (Philadelphia) to Brown & Ives, November 6, 1816, Miscellaneous Letters.

33. Brown & Ives to Loomis & Learned (New York), February 24, 1816; and Brown & Ives to James Lloyd, October 21, 1816, Miscellaneous Letters.

34. James Lloyd to Brown & Ives, November 30, 1816, Miscellaneous Letters.

35. Samuel Aborn (at New York City) to Brown & Ives, January 3, 1817, Miscellaneous Letters.

36. Samuel Aborn (at New York City) to Brown & Ives, January 4, 1817, Miscellaneous Letters.

37. Brown & Ives to Thomas Willing, January 3, 1817, Miscellaneous Letters.

38. Brown & Ives to Thomas Willing, January 6, 1817, Miscellaneous Letters.

39. Brown & Ives to Robert Ralston, January 8, 1817, Miscellaneous Letters.

40. Brown & Ives to Gilman & Ammidon (Philadelphia), December 10 and 20, 1816, and January 8 and February 4 and 15, 1817, P G57.

41. Brown & Ives to Gilman & Ammidon, December 20, 1816, P G57.

42. Brown & Ives to Samuel Aborn and Edward Carrington, January 8, 1817, P C3.

43. Brown & Ives to Gilman & Ammidon, November 26, 1816, P G57.

44. Gilman & Ammidon to Brown & Ives, January 27, 1817, P G57.

45. Brown & Ives to Thomas Willing, January 16, 1817, Miscellaneous Letters.

46. Brown & Ives to Gilman & Ammidon, February 4, 1817, P G57.

47. Brown & Ives to Gilman & Ammidon, February 13, 1817, P G57.

48. Benjamin Ives Gilman (Philadelphia) to Brown & Ives, February 15, 1817, P G57.

49. Gilman & Ammidon to Brown & Ives, September 3, 1817; and Brown & Ives to Gilman & Ammidon, September 9, 1817, both in P G57. The two lists contain the same names but arranged in different order.

50. Both Benjamin Ives Gilman and Otis Ammidon were natives of New England. See Brown & Ives to Gilman & Ammidon, October 28, 1817; and Gilman & Ammidon to Brown & Ives, November 1 and 25 and December 9, 1817, and January 5, 1818, all in P G57.

51. See Brown & Ives to Loomis & Learned, January 7, 1817, P L59; and Gilman & Ammidon to Brown & Ives, October 4, 1817, P G57.

52. See the statement by Olney Winsor, cashier of the Providence Bank, March 3, 1806, Miscellaneous Letters.

53. See Redlich, *The Molding of American Banking,* Part I, pp. 208–17, for a clear discussion of the beginnings of savings banks in Europe and the United States.

54. Charters, Vol. VI (1818–19), entry 57, Rhode Island State Archives.

55. William Greene Roelker and Clarkson A. Collins, III, *One Hundred and Fifty Years of the Providence Washington Insurance Company, 1799–1949* (Providence, 1949), p. 8.

56. John Brown to Moses Lippitt, John Corlis, Thomas P. Ives, Amos Atwell, and James Burrill, January 4, 1799, P B72.

57. Roelker and Collins, *The Providence Washington Insurance Company,* p. 13.

58. Ibid.

59. Brown & Ives to John Brown, January 17, 1800, P B72.

60. John Brown (at Washington, D.C.) to Brown & Ives, January 17, 1801, P B72.

61. Roelker and Collins, *The Providence Washington Insurance Company,* pp. 20–21.

62. Ibid., pp. 37–41.

63. Coleman, *The Transformation of Rhode Island,* pp. 166–67.

64. Charters, Vol. I (1790–1800), entry 34, Rhode Island State Archives; for their investments in other turnpike companies see P T9, Vol. I.

65. Coleman, *The Transformation of Rhode Island,* p. 171.

66. See the minutes of annual meetings, P T9RN, Vol. I.

67. Charters, Vol. I (1790–1800), entry 12, Rhode Island State Archives; Thompson, *Moses Brown,* pp. 254–55; and Welcome Arnold Greene, *History of Providence Plantations for 250 Years* (Providence, 1886), p. 68.

68. See the memorial to the General Assembly, Charters, Vol. I (1790–1800), entry 46, Rhode Island State Archives; see also William Greene Roelker, "The Providence Plantations Canal," *Rhode Island History,* V, No. 1 (January, 1946), 19–25, 54–56, where the memorial is printed in full.

69. Roelker, "The Providence Plantations Canal," p. 19.

70. See the petition in Charters, Vol. I (1790–1800), entry 46, Rhode Island State Archives; see also Roelker, "The Providence Plantations Canal," p. 22.

71. Providence Gazette, February 6, 1796.

72. Roelker, "The Providence Plantations Canal," p. 56.

73. An Account of the Proposed Canal from Worcester to Providence (Worcester, Mass., 1822), p. 4; see a copy of the pamphlet, which belonged to Moses Brown Ives, in P B52.

74. See a copy of the act in P B52.

75. See a copy of the vote of the Blackstone Canal Company authorizing a committee to raise money, July 5, 1828, P B52.

76. See the list, August 12, 1828, P B52.

77. For the letter to the various banks, dated August 16, 1828, see P B52.

78. See the report and list of subscribers, P B52.

79. See the report, P B52.

80. Thomas P. Ives, Sullivan Dorr, and Benjamin Hoppin to Philip Allen, December 29, 1828, P B52.

81. Philip Allen to Nicholas Biddle, January 1, 1829, P B52.

82. Nicholas Biddle (Philadelphia) to Philip Allen, January 7, 1829, P B52.

83. In the Brown Papers are copies of two letters of the committee to Samuel Wetmore, both dated March 7, 1829, P B52. Of one of the letters there is a draft in the hand of Thomas P. Ives with a fair copy setting forth the data that Wetmore would need to show the prospective lenders. The other letter is of a more personal nature, containing instructions for his guidance.

84. See the circular letter of Thomas P. Ives, Sullivan Dorr, and Benjamin Hoppin to the stockholders of the Blackstone Canal Company, reviewing the course of events of the past two years, January 18, 1831, P B192. On the general subject of improvement banks see Redlich, *The Molding of American Banking,* Part II, p. 326.

85. See the circular letter of Thomas P. Ives, Sullivan Dorr, and Benjamin Hoppin to the stockholders of the Blackstone Canal Company, January 18, 1831; and a copy of the charter of the Blackstone Canal Bank, both in P B192.

86. See the certificates, dated October 3, 1831, P B192.

87. See Journal No. 11, June 1, 1831.

88. See the circular letter of F. B. Fenner, cashier of the Blackstone Canal Bank, which contains the amendment to the charter, September 30, 1834, P B192.

89. See the receipts of F. B. Fenner, December 18 and 23, 1834, P B192.

90. Coleman, *The Transformation of Rhode Island,* pp. 172–73.

91. Roelker and Collins, *The Providence Washington Insurance Company,* p. 65.

92. See the list, P B52, Vol. II.

CHAPTER 10. SPECULATION ON NEW FRONTIERS

1. For the price paid see the quitclaim deed, July 23, 1781; for the acreage see Stephen Atwater to Brown & Ives, March 21, 1853, both in P L2V. All the original proprietors of the township of Random seem to have been Rhode Islanders.

2. See power of attorney by Nicholas Brown and others to Jonathan Arnold, February 19, 1789, P L2V.

3. James Whitelow (Ryegate, Vt.) to Nicholas Brown, May 13, 1799, P L2V.

4. Brown & Ives to Abner Allyn, November 11, 1824, P L2V.

5. Abner Allyn (Navy, Vt.) to Brown & Ives, January 11, 1827, P L2V.

6. Isaac Dennison (Burke, Vt.) to Brown & Ives, July 4, 1834, P L2V.

7. Brown & Ives to Isaac Dennison, July 24, 1835, P L2V.

8. Town Clerk (Brighton, Vt.) to Brown & Ives, March 23, 1853, P L2V.

9. Stephen Atwater to Brown & Ives, November 21, 1853, P L2V.

10. Harvey Coe (Island Pond, Vt.) to Brown & Ives, November 16, 1866; October 24, 1870; January 20, November 1, and December 9, 1871; (Brighton, Vt.) August 15, 1872; and (Island Pond) February 4 and March 29, 1875, all in P L2V.

11. *Ibid.*

12. He wrote to Capt. Daniel Folger asking him to "purchase for us from Twenty to Thirty Thousand Dollars worth of Good Land within Twenty or Thirty Miles of Allbaney on the best terms you can and in as Large Tracts as you can, to pay in Continental Notes or Money," June 23, 1777, P L2NY.

13. See the list of certificates in a memorandum, October 16, 1786, P L2NY.

14. See the indenture, November 8, 1786; and the deed, November 9, 1786, both in P L2NY.

15. The final settlement notes with a nominal value of $13,403 received in exchange for loan office certificates with a specie value of $4,174 not only paid for Nicholas Brown's two-thirds part of the two purchases but left a balance in his hands of $953 nominal value; see Nicholas Brown's account with Joseph Bennet, December 6, 1787, P L2NY.

16. See Benjamin Bowen's account "respecting the Mohawk Lands that have been sold by him," P L2NY; the document is undated, but sales mentioned had been made in 1796 and 1797.

17. J. Franklin Jameson, *The American Revolution Considered as a Social Movement* (Boston, 1950), pp. 27–47; Charles

and Mary Beard, *The Rise of American Civilization* (4 vols.; New York, 1927–42), I, 228–96; Harry B. Yoshpe, *The Disposition of Loyalist Estates in the Southern District of the State of New York* (New York, 1939), pp. 59–60, 63–78, 114–15.

18. For an excellent discussion of land speculation in New York at that time see Ray A. Billington, *Westward Expansion* (New York, 1949), pp. 251–61.

19. See Helen I. Cowan, *Charles Williamson: Genesee Promoter* ("Rochester Historical Society Publications," Vol. XIX [Rochester, N.Y., 1941]).

20. See Paul D. Evans, *The Holland Land Company* ("Buffalo Historical Society Publications," Vol. XXVIII [Buffalo, 1924]).

21. Billington, *Westward Expansion,* pp. 260–61.

22. Only one person in the past fifty years, Alfred L. Donaldson, has been permitted to research and use portions of the Herreshoff family papers to write a history of the Adirondacks. The account given here for the most part was derived from his *A History of the Adirondacks* (2 vols.; New York, 1921), I, 88–116. Collateral evidence from the Brown Papers would tend to support the judgment that Donaldson's is a fair report. See also Nathaniel S. Benton, *A History of Herkimer County, Including the Upper Mohawk Valley* (Albany, 1856), pp. 467–70; and Charles E. Snyder, "The John Brown Tract," *Herkimer County Transactions* (Herkimer, N.Y., 1896), I, 94–107.

23. See the will in the Providence Court of Probate.

24. The account of Charles Frederick Herreshoff which follows is based on Donaldson, *A History of the Adirondacks,* I, 103–16.

25. Charles Frederick Herreshoff (Brown Tract) to Brown & Ives, August 12, 1816, P L2NY.

26. Brown & Ives to Charles Frederick Herreshoff, November 26, 1816, P L2NY.

27. Charles Frederick Herreshoff to Brown & Ives, September 18, 1817, P L2NY.

28. Charles Frederick Herreshoff to Brown & Ives, April 3, 1818, P L2NY.

29. Although Herreshoff repeatedly referred in his letters to his "forge" on the John Brown Tract, in the context of his letters the term furnace would appear more appropriate. His plan was to process iron

ore directly from the mine. This would ordinarily be done in a blast furnace rather than in a forge. Donaldson, *A History of the Adirondacks,* I, 109, says, "some iron ore was mined and smelted." Iron ore is ordinarily smelted in a furnace rather than a forge. The present-day village of Old Forge near the site of Herreshoff's settlement would seem to indicate that the word forge was generally used in the neighborhood in reference to his iron works. But this may merely mean that the entire community was imprecise in describing the works.

30. Charles Frederick Herreshoff to Brown & Ives, May 14, 1818, P L2NY.

31. Brown & Ives to Charles Frederick Herreshoff, May 27, 1818, P L2NY; James Brown was the son of John Brown, and Mason was the son-in-law.

32. Brown & Ives to Charles Frederick Herreshoff, December 17, 1818, P L2NY.

33. Charles Frederick Herreshoff to Brown & Ives, April 22, 1819, P L2NY.

34. Donaldson, *A History of the Adirondacks,* I, 114.

35. Ibid., p. 116.

36. Asa B. Hogins (Boston) to John Carter Brown, June 15, 1850, P L2NY.

37. Brown & Ives to Asa B. Hogins, June 21, 1850, P L2NY.

38. For a clear and readable account of the Ohio Company and its land purchase see Billington, *Westward Expansion,* pp. 212–14.

39. Ibid., p. 213.

40. Ibid., p. 214.

41. See *The Records of the Original Proceedings of the Ohio Company,* ed. Archer B. Halbert (2 vols.; Marietta, Ohio, 1917), II, 236.

42. Benjamin P. Putnam (Marietta) to Brown & Ives, February 21, 1820, P L2OC, enclosing receipts from the state auditor of Ohio for taxes paid by them on December 31, 1819. The original proprietors of the land had been Nicholas Brown, Sr.; Nicholas Brown, Jr.; Moses Brown; Sally Brown; Ebenezer Macomber; William Peck; and George Corlis, all Rhode Islanders.

43. See Jabez Bowen, John Mowney, and Thomas P. Ives to Benjamin Ives Gilman, December 24, 1800; and Benjamin Ives Gilman (Marietta) to Jabez Bowen, John Mowney, and Thomas P. Ives, February 5, 1801, both in P L2OC.

44. Benjamin Ives Gilman to Jabez Bowen, John Mowney, and Thomas P. Ives, February 5, 1801, P L2OC.

45. Benjamin Ives Gilman to Brown & Ives, August 19, 1813; and Paul Fearing (Marietta) to Brown & Ives, December 14, 1818, both in P L2OC.

46. See the circular letter of Putnam & Turner (Marietta) to Brown & Ives, January 1, 1820, P L2OC.

47. Paul Fearing to Brown & Ives, December 14, 1818, P L2OC.

48. See the circular letter, January 1, 1820, P L2OC.

49. Putnam & Turner to Brown & Ives, August 25 and March 19, 1820, P L2OC.

50. Putnam & Turner to Brown & Ives, January 24, 1821, and February 5, 1823, P L2OC.

51. Six different sales reported in 1853 were made at $2.00, $2.50, $2.67, $3.25, and $4.00 an acre; see Douglas Putnam (Marietta) to Brown & Ives, January 8, 1853, P L2OC. Three different sales reported in 1860 were made at $6.25, $7.00, and $8.50 an acre; see Douglas Putnam to Brown & Ives, October 13, 1860, P L2OC.

52. Douglas Putnam to Brown & Ives, July 9, 1873, P L2OC.

53. See Benjamin P. Putnam to Brown & Ives, February 21, 1820; and Douglas Putnam to Brown & Ives, September 16, 1845, December 21, 1854, and February 20, 1858, all in P L2OC.

54. Charles H. Haskins, "The Yazoo Land Companies," *Papers of the American Historical Association* (5 vols.; New York and London, 1891), V, Part 4, 61–103; see especially pp. 65–80.

55. Ibid., pp. 80–83.

56. Ibid., pp. 84–87.

57. Brown & Ives to D. & I. Mason (Boston), February 4, 1803, P L2OC.

58. Haskins, "The Yazoo Land Companies," V, Part 4, 87–103; and *Annals of the Congress of the United States,* 13th Cong., March 26, 1814, Cols. 1924–25.

59. William Hunter (Newport) to Brown & Ives, March 21, 1817, P H76; Hunter was attorney for Brown & Ives.

60. The deed is to be found in Deed Book No. 4, p. 127, in the office of the recorder of deeds of Luzerne County, Wilkes-Barre, Pa.; see also Brown & Ives to John B. Wallace, October 4, 1809, P L2OC. Associated with Brown & Ives in the purchase was Ebenezer Bowman of Philadelphia, who represented himself and John Davis. Brown & Ives became the owners of five sixths of the land, Bowman and Davis of one sixth.

61. Brown & Ives to Caleb Jenks, February 11, 1802, P L2P.

62. See the agreement between Brown & Ives and Samuel Mason, May 27, 1802, P L2P.

63. See the agreement between Brown & Ives and Richard Burke, June 29, 1802, P L2P.

64. Brown & Ives to James Bowen, July 3, 1803, P L2P.

65. Brown & Ives to Charles Sutton, January 6 and December 5, 1807, P L2P.

66. Brown & Ives to James Bowen, December 30, 1803, P L2P.

67. Brown & Ives to Capt. Nathan Olney, April 14, 1802, P L2P.

68. Brown & Ives to James Bowen, February 10, 1810; Brown & Ives to William Arnold, February 10, 1810; Brown & Ives to Henry Billings, February 10, 1810; Brown & Ives to Parly Coburn, October 19, 1814; and Brown & Ives to Charles Sutton, October 19, 1814, all in P L2P.

69. "Transcript of taxes on Bradford County lands of Brown and Ives," April 5, 1815; and "Transcript of taxes on land belonging to Brown and Ives in Susquehanna County," June 3, 1816, both in P L2P.

70. Brown & Ives to Charles Sutton, November 3, 1808, and May 4, 1811, P L2P.

71. See the agreement, June 12, 1823, P L2P.

72. One of the handbills, dated June, 1823, is to be found in P L2P.

73. Parly Coburn (Warren, Pa.) to Brown & Ives, January 8 and March 28, 1828, P L2P.

74. The document is undated but is to be found in P L2P, Vol. VI.

75. The schedule is in P L2P.

76. Charles F. Tillinghast to Brown & Ives, July 22, 1836, P L2P.

77. The petition is in P L2P.

78. See this communication, July 11, 1856, P L2P.

79. C. R. Coburn (Warrenham, Pa.) to Brown & Ives, October 31, 1860, P L2P.

80. John Carter Brown (at Saratoga Springs) to Robert H. Ives, July 24, 1835, Miscellaneous Letters.

81. See the account of John Whipple with Brown & Ives, July 10, 1820, P L2M.

82. See the agreement between Joseph N. Greene, Brown & Ives, and Elizabeth Nightingale for the division of notes received for land sold, August 20, 1831, P L2M.

83. See the deed by Brown & Ives to Joseph N. Greene, April 2, 1836, P L2M.

84. Paul W. Gates, *The Illinois Central Railroad and Its Colonization Work* (Cambridge, Mass., 1934), p. 99 and note.

85. Davis & Krum (Lower Alton, Ill.) to Nicholas Brown, August 1 and September 10, 1835, P L2I.

86. Winthrop S. Gilman (Lower Alton, Ill.) to Nicholas Brown, November 9, 1835, P L2I.

87. These data have been compiled from the following documents: "Lands owned by Nicholas Brown in Illinois in 1838"; "Purchase of Lands in Illinois," September 7, 1838; "List of Lands subject to tax in Henry County, Illinois," 1841; "Joshua Harper's Schedule of lands in Henry County," 1843; "Joshua Harper's Memo re lands," 1843; "Statement of lands bought for heirs of Nicholas Brown at tax sales," 1843; and uncalendared tax receipts, all in P L2I.

88. Winthrop S. Gilman (New York) to Brown & Ives, May 17, 1853, P L2.

89. United Fund accounts, 1854; the memorandum contains the following data:

Purchased on May 14, 1836—5,900.86 acres @ $1.25		$ 7,376.08
Add compound interest, May 14, 1836, to August 1, 1854		13,947.92
Add taxes paid from May 25, 1848, to August 1, 1854	$1,980.29	
Add compound interest for 6 years, 2 months, and 5 days	859.25	
	$2,839.54	2,839.54
	Total cost	$24,163.54

Sale of Lands:

80.00 acres @ $00.25	$	20.00
80.00 acres @ .30		24.00
520.00 acres @ .50		260.00
160.00 acres @ .75		120.00
160.00 acres @ 1.00		160.00
80.00 acres @ 1.50		120.00
120.00 acres @ 2.50		300.00
200.00 acres @ 3.00		600.00
40.00 acres @ 3.50		140.00
3,260.86 acres @ 4.00		13,043.44
200.00 acres @ 5.00		1,000.00
40.00 acres @ 6.00		240.00
80.00 acres @ 8.00		640.00
360.00 acres @ 10.00		3,600.00
40.00 acres @ 12.00		480.00
160.00 acres @ 15.00		2,400.00
40.00 acres @ 16.00		640.00
40.00 acres @ 18.00		720.00
240.00 acres @ 20.00		4,800.00
5,900.86 acres		$29,307.44

Total proceeds $29,307.44

Net profit $ 5,143.90

CHAPTER 11. A NEW GENERATION OF BUSINESSMEN

1. Francis Wayland, *A Discourse in Commemoration of the Life and Character of Moses Brown Ives* (Providence, 1857), p. 7.

2. Wayland, *Moses Brown Ives,* pp. 8–10.

3. See the many letters in P I9.

4. Wayland, *Moses Brown Ives,* p. 11.

5. John Carter Brown (at Saratoga Springs) to Robert H. Ives, July 24, 1835, Miscellaneous Letters.

6. Charters, Vol. XIV (1839–42), entries 48 and 50, Rhode Island State Archives; the charter was granted on January 20, 1841.

7. This account of the Hope Co. is based on William Bagnall, *The Textile Industries of the United States* (2 vols.; New York, 1893), I, 442–43.

8. Charters, Vol. XV (1843–47), entry 113, Rhode Island State Archives; the charter was granted June 24, 1847.

9. Robert H. Ives to Horace Waldo, Esq., June 17, 1851, Miscellaneous Letters.

10. See Letters, Lonsdale Co., December 24, 1853–February 17, 1855, p. 662, RIHS.

11. See letters of Goddard Brothers to A. I. Stewart & Co., June 1 and 4, July 25, October 31, and November 16, 1867, Letter Book, Blackstone Manufacturing Co., May 24, 1867–February 2, 1870, RIHS.

12. Caroline Ware, *The Early New England Cotton Manufacture* (Boston and New York, 1931; reprint, New York, 1966), pp. 179–80.

13. Ibid., pp. 180–81.

14. Ibid., p. 185.

15. Compiled from Receipt Book, February 1, 1839–December 8, 1843; from Receipts A, June 4, 1838–July 15, 1850; and from Receipts, June 6, 1859–September 10, 1860.

16. Annual Statement, Lonsdale Co., December 31, 1841, p. 47, RIHS.

17. See Blackstone Manufacturing Co. Receipt Book for Dividends, RIHS.

18. Victor S. Clark, *A History of Manufacturers in the United States* (2 vols.; New York, 1929), I, 553.

19. Annual Statements, Hope Co., RIHS.

20. Compiled from the Annual Statements, Blackstone Manufacturing Co. and Hope Co., RIHS.

21. Annual Statement, Blackstone Manufacturing Co., RIHS.

22. Annual Statements, Hope Co., RIHS.

23. Compiled from Unclassified Papers for Civil War Years.

24. Unclassified Papers; Annual Statement for 1872, Blackstone Manufacturing Co., RIHS.

25. Acts and Resolves of the Rhode Island General Assembly, LVI (May, 1863), 14, Rhode Island State Archives.

26. Ibid., XXIX (May, 1872), 21.

27. Certificate Transfers, Berkeley Co., RIHS (with Bonds of the Blackstone Manufacturing Co.).

28. Edward Stanwood, "Cotton Manufacture in New England," in *The New England States: Their Constitutional, Educational, Commercial, Professional, and Industrial History,* ed. William T. Davis (3 vols.; Boston, 1897), I, 158.

29. No statement has been found regarding the number of spindles of the Berkeley Co.; the Annual Statements of the company contain no data on this point.

30. Stanwood, "Cotton Manufacture in New England," pp. 161–62; and Zachariah Chafee, Jr., "Weathering the Panic of '73, An Episode in Rhode Island Business History," *Proceedings of the Massachusetts Historical Society,* LXVI (October, 1936–May, 1941), pp. 270–93.

31. The originals are in the Library of Congress.

CHAPTER 12. INVESTING CAPITAL IN THE WEST

1. Winthrop S. Gilman was the son of Benjamin Ives Gilman.

2. Winthrop S. Gilman (New York) to Brown & Ives, February 26, 1851, and February 16 and March 9, 1852; and Brown & Ives to Winthrop S. Gilman, February 12, 1852, all in P G58. Gilman bought bonds at 68¾, expecting them to appreciate.

3. Winthrop S. Gilman to Brown & Ives, January 3, 1853, P G58.

4. Winthrop S. Gilman (at St. Louis) to Brown & Ives, May 28, 1852, P G58.

5. Paul W. Gates, *The Illinois Central Railroad and Its Colonization Work* (Cambridge, Mass., 1934), p. 109.

6. Brown & Ives to Winthrop S. Gilman, June 10, 1852, P G58.

7. Winthrop S. Gilman (at St. Louis) to Brown & Ives, May 28, 1852; and Brown & Ives to Winthrop S. Gilman, June 7 and June 10, 1852, all in P G58.

8. Compiled from Winthrop S. Gilman's reports of June 30 and July 24, 1852, and February 12 and 28 and May 30, 1853, all in P L2, 1852–67.

9. Winthrop S. Gilman to Brown & Ives, July 14, 1852, P G58.

10. Winthrop S. Gilman to Robert H. Ives, July 8, 1852, P G58; Gilman's account of cash paid on the $2.50 lands is located under a memorandum of Robert H. Ives, dated May 27, 1853, P L2I.

11. Winthrop S. Gilman to Robert H. Ives, July 8, 1852, P G58.

12. Winthrop S. Gilman (at St. Louis) to Brown & Ives, October 22, 1852, P G58.

13. Winthrop S. Gilman (at St. Louis) to Brown & Ives, November 25, 1852, P G58.

14. This was the form of the proposed addition to the contract regarding lands, January 25, 1853, P G58.

15. See data for June 1, 1853–October 18, 1855, P L2I.

16. See Winthrop S. Gilman to Brown & Ives, June 27 and August 14, 1855; and Winthrop S. Gilman to E. R. Helmbold, June 29, 1855, all in P G58.

17. See the statement of sale, October 18, 1855, P L2I.

18. See Winthrop S. Gilman to Brown & Ives, July 22, 1853, and February 2 and 4 and April 4, 1854, P G58.

19. Winthrop S. Gilman to Brown & Ives, March 8, 1856, P G58.

20. Winthrop S. Gilman to Brown & Ives, July 3, 1856, P G58.

21. See letters of Gilman, Son, & Co. (New York) to Brown & Ives, Inland Letters.

22. Gilman, Son, & Co. to Brown & Ives, November 21, 1892, Correspondence.

23. Gilman, Son, & Co. to Brown & Ives, September 10, 1901, Correspondence.

Index

INDEX